P9-BYV-943

What's in It for Me?

ALSO BY DARY MATERA

Quitting the Mob

Get Me Ellis Rubin!

Are You Lonesome Tonight?

What's in It for Me?

JOSEPH STEDINO
with Dary Matera

HarperCollins*Publishers*

WHAT'S IN IT FOR ME? Copyright © 1992 by Joseph Stedino with Dary Matera. All rights reserved. Printed in the United States of America. No part of this book may be used or reproduced in any manner whatsoever without written permission except in the case of brief quotations embodied in critical articles and reviews. For information, address HarperCollins Publishers, Inc., 10 East 53rd Street, New York, NY 10022.

HarperCollins books may be purchased for educational, business, or sales promotional use. For information, please call or write: Special Markets Department, HarperCollins Publishers, Inc., 10 East 53rd Street, New York, NY 10022.

FIRST EDITION

Designed by George McKeon

LIBRARY OF CONGRESS CATALOGING-IN-PUBLICATION DATA

Stedino, Joseph, 1937–
    What's in it for me? / Joseph Stedino with Dary Matera. — 1st ed.
        p.   cm.
    Includes index.
    ISBN 0-06-017973-2
    1. Political corruption—Arizona. 2. Arizona—Politics and government—1951– 3. Stedino, Joseph, 1937– I. Matera, Dary, 1955– II. Title.
F815.S74   1992
320.9791—dc20   91-58358

92 93 94 95 96 ❖/HC 10 9 8 7 6 5 4 3 2 1

To Gail — my wife, my friend, whose love made it all possible

Acknowledgments

Special thanks for the extensive editorial assistance provided by: Fran Matera, Ph.D., The Walter Cronkite School of Journalism and Telecommunication, Arizona State University.

And to: Detectives Gary Ball, Mark Stribling, Ron Sterrett, Dave Kerr, Rick Lopez, Jorge Escobar, Rick Harris, Dave Gustafson, John Williams, Jack Ballentine; Lieutenant Jack Bentley; Sergeants D. P. Davis, Dennis Duncan, Pat Pezzelle, and M. Hobel; Captain Tim Black, Assistant Chief Benny Click, Chief Ruben Ortega; Officers Michelle Thiry, Michelle Carlton; County Attorney Richard Romley, Chief Deputy James Keppel, Chief of Major Crimes Unit George Mount; Sheriff John Moran and Undersheriff Eric Cooper, Las Vegas; Special Agent Michael McKinley, FBI Reno; Special Agent Daniel Camillo, FBI Las Vegas; Eric Christensen, FBI retired; Jim Perry, FBI Washington, D.C.; Kevin O'Grady, FBI New Jersey; Roger Greenbank, FBI Pittsburgh; Esquires Jud Roberts, Myrna Parker, Ellis Rubin, Bill Friedl, Cal Dunlap, Pete Perry, Bill Marchese, James Ecker, John Vetica, Dan Barr, Grant Koppelman.

Ann Levine, Todd Harris, Sheldon Kaplan, Bill Roberts, John Genzale, Bart Graves, Norman Mallinger, Gerald Arenberg, Derek Van Brode, Tom Walshire, Susan and Woody Harrell; Father Luis Salca, Father John Wellinger, Father Francis Timoney, Father John Kane, born to eternal life January 1, 1991; the order of "Sisters of Mercy." All my brothers and sisters at the Larimer Avenue Social Club, the Rulli Family, Betty and Joe, a.k.a Mom and Pap.

John Berentz, Harold and Gladys Lister; Dr. Joe Fink, Dr. Stephen Groban, Dr. Edward Zivic, Dr. David Jacobs, Dr. George Lopez, Dr. Joseph Massaro; Chuck Astrin, Howard Bixler, Dave Brattain and family; Pete Tapia and Jim Anderson, Sydney, Australia; Harry Rocklin,

The Treniers—my brothers, Martin Clancy—who gave me immortality, John and Ann Dick, Aunt Louise and Uncle Ralph, Lawson and Ruth Worsham, Les and Irene Ferguson, Joe and Shirley Baker, Laurie, Michael and Jill; Harry Rocklin, George and Alma Welch, Gloria Grossblatt, Rich and Terry Shurtleff, Jimmy Robinson, Dave and Pauline Shorr, Ted and Kathy Topolski, Paul Balletti, Michael Franzese, Leo Suarez, Les Share, Cody Matera, Leen and Fiddy, Bruce Weigand.

To all those who helped me along the way, "Thank you." And thanks to God!

Special thanks to Larry Ashmead, our editor Eamon Dolan, and to our agent, Connie Clausen.

In memoriuam, Matthew Roberts.

THE CAST OF CHARACTERS

The White Hats

Joseph Stedino, fifty-three, a.k.a. Joe Stead, a.k.a. J. Anthony Vincent: Slick, fast-talking, six-foot-four, 250-pound front man in the operation. Longtime Mafia associate. Former host of "Vegas Nite Life" television show. The ex-con turned government agent played the part of Tony Vincent, a rich Mafioso determined to bring casino gambling to Arizona.

Gary E. Ball, Phoenix Police, Organized Crime Bureau, undercover detective: Lead police detective in operation.

Michelle Carlton, police undercover officer: Acted as "Tony Vincent's" first secretary.

Representative Jack Jewett, Republican–Tucson, newspaper publisher: The only Arizona politician credited with immediately taking the right action after meeting Vincent.

Ruben Ortega, Phoenix Police Chief: Tough veteran police boss lambasted by American Civil Liberties Union, Arizona law professors, and defense attorneys for okaying the sting.

Richard M. Romley, Maricopa County Attorney: Vietnam veteran who lost parts of both legs during the war. Honest and tough.

Michelle Thiry, a.k.a. Rosa Marie Donato: Carlton's replacement as Vincent's girl Friday. Played the part of Vincent's niece to keep from being preyed upon by the sex-hungry lawmakers.

The Black Hats

Gary Bartlett, former Guadalupe town magistrate, lobbyist, private detective: Vincent's first political contact.

Jim Davis, former Yavapai County Sheriff, bounty hunter for bail jumpers: A ruthless Vietnam veteran, who lost his right leg in the Vietnam war.

Representative Bill English, Republican–Sierra Vista, eighteen-year-veteran lawmaker: Two-fisted drinker.

Shiree Foster, administrative assistant, Arizona Chamber of Commerce: Sexy blonde who had her own mysterious agenda.

Representative Art Hamilton, Democrat–Phoenix, House minority leader: One of Arizona's most powerful legislators.

Representative Jim Hartdegen, Republican–Casa Grande, Speaker Pro Tem: Tall, lanky, Will Rogerstype.

Senator Jesus "Chuy" Higuera, Democrat–Tucson, chairman, Senate Government Committee: Burly Mexican.

Al Hill, former professional football player: Kiddie-porn dealer.

Ernest Hoffman, public relations executive and lobbyist for tobacco and insurance interests: Bagman for legislators.

David Horwitz, lobbyist, union representative for state, county, and municipal employees: Helped Vincent troll for receptive legislators.

Representative Don Kenney, Republican–Phoenix, chairman, House Judiciary Committee: The first to fall under Tony Vincent's spell. Became the "quarterback" of the operation.

Representative Sue Laybe, Democrat–Phoenix: Soft-spoken, ambitious.

David Manley, chairman, Maricopa County Democratic party: Had great difficulty setting his price.

Representative Jim Meredith, Republican–Phoenix, House majority leader, ten-year House veteran: Funneled Vincent's money to fellow Republicans to bolster their reelection campaigns.

Representative Candice Nagel, Republican–Phoenix: Attractive blonde, turned political gossip into an art form.

Representative Bobby Raymond, Democrat–Phoenix: A suave lawmaker from Muleshoe, Texas. A vicious political infighter who repeatedly disavowed any interests outside his own profit.

Richard Scheffel, high-powered lobbyist, represented tobacco, beer, and gasoline industries: Bagman for legislators.

Senator Alan Stephens, Democrat–Phoenix, Senate majority leader: Took money from Vincent but escaped criminal prosecution.

George Stragalas, former executive director of the Arizona Democratic party: Eagerly accepted salaried position of "Executive Vice President in Charge of Bribery."

Donald Stump, justice of the peace, Tolleson: Accepted a bribe twenty minutes after meeting Vincent.

Ronald Tapp, private detective, lobbyist for bail bondsmen: Conspired with Vincent to have rival private detective murdered.

Senator Carolyn Walker, Democrat–Phoenix, Senate majority whip: A national spokesperson in the Martin Luther King holiday controversy.

Fringe Players

Terry Goddard, former Phoenix mayor, Democratic candidate for governor, son of former Arizona governor Sam Goddard: Became the victim of a snowballing gossip campaign regarding his personal life.

Evan Mecham, impeached former Arizona governor: Anti–Martin Luther King Day crusader.

Rose Mofford, governor of Arizona during the sting: Sported a white, beehive hairdo.

J. Fife Symington, governor of Arizona: Currently being sued by the Federal Resolution Trust Corporation for past actions as a board member of a failed savings and loan.

The following chapters contain quotes and conversations gleaned from the "Desert Sting" undercover police transcripts. They involve politicians and political insiders accusing one another of criminal acts, immoral and unethical behavior, hidden sexual persuasions, peccadilloes, and/or perversions, and myriad antisocial activities. None of these accusations should be taken as fact on their face: They are included here to illustrate how American politics is fueled by gossip, extortion, coercion, blackmail, smear campaigns, espionage, threats, and the art of holding a "hammer" over a political enemy.

In addition, some of the taped conversations have been edited slightly to correct poor English and to eliminate excessive profanity.

I

The whole idea was crazy. I'd been called in for a job interview by the county attorney's office for a position as a "special undercover agent" assigned to infiltrate the gambling scene in and around Phoenix, Arizona. My credentials? I was a longtime, ex-con wise guy with three felony raps and a lifetime of running with the mob.

Even the task itself was bizarre. Arizona had some weird loophole in the law that allowed people to set up blackjack and poker tables in bars and nightclubs and run mini-casinos under the guise of "social gambling." As long as the bar and nightclub owners didn't profit or participate in the games, it was considered the same as playing for matchsticks on the kitchen table with your bowling pals.

They weren't playing for matchsticks in Arizona. In fact, the action in the bars, nightclubs, and poolrooms was getting pretty heavy. Hundreds of thousands of dollars were passing over the portable tables each night. The games weren't regulated and were crooked as hell; the bar owners were damn sure taking a cut; dealers sometimes got mugged in the parking lots; Mobsters were moving in: It was a disorganized mess.

But that was Arizona's problem. I was living in Reno, Nevada, and balked at willfully venturing into the withering desert of Phoenix. The two Western cities are separated by little more than a zillion acres of sun-baked dirt with an occasional saguaro cactus jutting up like a prop from an old Western movie. With no moisture in the air, the sun slams down on a speeding car like a little kid frying an ant with a magnifying glass. The temperature can hit 122 degrees. A car's sheet-metal body can soar to 150, 160 degrees, easy: Lift the hood and the heat will sear the skin off your hand. Blow a radiator hose on one of the deserted stretches, and you'll be crawling on your hands and knees, sucking dust, and bumping your head on bleached cattle skulls.

I argued with my wife for nearly ten hours before I agreed to go. I didn't think I had one chance in hell of getting a law enforcement job in Arizona. And even if I did, I wasn't sure I wanted it. I didn't know who or what I was anymore. Was I a good guy or a bad guy? Was I a talk-show host or a mobster? A cop or a robber? I'd worked both sides of the fence all my life, but it was never as cut-and-dried as this. I was either breaking the law or struggling to obey it.

I never considered joining up with those who try to enforce it.

The long, monotonous drive across the desert gave me a chance to sift through my confusion and figure out who I'd been and who I wanted to be. I was fifty-one. I had a wife, my fourth, and three teenage kids to support. Times were tough. Ever since I helped the FBI in 1987 break up a billion-dollar hashish ring, I was on the outs with everybody. The bad guys thought I was a rat. The casinos wouldn't hire me anymore because they either couldn't employ an ex-felon or didn't want a rat sniffing around their operation. Nobody trusted me, good guys or bad. The past four years had been the worst of my life.

I hadn't planned to sell out the drug dealers, even though I think they should all rot in hell. The situation just fell into my lap. Their money-men wanted me to wash $100 million through a Reno casino at $10 million a week. I'd pocket 4 percent for my troubles—a crisp $4 million in cash for ten weeks' work. It was a wise guy's dream come true. But it was too good to be true. It smelled like an FBI setup. I'd fallen into the Feds' trap once before on a traveler's check scam. That little indiscretion lead to hard time in a rancid federal pen in Missouri. I was getting too old for that. I didn't want to take another fall.

When the drug lords contacted me, I had three options: I could play along, hit the couriers with a stun gun, steal the $10 million, and beat it to South America; I could play it straight, wash the money, and collect $400,000 a week, half of which I'd have to share with a casino boss; or, I could cover my ass and sing to the FBI. For most of the week, Plan A seemed to be the way to go. Stun 'em, take the money, and let the bastards explain it to the dealers. As the date drew near, nightmares of the isolation hole in Missouri began stabbing my brain.

I called the FBI. The deal went down. The Feds swooped in, grabbed the money, arrested the bagmen, and persuaded them to roll on their bosses. The FBI eventually confiscated seventy tons of hash, arrested twenty-seven more conspirators, and destroyed the whole intricate, Thailand-to-America smuggling ring.

I was free. I was a hero.

My life was ruined.

Now, four miserable years later, someone had recommended me for the unusual job in Phoenix. My wife told me in no uncertain terms that I'd better at least show for the interview. If I didn't get it, so what? Nothing lost. If I did, it could lead to a whole new life, for my family as well as for me.

As I crossed the state line into Arizona, I thought of another time when I had been at a crossroads. It was thirteen years earlier, in 1976. I had driven out to the San Diego airport to pick up mob boss Frank "Bomp" Bompensiero. He had spent the week in Chicago attending some major Mafia "heads of state" powwow to settle a territorial dispute between two families. Bomp was in his late sixties then. He was a short, gruff, solid man who could be a sweetheart or a beast, depending upon the circumstances. A renowned hit man, Bompensiero was respected in mob circles for being especially handy with "the Italian rope trick," a type of deadly garrote.

I had met Bomp when he tried to muscle in on a lucrative law firm I had opened near the San Diego courthouse. Although I never finished the ninth grade, I created the firm, managed the office, and hustled up the clients. To make it legal, I hired some young attorneys for their credentials. Somewhat to my surprise, we began making a killing. When word got out, Bomp came to see me. I smelled shakedown all the way. But a funny thing happened on the way to the squeeze. Bomp and I began talking about Las Vegas, my days mingling with Frank Sinatra and the Rat Pack, my stint as a Vegas television talk-show host, and my education on the street as a mob associate in Pittsburgh. He knew I knew the score and took a liking to me. The play never came. Instead, I signed him as a client. We began having lunch together two or three times a week. In six months, I went from being a potential mark to one of his top advisors. It was typical of my life. The moment I became legitimately successful in a respected profession, the doors to the top of the underworld cracked open.

They would swing completely open that afternoon in 1976 after I picked him up at the airport. We drove directly to the Cuyamaca Club, an exclusive restaurant in downtown San Diego. After lunch, a strange, fatherly look came over the mob boss's face.

"You know, Joe, you've proven yourself time and time again to be intelligent, dependable, and loyal. It's time you should meet some people and come in."

I knew exactly what he was saying, but it still took a few moments to sink in. Frank "Bomp" Bompensiero was offering me the chance of a poor, street punk's lifetime. He wanted me to go through the Mafia's secret ceremony to become a "made man." I would swear a blood oath to the mob and would be inducted into one of the tightest fraternities of men on the planet, the thousand-or-so Italian Mafia brothers world-wide.

It was not an invitation to accept, or turn down, lightly. My mind spun. Ten years before, I would have jumped at it. I would have said "When, where, and who do I have to kill?" That last part was no figure of speech. I knew that in order to become part of the mob, I had to "make my bones." I had to kill someone.

That was the snag. I didn't want to kill anybody, not even a stranger on a street corner. A decade before, when I was young, tough, and hungry, yeah, maybe. But not then. Not at age thirty-nine. Not when I was running a successful law firm and had my act together.

Bomp's offer was the chance of a lifetime—but a different lifetime.

Saying no wasn't going to be easy. I had to walk a verbal tightrope to make certain that Bomp wouldn't be insulted by my refusal. He was an old-school Don who loved the Mafia and viewed the initiation cere-mony as a sacred honor.

"Thank you, but no Don Bompensiero. I don't want to get mar-ried."

A smile cut through the old mob boss's face. I knew the talk, and I had selected the right word. Joining the mob was like a marriage, even more so. Becoming a "made man" meant giving up your old way of life forever. There was no quitting. Ever. You lived by their laws, or died by them. You followed their orders, or got whacked. You had to kill to get in, and you might have to kill again and again when the need arose. Slip up once, show mercy, refuse an assigned hit, and there was no judge or jury to defend you. You were history.

No doubt, being "made" would have given me unprecedented power and respect on the street, but it would also have invariably led to my death. Very few "made men" die of natural causes.

I could have simply let my "no marriage" answer ride and Bomp would have understood. But we had grown close over the years. I felt he deserved a better explanation.

"It's not the same anymore," I said. "It's not like it was back in Pittsburgh. People are rolling over left and right now. You do a deal with someone today, and he's kissing up with the FBI tomorrow. And the drugs, the drugs, Don Bompensiero, are everywhere. As much as decent men like yourself tried to keep them out, it didn't work. La Cosa Nostra isn't clean anymore. And that life, the drug dealers, there's no honor. They steal from each other. They kill each other. They murder each other's wives and children. They rat on each other to the first cop who slams on the cuffs. In the drug business, you're only as safe as your last deal. And you'll probably get killed on your next one."

Bompensiero wearily nodded his head. I could tell my words were hitting home. He was a Don from the era when drugs had been outlawed under penalty of death. The old Dons knew that drugs would be a cancer. They hated narcotics, hated the physical and mental destruction they caused, hated the way drugs preyed upon the young. They had the foresight to ban drug dealers from their brotherhood. Bompensiero ached over the way the mob had slowly succumbed to the fast money and temptation and had been poisoned by the drug trade.

"You're right, Joey," he said. "It's not the same. But there're still some of us who keep to the old ways. The door will be open for you if you change your mind."

I never changed my mind, and it turned out to be a good thing. Within a year, Bomp would be dead, the victim of the crazed ambition of Los Angeles mob boss Dominic Brooklier and sociopathic San Francisco boss Jimmy "the Weasel" Fratianno. Fratianno lured Bompensiero to a phone booth four blocks from his Pacific Beach home to return a call—which Bompensiero made using my AT&T credit card. Jimmy the Weasel then had an assassin blow the aging Don away as he walked back to his house.

I had some tense moments explaining to the cops why Bomp's last call—to Fratianno no less—was on my credit card. I told them the truth. It was one of the services I provided my friend. He used my account number and I sent him the bills, unopened.

Driving to Phoenix, I began, for the first time, to feel twinges of regret that I hadn't accepted Bompensiero's offer. At least it would have clearly delineated my life. And it would have made the bad times a lot easier. The cops and the prison guards treat "made" guys with respect. They'll rough up, roust, and billy club a mob associate with little or no provocation, but they won't touch a made man. Even the news media portray the made guys in a more romantic light. Had I been made, I would have been able to do soft time in Missouri, with better food and drink, and the guards would have fallen over themselves giving me special privileges.

Then again, I probably would have been splattered by one of Fratianno's soldiers. I hated that devious slimeball from the moment I met him at a party celebrating Frank Sinatra's induction into the Knights of Malta. Fratianno no doubt picked up on my revulsion. Had I been made, I probably would have bought it the same day as Bompensiero.

As the endless acres of brown dirt and scrub brush continued to whiz by my window, I thought of more pleasant things. My "Vegas Nite Life" talk show days from 1964 to 1967, then again in the early 1980s, were the best of the best. It was just a local program, and I was more of an all-night movie host than a Phil Donahue–type, but the show was successful and I made a killing off of it—usually about $10,000 a month. And since Las Vegas was a hotbed of entertainment, I had no trouble getting the top stars to drop by and chat during the commercial breaks. They'd plug their casino shows and I'd spin movies and rake in the advertising money. Everybody came on my show—Dean Martin, Judy Garland, Red Skelton, Jack Benny, Steve Lawrence and Eydie Gorme, Danny Thomas, Vic Damone, Lena Horne, Sammy Davis, Jr., Jerry Lewis, Bobby Vinton, Liberace, Jimmy Durante, Milton Berle, Eddie Fisher, Woody Allen, Buddy Hackett, Bill Cosby, Richard Pryor, Don Rickles, Della Reese, Flip Wilson, and dozens of others. If they played Vegas in the 1960s, they were on "Vegas Nite Life."

The memories came back in rushes. Partying. Gambling. Strutting around Vegas like a wise guy. Dating an endless supply of long-legged showgirls. Smooth-talking the TV audience. Scooping up the advertisers' cash. Those were definitely the good ol' days.

Mixed in were some equally dramatic bad ol' days. None were worse than my ill-conceived plan to be an instant loving father to my long-lost, nineteen-year-old illegitimate daughter. I swooped in unannounced on her tranquil life in Pennsylvania, tossed wads of money around, and convinced her to move in with daddy in sunny San Diego. In a brilliant move, the first person I invited over to meet my beautiful new daughter was Chris Petti, San Diego's current mob boss. Petti might as well have been John Gotti. He reeked stone-cold killer gangster from every pore.

When the evening ended and our guest left, my daughter cornered me in the kitchen. In an emotionless voice, she asked the $64,000 question.

"Are you in the Mafia?"

I smiled and answered softly, "Jolene, I have friends in all walks of life."

A few days later, we were walking from the car to a movie theater when a gust of wind swept through the parking lot. I reached over to put my arm around her shoulders to shelter her from the chill. She jerked away. It was as if she stuck a knife in my heart. In her eyes, I became too vile to even touch.

The tension in the house grew so thick you couldn't puncture it with an ice pick. Something had to break. Two weeks later, it did. She came home at 2 a.m. Alcohol had apparently loosened her tongue. Her feelings came pouring out. She started screaming at me, castigating me for deserting her two decades before.

"Where were you all my life?" she yelled. "Where were you, you son-of-a-bitch, when I needed you?"

I couldn't deal with it, so I went to bed. She wasn't about to let me off that easy. She burst through the bedroom door hissing like a bobcat and spoiling for a fight. She stood in front of my bed, screaming.

"Where were you for nineteen years, you son-of-a-bitch? Where were you?"

"Jolene, calm down," I said. "I tried to see you. I tried to come. But your mother and aunt told me to stay away. They said it was best for you."

She wasn't buying it.

"You bastard! You owe me $50,000. I want $50,000 for all the years you weren't there!"

This was a twist. I was being shaken down by my own long-lost daughter.

"Who the hell do you think you're talking to?" I screamed. "I'm not some asshole off the street. I'm your father! You talk to me with respect!"

She reacted by taking a wild swing at me. I caught her fist in my hand. As I looked in her eyes, I could see nothing but hate and revulsion. I realized then that my daughter, my blood, would never be able to accept me, much less love me. She left the next day.

I spent the next few months wandering around aimlessly in my big, lonely house. Finally, I couldn't stand it another second. I couldn't even walk into Jolene's room. I called Chris Petti and told him I was on my way out of town and I wanted to stop by and say good-bye. I drove to his house and we talked for three hours about our lives, mainly about the wise-guy life. I poured it all out, the short-term careers, life on the streets, my miserable marriages, the fiasco with my daughter, Bomp's offer to be "made," everything. I told him that I was selling my house and moving back to Las Vegas. He asked me if I needed help getting settled there. I thanked him and declined. I wanted to cut all ties to the mob.

I didn't tell Petti about my misgivings concerning the wise-guy life-style. We always think that we're the heroes of the neighborhood. We think we have life by the balls. We have money, power, women, big homes, sleek cars, anything we want. We laugh at those who carry a lunch pail and slave away at some nine-to-five job for chump change. In our eyes, we are the kings.

But in the eyes of most decent people, we're slime. I never could see it until I saw my reflection that night in my daughter's hate-filled eyes. Jolene had looked at the Emperor, and saw that he was naked. She made me feel ashamed and dirty.

I became determined to set things straight. I was ready to mature and clean up my act. I was going to leave the wise-guy life behind and make something out of whatever time I had left. I was only forty-three. I could turn it around. I would become something my daughter could be proud of.

Petti followed me to my car. We hugged and kissed mob-style.

With tears in his eyes, he said the gut-wrenching words I had heard from wise guys so many times before.

"As I look back over my life, I wish things could have been different. But this is the life I chose. It's too late for me."

We hugged again and said good-bye. As I drove away, I remembered that Chris Petti had two young children that he adored. I realized why my anguish hit him so hard. He lived in fear that one day he would see the same look in his children's eyes that I saw in my daughter's.

As the sun was setting over the bare mountains that ring Phoenix, I thought again about my vow to turn my life around. In doing so, I figured that my days and nights of fast times and wild thrills were over. I couldn't have been more wrong. In seventeen months, the havoc I would wreck in Phoenix would bounce the war in Iraq off the front pages of newspapers across the state and around the country.

2

After arriving in Phoenix, I met with County Attorney George Mount and Phoenix Detective Gary Ball in Mount's corner office on the seventeenth floor of a downtown Phoenix skyscraper. The view of the desert city was spectacular. Mount, the head of the Maricopa County Major Crimes Unit, was a slight, handsome man in his fifties with neatly trimmed, graying hair. Ball was a stoic, seventeen-year veteran undercover agent who had spearheaded a controversial drug sting against members of the Phoenix Suns basketball team a few years earlier. Although I'm six-four, 240 pounds, I felt small standing next to Detective Ball. He was a massive walrus of a man in his late thirties who stood six-six, 260 pounds, with brown hair and a thick mustache.

Mount and I did all the talking. Ball sat expressionless, sipping a Coke, while Mount grilled me on my knowledge of gambling and outlined the problem they were having. I tried to be as upbeat and personable as possible. I could tell Mount liked me. I figured Ball hated my guts. He was a cop. I was a crook. We were natural enemies.

After Mount finished, he asked Ball if he had any questions.

"No, but he knows what he's talking about," Ball said.

Mount thanked me and said they might get in touch. I figured that was the last I'd hear from them. I called Gail. "No way. The cop hated me."

The phone rang the next morning at nine. It was Mount. He asked me how soon I could be at another meeting. Since my hotel was only two blocks away, I told him I'd be over in twenty minutes.

The room was crowded when I walked in. I was introduced to Jim Keppel, a tall, thin man with reddish hair who was the chief deputy of the Maricopa County Attorney's Office. I was then introduced, in order of rank, to Captain Tim Black and Sergeant D. P. Davis from the Phoenix Police Department. We went through the same conversation as before, only now I was playing to a larger audience. After an hour or so, Keppel said, "I don't know about you guys, but I want to hire him." They then started talking about me as if I wasn't there.

"It might be best if I wait outside," I offered. Ten minutes later, Mount and Keppel walked into the lobby sporting big smiles. Mount extended his hand. "Congratulations. You're hired."

I was designated an "agent/consultant" to the Maricopa County Organized Crime Bureau, but I would be working with Ball and Davis under the direction of the Phoenix Police Department. After a few rounds of negotiations, we agreed upon a salary of $3,000 a month, plus a car—a blue 1989 Mustang—a cellular phone, and a housing allowance.

The police gave me carte blanche in naming, creating, and breathing life into my undercover identity. I dubbed myself Giuseppe (Joseph) Anthony Vincent, translated to J. Anthony Vincent, or just Tony Vincent for short. I picked the name because of the initials, T.V. I was a fan of the television show "Wiseguy" in which Ken Wahl played an undercover FBI agent named Vincent Terranova—initials V.T. Vinnie Terranova became my role model and inspiration. I then went to the local flea market and acquired some phony identification. After that, I drove to Valley National Bank, flashed my new ID, opened a checking account and accepted their offer of a credit card. I made a mental note not to bank at that chain in the future.

Tony Vincent began hitting the streets in early September 1989. The first gambling bar I scoped was a place called Tong's in north-central Phoenix, which was owned by a Chinese man named Steve Tong. I was floored from the moment I walked inside. There were fourteen blackjack tables, a crap table, plus a poker and gin rummy room in the back. The place was jammed and money was flying.

I sat at the bar, ordered a Pepsi, and watched in amazement. The independent blackjack dealers were playing with marked cards, dealing from the bottom of the deck, scooping up winning hands before the player noticed, hitting winning hands to bust them out, and playing with "short" decks that were missing face cards. A couple of dealers had "glitter fingers"—tiny prisms glued to their fingers, which they used to view the underside of the cards they dealt. The dice at the crap table were as loaded as a wino on a Saturday night. The poker tables were stacked with teams of insiders playing against a designated sucker. I saw more cheating in ten minutes than I had in ten years in Las Vegas. Harry Houdini and Amarillo Slim couldn't have won a dime in the joint. The only things missing were masks and guns.

I shook my head and ventured to another joint, the El Coyote. It was the same scene, only it had a crooked roulette wheel with a magical dancing ball. I left, returned to Tong's, and struck up a conversation with a dignified-looking man named Vito. He told me he used to own a jewelry store, and added that he gambled at Tong's every day.

"How much have you won?" I inquired.

"I've never won!" he exclaimed, laughing heartily.

"You think they're cheating?"

"What's the difference?" he shrugged. "I like to play."

I suddenly realized why every slimeball bunco artist was now in Phoenix. It was a predator's paradise.

Within a month, I was wired into the gambling scene. Many of the bar owners were unlawfully cutting into the action. The cheating at the tables was so prevalent that I was unable to find an honest game anywhere in the county. And I had flushed out, and bet into, eight separate bookmaking operations.

The only problem I encountered was with the bookies. I wagered heavily on professional football and kept winning $500 to $1,000 a week, which I turned over to Detective Ball. He wasn't happy.

"We ain't paying you to win!" he barked.

Ball's attitude was understandable. The crime committed by bookmakers involves the "vig" — the percentage they take off the top of losing bets. If you win, there's no vigorish and no crime.

Sixty days into the investigation, Ball surprised me with a compliment.

"You've done nine months' worth of undercover work in two months," he said. "You're making good cases, getting solid information. It's good cop work. When I first met you in Mount's office, I figured you were just another bullshitter. But you're honest. You're for real."

I appreciated that more than Ball knew. This was a guy who didn't toss around bouquets. It took a lot for him to praise an ex-con. I later learned that they had undercover cops shadowing me the first few weeks. They counted how much I was losing at the tables and compared it to what I was reporting on my expense sheets. Everything added up.

What also impressed him was that it was a dangerous job. In some of the bars, nearly everybody in the place was packing a gun or knife. I was wearing a body mike by then, and one false move could have cost me my life. Plus, I had been made three times by dealers from Vegas. I either ducked out before it got ugly, or fast-talked my way out of the situation. Being recognized wasn't that critical. With my background, taking on a new identity in Phoenix wasn't out of the ordinary. However, anyone who knew enough to connect me to the Reno sting could have caused major trouble.

Increasing the danger was the growing subculture of self-professed "collectors" hovering around the bars. These were lean, hardened killers who were hired to collect from tough guys, smart alecks, fellow criminals, and players who got in too deep. After meeting a few of these beasts, I began carrying some heat of my own—a .357 Magnum on my hip and a .380 in my pocket. Sometimes, I added a third weapon, a double-barreled derringer that fired .410 shotgun shells. Not only could it blow someone's head off, the kick could snap the bones in the shooter's wrist. I had to fire it with both hands locked tight, and it would still kick my arms over my head.

All along my honky-tonk travels, I kept hearing that there was a judge who hung out at the clubs and sometimes ran his own blackjack game. The crooks bragged about knowing him. That piqued my interest. At the Uptown Lounge one evening, I heard everyone yell "Hey Judge" like they yell "Norm" on the TV show "Cheers." I turned and spotted a huge bear of a man, about six-two, 260 pounds, forty-five years old, with short, salt-and-pepper hair and a full beard. He had a young woman on each arm. Everybody in the place immediately began kissing up to him.

We were introduced. His name was Gary Leon Bartlett, and his business card listed him as a private detective. I later learned that although he wasn't even an attorney, he had once served as a magistrate for the small, heavily Mexican community of Guadalupe southeast of Phoenix. He had also held various county hearing officer positions, and ran unsuccessfully for a justice of the peace post. Whatever his credentials, in the bars he was "the Judge."

Bartlett swept in again a week later. This time we talked at length. He professed to be a close friend of then-governor Rose Mofford, a strange woman with a massive white beehive hairdo. Mofford ascended to Arizona's highest office after another odd creature, Evan Mecham, was impeached in 1988 for campaign violations. Bartlett bragged that he had many political connections.

The Judge asked me what my game was. I told him that I was from Reno and was in town studying the gambling scene. I said I represented some heavy backers who were interested in getting real casino gambling passed in Arizona. Where did that story come from? Who knows? I just pulled it out of my butt at the bar.

Bartlett listened intently. He told me the Arizona legislature was full of crooks who could be easily bought.

"Some can be bought with money, some with whores. Others prefer whiskey or dope. Whatever their vice, they're all crooked," he said. As an example, he claimed that both he and Mofford were privy to a transaction in which U.S. Senator Dennis DeConcini gave then-governor Bruce Babbitt a million dollars not to run for the Senate. Despite the privileged nature of this revelation, he was talking loud enough for half the bar to hear.

After the meeting, Detective Ball and I talked about what Bartlett said. He advised me to stay on it. However, the police and prosecutors later ordered me to "lay off" the accusation made against Mofford, DeConcini, and Babbitt. It was either too hot or total bull.

I met with Bartlett in early January 1990 at Furr's Cafeteria on Thomas Road in east Phoenix, and again at Tony Roma's. He continued to brag about all the contacts he had in the legislature, and rattled off the names of politicians and judges he said were dirty. He also knew who all the players were in the county attorney's office, including Mount, Keppel, and their boss, County Attorney Richard Romley. They were clean, he said.

"Jim Keppel, he's an asshole," Bartlett said on a tape that Keppel would be hearing within the next few hours.

That evening, I typed a report for the police and county attorney suggesting that we shift the entire "Tony Vincent" operation from gambling to politics. Using Bartlett's connections and my new, ad-libbed Tony Vincent cover story, I could set up shop and troll for dirty politicians.

"If Bartlett is telling 10 percent of the truth, we'll fire the shot heard around the world," I wrote.

On January 14, the new operation almost died in the womb. I bumped into Bartlett at the Uptown Lounge.

"Hey Tony," he said. "I hear you're a snitch, that you testified for the Feds in Las Vegas!"

"That's bull," I said calmly. "Who's spreading that around?"

The Judge quizzed me a few more minutes, then changed the subject back to our plan to push for casino gambling. I had talked about hiring him as my lobbyist, at $1,000 a week, and his greed was more overpowering than his instinct for caution. To prove himself worthy of the job, we drove to the capitol. My car was equipped with a bug planted between the twin visors. It transmitted to a tape recorder in the trunk.

"There's quite a few of them [legislators] we can do business with, some of them are going to be ours because they believe in us, and then the rest of them that don't believe in us, we can switch 'em," Bartlett claimed. "I'll tell you what, [Representative] Don Kenney, you run a whore in front of him and that son-of-a-bitch will go absolutely ape shit! He'd vote for the devil himself. Wait 'til you meet this guy. He's a real shyster."

At the capitol, Bartlett marched right into the office of Jim Shumway, Arizona's secretary of state. Shumway greeted him warmly. Bartlett then introduced me to Senate Minority Leader Alan Stephens, a man he had frequently mentioned among those he felt would jump on the casino bandwagon. We also bumped into Representative Bobby Raymond, a suave, handsome man with an air of confidence.

I was impressed with Bartlett's contacts. He was such a bullshit artist, I expected him to crap out. But everyone greeted him like an old friend. We discussed our day on the way back to the office.

"I'll tell you what encouraged me about Stephens," I said. "He knows it's [socialized gambling] going on. He knows the owners are getting money from it and he don't seem to give a fuck, so that tells me that he's pro-gaming."

"Yeah, he's pro-gaming," Bartlett confirmed. "Did you hear me when I said I like to play? He said, 'So do I.'"

"I like Bobby [Raymond]. I think he's cute," I added jokingly.

". . . Bobby's married though, I know his wife and kids. He's got a bunch of kids, but I still think he'll suck a dick," Bartlett said.

"There's something wrong with him?" I wondered aloud.

"Yeah," he repeated.

". . . Maybe he's just a gentleman."

The Judge wasn't buying my argument. To him, a nice suit and well-coiffed hair meant you had to be gay.

"The big Democrats, the big ones are Stephens, the black guy Art Hamilton, the Mexican . . ." Bartlett continued.

"Does he hold office? The black guy?" I asked, referring to Representative Art Hamilton.

"He's the minority whip . . . He's number one in the House of Representatives!"

"How do we stand with him?"

"Oh shit, he's one of my best, closest friends . . . !"

"Do you think he'd be pro-gaming?"

"He'll be pro-Bartlett."

I shifted the conversation to his plan to compromise his legislator friend.

"Where are we going to find a whore that's not going to give this guy [Representative Kenney] AIDS?" I inquired.

"I know this nineteen-year-old girl that's been wanting to do it and wanting to do it," Bartlett answered. "She's never done it before, but she's a beauty. Couple of hundred bucks, but that's worth it for her."

A beautiful, nineteen-year-old virgin prostitute for a mere $200? Hell, that might bring Elvis out of hiding. Either Bartlett lived on Fantasy Island, or Arizona's economy was in serious straits.

By now, I was trying out my new cover story on my other buddies in the gambling bars. One old-timer I befriended, Popsy, professed to have his own political connections. I didn't pay much attention to him. Popsy was a white-maned, gray-bearded beatnik type in his sixties who danced to his own bongos. He set up a lunch meet with a guy named George Stragalas, the former executive director of the Arizona Democratic party. Stragalas was preparing to run for state treasurer. I didn't expect him to show.

Stragalas appeared, right on schedule. He was a short, round-faced, heavy-set Greek in his forties who was articulate and upbeat. I instantly smoothed Tony's persona from the "dis and dat" street guy he'd been in the bars to a more stylish crook. That enabled me to give Stragalas a slicker version of my new rap, which I continued to embellish with each new telling. The ex-Democratic party head listened intently, but said little. After lunch, he promised to get back to me.

Buoyed by the second connection, I pushed the police for a decision on my grand plan to take Tony uptown. Thanks to Bartlett's tour of the capitol and the positive meeting with Stragalas, the decision was made to pull Tony Vincent out of the dark bars and bring him into the sunshine of American politics.

I put Bartlett on the payroll and rented a four-room office suite on Camelback Road just north of the state capitol and downtown Phoenix. The suite was perfect because the landlord was able to wall off the fourth room and construct a separate entrance. That became the police's surveillance headquarters. They moved in and wired the office for sound and video. The police assigned a young woman fresh out of the police academy as my secretary and receptionist. She was a tall, bulky, muscular blonde named Michelle Carlton who was a body-building enthusiast. Her cover was that she was the girlfriend of my partner Carmine in Reno. I had to do some of my best acting to sell the line that Carmine "liked them husky." The police gave Michelle a gleaming silver and black Corvette they had confiscated from some high-flying criminal to enhance her Mob moll image.

It was late March 1990. We were in the vote-buying business.

One of the first things Bartlett did was introduce me to Ron Tapp, a forty-nine-year-old bail bondsman who doubled as a lobbyist for a unified group of fellow bail bondsmen. Tapp had a big gut, graying hair, wore Coke-bottle glasses, and had a loud, grating, hyena laugh. After talking to him, I could see that he was wired into the state legislature better than Bartlett. In fact, it appeared that Bartlett had made his connections through Tapp. That was good to know because Bartlett was proving to be a pain. He nitpicked about the office decor, then began making outlandish demands, including a computer, a new Cadillac, a wardrobe, and extensive dental work.

I met with Tapp privately and told him I wasn't happy with Bartlett. Tapp confessed that he didn't like the man either. I asked Tapp whether he would take Bartlett's place, and his $1,000 a week salary, if I fired Bartlett. Tapp was barely able to contain his eagerness.

The changing of the "coaches" enabled me to correct a bad strategy decision. With the cops and county attorneys ducking in and out of the fourth room, we didn't want someone around all the time who wasn't in on the sting. Tapp was allowed to work for me out of his bail bonds office.

Unlike Bartlett, Tapp turned out to be a good hire. He was also devious and creative. In one of our first meetings, he outlined plans to wire hotel rooms for video, then set up lusty lawmakers with high-class hookers. We'd then use the tapes to extort them for their pro-casino vote. That would have been fun. Unfortunately, the cops and county attorney reiterated their "no broads, no sex" directive.

Tapp quickly began to educate me how lobbyists did business. Particularly interesting was the way they got around the $220 limit that an individual could give as a campaign contribution to a state legislator. The technique was called "bundling" and involved various ways of filtering the money into individual $220 checks made out from long lists of bogus contributors. Fund-raisers were also a favorite way of washing illegal contributions. If a deep-pocket special interest group wanted to give its puppet legislator say, $5,000, the politician's aides would arrange a fund-raiser. They'd then let most everyone in free, and later fix the books so it looked like each guest paid $100.

I explained to Tapp that I wasn't interested in operating that way. Tony was a face-to-face kind of guy. Tony wanted to look in people's eyes, tell them it's my dough, and get their personal commitment. Although I sold this idea forcefully, it was a tip-off that things weren't right. A real Tony Vincent wouldn't have cared how the money got to the legislators as long as they voted as ordered. In fact, a real Tony would have had a skilled bagman make the drops in order to insulate himself from bribery charges. Anybody who knew how the Mob operates would have smelled a rat. In Phoenix, no one had a clue.

During one of our meetings, Tapp took a shot at County Attorney Rick Romley, the man who would eventually hold the key to his fate.

"This guy's a war hero and he's straight," I said. "He's supposed to have a helluva war record."

"No, he doesn't!" Tapp cracked. "He does not. He lost both legs, okay, on a land mine!"

"It blew both his legs?"

"Yeah."

"You don't call that a helluva war record?"

"No!"

You can guess where that transcript went—straight to Romley.

From the moment Tapp signed on, he pushed me to meet with his friend, Don Kenney. Representative Kenney sat on the influential House Judiciary Committee, the body that drafts state laws. Tapp pitched Kenney as our "quarterback," the guy who could lead the way and shepherd all his powerful peers. The first meeting Tapp arranged was canceled due to scheduling problems. The second, a dinner at Marie Callender's restaurant on April 11, kicked Desert Sting into motion.

3

The prospect of meeting with Representative Don Kenney excited the police and prosecutors. Kenney, fifty-two, was positioning himself to become chairman of the House Judiciary Committee. He was a prominent tax attorney with multiple real estate holdings in and around Phoenix. He was also a father of four and a devout Mormon who had graduated from Brigham Young University. He earned his law degree from the University of Arizona, and added a postgraduate degree in tax law from the University of Southern California.

To me, Kenney seemed to fit the profile of those least likely to dive headfirst into the sleaze. He had a law degree that was a ticket to $150 to $300 an hour for the rest of his life. He lived in a large home. He had a powerful political position that no doubt helped feed his private law practice to the tune of hundreds of thousands of dollars a year. His ambition was to become Speaker of the House, then make a run for the U.S. Congress. I felt he had the background, style, and look to accomplish his dreams.

Even if he did make a few passes at the money, Kenney seemed intelligent enough to smell a trap.

Still, Tapp was insistent, so I went along.

The first meeting was a dinner. The restaurant they picked should have tipped me that these guys didn't fly as high as I imagined. Tapp knew I had hundreds of thousands in cash at my disposal. He could have picked the fanciest, five-star, mountaintop restaurant in town. Something with a Western flair like Rustlers' Roost at the Pointe at South Mountain. Or maybe the Top of the Rock, dug into the mountainside at Westcourt in the Buttes. Or better yet, one of the gold-plated, rip-off joints in savings-and-loan thug Charles Keating's $200 million Phoenician Hotel.

Tapp and Kenney chose Marie Callender's, a pie shop in west Phoenix that microwaves food and makes a run for the Denny's crowd. It was their show, so I agreed.

Before I arrived, Detective Gary Ball and Sergeant D. P. Davis gave me a beeper-looking device that would transmit our conversation to the tape recorders in a van parked outside. I hooked it on my belt, right in plain sight.

Tapp and I arrived at the restaurant first. I was wearing my $800 good-old-boy outfit—cowboy boots, an embroidered cowboy shirt, Western-cut pants, and a Sheriff McCloud jacket, everything but a ten-gallon hat. Tapp advised me that such an outfit would make the Arizona legislators more comfortable. Personally, I felt like a dope.

Kenney appeared a few minutes later. He was a dignified, good-looking man, about five-nine, with a round face, wavy hair, and a thick mustache. He was wearing a business suit. He introduced himself in that politician's way, using a pat, radio announcer's voice.

"Gentlemen, how are you? Don Kenney."

Hi, I'm Roy Rogers, I thought.

The dinner started out somber. For the first hour or so, as we ate, I educated Kenney on the social gambling problem in Arizona, a quickly spreading plague that appeared to be news to him. I explained that there were more than a hundred bars and restaurants running nightly poker and blackjack games, and that the number was rapidly increasing. When he expressed surprise, I turned to Tapp and instructed him to take Kenney on a tour—at my expense. Kenney immediately warmed to the idea. Still, he maintained a safe, standoffish attitude.

By the end of the second hour, the conversation took a dramatic turn. We started talking about what I would soon learn was a topic that consumed the thoughts of most of Arizona's male politicians—sex. They would spend hours detailing how much they got in the past, how much they were currently getting, and how they longed for more in the future. Kenney was no exception. He began entertaining us with tales of his law school days at the University of Arizona. He said he and a buddy of his, a fellow future state senator, would regularly drive south from Tucson, cross the border, and indulge in an orgy of booze and babes at a variety of Mexican whorehouses. Kenney seemed to come alive as the talk grew raunchier. Apparently exciting himself with his own stories, he began coming on to the waitress, a pretty teenager about eighteen years old.

It quickly became clear that the sex talk and waitress hustle wasn't idle bragging. Kenney was letting me know what he liked. I knew then that I could have imported a gorgeous, $500-an-hour Vegas hooker, thrown her his way, and he would have voted to award Saddam Hussein the Congressional Medal of Honor if that's what I wanted. Hell, I probably could have done it with a $20 Jimmy-Swaggart-Special streetwalker.

It wasn't going to be that easy. Hookers weren't part of the bait. The cops' rules were that I couldn't commit a crime to lure anyone into committing a crime. Setting a guy up with a bed warmer was a crime.

Actually, so was bribing state lawmakers for their votes. It was hard to see a difference, especially when considering that the FBI set up former Washington, D.C., mayor Marion Barry with the lure of a woman and crack cocaine. Then again, Barry nearly walked, so maybe the cops and prosecutors felt the bust would be cleaner in the public's eye if it was just money. Whatever, my orders were clear. No women.

At that point, the three of us had eaten and talked trash for about two hours. Suddenly, I looked up and spotted Detective Dave Kerr, one of the van cops. He strolled by, circled, and passed me again. This time he gave me an ever-so-subtle command to follow him. He then disappeared into the men's room.

"I'm gonna get some cigarettes," I said.

When I entered the restroom, Detective Kerr braced the door, then snatched the beeper off my belt.

"The battery's dead! Didn't they tell you the time limit?" he said, quickly popping off the back cover and plugging in a new power cell.

"No. Nobody told me nothing," I said. "They damn well should have. If the battery has a time limit, let me know and we'll work it out. This is crazy."

"They probably didn't think you guys would be in here longer than two hours," he said.

"Hey, time flies when you're having fun. You didn't miss anything. Just a lot of boy talk 'bout fuckin'," I explained.

Kerr laughed. Missing that wasn't a problem. It's not against the law to boast or lie about one's sexual prowess. If that was a crime, every politician would be in jail.

I returned to the table, transmitting once again. My brief departure enabled me to steer the conversation away from the waitress's crotch. Tapp began explaining to Representative Kenney what my goals were regarding casino gambling. Kenney said he had no problem with casinos, but that some of his right-wing, Mormon constituents were strongly against it. He added that despite that handicap, he could still help out if things were kept quiet.

I asked Kenney to prepare a budget for what he needed to get my campaign rolling. It could be for legal services, campaign contributions, expenses, whatever he felt was necessary. He agreed and we scheduled a meeting for a week later.

Outside in the parking lot, Tapp was flying. I was paying the bail bondsman and capital lobbyist $1,000 a week for such introductions, not to mention my promise that he would handle the insurance—workers' comp, fire, theft—on all my phantom casino hotels. It was a perk that, if real, would earn him millions in commissions. His elation in the parking lot was based on two factors: First, he had justified his salary by bringing me a big fish. Second, the closer we came to passing a bill legalizing casino gambling, the closer he felt he was to the millions in insurance commissions. Essentially, he was dirtying his friend to feed his own greed.

Tapp also felt that he had earned the right to know more about my operation. "I am gonna find out who Tony Vincent is."

"Do it," I said. "Do what you got to do."

"That was part of my deal with Don that I would make sure everything is kosher and clean . . . up front . . ." he explained. "'Cause we don't need our pictures in the newspaper."

I didn't know what he was up to, or what sources he had, but I wasn't worried. The basic Tony Vincent story was that I had four deep-pocket, mobster partners and together we were prepared to spend $10 to $20 million on the campaign to legalize gambling in Arizona. I arranged to have a file on J. Anthony Vincent punched into the police computers. Anyone tapping in would learn that Vincent was formerly the casino manager at the Sands Hotel in Las Vegas, a longtime mob front, and later a casino executive at Harvey's Wagon Wheel, a huge hotel in Reno. I also put in a few traffic tickets and a notation that "Vincent" had once reported that his car had been stolen. For an address, I used the office of a Reno veterinarian who had treated my cat for feline leukemia.

I never knew what Tapp actually did to investigate my background. All I know is from that point on, he bragged to everybody that he had "checked me out better than the CIA." He assured them I was everything I said I was—and more. Which meant I was indeed the Mafia honcho he had convinced himself I was. Either he hooked into the police computer, crossed paths with some sources who knew my cover, or as I suspect, did nothing and just somehow, blinded by greed and power, deluded himself into thinking that he had "checked me out better than the CIA." Whatever, he was my best promoter from that point on.

A week or so later, Tapp walked into my three-room office suite with a copy of Representative Kenney's budget. The judiciary chairman had submitted some piece of work. There were facts and figures all neatly typed. Kenney wanted a total of $55,000: $10,000 for his fellow legislators, $42,000 in assorted legal fees, and another $3,000 for wining, dining, and other miscellaneous expenses. I looked it over, told Tapp it was okay, and had him set up a meeting. Tapp arranged it for the following Monday, April 30, 1990.

On the Friday before the meeting, Tapp dropped a bomb. He decided that he wanted to have the office swept for bugs. I explained that I had a bug man go over it twice a week. Tapp persisted, claiming to know a super technician who had worked, or was working, for the Mossad, the Israeli intelligence agency. What a Mossad agent was doing in Phoenix, Arizona, baffled me, but Tapp remained adamant. I just shrugged and told him to go ahead.

The next day, the police sent a crew of four police technicians to strip the suite of all the miniature hidden cameras, recording devices, and microphones, along with the yards of wire that supported them. They had to cut through walls and then patch and repaint them. It took the harried specialists six hours to clean the rooms.

Tapp showed up the following day at noon with two guys in tow. The lead man, the "Mossad agent," was a skinny little guy named Eric Levenson. He appeared to be in his mid-thirties, and had hair sticking out from both sides of his head like Larry from "The Three Stooges." He brought an "assistant sweeper," a young Jewish kid with brown hair and pale skin. Together they lugged in enough electronic equipment to fly a spaceship—about $50,000 to $60,000 worth of state-of-the-art, anti-espionage hardware. Levenson mumbled something about being able to detect both "hard wired" bugs or "radio frequency devices." He and his apprentice donned headphones, strapped on some equipment like those Ghostbuster guys, and then proceeded, over the next six and a half hours, to comb every inch of my office.

After the first hour, my patience began to wear thin. When the kid sweeper knocked over a ceramic Indian piece I had on my desk, I kicked him in the ass.

"Be careful," I ordered.

Tapp and Levenson looked up for a second, then went about their business. Such aggressive behavior was expected of big Tony Vincent.

By hour three, I was ready to kick all their asses, especially Tapp's. I couldn't believe they were putting me through this on a Sunday when I could have been at home with my wife.

When Levenson reached the window, he told me that the Arizona attorney general had a listening device that worked on a laser beam. He said they could shoot the invisible beam through my window and it would act like a telephone wire. In order to thwart such a space-age device, he said I could adjust the angle of my miniblinds. If they were closed facing downward, then I should reverse them to close facing upward. Since the attorney general's laser would be calibrated to penetrate a blind that was closed facing downward, moving them upward would screw up the beam and throw them off.

I wanted to throw them off all right, I wanted to throw these two clowns off the top of the building!

Finally, as the sun set and the office grew dark and dreary, and I was searching the ceiling for a beam to hang myself from, Levenson took off his headphones and pronounced the place "clean."

"How much do I owe you?" I asked.

"Nothing," Levenson said. "Don't worry about it."

Aha, I thought. Now comes the move. Everyone, even "Mossad agents," were looking for their piece of Tony's action. Casino hotels use millions of dollars of surveillance equipment. Security cameras train on every dealer, every game, every keno girl, to check for scams and employees on the take. As with the insurance, shrimp, mushrooms, restaurants, and dozens of other hotel concessions, a surveillance equipment contract for two or three casino hotels could turn a couple of yo-yos scanning an office suite on a Sunday afternoon into millionaires. That devious son-of-a-bitch Tapp not only wanted to sweep the room, he wanted to get his guys in on the ground floor. He no doubt had carved himself a slice of their business should things work out.

"I tell you what," I said to Levenson, instantly picking up on the scheme. "I'll let you do the surveillance in the hotels."

"I'd appreciate it," he chirped.

"I'd also like to wire my executive offices to check on my people, spy on my employees," I said.

"I can do that," he assured me.

"Come on, let me take you guys to dinner," I said. "Let's go to Tony Roma's."

"I don't like Italian food," Tapp piped up.

I shook my head.

"That's a rib joint, you moron."

As I drove to the restaurant, I had to fight to keep from laughing. For all of Levenson's expensive equipment and technical skill, and despite the excruciatingly detailed sweep, the guy screwed up. Although even the fourth room had been stripped of the surveillance equipment, there were still holes in the wall and counter stands where some of the stuff had been positioned. Any semi-intelligent person walking in there could figure out what was going on.

But hell, the door said "Private." The superduper "Mossad agent," like everybody else, treated it like Poe's purloined letter—even though it was right in their line of sight and was usually packed with police and prosecutors gathering evidence destined to screw up the lives of all who entered my lair.

After dinner, Tapp and I bid the sweepers farewell and made arrangements to rendezvous at Judge Don Stump's house in Tolleson, a town west of Phoenix. Stump was the Tolleson justice of the peace. Tapp said he had trained Stump to sign blank bail bonds, a process that made Tapp's life considerably easier, but was illegal. When Tapp went to his office to pick up the bonds, I huddled with the police. They snapped the "beeper" back on my belt and swung the spy van into action.

Judge Stump was a short, heavy man in his fifties with thick, gray hair and a leathery, sun-baked face. He was a crusty desert cowboy who loved to talk snow skiing, horses, and cattle. From the outside, his house was large, inviting, and set in a nice neighborhood. Inside, however, it looked like it belonged to Dr. Frankenstein. The place was so filthy I didn't want to sit down. There was paper and junk strewn about, and everything was coated with a thick layer of dust. I could have written the words "Helter Skelter" with my finger on his living room wall. If that wasn't bad enough, there were about twenty cats and kittens scurrying about, inside and out, perfuming the rooms with their own special fragrance. In the bathroom, the water in the toilet bowl was dark brown.

"I'm just a total lazy bum," the judge admitted. "Now one of these days . . . I'll get a vacuum cleaner and then I'll throw all this bullshit out and it'll actually look like a human lived here."

When I reached up to light a cigarette, the judge stopped me. He didn't allow people to smoke in his house. We went out to the front yard so I wouldn't pollute the fresh air inside his pristine home. I glanced across the street. About thirty yards away, parked in a church parking lot, was the police van.

Fifteen minutes into our chat, the talk turned to the judge's financial needs.

"Could you use a little campaign donation?" I offered.

"I never say no to that," he replied.

I peeled off $1,500 to support his reelection campaign—a healthy sum considering that he was running unopposed. It was also $1,280 over the $220 limit an individual is allowed to contribute in Arizona. Judge Stump took the money and buried it in his pocket like a veteran.

"Maybe it'll help you get reelected," I said.

"You better believe it, man. I appreciate this."

He was sincere. Judge Stump later sent me a thank-you card. A thank-you card from a judge for a bribe! That was a new one. He was a crooked bastard, but he had impeccable manners.

In return for my gift, the judge promised to fix traffic tickets and "OR" anybody I wanted who got arrested anywhere in the Phoenix area. "OR" means to release them without bail on their "own recognizance." It was a handy thing to have if you had the kind of friends I was supposed to have.

The judge gave me a list of telephone numbers where I could reach him at his home or office, or reach his secretary at her home or office, night and day.

This guy should be locked up, I thought as I drove away.

A half mile or so down the road, I pulled into an empty parking lot and drove the car to the service area behind a store. The spy van appeared shortly afterward. I gave Detective Ball the beeper.

"Nice work," he said.

"Thanks. Splendid legal system you have here."

Meanwhile, back at my office, the police technicians were working into the morning reinstalling the video and audio equipment in preparation for Representative Kenney's visit later that day. By the time I showed up at 10 a.m., everything was back in place. The stage was set.

Kenney appeared on schedule at 6 p.m. carrying an empty gym bag under his left arm. I liked that. Most people don't realize how big a load $55,000 in cash bribes can be. Kenney came prepared.

In the "Private" room, Detective Ball and Sergeant Davis fired up the video equipment and motioned for County Attorneys Jim Keppel and George Mount to watch the monitor. Kenney and I were going over his budget when Tapp arrived and took his place in an overstuffed chair at my right. Kenney was sitting in front of us on the couch. After discussing the budget another minute or so, I cut to the chase.

"So I'll be pumpin' twelve into your campaign. Legal fees for the next twelve months, $2,500 a month. I don't have a problem with that," I explained. "I just wanna be sure you understand that I don't expect you to do any tax attorney work for me. Do you understand that?"

"Okay . . ." he replied.

We chatted some more. Tapp saw an opening and decided to slander Bob Corbin, Arizona's attorney general.

"What we intend to do is we know that you [Tony] will attract attention from the attorney general and I hate to break this to you, but the attorney general is so damn corrupt that it's absolutely unreal!"

"Is that right?" Kenney asked.

Tapp assured him it was.

I made a note to see if we could invite Mr. Corbin to one of my little office parties. Then I got back to the business at hand.

"You can call this anything . . . call it a gift, call it legal fees, the bottom line is that I want you to leave here today with your $55,000 understanding that it's really, in reality, it's for your vote . . ."

"I understand that exactly," Kenney replied.

Shortly thereafter, my pager started beeping. That was a sign from the county attorneys in the next room that Kenney had sold his vote. The beeps, combined with the number 702 that flashed across the pager's tiny screen, were signals to release the money. I switched the beeper off and walked to my drawer to retrieve the cash.

As I gathered the money, I kept glancing to see if Kenney was still sitting there. He was. That surprised me. My little speech was made to order by the prosecutors. They wanted to make it 100 percent clear to a jury, and to the public, that Kenney knew he was accepting a bribe instead of contracting for legal services. A normal bribe wouldn't have gone down like that. Nobody makes those kind of speeches unless they're being advised by a prosecutor. Maybe some of the other legislators would miss it, but a skilled lawyer like Don Kenney should have sensed I was setting the hook and gotten the hell out of there.

Not Representative Kenney. He just stroked his gym bag, waiting to fill it.

Before turning over the money, I informed Kenney and Tapp that I was going to burn Kenney's budget sheet. They nodded in agreement. The payoff wouldn't even have a pretense of legitimacy.

With that, I handed Tapp $20,000 in neat stacks of hundreds and reached over and handed Kenney the other $35,000. Tapp immediately passed the $20,000 to his friend.

"You sure there isn't a camera? Wave to the camera," Kenney said, waving at the ceiling.

I waved. "There's no camera," I assured.

As Kenney began counting the money, something inside me began to scream. Tapp was a low life. That had long been established. But Kenney? I still couldn't figure it.

Don't take it you bastard! I thought. Do you know what you're doing? You're throwing your life away for $55,000. You don't need the money. You have a law degree, a nice family, your daughter dates a U.S. senator's kid. You own chunks of real estate all over the county. Why are you doing this? Are you nuts? I wouldn't take ten cents from a guy like me if I were in your shoes.

For a moment, I thought Representative Kenney read my mind. He stood up and put the whole pile of cash back on my desk.

"Remember those videotapes of the AbScam trial?" he said, referring to the Washington, D.C., sting operation that nabbed some congressmen.

"Believe me, there's no video camera in here," Tapp insisted.

Kenney sat back down on the couch. Something—his conscience, his religion, his principles, his fear—was eating him.

"Are you giving this back?" I asked, nodding to the pile on the desk.

He shook his head no.

"Then why's it over here?" I picked up the pile and handed it to Tapp, who handed it back to Kenney. This time, he began stuffing it into his gym bag.

"Let's shake hands on our deal," I said a while later. "Do I have your vote on legalized gaming?"

"Yes."

"You have my $55,000 and I have your support and your sponsorship . . ."

"Okay, like, again, I'm just the quarterback. You guys are the coaches . . ." Kenney said, obviously vanquishing the last remaining tinges of guilt.

You're my Judas goat, I thought. You're going to lead all your fellow legislators to the slaughter.

I had previously explained to Kenney that his peers weren't going to get $55,000. I told him he was special and deserved that much, but the others could expect less. That suited him fine. I then decided to show Representative Kenney the playing field. We walked down the hall, where there was eight thousand square feet of office space available.

"This is where I'm going to set up my operation," I said. "I'm bringing in my P.R. people, my law firm, my marketing team. This is where it'll all happen."

"Can I have an office here?" Kenney asked.

I raised my eyebrows. What the hell did he think he was going to be? "Executive Director of Politicians on the Take?" The only office he was setting himself up for was a twelve-by-twelve prison cell.

"No problem," I said.

As we walked back, Kenney started talking at length about his hemorrhoids. Why? Who knows? The more he talked, the more I cringed. Since the hallway conversations were away from the cameras and tapes, I would have to write a detailed report on everything that was said while we were out of the office. That meant I'd have to spend a half hour writing about Don Kenney's hemorrhoids.

"For your information guys," Kenney said, "I work late every Monday evening, so Monday's a good time to meet, [to] bullshit. I don't have the pressure to get home. My wife understands . . . It's my night to go out tomcatting, screwing, working late, whatever, she doesn't ask any questions . . ."

We talked a little while longer in my office, then broke for another big dinner. As I was about to leave with my two pals, the phone rang. It was Sergeant Davis in the fourth room.

"Don't go to dinner with them," he instructed. "You're not wired. He can say he gave you the money back."

That was a good point. My hands-on education as an undercover agent was continuing. I turned to Kenney and Tapp and said there was a problem with one of our overseas casinos and I had to make some calls. I then handed Tapp $50 and told them to enjoy their dinner. Given their culinary standards, that would cover their meal with enough left over to share a streetwalker at a Motel 6 on the way home.

After they left, I knocked on the "Private" door and told them it was Tony. Detective Ball let me in. He had a big smile on his face.

"Hell of a job," he said.

Inside, the cops and prosecutors were pumped. Even Ball, who is usually so cool he barely has a pulse, was hyped.

"Great job. Nice work. He's history," they chanted.

We all slapped high fives like I just scored a touchdown to win the Super Bowl. It was so new, so strange to be slapping skin with cops and prosecutors after snaring a dirty politician in a sting. For fifty years, the cops and prosecutors had been my greatest enemies. They had set me up like a stooge in Vegas and put me away a few times. Now we were a team. It felt weird, but it also felt good. Whatever the deep implications of what we were doing, at least I was on the right side. For once in my life, I was playing ball with the good guys. After living a life like mine, you can't imagine how satisfying that was.

On the way home, I realized that if Kenney brought me half the people he promised, they were going to have to put a revolving door on my office.

The good feeling lasted only until I got home. I was greeted by a ringing telephone. I instinctively punched the record button. It was Ron Tapp.

"We had a bad body count."

"What's that mean?"

"The count was bad . . . it was thirty-five, not fifty-five."

My mind spun. Tapp was telling me that $20,000 was missing from the payoff to Representative Kenney. I got pretty hot. What kind of hustle were these two playing? What did Don Kenney think he was doing? I calmed myself and told Tapp that something was wrong and I'd check it out.

I called Kenney at his house.

"Was there four stacks in them pancakes," I said.

"No, just three."

"Only three?"

"Yeah, only three."

I was beginning to squirm. It was our first "sting," and already it had gone bad. I considered who the cops and prosecutors would suspect. Would they think that one of the law enforcement officers had pulled a fast one? No way. Tapp? No, he was too stupid. Kenney? No, he was the next chairman of the House Judiciary Committee, a respected citizen. What about the ex-felon, ex-mobster undercover agent? Bingo. The missing $20,000 would fall on my ass.

I called the cops and explained what happened. They weren't pleased. They told me to go back to the office and search the place for the money. I did. I looked high and low, in drawers, trash cans, under the sofa cushions, everywhere, and no $20,000. Now I was really starting to sweat. I left the office and returned to my car. The moment I got in, the car phone rang. It was Tapp. He said Kenney had looked in his trunk again and found the money.

When I got home, I called Kenney. I wanted to confirm the find on a taped line. He didn't answer. I called Tapp and had him repeat what he told me on the car phone.

Kenney called three days later.

"Tony, first let me apologize for the snafu the other night. I bet you think I'm just a real schmuck."

"Well . . ."

"I put that stuff in the bag and then we threw it in the back of the car . . . we went over to the restaurant, BS'd and I went home. It was dark and I pulled the bag outta the thing and got in there, locked myself in my bathroom, started counting it and when I threw it in there [the trunk] from when we left your office, it just must have fell out . . . So it was a complete mess and I apologize . . . I hope you realize I'm not a complete schmuck."

No Don, I thought, I don't think you're a complete schmuck. You are, however, the dumbest cocksucker I've ever come across in my life! If you didn't have your head in your dick and ass all the time, you might have noticed $20,000 in your trunk!

"Hey, that could have happened to any human being . . ." I said instead. "Don't you have a zipper on that bag?"

"A what?"

"A zipper?"

"Yeah, but it's half broken."

"Oh."

Kenney then shifted into what he would do to earn his money.

"Tony, I have to start setting up my game plan . . . I think the first man we need to hit is my friend from law school days, Leo Corbet. Leo is currently chairman of the Senate judiciary. Leo is past president of the Senate. Leo ran for governor . . . Leo and I have been friends for gosh, twenty-five, thirty years, since we were in high school or college together at the U. of A. [University of Arizona]. We drink together and wench together and screw around together and . . ."

"Is that 'wench,' excuse me?" I baited.

"Wenching, don't you ever go wenching?"

"I don't know what it is."

"Oh, bullshit."

"Wench?"

"Go out wenching, don't you ever . . ."

"I'm fifty-two. We're close in age, but that word, I don't know maybe my . . ."

"Go out with wild chicks!"

"Oh, okay, I'm sorry."

"Wenching, go out lookin' for wenches . . ." he clarified again.

"Okay, I gotcha."

"So anyway Leo . . . is hurtin' for dough. He's a lawyer but he hasn't practiced law in years . . . I know he needs campaign contributions . . . Leo is a good guy, he can be kinda the, I'm the quarterback, but he can be the halfback . . ."

We chatted some more about political football, then Kenney shifted metaphors to gardening.

"My second comment is we'll be glad to come to your office and those that aren't half, aren't quite that ripe yet, oh you know, we'll go through Ron [Tapp] and between the two of us, we'll get 'em ripe for ya!"

A ripe bunch of halfbacks. What a pleasant thought!

I sat quietly in my chair for a long time after the call. These guys, these so-called good guys, not only were they crooked, they were completely goofy. I had overestimated them. In my world, in the cutthroat world of the Mafia, they'd be instantly eaten alive. I made a mental note for my future dealings. The biggest risk in the operation was not the chance of being discovered, nor was it the possibility of being made or doing something to blow my cover. It wasn't even a potential foul-up with the electronic equipment. My biggest battle would be against the intangibles presented by the mental instability and sheer ineptitude of Arizona's politicians.

Operation Desert Sting would get bigger. And it would get a whole lot crazier.

4

After Judge Stump and Representative Don Kenney took the bait, I figured that the rest of their pals would come running after the money. It didn't happen that way. The problem was what I called the "prime directive." In the "Star Trek" television series and movies, the prime directive states that the members of the Federation, including the crew of the Starship *Enterprise* can't interfere with other cultures and upset their natural development.

For space travelers, it's a good policy.

My prime directive was similar, but I'm not sure it was quite as noble. I was not allowed to chase, seduce, push, hustle, or entice a politician in any way. In essense, I was not to alter the natural development of a crooked politician. My duty was to purge the legislature of those politicans already predisposed to break the law. I was under strict instructions to merely let the word go out across the desert that money could be had, then wait in my office for people to grab it. I couldn't even offer specific amounts. I was instructed to ask only what they wanted.

My employees and political point men weren't bound by such restraints. They could hustle their hearts out. But Big Tony couldn't so much as pick up the telephone. This really slowed us down. If they had let Tony dance, he could have roared through the legislature like Pac Man. In ninety days, I may have convinced fifty to sixty of the legislators to take the bait—everyone except the staunchest Mormons, the born-again Christians, and a few scattered honest politicians. But because of the prime directive, Tony couldn't dance. Tony had to sit. That was the hardest part.

The reason was that some people caught in past stings — Marion Barry, John DeLorean — cried "entrapment" and the jurors listened. The Arizona cops and prosecutors learned from those mistakes. Our motto became, "If they're dirty, buy 'em. If they're clean, let 'em walk."

However, the waiting grew to be a problem on another front. Captain Black, in my opinion, had made a terrible mistake in placing a raw recruit in the critical role as my girl Friday. Michelle Carlton didn't have the experience, skill, or mindset to handle the undercover assignment. The old cliché that any operation is "only as strong as its weakest link" applies to stings. Carlton was our weakest link.

The long periods of inactivity made the young woman extremely restless. She wandered the building and made friends with the other occupants, including the maids. She hung out in the building coffee shop, and of course, made good use of the downstairs weight room. If she had been more skilled, such meanderings may have paid off in tips and information. With her, it had the opposite effect.

One of the employees of the exercise room was a high school classmate of Carlton's. Michelle wasted no time in telling her chum that she was an undercover cop and was supposed to be some mobster's girlfriend. That could have compromised the operation. The whole building shared the weight room. Michelle's friend could have spread the news in an hour.

Plus, to illustrate how such innocent confessions can have devastating consequences, the building's wholesome exercise girl lived a secret life. After pumping iron all day, she liked to display the results at a local topless bar — a place frequented by Gary Bartlett and many legislators.

Carlton had sense enough to tell Ball and I what she had done. It was my life on the line so I wanted her out. The cops scolded her but let her stay. Apparently, she had become some kind of blind spot with Captain Black. To pull her off the detail was to admit that he screwed up. He wasn't about to do that.

Carlton followed that mistake with an even bigger one. Driving the sleek Corvette was such a turn on, she took to cruising the boulevards, showing off and flirting. Driving home from work one evening, she picked up a tough Mexican kid named Eddie at a stoplight. They pulled over, chatted, then had dinner at Denny's. The dinner went so well, they ended up at her apartment where Michelle, true to form, blurted out that she was working for Tony Vincent.

"I know Tony!" Eddie piped up.

I knew Eddie all right. He was a raging bull who liked to go to the toughest bars in town and see if he could coldcock the bouncers with one punch. I bought him dinner one night at Foxxy's, another gambling joint. After dinner, he tried to hit me up for $100. I smelled shakedown all the way. When I refused, he asked for a ride.

"I ain't going that way," I said.

"I haven't even told you where I'm going."

"I don't care. Wherever you're going, I ain't going that way."

Eddie left, but skulked around outside. I guessed that he was going to try to jump me in the parking lot. If that happened, I was going to have to kill him. I called Ball. He advised me to wait him out. I watched through the window. Finally, someone Eddie knew walked out of Tong's bar across the street. He ran over to talk, or mug the guy, or rape his girlfriend, or whatever.

I shot out of the place, got in my car, and drove off. In my rearview mirror, I saw Eddie running after me shouting, "Tony! Tony!"

Michelle told me the next day that she met someone who knew me. I told Ball and Davis and they were as livid as I was. They brought her downtown and interrogated her. They then moved the rookie out of her apartment and changed her phone number, but they left her on the job.

The police gambled that Eddie's street world did not cross with the high society I was now in, so the risk was low. It was a logical assumption, but of course, it had already proven faulty. It was also no sweat off their behinds. My ass was on the front line, not theirs. But I was an ex-con. I was expendable.

As the weeks progressed, I gave Carlton an increasingly wide berth. Her mere presence in the office ate at me. I couldn't stop wondering how many more people she was spilling her guts to. When I raged about her, Ball and Davis came up with a new line. They said they were in a catch-22 situation. If they pulled her and put her out on the streets, she'd start blabbing to other cops. Since all police departments are rife with leaks, that would be worse. That was stellar logic. The police's best solution was to leave her in my office—where she could do the most damage.

In between battles with my secretary, I began fielding calls from George Stragalas, the former Democratic party head who was also an ex-Air Force captain and a graduate of the University of Denver Law School. He had warmed considerably and was itching to join my team full-time like Tapp. I considered it, but held him off.

On April 24, Tapp came to my office and did a jig that would become common among the politicians and lobbyists I enountered. He brought me the legislative directory, which featured all the names and photos of the current state legislators. Together, we gave it a going over. Tapp pointed out each representative and senator and advised me whether he felt they could be bought. As with everyone who went through this waltz, Tapp didn't stop there. He insulted the legislators, gossiped about them, told me who they were sleeping with, what jerks they had married, and any other dirt he knew.

"[Representative John] Wettaw is a player, no doubt in my mind . . . He's a drinker. He also likes the young honeys . . . This guy is . . . a professor . . . mathematical chemistry . . . a mad fuckin' scientist, does that give you a clue?" Tapp began. "[Senator] Jim Henderson, Jr. [a Navajo Indian], he can be bought. I'll tell you why he can be bought. I got his kid outta jail. The only motherfucker I ever lost in my life."

"He ran?" I asked.

"Yeah, but I knew where he was at."

"On the reservation?"

"You got it . . . [Senator] Tony Gabaldon. Appropriations, son-of-a-bitch, commerce, labor, insurance, banking and finance," Tapp continued, outlining the committees Gabaldon sat on. "We need to know him."

"What does Henderson serve on?" I asked.

"Education, welfare, health, aging and environment, transportation . . . We don't need to get to know him real good, but we need to make sure that he's in our hip pocket . . . Alan Stephens, you met with Stephens, didn't ya?"

"Yeah . . ." I said.

". . . So we'll put a 'B' [for "buy"] around him . . . we're gonna put a check mark and a star on him."

At this point, Tapp broadened his scope from legislators to other community leaders.

". . . So what occurred and the reason this governor [Mecham] went bye-bye, he had a scumbag that was head of the DPS [Department of Public Safety] by the name of Ralph Milstead. Ralph is a career cop. Come out of Phoenix P.D. as a captain on the take, no fuckin' doubt in my mind. Loves the ladies. I mean this motherfucker runs a string of girls like you wouldn't believe . . . I'm not talking about runnin' whores, okay, but he runs the ladies hard. He's a ladies' man. And he runs with good lookin' honeys . . ."

"This guy, we don't wanna get to know this guy, this former head of the DPS," I warned. "He don't sound like our kinda guy."

"But this is how this state has operated for years," Tapp argued.

The conversation took an unexpected twist, one that caught my attention.

". . . Over the years I made close associations with certain cops . . ." Tapp said. "That's one of the reasons I can spot a lot of these undercover cops in these joints 'cause I know a lot of 'em. Once a cop goes under, it's awful hard. [If] he's been under for a long time, you can't hardly bring that motherfucker back out into normal civilian life."

"Why? What happens to them? What happens?"

"These fuckers become almost like what the hell they're out there in the streets chasin'. Absolutely unreal. They ruin a lot of good street cops by makin' them undercover cops. They just can't function in society . . . I mean, they start livin' in a whole different world."

As I contemplated that phenomenon—which would indeed affect me—Tapp continued through the legislative book.

"[Senator] David C. Bartlett, now this guy's kind of interesting. He's an attorney. He's a full-time legislator . . . this guy's very interesting in that he does not take any PAC [Political Action Committee] monies . . . So we gotta find out a hot button for him."

We ran down a few more, then the talk shifted to the governor's race.

"They say [Terry] Goddard can beat either one of them, [Republicans] Symington or Steiger," I said.

"I hope so . . . If they vote party line, the Republicans have a margin of 89,000 in the state."

"But isn't Goddard popular?" I said, offering what little I knew about the former Phoenix mayor, a Democrat.

"They're gonna hit this motherfucker with being a queer, okay. Now that's not going to make any difference to some people, but my friend, when you do that to the conservative right-wing people out there, they're gonna send his ass back to San Francisco!"*

After that brief diversion into the Twilight Zone, we dove back into the legislative dung heap.

"[Senator] Bob Denny . . . he's a retired U.S. Air Force colonel . . . The guy's kind of a wacko sometimes. He's always dressed in golf attire like he's ready to hit the course at any minute. He wears sports coats that a lot of used-car salesmen would love to have."

"So we put him down for a bucket of balls and a set of clubs?" I offered.

"I understand he can be bought," Tapp answered. "That's just scuttlebutt, okay. It would have to be done with class.

"[Representative] Bill English, there's no doubt he'll play, but I cannot approach English until Rebecca leaves town. She is a . . ."

---

*Terry Goddard has publicly denied that he is a homosexual on numerous occasions in the past. The rumors have dogged him through much of his political life.

"That his wife?" I asked.

"Fuck no."

"Who's Rebecca?"

"The gal that works for me. She was out partyin' with English and [lobbyist] Ernie Hoffman last night 'til one o'clock in the morning. Goin' home shit-faced . . . Ernie, down the road, we may just want to get Ernie involved. Probably would cost us a hundred grand a year."

"Is he worth it on a hundred grand a year?"

"Yeah . . . English is quite a powerful son-of-a-bitch. And he and English are bosom buddies . . . I've met Ernie through Becky . . . Ernie likes to make money and he's a whore, there's no doubt in my mind. And he's an expensive whore, but he is also a good whore. He gets what he sets out to accomplish and he's also very highly respected because when he tells them something, they can put it in the bank."

"Let's get back to where we were, who's next? [Senator] Wayne Stump," I continued.

"Wayne Stump is a wacko," Tapp announced. "Chiropractor . . . you never know where the hell Wayne's comin' from. And you can never get a read on Wayne . . . I think it would be a mistake to approach him 'cause everyone in town might know what the hell we're doin'.

"[Senator] Jerry Gillespie, I think could probably be purchased. The reason I say that . . ."

"You mean like the Louisiana Purchase?" I chuckled.

"I think so."

"We're gonna have the Gillespie Purchase?"

"Yes."

"Okay, I'm sorry for laughin', it's just a funny line. He can be 'purchased.' I like that."

"The reason being, Jerry Gillespie got into a big-time problem in the insurance business not too long ago. In fact, he damn-near lost his license. The attorney general even took a look at him and he was doing some unquestionable, some questionable practices. Even though Jerry Gillespie is a Mormon, he is also a cripple, which looks to me like it's probably genetic, at birth, the way he walks. It doesn't look like an accident deal . . . We just need to find his hot button and how to buy him."

"Okay, how about Mr. Pena [Senator Manuel Pena, Jr.]?" I asked, moving the process along.

"I think we can probably purchase Manuel, better known as Manny."

"[Senator] Pete Corpstein?"

"[Senator] Jan Brewer told me something interesting about Pete

Corpstein," Tapp said. "She said he's 'a fuckin' wimp' . . . When I was trying to get a bill heard, she told me to corner him and turn the heat on him, he's a wimp. Which tells me that probably he is a player . . . [Senator] Jacque Steiner can be a first-class bitch. We gotta be careful with her . . . [Representative] Bobby Raymond . . ."

"You tell me if I'm wrong," I interjected. "I read him like an open book. If I can't buy him, there ain't a cow in Texas."

"I think you're right. [Senator] Tom Patterson . . . a doctor. Now how the hell do we approach a fuckin' doctor?" Tapp wondered out loud.

"I give up. Is that a question?"

"You can't buy the motherfucker, I don't think. Emergency room physician, which tells me he's probably makin' pretty close to two hundred grand a year."

"Burn down his emergency room," I suggested, ever the wise guy. "Would that get his attention?"

"Not with that many hospitals in town . . . [Senator] Lester Pearce," Tapp continued. "Captain Pearce, Maricopa County Sheriff's Department, is his brother. Captain Pearce has twenty years in next year. Good lookin' son-of-a-bitch, ladies' man. Probably keep the security at some casino . . . that's the way to control Lester Pearce."

"No argument. We could start his salary now if he wants," I offered.

"[Representative] Mike Palmer. I really don't have a feel for him other than he's a very honest individual. Although Mike Palmer kind of impressed me as the type of guy that was a player when it came to ladies . . ."

Tapp's accusing little finger moved across the page from Palmer to Representative Bill English. "The only thing which I got down is a 'party boy' since he's fuckin' your secretary, I guess that's fair to put down?" I asked.

"Yeah, I gotta hunch we can just put a big 'P' [purchase] by him. [Representative] Kyle Hindman," Tapp continued. "I know Kyle very well. Honest individual. Amazing as it seems. You couldn't buy Kyle."

Ah! Put away the lantern, I thought. We found our honest politician!

"[Representative] Nancy Wessel, we're just gonna put a big 'B' [buy] on Nancy 'cause I know Nancy very well . . . You bet your ass I can buy her . . . and she'll keep her mouth shut! . . . Her husband's a worthless son-of-a-bitch. He works for Honeywell."

By the time he finished, Tapp had designated 70 to 80 percent of Arizona's legislators as capable of being "purchased."

"This little conversation that we just had here today would constitute conspiracy," he announced into the video cameras.

"Conspiracy to do what?"

"Conspiracy is 'knowledge thereof.'"

I quickly changed the subject. Tapp foolishly came back to it a few minutes later.

"Did you hear me, our conversation today, we don't ever want anybody else to listen to our conversations. That constituted conspiracy."

"What did we do?"

"Conspiracy to buy public officials!"

"I told you never to use that word 'buy' in front of me," I replied. "It's 'purchase.'"

Stragalas called after the meeting with Tapp. He said he had officially decided to run for state treasurer and wanted to know if I'd support him. If elected, he promised to be my eyes and ears in the governor's office. I told him that was a fair trade.

On May 3, 1990, the Arizona legislature passed a bill outlawing socialized gambling. There was wailing and rending of clothes across the underworld landscape, especially in my old haunts. That night, as I drove home, I realized that Tony Vincent was now mirroring the life of his alter ego, Joe Stedino. He had dodged a bullet. If the operation hadn't shifted to politicians, the bill would have put Tony out of business.

The next morning, Stragalas brought me a new fish, freshman Representative Sue Laybe, a Democrat from Phoenix. Laybe was a tall, skinny, Olive Oyl–looking woman, about thirty-five, with wispy hair and horn-rimmed glasses. Although she wasn't unattractive, she dressed like an old-maidish schoolteacher—lots of simple cotton dresses with small-check prints and lace around the collar. Despite her bland attire, she knew the bar scene. She was a former cocktail waitress and bartender.

Laybe had an interesting political background. She was one of the first Arizona politicians to openly court the gay vote. In Phoenix, the land of redneck cowboys, wacko Mormons, and Evan Mecham, that was a high-wire act. Demographically though, it made sense. Laybe's district encompassed the area where nineteen of the city's twenty-two gay bars operated, and where it is estimated that 40 percent of Phoenix's gays live.

Her battle to win this untapped, politically active voting bloc was a tough one. Sue wasn't their kind of woman. They openly ridiculed her clothes, hair, and lack of flash. *New Times*, Phoenix's feisty alternative weekly, noted one confrontation Laybe had early in her campaign. Speaking at a gay club, she was interrupted by a heckler.

"Shut up," he cried. "You were here last week wearing that same dress!"

"Yes, and you were drunk then, too!" she shot back.

Despite such barbs, she hung in there. Her perseverance and thick skin earned their respect and affection. The gays were moved by the sheer effort she put into winning their support. She made them feel like they counted. They responded by turning out at the polls. Laybe, an underdog given little chance, won the election by four hundred votes—no doubt four hundred gay votes. Once in office, the string-bean freshman didn't forget her constituency. She regularly trekked to the gay bars and updated her constituents on various AIDS and civil rights bills.

We had a nice breakfast meeting. She was a bit jittery and uncomfortable, especially when I went into my Brooklyn Tony act. Still, she agreed to follow me to my office, talk some more, and pick up a contribution. While I was waiting for her, Representative Don Kenney called. He said he was working on his friend, Senator Leo Corbet, and another representative, a man named Jim Hartdegen. Kenney appeared to be earning his money.

Laybe arrived right as I was hanging up. When I asked her what she wanted, she said she needed people to canvass her district, lick envelopes, and work the phones. I told her Tony didn't lick. She then asked for a $220 contribution, the legal limit. I told her I was "maxed out," meaning I had already spread around $2,200, the total amount that one individual could pump into any legislative election. However, I said my wife, Gail, still had some space. She agreed to accept a check in Gail's name, which was perfectly legal. Laybe walked out with my $220.

God bless her, I thought. She was a nice lady who had worked her way from hustling tables to the state legislature. She had found a voiceless and reviled pocket of society and become their champion. Still, she had to survive in her frumpy dresses among the doctors' wives and high society dames who play at politics and populate state legislatures everywhere. In my book, Sue Laybe was a "good broad," the highest compliment a wise guy could give. I figured that she'd stay clean and I'd never see her again.

After that, it was back to dealing with my main diversion. Whenever things got slow, I always had my goofball secretary to get my adrenaline going by putting my life in danger. Michelle, in a dreamy moment, told a cleaning girl that she was in love with some guy named Alan in London. That was interesting, especially since she was supposed to be my friend Carmine's girlfriend.

I was certain Michelle's next mistake was going result in a hollow-point bullet ripping through my brain.

Ron Tapp continued to earn his money. He mentioned that he was working on Senator Jan Brewer. I advised him not to bring the sheep to me unless he was sure they could be sheared. Or as Kenney said, unless they were "ripe." I didn't want my point men bringing me some born-again Christian who would run straight to the attorney general after the meeting.

Tapp advised me to broaden my issue base in order to buy politicians who were already in favor of casino gambling. That was a good tip. He had two suggestions: He advised that we push for private prisons, an innovative concept where prisons are built, owned, and operated as private enterprises that contract with the state for the housing of prisoners.

Tapp also wanted to press for "house arrests" in which a judge sentences someone to stay inside their home for the length of their sentence. Unless they were convicted for obscene calls or running a boiler room telemarketing scam, it would work as well as a prison. The profit was in providing the systems used to monitor the prisoners. These devices, worn on the wrist or ankle, had to be manufactured, rented, and monitored twenty-four hours. It could, and probably will, turn into a billion-dollar industry.

On May 16, Tapp arrived at the office with a tough-looking man who walked with a limp. The stranger was about five-ten, with short brown hair, and a ruddy complexion. Tapp introduced him as Jim Davis, a Yavapai County extradition officer and bounty hunter who was running for justice of the peace (JP) in Mayer, a small town north of Phoenix. Davis, fifty, was a martial arts expert who had won a gold medal in the Arizona Police Olympics in 1988—a remarkable feat considering he only had one leg. His right leg was amputated at the knee after a Viet Cong mortar struck his jeep during the war. The mortar killed two of his buddies and left the third a quadriplegic.

The meet with Davis was a quick burn. He had served as a judge pro tem for civil cases in a Mayer court, and said he was the acting JP. He agreed to "OR" (release on their own recognizance) people from jail for me, run license tags, and do other little things in return for a $2,000 campaign contribution—$1,780 over the limit.

"Can you fix a ticket?" I asked.

"Can I fix one? I can dismiss 'em . . . How fixed is that? . . ."

"How 'bout drunk drivin' and things like that? Somebody gets arrested on a DUI down here [outside Davis' jurisdiction]? . . ."

"I don't think it's any problem. Like I said, the JPs stick real close together."

As usual, the talk turned to sex.

". . . The female [prison] guards are puttin' out," Davis said.

"Are you kiddin' me?"

"No, it's a fact . . . I picked up this guy up in Winslow and he said 'I don't wanna leave!' I said 'You gotta go back down because they're gonna take you to court.' He said, 'Yeah, but look at it this way, I'm gonna lose my [prison] job . . . somebody else's gonna run my still . . . they're gonna get in my pussy while I'm gone!'"

"Meanin' the female guard?"

"Yeah."

That was good to know. I wouldn't feel so sorry for Representative Kenney and the other horny bastards who were about to do some time. They could amuse themselves wenching prison guards while they were doing their time.

After Davis pocketed the two grand, the scorecard read two judges and a politician taken down—and counting.

Around this time, Tapp began pushing a new issue. He wanted to pass a law that called for the election of superior court judges instead of having them appointed. He felt they would be easier to bribe if they had to run for office.

A week later, Judge Stump paid me a visit. Seeing him reminded me of an old wise-guy joke, "He's so crooked that when he dies they're gonna hafta screw him into the ground." I gave him another $500—he was still running unopposed—and sent him on his merry way. The judge was now on video.

The next day, I received a letter from another "judge," Gary Bartlett. He claimed I owed him $3,088 for the time he spent in Reno attending some judicial college. I mumbled "screw him" and blew it off, but the prosecutors in the fourth room were upset. They said if Bartlett sued to get his money, the jig was up. I could not represent myself in court as Tony Vincent. If Bartlett pushed for the money, we'd have to fork it over. I hated to hear that. Even though Tony was created in part to be played a sucker, the machismo in Joe didn't take to being squeezed.

On June 6, I hopped in my burgundy 1990 Camaro—the cops had switched it for the Mustang—drove out to I-10 in west Phoenix, spotted a radar cop "taking pictures" on the side of the road, and put the pedal to the metal. I passed him once at seventy miles an hour. He didn't move. I turned around and passed him at eighty. Nothing. I did a U-turn and blew by the guy at ninety. No response. I did it twice more. Nothing. Finally, I pulled up behind him to see if he was alive. He was. I peeled rubber around him, kicking sand, blowing dust, and squealing like a pig at a pork chop factory.

This got his attention.

"Why are you speeding?" he said politely when he pulled me over.

"I just got this car and I wanted to see what it would do," I said.

"Well, I'm gonna hafta write you a ticket."

Please do, I thought.

The point of this insanity was that I needed a ticket for my pal Judge Stump to fix to bolster the bribery charge. After I got the ticket, I called him and he agreed to come over and take care of it.

Stump arrived at my office late in the afternoon.

"I don't have any points comin' at me, right?" I inquired, handing him my ticket and $200.

"Well, when I take this, we're just gonna wipe this out, period."

"What about the cop's copy?"

"That won't make any difference . . . At this point, I'm gonna forty-three this thing. I'm going out and take it and burn it."

"What's forty-three?"

"Forty-three means a dismissal. I just dismiss the thing to nothin' . . . I just took it and said to the officer, 'Well, you can take it and clean your hinder parts with the rest.'"

So that's what the cops do with the carbon copies. Another mystery solved.

"Well, now you see why a fella like me can get embarrassed," I said. "That's why a fellow like me gives up $2,000 because he knows that some day somethin' stupid like this is gonna happen, and he's gonna need a fella like you to help him out."

"I'm here to help you any way I can . . ." Stump promised.

"See, that's like I tell you, I mean, a fella says, 'Well, I want you to give a judge $2,000.' I never balk because you never know when you're gonna need a judge."

"Well, that's right . . . My girlfriend, she calls this thing down here the buttercup. She says, the little butter, you know . . ."

I didn't know how or why the judge suddenly decided to slip his dick into the conversation, only that it was typical.

"There's a place and a time for everything," the judge continued a few minutes later. "If you just decide to do your racing in the Tolleson precinct, and Don Stump's still the judge, why probably all things can come out satisfactorily."

Hot damn!

On June 13, Popsy strolled into the office with two ominous shadows, Romano Sbrocca and George Sikokis, a.k.a. Big George, George Drake, Nick the Greek, and Theodore Sorenson. This was the move I'd been waiting for. Sbrocca operated out of his popular east Phoenix restaurant, Ernesto's Backstreet. Although the Feds suspected that he was laundering drug profits, he'd never taken a fall. He was a short man in his fifties with reddish hair. That afternoon, he was dressed to the teeth in a pinstriped Godfather suit. *

Big George, who had been arrested on numerous felonies, was a tall Greek who arched his nose in the air like he was smelling shit.

This was going to be fun.

Sbrocca began pumping me about my operation. I gave him my heaviest Brooklyn Tony rap. Big George appeared skeptical. He didn't feel I could get the gambling legislation passed. Sbrocca looked jealous. Tony Vincent was everything he always wanted to be. We chatted for about forty minutes. It was a preliminary meeting, a feeling-out session. The move against me, if it came, would come later.

Actually, the meeting turned out to be far more troublesome than the police and prosecutors realized. At the time, Sbrocca was in the midst of a nineteen-month FBI drug money–laundering sting. Thus, two massive law enforcement operations—Desert Sting and "Steep Chase"—crossed paths in my office that afternoon. Theoretically, all hell could have broken loose with cops and county attorneys pouring out one door, and FBI agents and Federal prosecutors swarming in another.

The next day, Tapp and Jim Davis visited. I gave Davis another $500 for his continuing services. During the chitchat, I mentioned that the Camaro was killing my back. Davis offered to get rid of it for me, that is, steal it, deliver it to a chop shop, and let me collect the insurance. That's known as "selling it to the insurance company." I told him I'd consider his offer.

*In May 1991, the *Phoenix Gazette* published an article which quoted Joseph Stedino as saying, "I'm 90 percent sure they [Romano Sbrocca and George Sikokis] are the closest thing I've found to organized crime in this town." The article went on to quote an attorney for Sbrocca as saying, "There's no organized crime here." When asked why his name was associated with certain underworld characters, Sikokis was quoted as saying: "I have no idea." As this book was being completed in May of 1992, Sbrocca sued Joseph Stedino, the publisher of the *Phoenix Gazette*, and one of its reporters for defamation based, in part, on Stedino's quote.

After the meet, I huddled with Ball and Sergeant Davis. We decided to pitch the idea of letting Davis pinch the car. Five days later, the word came down that "Operation Chop Shop" was a go. Since Davis was a form of police officer, they were eager to nail him.

Operation Chop Shop had a neat little twist. Instead of the Camaro, which the county had paid for, it was decided to let Davis grab my secretary's 1986 Corvette. What a wonderful idea! Michelle would be given the Camaro and I'd get another car. When told the good news, Michelle whined that she "wouldn't get as much attention" in the Camaro.

I called Jim Davis and gave him the skinny. He said he would arrange to bring the car to a chop shop in Prescott. I asked him if he was going to be taken care of on the other end, meaning the chop shop people would pay for the car. He said no. That was interesting. I offered him $1,000 to handle it for me. He accepted.

After I hung up, I analyzed Davis' plan. He was telling me he was going to steal a $15,000 Corvette and deliver it to a chop shop for free. He wanted me to believe it was a public service he provided to organized crime. And Davis bought the line that Tony Vincent, a mobster with $10 million to throw around, wanted to risk his freedom on a $15,000 insurance scam. Best yet, he believed that Tony would pay him a cool grand to steal his car.

When I returned to the office after lunch, Michelle was gone. I called Detective Ball. He didn't know where she was. A half hour, an hour passed, no Michelle. People were calling to arrange meetings and take bribes, but no Michelle. When I left just before 5 p.m., she still hadn't returned.

The next morning as I drove to the office, Ball called to explain the mystery of Michelle's lost afternoon. It seems she left to take an emotional last ride in her gleaming Corvette. During her drive, she said she spotted a turtle crawling across the road. She stopped the 'Vette, jumped out, and picked up the turtle. She then hunted for a pet shop. When she found one, they refused to take the reptile. She claimed they told her it was a water turtle—in the desert?—and suggested that she drop it into an irrigation canal. She insisted that she spent the rest of the afternoon searching the desert around Phoenix for just such a canal.

It got better. Sergeant Davis was said to be so enraged by the apparently "hokey" story that he would spare no resources to disprove it, and then bounce Michelle off the case.

I was elated. The thorn in my side was finally going to be

removed. The paper-thin link in our chain was about to be burned away and a new iron ring would be welded in its place. It was the happiest I'd been in months.

Ball called back a few hours later. "It's true, Tony."

"What?"

"Her story, the turtle, all true," he said.

"You gotta be kidding."

"No. We checked with the pet store. A woman fitting her description did bring them a turtle. They did refuse to accept it. They did tell her to take it to a canal. It's all true."

I let out a string of obscenities.

"We're gonna have to keep her on," Ball said.

"What!" I screamed. "Even if it's true, she should be dumped. Hell, especially if it's true!"

I raged on, arguing that any undercover agent who would abandon her post in a critical operation to spend an afternoon trying to rescue a water turtle in the middle of the Sonoran Desert should be drummed out of the force without delay. Ball countered that the deal was, if the story was a lie, she was gone. No one considered that it might be true.

So, as Michelle's turtle went its way, doing the breast stroke in some irrigation canal, I went back to work and waited for the next rod to get thrown through the engine of Operation Desert Sting.

5

Operation Chop Shop swung into action on June 22, 1990. Davis arrived at my office after hours, around 5:30 p.m. The Corvette was across the street in a restaurant parking lot. I could see it from my office window. I gave Davis the car keys and $1,200—the extra $200 was for running a police check on Sbrocca and Sikokis—and told him that I wouldn't call the cops and report the car stolen until he gave the word that it was being dismantled inside the chop shop. Davis said he was going to pick up an accomplice, and would return for the Corvette later that evening. I stressed that I wanted it chopped as planned so it could never be found.

"I mean no trace," I ordered. "It's not gonna be a taxi cab in Tijuana. That's the old gaff that gets people fucked up. If they chop it, it can't come back to me."

"Right," Davis assured.

After he left, Ball, Sergeant Davis, and Mount came into my office. We turned out the lights and watched the drama unfold. The police had arranged for the 'Vette to be followed by a posse of detectives in a van and two separate cars. It would also be shadowed by a police airplane.

Jim Davis pulled out of the parking lot in his own car and promptly spotted one of the detectives sitting in his vehicle chatting away on the police radio. What a crack police operation. Davis drove away, glanced in his rearview mirror, and determined that three sets of police officers were following him. He pulled over and found a pay phone.

"Tony, I've picked up some heat somewhere. I got three cops on my ass!"

"I don't know what that's about," I said. "They must have been staking out the building for someone else."

"What do you want me to do?"

"Do what you want. If you don't want the car, don't take it."

Meanwhile, Sergeant Davis ordered the three shadow cars pulled off. We'd go with the airplane and pick up the trail when he came for the Corvette—if he was stupid enough to return for it.

Davis called again a few minutes later. He said he had shaken two cops but still had one on his tail. If you've got one cop on your tail, you might as well have the whole force. I told him that he was getting paranoid.

He called back again. He had picked up his accomplice, a woman in her fifties wearing a red-and-white striped blouse, and said he was on his way to pinch the Corvette.

"They were thicker, thicker on me than flies. I'm tellin' you that. I mean, I went from here to Glendale, and movin'."

"Hey, I'm with you," I said. "If you want to call it off. Whatever you want to do."

". . . Okay, if they jump up again, I'll be gettin' plate numbers . . . I know they came out of the street right across from you. I watched him come out."

"They could be layin' on one of these stockbrokers and then grabbed you," I winged, laughing. ". . . What would the connection be between me and you? You're a cop and a judge. And I'm a business-man with no criminal record. So I don't see any connection there at all."

"Okay . . . Maybe they figured I was seeing somebody else."

"There could be heat on anybody in this building. But I don't think there's any heat on me."

"Okay. If anything pops up, I'll call you again."

Davis pulled into the restaurant parking lot. The woman got out and hopped into the 'Vette. Smooth. If they were busted, the woman would take the fall. Detectives Ron Sterrett and Mark Stribling, driving separate vehicles, fanned out behind them. Ball and Sergeant Davis sprinted down from my office, jumped into their cars and joined the caravan. The detectives expected Davis to lead them to a bustling chop shop in Prescott. They would then stake out the place, radio for rein-forcements from police departments with proper jurisdiction, and bust what they were certain would be a multimillion-dollar stolen auto parts operation.

The four-car caravan followed Davis and the mystery woman—and followed, and followed, for two hundred miles all the way to Nogales, Arizona, near Mexico. Davis was going to sell the car south of the border, a common move among Arizona car thieves. They could command a higher price in Mexico, especially if the buyer was a big shot with political connections. Phoenix Police auto theft detectives estimated that such a Corvette could be sold in Mexico for as much as $7,000. An Arizona chop shop would have paid $200 to $500.

Davis called the next day to report that he had successfully delivered the car to the chop shop. He also made a point of saying that he spent the night in Phoenix. I thanked him for his diligent service.

The police, interestingly enough, let the expensive car vanish behind the border where it is no doubt helping some Mexican playboy get laid to this day. For the auto theft charges to stick, it had to be a done deal. And once it was done in Mexico, it was done. Adios, silver and black Corvette.

For the umpteenth time, I marveled at the dangerous stupidity of the players in this political farce. Arizona has no Mafia family, so nobody knows how to deal with the Mob. Had Tony Vincent been real, the next morning would find wild javelinas nibbling on Jim Davis' mutilated body—right at the foot of a tall saguaro cactus.

This yo-yo was lucky this was just a sting.

At the end of June, as the temperature dipped from recent highs of 122 degrees to a chilly 115 degrees, the decision was made that Tony needed a high-line apartment as an alternate operations site. It was felt that the politicians might be more comfortable in an informal setting. I suspected a second, stronger motivation. The cops and county attorneys were getting tired of spending hours on end cramped together in the fourth room getting on each other's nerves. They wanted a place where they could be more comfortable while they waited for something to happen.

I located an upscale complex five blocks from the office and rented two adjacent apartments. I set up house in one and gave the cops the keys to the other. My place was wired for sound and color video. The spider had a new web.

What the spider didn't have was a single shirt in the bedroom closet, or so much as an errant sock in a drawer. I didn't see that as a problem. I had told everybody that I was living with my girlfriend, and this place was just for when my wife came to town. And I wasn't planning to let anyone into the master bedroom anyway. Besides, dancing on the edge keeps the senses sharp.

Tapp came to the office on July 2 and told me he was softening two more legislators, Representatives Candice Nagel and William Mundell. I looked them up in the book. Nagel was a mature, attractive blonde who worked in the hotel industry. Mundell was a young attorney who looked like an FBI poster boy. I looked forward to meeting them both.

Tapp also informed me that he had a purchased a classic 1966 Mustang convertible, no doubt with Tony's money. He claimed the purchase price came from money he and his wife, a former nun, earned from the bail bonds business. At this point, Ron Tapp had confessed to everything but the Kennedy assassination, and that wasn't out of the question.

Four days later, I had a meet with Representative Kenney and Tapp. Kenney was in rare form. He referred to me as his "compadre" and "padrone" and offered an update on his efforts to bring Representative Jim Hartdegen and other lawmakers into the fold.

"Let me give you a little background on Hartdegen . . . Hartdegen's the type that's never made probably over eight bucks an hour in his life . . . He doesn't think of big things. To him a new car is a three-year-old pickup . . . But we'll make an A-player out of him . . . He's what you call an unsophisticated whore, and they're so gorgeous, they don't realize they're gorgeous . . . They roll over for nothing . . ."

"I want to make it clear that I don't expect either one of you, you as quarterback and him as coach, I don't expect you to chase these people," I said, laying down a modified version of the prime directive.

"Hey, we're not," Kenney protested. "We just reel 'em in."

Kenney continued his discourse on Arizona politics.

"Okay, remember each individual has entirely different backgrounds. The scope of experiences and influence are high. They're all gun-shy as shit. They have, every night on TV, some poor mayor of Washington, D.C., or some poor congressman caught in the AbScam trial, or something like that, so they're gun-shy. That's Leo's [Senator Corbet's] situation. He's been burned. He's on the verge of being disbarred. One more complaint, he'll be out of the state bar."

Corbet, Kenney explained, got toasted big time in some cantaloupe deal involving the Dominican Republic that went sour. Cantaloupes! What a way to go.

"What I'm shooting for are guys that, four o'clock in the morning, the last day of the session . . . they don't give a fuck what they vote for," Kenney continued. "Just tell him 'You vote, this is the five thou-

paigns. If Kenney could salt their war chests, they'd in turn be
;ated to support his bid for Speaker of the House or chairman of
House Judiciary Committee, whatever he had his eye on. Kenney
previously come to me requesting $10,000 to purchase "Vote for
signs for his supporters. I repeated "Tony's Golden Rule" which
"He who has the gold, makes the rules," and my rule was face-to-
meetings. I wasn't going to fund the campaigns of politicians who
:n't in my pocket.

Ball called the next day looking for Michelle. She had gone AWOL
1.

"Check the coffee shop," I cracked. "That's where she works now."

Tapp phoned and said he was going to meet with a "Captain
ce" of the Maricopa County Sheriff's Department. He claimed that
ce was still angling for a security job at one of my casino hotels. I
sed Tapp to be careful. The fourth room boys weren't enthusiastic
it pursuing this lead. They felt it would be stirring up a hornet's
to take on the sheriff's department.

Tapp had set a meeting for the following day with Senator Jan
'er, a name tossed around frequently as a possible player. Brewer
the senator in Representative Kenney's "Sun City" district north-
of Phoenix. Ball delivered $10,000 for the buy, then retreated to
ourth room with his partners in anticrime.

At 2:30 p.m. Tapp called and said Brewer had gotten cold feet. He
rted that she was "paranoid of Mafioso" and didn't want any
ey. "She has a tremendous right-wing Christian element in her
ict," Tapp said.

"So does D. K. [Don Kenney]. It doesn't bother him."

"Yeah, but you have to remember, D. K. is a real whore."

Tapp found Brewer's reluctance surprising because she was, he
ied, a woman of loose morals.

"I think that, honestly, Jan would like to get into my drawers."

"Is she single?"

"No, but when I'm around Jan, she seems to be highly attracted to
and John, her husband, seems to be highly attracted to Helen
p's wife] . . . Does that give you a clue?"

"Swappers?"

"Could be. Could very well be."

This I found hard to believe. Tapp was a pig. I couldn't imagine
ne longing to get into his drawers.

t got worse. Tapp said he suspected that Brewer was a reformed
.er from Las Vegas, and that when she worked as a private detec-
she used to sleep around for information.

sand bucks' . . . That's my idea of the A-Team.
Rhodes scholars . . . They're not gonna go out and
Women Voters with some asshole from the chur
go out there and vote '*qui*' when I tell them to vot

"That's the A-Team," I said. "We're all on the

". . . All you need is thirty-one votes, you do
[in the House] . . ." Kenney said. "Again, the a
dividual is different. My assessment of Hartdege
titute. He doesn't know what he's worth . . .
Arizona's fairly unsophisticated in that regard.
legislator for ten years, I've never had anyone [o
degen has a great line, 'I've had my hand un
fifteen years and all I've gotten is some stale
Which is the truth. This is a relatively naive state

"I can understand why nobody came to you,
"Why?"
"You lose it!" I said, referring to his car trunk
"I was so nervous that day when I came in
shaking," Kenney said laughing. "I was absolute
camera watching us up there."

Kenney proceeded to outline who I should
bents and challengers, in the upcoming electic
what was becoming a very educational meeting.

"Remember, money is not the only way to h
indebted to you . . . Let me give you some idea
about. Puttin' up [campaign] signs is a bitch. V
sign when it's 120 degrees?"

"This nut," I said, pointing to Tapp.

"Well, we don't want Ron to do it . . . I kno
it's a bitch to get volunteers to put up signs. So
put up signs, you know, get a crew for two week
didates' signs, hey, they're indebted to us . . . R
ing between now and the first of January when
sion starts to finalize the A-Team. Ron and I v
these guys two or three times and gradually ov
bring 'em in to you so that when we start t
maybe five to ten solid Republicans and we sa
what the three thousand bucks I gave you is fo
night of the session you vote for [bill] 2175, peri

Sounded like a hell of a plan to me.

On July 16, Kenney returned for another m
to lay out a few grand for him to distribute int

"Well, let's not put a whore jacket on this broad," I said, trying to tone down the load of malicious bullshit. "But I mean, if you're telling me —"

"That's exactly what we're doing!"

"This guy [an ex-cop] told you she'd fuck for information?"

"Yeah."

After Tapp left, I walked into the fourth room and asked the prosecutors if there was such as thing as "felony gossip." They laughed and said if such a law existed, all the politicians would be in jail.

Tapp called the next day and reported that a lunch meeting with Candice Nagel had not gone well. She professed to vote her convictions and wasn't interested in tainted money.

Kenney phoned and dropped the hint that if I wanted to meet him without Tapp being around, that would be okay. I got the feeling that he felt Tapp blew it with Brewer and Nagel because he came on too strong, or wrong, or they just didn't like him. Kenney said he'd talk to the women and see where they really stood.

On July 23, Stragalas called on the cellular phone and said Representative Laybe wanted another sit-down. My heart sank.

"What's she want?"

"Money," he said.

Laybe called about five minutes later and we set a meet for August 2, at 10 a.m. She talked so softly I could hardly hear her. I made a mental note that I'd have to find a way to make her speak up during the meeting.

Jim Davis phoned next. He said he had to take a leave from his sheriff's office job until after the election, and that put him into financial straits. He wanted a $2,000 loan, and offered to pay ten points a week for two months. That amounted to a hefty $1,600 in juice piled on top of the $2,000 principal. Tony had a better idea.

"If I had a situation that occurred similar to what that fellow in Houston does, are you available?"

"Yeah," Davis said without blinking.

The guy in Houston was a hit man Tapp had told us about. Davis mentioned during a previous conversation that he could do that kind of work. I filed it away, waiting for the right opening.

"What ballpark are we in?" I wondered.

"That's all accordin' to just how much you want done . . . How elaborate do I have to get?"

It appeared that Deputy Davis murdered people on a sliding scale.

"Okay," I said. "Let me kick that around . . ."

I mentioned a television program I had seen, "America's Most

Wanted," where one segment was about Mexican police using stolen American cars. I was jerking Davis' chain to see if he would confess to the Corvette scam. He didn't. I also reminded him about his offer to get me an "orphan," which is an unregistered pistol, and promised that I'd "keep my ear to the grindstone" regarding his financial problems. It was a painful mix of metaphors. I wondered how much it would cost to get Davis to waste somebody that way? The old "ear to the grindstone" method would certainly sow fear into the hearts of Tony's enemies.

The phone rang again. It was Jack Smyth, a guy I'd met during the gambling investigation who owned a strip joint called The Dancing Sunshine. Smyth had heard about my new game and wanted to help. He said he knew a dozen legislators who were pro-gaming. He specifically mentioned Phoenix Senator Carolyn Walker, who had proposed gambling bills in the past, and Representative Mike Palmer, a Democrat from Cochise County in the southeast corner of the state.

"Carolyn Walker, her biggest thing is 'What's in it for me?'" Smyth said.

Sounds like my kind of gal, I thought.

"Mike wasn't that way. Mike's a gambler," Smyth continued.

In return for the intros, Smyth wanted to make sure I'd "throw a bone" of gaming action to the smaller bars and lap dance dens. He envisioned slots and video poker and blackjack games in his place. What was interesting was the way my two operations were starting to merge. The social gambling crowd, left in the cold after the legislature shut down their crooked action, was now viewing me as their messiah.

George Stragalas called at home on my untraceable, undercover line shortly before 7 p.m. on July 23.

"What made you think that [Representative Laybe] wanted money today?" I asked.

"Well, what she said to me. She said, 'Is there a way that your friend, which is a mutual friend of mine as well, can help out by makin' donations to the Democratic party?'"

Laybe wanted to channel my money into the party in order to score points with the Democratic bigwigs. I told George she could do whatever she wanted with it as long as she committed to me.

Two days later, I met with a short, fat, and fortyish lobbyist named David Horwitz who Don Kenney sent my way. An upbeat fellow with a cherubic face, Horwitz fronted for the Arizona chapter of the American Federation of State, County, and Municipal Employees. We talked for a couple of hours. After he warmed, the union man said he could help me "shuffle" contributions to the politicians.

"Legally, labor is only allowed to solicit its own members for political contributions," he said. "However, we can solicit other folks to do internal-education of community service projects . . . and who is to say that the gasoline that went into this truck or to put up signs wasn't a community service project?"

He was saying that he could help me indirectly funnel money to legislators. But that wasn't Tony's action. Even so, I figured I'd see him again. He smelled money.

Michelle made a rare appearance at her desk the next day and informed me that Jim Davis called and said his car had broken down. "He said you would know what that meant."

I had no idea what that meant. I called Davis. He said his car had broken down. That's what it meant. Shrewd code system we had developed. The police had decided to pursue Davis' offer to become Tony's hit man and now Davis needed to rent a car to make the murder meet. I told him he could rent one on my tab.

Davis showed at 1:25 p.m. looking like he just finished rustling some cattle. I explained who I wanted taken out. The target was a man in his fifties with no family who had done me wrong. I explained that I'd bring the guy to town, set him up in a motel, and let Davis take it from there.

I asked Davis how he would do it.

"I'd most likely blow him away. Just put a silencer on it."

At that moment, looking into this psychotic cowboy's cold, dead eyes, I knew he was serious.

"Are you available even after the election? If you're elected [JP] or not, can you still come down and fulfill the contract?" I asked.

"Yeah."

"Even if you lose the race and get back on the [police] force, then you'd still come down and finish it for me?"

He nodded yes.

"If he [the target] has ten [thousand] in his pocket that's yours . . . Leave the plastic. Leave the credit cards. Leave the jewelry," I instructed.

"Done."

"Unless you're dumb enough to take it."

"No, I don't do that."

Davis said he wanted $5,000 for the clip. I agreed and gave him $2,000 in advance to tide him over, plus another C-note for the rental car.

"Uh, I might have another one of these comin' up where it would require a trip to Nevada . . .," I said, doubling the jeopardy. "The guy has a limp. The guy wears a cowboy hat. Very common in Reno."

"Is that where we're talking?" Davis asked. ". . . Might be up there goin' to school."

"At the judicial college? When are you going?"

"After the election . . . I'll be there a couple of weeks."

"You're right there! What a perfect thing to walk away for an evening."

"Yeah."

There was a novel thought. A newly elected justice smoking somebody for hire in between classes on how to uphold the law.

"You know how to break somebody's neck?" I asked.

"Easy," Davis replied, the ice crackling in his veins.

At the end of the day, I recorded what has to be one of the more interesting notations on an official police expense sheet: "Jim Davis— $100 for rental car. $2,000 for murder."

Sergeant D. P. Davis called the next day with some wonderful news. They had grilled Michelle about her latest lost afternoon and were told that she had gone to Smitty's supermarket to pick up some food for the office. When they traced the receipt, it turned out she had gone to a Smitty's all right, but not the one nearby. That was the last straw, even for them. She was going to be phased out of the detail and buried in the transcript room at police headquarters where a staff of cops and typists were already busily working on the tapes. I suspected there was more to that story than a supermarket jaunt.

My elation soon gave way to empathy. Sure, I wanted her out of there, but I still felt bad for her. It wasn't her fault, it was Captain Black's. He wasn't 100 percent behind the operation in the beginning and telegraphed his feelings by putting a raw rookie on the job. This particular rookie was especially ill-equipped for the task. She had lived at home all her life, and her previous job had been as a veterinarian's assistant, which explained her sympathy for wandering turtles. The changes in her life had come fast. She was suddenly taking home a much bigger paycheck, and was handed a Corvette to cruise around in. Professionally, she was thrust headfirst into a tense undercover operation that initially involved doing practically nothing. As for maintaining her cover, her background made it difficult. She had lived in Phoenix for years and attended high school there. That made it hard to envelop herself in a new identity, especially when she frequently bumped into or socialized with old friends.

On the other hand, she was a real airhead.

By then, frightening as it seemed, I was beginning to understand police thinking. Michelle probably would have been a greater risk working the streets. Police departments leak like spaghetti colanders. The detectives and officers intermingle professionally and socially with the judges and legislators, and no doubt would have "quietly" warned their friends, associates, or lovers about the sting. A politician given such information would have whispered warnings to his closest friends, and so on, until everyone was alerted. This supported what a close friend of mine, Gerald Arenberg, had warned me about.

"Joe, be careful when you deal with the police," he advised. "They talk too much."

Arenberg's words carried weight. He's the executive director of the American Federation of Police (AFP), and heads the National Association of Chiefs of Police. I met him in Vegas when I emceed an AFP fund-raiser. During the entire "AzScam" operation, he acted as my "deep throat," advising me how to handle certain situations, mostly how to deal with the police. I'd relay what was happening, and he'd educate me on what each particular police action, decision, or comment really meant. His warning about blabbermouth cops was extremely disquieting. Whether you're a good guy or bad, the worst way to fall is to be sabotaged from within.

I was introduced to my new secretary at the apartment a few weeks prior to the switch. She was a petite brunette named Michelle Thiry. Another Michelle! Number II was pleasant in both looks and disposition, and had one year on the force under her belt. Better yet, she had brains. She had graduated from Northern Arizona University with a degree in criminal justice. Michelle II was on a fast-track to move up through the ranks, where female brass are in short supply. I perceived that she would view this assignment as a launching pad, and would do everything in her power to make it a success.

The first thing I did was change her name. She became Rosa Marie Donato. Her cover was that she was my niece. That was designed to keep all the prick-in-hand judges and politicians from hitting on her.

Representative Kenney caught me on the cellular phone during my drive home. These mobile calls couldn't be taped, so I usually mouthed static noises, claimed to be near one of the area's mountains, and requested that the person call me at home.

"[Representative] Candice Nagel is ripe and ready," Kenney said. "She needs $2,500, but wants it bundled. Tapp can give you a list of names."

"That's okay by me," I said. "But she's got to come to the office and get it."

As soon as I hung up, Tapp called.

"Did you hear the news about California?"

"No."

"They nailed a bunch of legislators in a sting!"

"So what else is new?" I said. "People have been buying politicians since time began."

My cool reaction calmed Tapp's nerves.

Tapp called first after I got home. He was still worried about the California legislators and wanted to meet my bug sweeper from Reno. I said that was okay by me. He also suggested that we form a corporation that could be used to distribute the bribes. I told him to proceed with the paperwork. We agreed to name the company Arizona Economic Resource Group.

Kenney called that Sunday, July 28. He knocked Tapp, saying the bail bondsman wasn't smooth enough to woo the more sophisticated lawmakers like Senator Brewer and Representative Nagel. He also said that he had talked with Senator Leo Corbet at length and Corbet remained extremely hinky. Cantaloupe problems and all. Kenney said Corbet had me figured for the Mob.

Kenney added that Nagel had phoned him wanting to know if Tapp was serious about me being a good source for cash. He said she was nibbling, but chilled every time the conversation hinted at doing something illegal. Nagel, Kenney explained, had yet to reach her "comfort level."

"Give these people checks," my quarterback advised. "Because as a candidate, these people would have a comfort level if you give 'em ten checks for $220. For example. Candice Nagel, that $220, they cash it, they Xerox it, their ass is covered . . ."

"[Tapp] was gonna swing by her office for her, I was gonna meet her and give her the money. And he had the names to give her," I explained.

"Well, as I understand, he was going to just give her $2,500 with ten names on it in cash."

"What's wrong with that? Is that different than the checks?"

"Well . . . it takes away from that comfort level . . ." Kenney said. "You just can't go out and give bags full of cash 'cause you're just attracting a red flag to yourself."

After that, the phrase "comfort level" became the second most important idiom in the Desert Sting operation, right below "prime directive." I learned that politicians have their own individual comfort levels that have to be attained before they would accept bribes and illegal donations. They wouldn't reach for Tony's loot until a deal was structured to meet an individual's comfort level.

The check requirement caught me by surprise. In every other area of society, people laugh at you if you try to bribe them with a check. Not politicians. In their insane world, they actually prefer checks.

Kenney's wrinkle about checks was okay because the two concepts, comfort level and prime directive, weren't necessarily in conflict. If the politician voluntarily suggested what had to be done to reach his or her comfort level, we could accommodate them—as long as the deal could also be structured to fit into a third precept—"Tony's Golden Rule," which stated that whatever shape the "bundle" took, Tony had to make the drop face-to-face.

Kenney continued taking me to school, teaching me more about dirty politics in this one conversation than most people learn in a lifetime. He advised me to open ten to twelve different bank accounts in the names of my aunts, uncles, brothers, and sisters, my secretary and her aunts, uncles, brothers, sisters, nieces, and nephews, etc., to bundle the checks. He added that what we had going for us with Nagel was that she was "PACed out," meaning she had accepted all the money she was legally allowed to from Political Action Committees [PACs]. PACs are special-interest organizations that many observers feel have no other purpose than to lawfully buy politicians. Nagel was also expecting to be blindsided by a hit piece from her opponent. A "hit piece" is a mailer that attacks the voting record, life-style, or personal foibles of an incumbent. The incumbent invariably reacts, or overreacts, by buying a newspaper advertisement or sending out his or her own mailer that either counterattacks or vigorously defends against the charges.

An incumbent who is PACed out and gets nailed with a hit piece is thus desperate for the infusion of cash needed to finance a response. That makes them vulnerable to the Tony Vincents of the world.

6

Although the undercover operation was going well, the job was becoming increasingly stressful. I'd come home exhausted from the pressure of being "on" ten to twelve hours a day. More and more people were circling Tony's treasure chest. There were meetings nearly every morning and afternoon. My phone rang constantly. When I wasn't "on," I was sleeping. And even then, even in my dreams, I was Tony Vincent.

If someone yelled "Tony," I'd instantly turn. When my wife called out to Joe, I wouldn't budge.

Joe Stedino was becoming a fading memory. I was under, and under deep.

George Stragalas came in at the end of July with news about a possible meet with former governor Sam Goddard. Sam's son Terry was entering the homestretch of a close and expensive gubernatorial race and needed all the money he could get. Although Terry Goddard had shot out of the gate as the favorite, the leading Republican challenger, J. Fife Symington, was charging up the rail. The fact that J. Fife was a rich boy "elitist" who sat on the board of a savings and loan that later failed wasn't enough to keep his supporters from rushing to the polls. The Symington groundswell prompted the Democrats to start sniffing around the cash-laden lair of Tony Vincent. Stragalas said Sam Goddard might be interested in doing business with me.

My coach and quarterback, Tapp and Kenney, breezed in for another huddle. We talked some more about comfort levels and bundling checks. Tapp didn't like the idea of setting up the phony checking accounts. He felt that was too risky. Instead, we concluded that postal money orders were the ticket. They're as good as cash, and you can write any donor's name on them. We had found the perfect way to deal with politicians who were afraid of cash.

A few days later, Tapp brought Representative Bill Mundell to a lunch at Stockyards, a restaurant in east Phoenix. Mundell represents Chandler, a half-farming, half-developed bedroom community southeast of Phoenix. I was in my cowboy outfit again, complete with a bolo tie and shit-kicker boots. I also wore a body mike. Mundell was so clean-cut he looked like he walked out of a Sears catalog. He was a tall, blond, good-looking attorney who appeared rather pleased with himself. I toned Tony down a bit, not Brooklyn Tony, but not quite Park Avenue Tony either. Mundell was an attorney, but he was also a kid. I gave my casino spiel then asked him what he needed. He said six or seven thousand would be nice.

At that point, it seemed like this was going to be another quick burn. However, when I asked how he wanted it, his eyes nearly popped out of his head. He proceeded to give me a speech on Proposition 200, the $220 limit law. The more he talked, the more nervous he became. When Tapp suggested we could wash the money through Tapp's bail bond company, Mundell begged off. He suggested, instead, that if we really wanted to help, we could provide transportation to the polling places. If I played this game, Tony would have become a real social activist. I'd be licking envelopes and walking a beat on the wild side for Representative Sue Laybe, and then driving a yellow school bus to Sun Lakes to herd all the geezers to the voting booth for Billy Mundell.

Screw that.

What Mundell needed was a nice warm body to push him over the edge. He had recently divorced and, according to Tapp and Kenney, was focusing most of his energy on skirt chasing. If I'd have stuck that seven grand in the garter of a prime Vegas bed warmer and plucked her down on his face, we might not have heard any more speeches about Proposition 200. But women weren't in Tony's arsenal, so I figured I wouldn't see the man from Chandler again.

The first week of August marked a new era for the operation. The police swept in, ushered Michelle I out, and plugged Michelle II in her place. Michelle I was told that six months was the longest they liked to keep someone under. My cover story was that Carmine missed her terribly and wanted her back in Reno. What was interesting about the move was that although the faces had changed, the car didn't.

Michelle I arrived that morning in the Camaro. Michelle II drove the Camaro home that evening. To Tony's secretary go the burgundy spoils.

From the moment Michelle II, a.k.a. Rosa Marie Donato, took her seat, Operation Desert Sting began to run smoothly. "Marie" was exactly the kind of intelligent, efficient operative I needed to assist me. She had worked the Desert Sting transcript room prior to coming on-line, so she was up-to-date on the operation. Mostly, however, she gave me peace of mind.

Representative Laybe arrived for her scheduled meet on Thursday, August 2, clad in a dress Minnie Pearl would have burned. She was nervous and hyper and got right to the point. She wanted $10,000. I gave my speech about buying her vote. She agreed. Ball beeped me, then I reached in my desk drawer where the cops had stashed $35,000 in confiscated drug money. Hold on. Labye didn't want the money yet. She hadn't figured out a way to funnel it into the Democratic party. She said she'd get back to me after she worked it out with her high-powered, mysterious "financial consultant."

Out the door she went, still a virgin.

Ironically, Laybe's exact opposite was next on the agenda. Popsy had pressed me for weeks to hook up with Shiree Foster, a young woman from the Phoenix Chamber of Commerce. Foster was Romano Sbrocca's mistress and was said to have a lot of political contacts. I figured it was a move to plant a spy on me. But the move told me a lot about Sbrocca. No Mafioso would even consider dropping his own woman on someone else. That would result in an instant loss of respect, which in turn could result in a visit from a raving homicidal maniac like Jim Davis.

Still, the move intrigued me. I didn't like Sbrocca from the instant I met him. I was itching to burn him. So I bent the prime directive a bit and reached out for Shiree—pronounced "Sure-REE" instead of "Sherry."

The thirty-year-old Texas native sashayed into my office like John Dillinger's lady in red an hour or so after Laybe exited. This was no virgin. Operation Desert Sting had a lot of sex talk, but until then, no full-bodied sex appeal. That changed the instant Ms. Foster marched her blonde, mini-skirted self into my office. The guys in the fourth room leaped from their stupor and crowded the monitors to get a closer look.

I was Brooklyn Tony all the way with this little moll. If she was filing reports to Sbrocca, I was going to give them a show. I did my casino bit, then pulled out two C-notes to join the Phoenix Chamber of

Commerce. Shiree grabbed the money like a pro. She was young, bubbly, giggly, inquisitive, and upbeat, but I could see that her nights traveling on the dark side of the force were already beginning to harden her. She wore more makeup than she needed, and the facial embellishment appeared to be a new affectation. She had yet to master the art of keeping her lipstick on her lips. Instead, it trailed behind her like Hansel and Gretel's crumbs. She spotted everything in her path, cups, Coke cans, her front teeth, my pen, you name it.

Since she worked for the Chamber, I asked her about Phoenix's image problems. "Why is this town becoming less palatable and less attractive to tourists? What's the problem? What's wrong here? Something is not right."

"We've had so much bad publicity with the governor [Mecham] . . ." she explained. "And okay, you know Charlie Keating caused a lot of negatives. And our two senators are crooks."

I could see the Chamber's brochures: "Arizona! Okay, we got Evan Mecham, Charlie Keating, and two crooked U.S. senators—but it's dry heat!"

Midway through our meeting, something strange happened. Shiree started pouring her heart out about her life, particularly about her sixteen-month relationship with Sbrocca, who, on top of being ugly, uncouth, and a quarter-century her senior, was married.

". . . All I demanded was some attention and some time. Not even that much . . . I'm a very supportive, understanding person and I'm dumped . . . I cried about it for the first time Saturday night. I'm still upset . . . I don't know why men do it to me. Promise me this and that and I really like to take people at what they say, but that's been the hardest thing of my life to overcome, to understand . . . I say, 'Okay God, what are you trying to show me through rejection and disappointment, hard times, being through some real extreme situations with my job, finances, family, relationships? What are you trying to tell me?'"

Perhaps God's trying to tell you that you need to hang with a better class of people, I thought.

"I mean, I just keep getting up and dusting myself off," she continued. ". . . I've come through kind of a crummy time and I thought maybe well, maybe you would understand."

I understood. All too well. If she was a spy sent in by Sbrocca, she deserved an Academy Award.

Shiree asked me about my meeting with Sbrocca. "What did they . . . what transpired? I mean, were they asking for money?"

It was time to deliver the message.

"No, oh no. I hope they don't make that mistake. You'll really be lookin' for a [new] boyfriend if he makes that mistake. You know, he's . . . connected with . . . shit. I hope they don't start playing them games . . . Don't play cowboys with me. You can take that back to him and the Greek [Sikokis]. I don't care who they know."

I made the mistake of asking her how she got involved with Sbrocca. She explained at length that she wandered into his restaurant and nightclub a few times, and it was magic.

The phone rang. It was the fourth room.

"Hey, she's breaking our hearts. We're all cried out in here and we're out of Kleenex. Wind it up."

"All right Carmine," I said, using the code name. "Who loves ya baby? Who loves ya? If I ever give up the broads, you're first. Good-bye."

Although the cops had wearied of Shiree, I knew she was going to pay off down the road. Our strange relationship was only beginning.

"I'm gonna be hurt if you don't come and see me," I said . . . I truly mean this, now look into my eyes. The eyes are the window to the soul."

"That's right . . . And I will get in to see you and I hope we stay friendly . . . Any time you wanna, like, if you're alone and you give me a call and say, 'Hey, meet me tonight somewhere, I'm gonna be at the Ritz' or wherever. I'll be with you in a heartbeat. I'd love it, 'cause I love your company."

After she left, her perfume stayed in the office the rest of the day. It would become a familiar scent.

On Tuesday, August 7, I was standing in line at a nearby post office when the cellular phone rang.

"Tony, Sue Laybe. I'm ready. How's 1:30 in your office?"

"Fine by me."

"See you there, bye."

I returned to the office and cleared my slate. A meet with Dave Horwitz, the union guy, was canceled. An introduction meet with Tapp and Representative Bill English was moved up a few hours. I didn't want Laybe and English running into each other in my hall like two church deacons exiting adjacent playrooms in a whorehouse. Laybe was coming in to cook herself, so she took precedence.

But first, I had to deal with English. He was a tall, lean, weather-beaten desert man in his early sixties who was known to have a short fuse. Horwitz told me that someone once had the misfortune of handing him a complicated union bill in his office. The veteran representative promptly threw it across the room, pages flying.

"I'm not going to piss on the floor for labor the rest of this session!" English announced, according to Horwitz. English then forgot where he was and stormed out of his own office, leaving everyone sitting there. Kenney had warned me that English was pretty deep in the bottle.

I started out Park Avenue Tony with this old fox, but quickly switched to the streets. He was a player all the way. Not only a player, but one with his own moves. It wasn't long before he was advising me of my need for a good public relations professional. And he just happened to know someone.

Let me guess, I thought, Ernie Hoffman, his party-animal pal. I nailed that one on the head.

I asked English what he needed to support my gambling bill. As expected, he ducked the question. Didn't matter. He'd already told me loud and clear what he needed—Hoffman. I shooed him out of my office, loaded up the money drawer, stuffed cotton in my ears, and waited for Laybe. The cotton was my idea. Laybe spoke so softly, the tape wasn't picking her up. I invented an ear infection to get her to project better.

She arrived wearing what looked like the same Minnie Pearl–reject dress. I loudly explained my ear problem.

"Every time I jump in the pool, I get an ear infection, so I got the drops in there and . . . it affects my hearing and I, if I yell at ya today, it doesn't mean I don't love ya, I just can't control my voice 'cause everything's an echo."

The ruse worked. Laybe spoke up. Her first move was to bum a cigarette. She didn't flinch when I handed her one of my unfiltered Camels. Tough broad.

Knowing she was one that cut to the chase, I made my move.

"You got it straightened out?" I asked, referring to her laundry problem and mysterious advisor.

"Yeah. It was easy."

"What are you gonna do?

"I'm just gonna hand somebody $10,000 and it's taken care of."

Brilliant. It took them five days to figure that out?

"So there's no trail back to me?" I asked.

"I said I found a sugar daddy fag and he doesn't want his name involved whatsoever . . . If he does say anything, I'll just say he's an Ed Buck type. Rich fag."

"Fag, geez, do I have to go limp-wristed?"

"No."

It was time to set the hook.

". . . You can call this a gift, call it Christmas time, call it whatever you want, just so . . . you're with me and you and I have an understanding that this is for your help and for you voting for my . . ."

"I'll even sign on as a cosponsor," she interrupted.

"Will ya? Oh, that'd be nice."

My phone rang. It was the fourth room.

"She's cooked herself," the voice said. "Give her the money."

I took $10,000 out of the drawer, handed it to her, and asked her to count it. She took the bundle and cracked the crisp bills like a nun slapping a ruler on the hand of a mischievous student. The C-notes snapped so loud the microphones picked it up. You could hardly hear her voice, but you could hear that dirty money popping halfway to Texas.

When Sue finished, she asked for an envelope, stuffed the cash inside, licked it, and dropped it into her purse. She politely thanked me and inched forward like she was ready to take the money and run. I set the hook again just in case something had gone wrong with the tapes.

". . . I appreciate your support and I appreciate your commitment to me and I'm committed to you, so one hand washes the other."

"That's what it's all about," she said.

I couldn't argue with that.

In the fourth room, the boys were lined up with their hands in the air and huge smiles on their face. I walked down the line and high-fived them all. It was one of my better acting jobs — not with Laybe, but with them. It was a solid burn. Another big fish was put in the pan. I had to act happy for the operation. In reality, Laybe's fall was tearing me up inside.

The fourth room crew left after the celebration, figuring that was enough excitement for one day. Not quite. Tapp called and said he was on the way back to tell me what English wanted. I interrupted him and said I already knew. English wanted the package given to Ernie, his bagman. Tapp was surprised at my perception, but a blind man could have spotted that move.

I called Sergeant Davis and Detective Ball and summoned them back to the fourth room. When Tapp arrived, I explained that Tony didn't do bagmen. He responded that we should at least meet the guy and hear him out.

Shiree dropped by the next day. She was wearing shorts and a blue top, and had snapped her heel in an air vent on the way up. When she limped over to the window, I received a call from "Carmine" in the fourth room.

"Get her back on the couch where we can see her legs!" one of the boys ordered.

I did as instructed, ordering her to stop flitting around.

Shiree said she knew Senator Jesus "Chuy" Higuera and Representative Stan Barnes and might send them my way. Chuy, pronounced "Chewy," was a Democrat from Tucson. Barnes was a Republican who represented Mesa, the second-largest city in the Phoenix metropolitan area. I encouraged Shiree to send them and gave her a Vegas $200 as an advance for her introductory services.

"I'm a Republican, but my money is apolitical," I announced. "My money is bisexual. My money is bipartisan. It doesn't care who I support."

Shiree's offer was a twist. I was certain she had come to spy on me for her Sbrocca. Now she was pimping legislators? What was the move? She called a couple hours later and said that she would try to arrange some meetings. She called a third time and reported that Barnes was antigambling, but had agreed to hear me out. She phoned on August 9 to give me Chuy's phone number in Tucson and to suggest that I soften him a bit. I dialed the senator as directed and we had a nice chat. When the talk turned to gambling and whether he opposed it, he had an interesting response.

"I'm not a Mormon!"

Horwitz showed at 2 p.m. and handed me a list of seven senators and fifteen representatives he felt were in tough campaigns and could use an infusion of cash. I said I'd met a guy who needed $7,000. Without missing a beat, Horwitz identified the $7,000 lawmaker as Bill Mundell. I told him someone set up another meet with a Mormon who was against gambling but still agreed to see me. He said that had to be Representative Stan Barnes. It was an impressive show. Name a figure or situation and these lobbyists knew the politician.

After playing "Horwitz the Magnificent," the union representative delivered some disturbing news about the gubernatorial primary.

"The latest word, and the most devastating word I've heard, is, as of today, it appears that in the Republican primary that Mecham is now ahead of Symington, which is absolutely insane . . . It could come down to Goddard and Mecham."

"This is amazing to me," I interjected. "How could a man get impeached and re-run and get elected again?"

"It's insane . . . The question that I think a lot of folks have is Symington's solvency . . . The banks are calling in their notes and we all know that moma has probably turned off the tap . . . She's the one that's got the money faucet there to turn on the money and turn it off. The word that I got was that she just turned it off. You know, the mother-in-law turned it off!"

I gave Horwitz $500 for his time and assistance.

Tapp called after I arrived at my lair on August 10. He said Representative English had researched the law and discovered that gambling was legal in Arizona until 1910. That meant that they might have to file a constitutional amendment before the legislature could vote. I didn't understand that nonsense — except that I suspected that whatever the problem was, Ernie Hoffman could take care of it. They were hard-selling Ernie.

Things were speeding up. Tony had six people trolling for dirty politicians — Tapp, Kenney, Horwitz, Jack Smyth, Shiree, and Stragalas — with more itching to come on board.

On Monday, August 13, Stan Barnes called to set a meet for that afternoon. He was supposed to be dead-set against gambling, so it was sure to be an interesting afternoon.

He appeared at 2:45, fifteen minutes late. He looked like a "Ken" doll, well scrubbed from head to toe. Barnes was a young Mormon stockbroker whose family hit it big farming cotton in the deep suburbs. I played Park Avenue Tony with this little yuppie as Brooklyn Tony would have terrified him. I wore a suit and didn't even curse! He said he personally liked to gamble and often went to Vegas, but that his constituents in Mesa were right-wing and would want him to oppose it. I gave him my rap.

"If nothing else," I said, "Stan will come in and play a little blackjack?"

"Oh man, I always lose," he laughed. "That's the problem. I love it. I do love it. I do love to go."

Barnes posed the often-repeated Indian question: Why not just build on the reservation?

"Who would be dumb enough to go out and build a hundred-million-dollar hotel on an Indian reservation where they can say, five days later, 'Italian white man, go! Our wampum!' And I'm history!" I laughed.

I quickly made Barnes for a nonplayer. He was too rich, too clean, and had a solid political future. He wouldn't be back.

The coach and quarterback, Tapp and Kenney, met me at the apartment around 4 p.m. They razzed me about my suit. I explained it was a show for Barnes. Kenney had just returned from some legislative conference in Tennessee where he had promised to pimp hard. He reported that his style was severely cramped by the fact that his wife went along. He wasn't able to juke and jive with her watching. I suspected that my QB was just lazy.

"Everybody I ran into—you have your name tag on for a solid week, ARIZONA—said, 'You still have that screwball, what's his name, Mecham, Mecham, Mecham.' You know, the first thing out of their mouth," Kenney complained.

"Is he still governor?"

"Who?"

"Mecham Mecham Mecham."

Kenney laughed and continued: "Okay, well [Representative] Patty Noland was back there. I had some good times with her. Very sharp gal. You gotta strike these women when they're emotional and nervous and they're both nervous. I tried to line up Patty Noland and [Representative] Ruth Eskesen, two good people who I know need money, need help."

I updated the duo about my meets with Laybe, Barnes, Mundell, and English. Kenney had a different slant on the two Mr. Cleans, Mundell and Barnes.

"This guy [Barnes] kind of likes to slip and slide. He's Mormon, so don't trust him with your wife . . . [Mundell] he sure likes the girls."

"That was my analysis of him . . ." I agreed. "Put some pussy on this kid and he'll do whatever you want to do."

"Yeah, yeah. That's his weakness."

Kenney advised me again to hold off on Senator Stephens and Representatives Raymond and Hartdegen until after the September primaries. The trio were running unopposed inside their parties and wouldn't need money until the general election.

The talk turned to Sue Laybe. Kenney felt she was going to lose her seat in the upcoming election and that I might have squandered my $10,000. I responded that I read the election differently, that she had strong support among the gay community.

"You've got a gay JP in Phoenix east [district] one," Tapp pointed out.

"Who's that?" Kenney asked.

"David Braun. He's queerer than a two-dollar bill."

"Is he really?"

"Oh, yeah," Tapp insisted. "He's been carrying that district for a long time. Now, they just ran a hit piece on him that said, 'We won't bring out his sexual preference . . . We want to campaign on the issues, we don't want to talk about his sexual preference and his personal life.'"

The "hit" point being that by talking about not talking about it, they talked about it.

Kenney brought up the changing of the secretaries. I explained that Michelle was in Paris with her beau. "It was too hot here and she was missin' Carmine."

"Fuck, weren't you takin' care of her?"

"Please, that's my partner's girl. We'll end up in a shootout."

"She's a big hussy momma," Kenney said.

The future judiciary committee chairman was warming up. He didn't miss a thing, including the possibilities presented by my new undercover apartment.

"This is a nice setup. Is it available for the boys' intergroup to come and have a sweet spiritual relationship with . . ."

"Any time. Any time you wanna use this for church purposes, to hold services . . ." I offered.

After another interlude into politics, the conversation again returned to the Twilight Zone.

"I will be out of state from the eighteenth of September until the twenty-fifth," Tapp informed us.

"Your anniversary," I wondered.

"Yes."

"Shit," Kenney cut in. "What, does it take you a week to celebrate your anniversary?"

"Yes."

"I take my wife to Wendy's and that's it, kid. Wendy's, a fifty-cent card, and I give her a little sex if she's nice . . . Shit, boy you guys are, you're just too nice!"

Us guys were starting to roll.

"[Representative Kyle] Hindman is an ex-MP . . . you know, he carries an assault weapon in his pickup," Kenney said. ". . . But again, I've seen this other side of Hindman too . . . We sit at a big conference table in the Republican caucus . . . It was kind of horseshoe type. I was sittin' on one side during the first part of the year and that's where all the smokers sit, because they're my buddies. I got so tired of the smoke. I got a bad cold, so I moved to the other side where Hindman was . . . He's not one of my spiritual brothers. I sat over there, and I said, 'Kyle, you son-of-a-bitch, I can see why you're sitting over here!' Because straight across there, the other side of the horseshoe table was [Representative] Susan Gerard, big tits and dress up to here, and you could see clear up to her panties! I said, 'Hindman, you son-of-a-bitch, I'm gonna sit over here every day from now on!' He said, 'You found out my secret!'"

After Kenney left, I talked with Tapp a while, picking his brain about what he got out of the meeting.

"I was surprised Susan Gerard's wearing panties," he said. "If she's wearin' panties, she may not be a player, cause most broads that wear pantyhose don't wear panties."

I'm sure there was some astute political insight there, but damned if I knew what it was.

On the way home, Stragalas called on the cellular phone and said Senator Stephens was primed and ready for a sit-down. I called Stephens at the capitol and set a meet for August 20.

Tapp phoned the homestead that evening. He reported that Kenney was stalling to try and get another $55,000. I told Tapp that there were a lot of ways to make bonus points with Tony, but stalling wasn't one of them.

Kenney called the next day and said that after chatting with Representative Mundell, the boy legislator was now ready to come on board. I'd believe that when I saw it.

Kenney rang again on August 16. He was calling from a strange location, bedside at St. Joseph's hospital. Candice Nagel had some kind of sudden pancreas problem and was there recovering. He put her on the phone. As she began speaking, I remembered Kenney's theory about women legislators: "You gotta strike these women when they're emotional and nervous."

I flipped through the legislative book and found Nagel's picture. She was a beautiful Doris Day clone. I was looking forward to a conversation where the word "fuck" wasn't in every sentence.

". . . And see, that's why I love Don Kenney," she said. "Because in our caucus, he turned out to be a statesman. We got a bunch of nuts in there that are just gonna fuck the state!"

So much for that great expectation. Nagel described herself as being in the "booze and bedroom business" and cursed worse than Tapp. She appeared ready to leap on Tony's bandwagon.

"Because we're in the hospitality industry . . . you know, you try to make liquor sound clean . . . I can look like Doris Day and talk about liquor and make it sound like something Jesus drank," she boasted.

Nagel confirmed what everyone had been telling me about my coach, Ron Tapp.

"You need to find somebody whose integrity is perceived as above reproach. They cannot have lobbied for pornography, or the movie industry, you know, those kind of things. You need to pick somebody that has the integrity and the air of absolute squeaky-cleanness."

As always, the conversation wandered.

"My husband is in remission, but he has rheumatoid arthritis. And you'd never know it . . . Well, like I told him, I was hopin' to be a rich widow and he'd die of a heart attack, but no, I'm gonna have to drag his crippled ass around!"

She laughed, but I was somewhat taken aback. I refocused the conversation. "What I've got going for me is I've got someone to introduce the bill. I've got a cosponsor for the bill and I have made rapid progress . . ."

"Then you need Ron outta your front line," she reiterated.

Kenney called that evening. I said I was caught off guard by the beautiful representative's spicy language, but he saw that as a good sign.

"You had a friend 'cause she doesn't talk that way in front of strangers."

We discussed the "Tapp problem" then wound down.

"All right, well, let me leave you with these words," I said. "In the words of Brigham Young, 'I don't care how you bring 'em, just bring 'em.'"

"In that regard," Kenney shot back, "I can't wait to meet your niece!"

"She's lookin' forward to meeting you, too."

What a guy. Still leading with his dick.

7

Tony Vincent was developing a strange, multifaceted personality. I had decided early on that I would become whatever the person in front of me wanted me to be. That meant Tony was proabortion, and fervently antiabortion. He was a champion for women's rights, and a sexist pig who felt, heh, heh, that women have no value standing up. He was a liberal civil rights activist who was one with his black, Mexican, and Indian brothers, and he was a stone-cold racist who sprinkled his conversations with ethnic and racial slurs. Tony was so pro-gay that one might expect him to lead parades in San Francisco, and he was a homophobic gay basher. Tony stood behind his union brothers, and felt the unions were destroying the country. He supported gun control, and the National Rifle Association. He felt the police had too much power, and protested that the cops had their hands tied by bleeding heart liberal judges who coddled criminals.

Tony could go with any flow. His purpose was not to create confrontations, but to become a spiritual, political, and ideological brother with the politicians and lobbyists who took the Ed McMahon seat in his office.

On the surface, this might seem to be a dangerous high-wire act fraught with the possibility of leaks. Hypothetically, if a proabortion senator and an antiabortion senator had lunch and the conversation turned to the strange Mafioso dude pushing for gambling, my conflicting views might have raised some eyebrows. In reality, this ideological fence-jumping posed virtually no threat to the operation. It's doubtful that the subtleties of Tony's political leanings would ever come up in idle chatter. More importantly, Tony was a one-issue guy: gambling.

Like most special interests, he coddled the politicians' and promoted their pet projects in order to gain their support on his issue. Far from raising a red flag, such hypocritical behavior is routine in American politics.

In analyzing the first six months of Desert Sting, I did note three potential mistakes I made that could have been critical. In dealing with Jim Davis, I twice created virtually the same, highly unusual murder victim. In order to make the hit appear like easy money, I described both potential targets as men with no families who would be alone somewhere waiting to receive a package. It would be difficult to find one human on the planet that fit that description, much less two. Bells should have clanged in Davis' head when I described the second, wonderfully convenient victim. For whatever reason—greed, bloodlust, stupidity—no such warnings sounded for Davis.

Second, the empty closets and drawers in the master bedroom of the apartment would have spooked anyone who stumbled in there.

The final potential mistake was that after telling everyone that I had a wife in Reno and a girlfriend in Phoenix, and was living with my girlfriend, I told Shiree Foster that I was separated from my wife and had broken up with my girlfriend. I played that tune because I wanted to lay a foundation for a personal confrontation with her boyfriend, Romano Sbrocca. It was a calculated risk, but I could always blow off the discrepancy as feeding her a line.

The biggest problem was that mistakes two and three together fused into a dangerously tangled web. My cover story for the empty closets was that I was really living with my girlfriend at her place. But if I'd dumped my girlfriend months before, I'd have to do some fast talking to mesh those stories.

Looking at the big picture, these contradictions were all part of a day's work. Tony Vincent had neither a past nor a future. He existed in the present and lived for the moment, for the quick kill. The odds were that some freak, unforeseen occurrence would expose the operation long before Tony's endless stream of conflicting stories could weave together into a hangman's noose.

George Stragalas, as usual, was overflowing with sharp political insight when he put in an appearance on August 16. He had some interesting things to say about savings and loan goon Charlie Keating, especially Keating's relationship with gubernatorial front-runner Terry Goddard.

"... So [Keating] buys the Lincoln Savings in California and runs it like a personal bank account and legally did it. His mistake was that he starts selling bonds and stock of Continental Corporation out of Lincoln Savings which weren't secure. And his second mistake was he started selling to little old ladies . . . and it got so crazy. I mean, he hires his son, a million dollars a year salary . . . his nephew, $800,000. It gets crazy."

"Did he have the [Arizona] legislators in his pocket?" I asked.

"He had the entire state in his pocket! . . . If you wanted to do anything in this town, you had to be on Keating's good side. And he was ruthless . . . He hired Terry's [Goddard] girlfriend . . . Terry didn't want her around anymore so he got her a job working at the Phoenix Police Department doing P.R., thirty thousand, she has three kids, she's divorced . . . So he was getting uncomfortable with her . . . 'cause people were saying the 'mayor's girlfriend, ex-girlfriend, police department,' so he actually got rid of her and she got pissed off and she said, 'Fine Terry. I've got to support my kids. I'm gonna go to work for your enemy, Keating!' . . . She was expecting $40,000, $45,000. He [Keating] says, 'Would $80,000 be okay? And a car? . . .'"

"What is Terry doing with a girlfriend?" I asked. "'Cause you said he was gay."

"There's a whole other side of Terry that people don't know. Terry met this girl, she brought him out of his shell. He's extremely shy. Doesn't like people . . . I mean, I didn't even think he went to bed with her to tell you the truth. I think it's one of these things where he liked the way she used to hang on him and just looked at him, stuff like that . . . When Terry was real down, she was there. And I think she loved him. And I think she would have married him, even if he never took her to bed. There's security. She has three kids . . . But the old man [Sam Goddard] killed it, would not allow the relationship to develop . . ."

There was, of course, a point to telling me all this.

"What you're gonna build up here," Stragalas continued, "what I maintain you're gonna build up, you're essentially gonna be a nice Keating."

Stragalas also had a novel idea on how to turn Terry Goddard from his antigambling stance.

"Goddard said he's not in favor of gambling. He said he's not gay, either. Isn't that great? . . . In other words, it's such a great comparison because if you ask them back to back, what he's gonna say about gays is 'Well, I think people ought to do what they want to do. It's not my preference.' Same thing with gaming. 'People ought to do what they want to do. It's not my preference.'"

Before Stragalas left, I made arrangements to give him another $2,750 for his campaign.

"I think I'll have my [business] cards redone," I said. "After my name, put N.C.K."

"What the hell is that?"

"Nice Charlie Keating."

"That's good!"

Senator Jesus "Chuy" Higuera met Brooklyn Tony on August 17. Marie had to pick him up at the capitol and escort him over because Chuy needed help finding the way. Higuera was a burly, barrel-chested man who had acted as a bodyguard for Cesar Chavez in the Chicano Rights days of the late 1970s. As he sat in my office and talked, my mind kept flashing disconnected scenes from a black-and-white movie. Finally, the correct scene scrolled behind my eyes. Higuera reminded me of the phony Mexican Federale in the movie *The Treasure of the Sierra Madre*, who uttered the famous line, "Badges? We don't need no stinkin' badges!"

Although Chuy Higuera was pro-gambling, he had a problem. He was friendly with the dog track people in Tucson. Traditionally, the pari-mutuel overlords at the dog and horse tracks are big guns in the war against casino gambling. I defused Higuera's concern by explaining how much money the tracks could make with slots and poker machines, and by promising to have a free shuttle service from the hotels to the tracks. I also offered to allow the pari-mutuel barons to buy into the casinos. These options seemed to make Higuera happy. We sent out for sandwiches and continued our get-to-know-each-other session.

"Tell you what," Higuera said. "I'd like to own a business that supplies your shrimp. That's what I'd like to do."

Shrimp! I thought. We don't need no stinkin' shrimp!

The truth was that casinos do need shrimp. Tons of it. Higuera wasn't as unsophisticated as his fellow lawmakers had warned. Casino hotels use shrimp cocktails as loss leaders to bring in the players. They're either free, or go for fifty cents to a buck. Higuera knew that whoever supplied the shrimp to the hotels would be a millionaire in five years. I told the senator the shrimp concession was his.

I also said that I envisioned him as a maitre d' at a big hotel scooping in the tips. He liked the sound of that.

"Tell you what, it'd be better paying than the job I've got," he cracked.

"Oh forget about it," I said. "I'm talking about you going home with $2,000 to $3,000 a night."

Higuera was warming fast.

"I could be valuable to you, I know I can," he insisted. "I know I can produce, you know."

Before he left, Higuera said that no matter what the dog track people said, he was in with me as casinos were the bigger issue. His quick turnaround didn't surprise me. They don't give away shrimp at the dog tracks.

Tapp called at 9 p.m. and reported that the Tucson dog track was owned by a Buffalo, New York, Mafia family. Where he came up with that nonsense was anyone's guess. The joint was actually owned by a group from Florida. Either way, I told Tapp I'd handle the dog people.

Tapp's eagerness to muddy the waters with rival mobsters brought a troubling mystery to the surface. Phoenix is known in the gangster business as an "open city," meaning there are no traditional Mafia families that rule. Still, there's always somebody around town who thinks they're "The Boss." It was long past time for Tony to be contacted by whomever had laid claim on the fast-growing desert city. There had to be someone, someone connected with a major New York, Chicago, or Los Angeles crime family.

Senator Higuera's link to the pari-mutuel business presented an opportunity to smoke out the Arizona mob. If such beasts existed, they'd probably have some connection with the tracks. Higuera would lead them to Tony.

Higuera had Mike Romaine, the manager of the Tucson dog track, call me on Sunday, August 19. I laid down a heavy Brooklyn Tony rap, outlining the plans my partners and I had for dotting the state with glittery casino hotels. None of it impressed Romaine. He said dog racing was already losing popularity and that casinos would be the final nail in the coffin. I repeated my offer to allow the pari-mutuel boys to buy a piece of my action "as a courtesy" and offered to fly him to Phoenix and set him up at the Ritz for a face-to-face sit-down anytime he wanted. He said he'd get back to me. I never heard from him again.

Stragalas dropped by on Monday, August 20, and picked up $3,000 for his state treasurer dash. We discussed the latest chilling development in the gubernatorial race. There were rumors that Evan Mecham was going to hit Goddard hard on the homosexual front—even before the primary.*

---

*Terry Goddard has publicly denied that he is a homosexual on numerous occasions in the past.

"If that comes out, he'll [Goddard] be able to turn around and say, 'I'm a good mayor. I'm a good governor. I'll be a good leader. That's what the issue is,'" Stragalas speculated. "There's still a certain portion of the population that will say, 'But he's a fag. You know, we don't want fags. We don't want that image. All the fags in the United States will look up to him as the governor in Arizona. We'll have them down here. They'll be down here for AIDS research, AIDS rehabilitation.' That's the way they'll build it up. That's what Mecham will build up."

There was a sense of urgency in Stragalas' voice. The prospect of a Mecham-Goddard election had many Arizonians paralyzed with fear. It would pit an angry, intolerant Mormon wounded by the shame of impeachment against an alleged closet homosexual. If Mecham snatched the Republican nod, he was sure to humiliate Goddard with a homophobic "AIDS is coming!" campaign that would probably power the crazy little geek back into office. If that happened, the Feds might as well drop a few nuclear bombs on Arizona and let the evolutionary process start over again.

Senator Alan Stephens, the minority leader, joined us after lunch. Although I had heard that Stephens was a player from day one, this was our first sit-down. He was a squat, weasely guy who slightly resembled Adolf Hitler. He sat with his arms crossed and reminded me of a rude little boy who hadn't gotten his way. He didn't say much; his body language did most of the talking. I perceived that he wasn't about to do anything naughty in front of Stragalas. Stephens arrived twenty minutes early, so I asked Stragalas to stay for the first ten minutes or so to bridge the meetings. It seemed like a good idea at the time. Stragalas was a Democrat running for state treasurer. Stephens was the Democratic minority leader in the Senate. I figured they were political brothers. But what appeared logical on the surface was, in retrospect, bad brain work. Politicians, like cockroaches, operate better in the dark. Stephens' face turned red the instant he saw Stragalas. It stayed red the whole meeting.

I was Park Avenue Tony with Stephens, complete with a suit and clean shave. The minority leader kept peppering me with negatives. He said the church groups, police, the newspapers, and other pockets of power would object strenuously to my drive. He mentioned my need for polls and studies to gauge public opinion and suggested I institute a feasibility study showing precisely how the state would benefit from the hundreds of millions in tax dollars gambling would generate. Since Stephens was an accountant by trade, these ideas were consistent with his thought pattern. Everybody viewed the issue from their own perspective.

I asked Stephens what I could do for him. I had $25,000 in the cash drawer ready to hand over. He requested a campaign contribution of $220. I gave him $440, one $220 from me and the second from my wife. That was legal.

He was a strange one. I couldn't get a fix on him. Was he dirty or clean? A player or a snitch for the attorney general?

Stragalas called afterward and said he was disappointed in Stephens' behavior. He then proceeded to rip and tear at the senator, referring to him as "a little guy" who struts around the capitol like "he's hot shit." He said that Stephens had double-crossed him in 1988 over some fund-raising for Representative Art Hamilton and presidential candidate Michael Dukakis.

"He's arrogant. He's rude. He is cocky. And he thinks he has the world by the ass. And he's a short little motherfucker!" Stragalas said.

It sounded to me like Stephens had all the right qualifications for a bright political future. Stragalas assured me that like Sue Laybe, Stephens would be back.

Representative Candice Nagel phoned and said she was back on the job, feeling frisky and wanted to see me at 8:30 a.m. the following day. That was too early for me, so I convinced her to come after 4 p.m. She agreed. She arrived the next afternoon like a ball of fire roaring up a parched mountain. She was a classy, attractive woman in her forties with blonde hair and freckles. Candice was the mother of three stunning daughters, ages twenty-two, nineteen, and eighteen, and talked like she had been vaccinated with a phonograph needle. She started off with Arizona's budget and population crisis, then grabbed one of my legislature directories and did a book dance to end all book dances. Nagel was the Rona Barrett of the Arizona legislature. She had molded raw gossip into an art form. However, unlike Tapp and the others, she refused to go through the pages person by person. She jumped around from page to page, senator to representative, back and forth in a blitzkrieg of stinging invectives.

"[Representative] Lela Steffey, she's not a player. She's stupid. I'd rather deal with an asshole than somebody stupid . . . [Representative] Stan Barnes. He's a wimp. He's a wannabe. He's a major wannabe . . . I know how to play my district, but behind me, and he's probably forty-five points behind me, is Gary Giordano, the champion wacko of all the wackos . . . The strategy we hafta do to get these three votes that Don [Kenney] needs for his [judiciary] chairman [seat] is for us to do whatever it is we wanna do, and what we wannna do is to make sure these three wackos lose! . . . That's absolutely critical! . . . I will sell my daughter to white slavery before I would vote for the wackos in lead-

ership . . . Didn't you know in Arizona for fifty cents and a cup of coffee at Denny's you can get your [real estate] license from the guy sittin'
next to you at the table? This place is a joke. We are babies. Nean-
derthals. People trust people here. It's scary . . . One of the main
wackos came to see me in the hospital. You know, the other ones called
me. I mean, they can't figure me out because I will not slam the door. I
mean, there are a couple that I hate their fucking guts. I hope they die!"

Nagel called time out and explained why gossip was so important
in politics.

"Do you remember high school? Do you remember it all ran on
popularity and rumors. Now if you wanna understand politics, you
remember if you can control the rumors, and you can create the
rumors, you are in control . . . You need to know who the fuckees are
and who the fuckers are and you need to know who's so honest that
this [gambling] will be very upsetting to them even talking about it . . .
And there's ego. There's this terrible jealousy. It's just like high school.
Go back to high school. If you're a slut, you're always a slut. If you
want a rumor started, you start it with a couple of folks and you get it
buzzed through like that . . .

". . . The city is run by the firemen. If you wanna know who the city
is, you bring in [firefighters union leaders] Pat Cantelme and Mike
Bielecki . . . [Cantelme] got paroled [charges dropped] on coke charges a
few years ago. The firemen are so powerful. The firemen play both parties. The firemen are the cleanest guys in the world unless they're protecting their brothers . . . They will jump off this building for their
friends. They go down with their friends. They die for their friends . . ."

After that trip through high school and the firehouse, we got back
to the yearbook.

"[Senator] Jeff Hill is evil. He would screw his mother . . . He wrote
a letter about another legislator out of his district to hurt him . . . To
help a Mormon. This guy's scary."

"What does this one . . ."

"I don't know if he's a wack," Nagel interrupted. "He could be a
closet wack."

"'Closet wack.' I love that."

"[Representative John] Kromko, never go near him. Kromko sees
conspiracy in everything, everything . . . He slept in his car for several
sessions . . . He's a nut . . . [Representative Earl] Wilcox is stupid. But
he's a player. He'll go for anything. He's so stupid! . . . [Representative]
Patty Noland is another one. She'd screw her mother, but she's tough . . .
She [Representative Brenda Burns] just got her tits and her nose done.

She's got divorce written all over her . . . She's [Representative Leslie Whiting Johnson] a hard-core wack."

"Oh, that's the dildo girl!" I cut in, recognizing Whiting's photograph.

"The dildo babe," Nagel confirmed.

"You can't have more than five dildos in your house," I said, citing one of Arizona's stranger attempts at lawmaking.

"Right. But they wanted to know if, you know, if cucumbers . . .? Are you talking motorized?"

"Did you really go through that? Were you in when she introduced that?"

"Not the original one, but the second one . . ."

"How could you sit through that? I mean, I'd be pissin' in my pants. I mean, that's hysterical legislation."

"It's a joke."

"[Representative] Art Hamilton?" I inquired, steering us out of the outer limits of fake dicks.

"You need to get with him and I would say the best way to figure him out is through [Representative] Debbie McCune. He has a soft spot in his heart for Debbie McCune . . . [Representative] Bobby Raymond will wanna play with you. He's disgusting . . . he's such a wannabe. His hair never moves . . . [Senator Tom] Dr. Patterson, the reason he hates me is because I hate elitists and he will probably be a player, but he will always consider you poor white trash and because, of course, that's what I am . . . He's the kinda guy that he's championing education because he doesn't want everybody to know that he's so pro–tort reform. He's a covert wacko . . . [Senator Lester] Pearce is a wack. This whole crowd's [Mesa's Mormon district] a wack ."

Nagel came up for air and confessed why she knew so much dirt.

"I have a profile on every legislator. I know what they do, who their cousins are. I know if they were adopted . . . I'm a salesman. Have you ever read *How to Swim with the Sharks Without Being Eaten?* Well, the number-one thing . . . you do a dossier on every person that you meet."

Back to the directory.

". . . This guy is [Representative] Mark Killian. He wants to be Speaker of the House. His daddy is the Godfather of Mesa. But see, he's adopted. He doesn't have the genes . . . Now [Senator] Leo Corbet, you can talk any way you want because he's as greasy as you, as any joker in this town. The guy is greasy."

Ouch! Candy nailed Big Tony pretty good there, but I let it slide.

"[Representative Bill Mundell] the first thing he said when he came into my hospital room is he . . . went around and looked at all the flowers, right. And he goes, 'Can I have this one. I hate this lobbyist the most.' Then he goes, 'Can you get AIDS from oral sex?' And I go, 'If she, if her gums are bleeding, I don't know, give me a fuckin' break!' So I mean, he's a neat guy."

We took another break so Candy could give me a few wardrobe lessons.

"Image is everything!" she scolded.

"So what you're tellin' me," I said, "is put the cowboy suit on, take the rings off, and stop the bullshit."

"That's the idea . . . the glasses are perfect."

There were still some people she had yet to skewer, so we dived back into the muck.

"[Representative] Bill English . . . this man is so smart drunk that I challenge him to anybody's intellect drunk and you sober . . . He's had three DUIs and still won his race every time by four thousand votes . . . He is a major player. He can get anything through. He's the rules chairman. He can make you or break you . . . You just want to get to know him when he comes to town. All you hafta do is buy his booze. You know, if you give him $220, he'll love you, but buy his booze . . . You need [Representative John] Wettaw. Wettaw is the appropriations chairman. He's the smartest son-of-a-bitch in the world. He just globs money for the universities because he's a professor . . . He looks sleazy, but he really isn't sleazy . . . [Representative Cindy] Resnick is the spider . . ."

"What's that mean?"

"They use you up and then they throw you away . . . This woman [Representative Polly Rosenbaum] you really need. She's like a million years old."

"Yeah, God love her. She's gotta be in her eighties . . . If she came up here and said to me, 'Tony, do me a favor, don't bring gaming to Arizona,' I think I'd have to consider it because of her looks."

"She wouldn't do that."

"You're gonna tell me this old broad's a player?"

"Not a player like out there doin' the deals. I mean there's a couple of deals she does, but they're dumb deals. She's got her own deals . . . [Representative] Kyle Hindman . . . would vote to take away Mother Teresa's wheelchair. And I say to him, everytime he does that, I go, 'You better hope there's no God!' . . . Chuy is gonna want some money. Just give him some money. You can have him . . . $2, $20, $50, take him to dinner, that's all he wants. He's so stupid. He's a barrio Mexican . . .

This guy [Senator Bob Denny] is the devil, but he'll vote with you. But he is the devil. Bob Denny is the devil."

"Is he the devil?"

"He's the devil. He looks like the devil. Doesn't he look like the devil?"

"All that's missin' are the horns."

". . . You talk about leadership, but we don't have such a terrible lack of leadership. We have an inability for followship. These people are all little kings, see all these little egos here . . . You wanna hear a great story?" Candy squealed. "The only time we ever had to find a [prostitute] was for Andy Williams. He is filthy. He is so disgusting that I wanna puke! . . . The Thunderbirds brought him in. The fathers of the community brought him in for some kind of benefit or somethin'."

"And you had to get him a whore?"

"It's disgusting . . . And you know what we had to do? You know how stupid, we had to look in the phone book! . . . We didn't know what to do. I mean, we're not in the business . . . And that's why I hate [Phoenix resident] Glen Campbell because they're very close and he's the religious wacko fundamentalist as a goof . . ."

"[Representative] Susan Gerard, what district is she in?" I asked.

"She's in the Speaker's district."

"She's a pleasant-looking woman," I baited.

"She's wonderful."

"Tell her to start crossin' her legs in the caucus meetings," I advised, spoiling my horny pal Don Kenney's fun.

". . . Kenney's a strange guy," Nagel understated. "He was married before to a very beautiful socialite type . . . a very bitter, bitter, bitter, bitter, bitter, bitter divorce . . . and see his church, his family, that's important to him. And that's status with him and, and so he decided he'd find a 'pleasant' woman that he could, you know, nest with."

"She's really fat?" I said, picking up on her hand motions.

"Huge!"

Ah ha! I thought. Therein lies the mystery of Kenney's perpetual state of lust.

"Mundell, I'm gonna talk to Mundell," Candy continued. "We're gonna have a little come-to-Jesus talk."

I didn't think she meant Senator Jesus "Chuy" Higuera.

After she ripped the House and Senate for me, it was time to offer Candy her reward. Her response was strange and convoluted.

"Okay, now, you wanna know," she started. "I'm sure before I stand up and look at you in the peepers and 'What can I do for you?' . . . let me tell you my situation . . . I am ahead in my poll so I'm safe, I'm fine. I'm wonderful. I'm gonna win. But there's a chance that this asshole, the king asshole of the assholes, may get in if I don't help this [Sue] Grace, so I've been doing all kinds of shit. Man, I've put signs up with her, you know, 'Nagel and Grace' and I've mailed the mailings with her. I've done this stuff . . . I know that the teachers are going to hit Giordano and I know this group called Mainstream Majority is gonna hit Giordano. And they're two people on the outside that hate him. They feel like if they could drive a stake through his heart, 'cause I beat him before, they can kill him this time. He'll never come back. I'm in the position right now, yeah, I'd like to have a couple thousand dollars. I'd like to have money orders with names on them. But I'm not, it will be extra money that I may or may not need. Whereas Sue Grace is desperate."

To translate, Candy was a lock in her race. However, the other representative seat in her north Maricopa County district was being sought by this character Gary Giordano, the alleged "King Asshole of the Assholes." So it was Candy's political duty to not only crush him, but to prevent him from coming in second and securing the other district seat. I later learned that the frightening "wacko" philosophy that so damned Giordano was the fact that he was a conservative Christian. He believed in honesty, integrity, the Ten Commandments, the Golden Rule, not bearing false witness against his fellow man, and all those other dangerously radical political ideas. I could understand why they wanted to keep a guy like him out of the Arizona legislature.

Whatever the deal, I told Candy that Tony's wad was behind her 100 percent. That led to some quizzical check bundling.

"Each one of these people [named on the checks] must be willing to get on a witness stand and say, 'I donated this to Candice Nagel for better government in Arizona.' "

"And you understand that's my money?"

"I understand."

At that point, it appeared to be a clean takedown. Not so fast. Candy wavered.

"But see, I want you to realize you're not giving me that money for my vote. I already agreed with your philosophy. I hafta, I hafta say that to you for my own sleep at night."

I could all but hear the groans in the fourth room. Candy had spit out the hook.

"So I can sleep tonight, off the record, this is not on the record," I began.

"I have no problem with gaming. It's a yes as far as I'm concerned," she cut in.

"So you will vote for my issue?"

"Yes."

"And I will support you."

"Yes."

"You commit to me. I commit to you."

"Yes. Yes. I have no problem . . . It's a deal."

That was better, but still not solid evidence of cash for votes. I tried again.

"Once I hand you the postal money orders, you can call it a gift, you can call it whatever you wanna call it, just so I know I got your vote, I don't care what you call it."

". . . But, but Tony. This is something I hafta, see, choose. These people are gonna have a real hard time sayin' that. You don't think people are gonna have a hard time sayin' that? 'I have your vote. I gave this commitment to you.' Don't you think they'll have a hard time sayin' that?"

No, but you sure as hell are, I thought. "I can't tell ya . . ." I said instead. "I mean why else? What am I, in love with everybody? . . . You think I'm gonna hand everybody $2,200, $5,000, $10,000 and just say, 'Okay, well, vote for me if you want to.' Come on."

"Integrity walks out the door when they get squeezed by their district," she said.

Candy was shrewd. I liked her. But I had danced with her so long I was dizzy. In a few more minutes, I'd have been accepting bribes from her. I decided to let the lawyers untangle her word games and end the meeting. Besides, I'd have another shot at her the next day when she came for her bundle and my mind wasn't reverberating with "closet wackos," "covert wackos," "champion wackos," "spiders," bleeding-gum blow jobs, "king assholes," nose and tit jobs, fat wives, superstar singers demanding Yellow Page whores, dildo counts, Jesus, Satan, "Mother Teresa's wheelchair," "white slavery," and bad genes.

Detective Ball called early the next morning to advise me of a change in plans. Instead of using Tapp's list of names, the police decided to go through the phone books and use their own list of phony names. This way, they wouldn't be setting themselves up for a future ordeal of having to drop subpoenas on Tapp's people to prove that it wasn't their money.

As I was driving to the office to make the drop, the cellular phone rang. It was Candy. She sounded pained and overwrought.

"Tony, I can't take the money," she said.

"Why?"

"I just can't."

Something spooked her. I told her the cellular phone was breaking up and I'd call her from the office. I wanted to get the conversation on tape. At the office, she told me that she trusted me and believed in my cause, but was hinky about the California sting.

"This is what I want to tell you. I believe you. I believe in you and I believe in what you're doing . . . I'm a very straightforward, down-to-the-gut person. What happened to me last night when I was driving away and my stomach started hurting, I said to myself, 'You know, you have never ever given any more than your word, and you have never out and out taken anything for anything . . .' What it is, it's a fine line of my gut check. What I want you to do is to trust me that I'm with you. But to understand that my guts won't let me take anything for it other than friendship. I know that down the road that I'll be able to help you and you'll be able to help me . . . but it has to be at a time when you don't want something for it. What you have to understand is . . . legislators will have a problem with saying the words 'I will vote for this. Thank you. You are doing this for me.' That has all the trappings of a sting."

"Oh God."

"No, it does. Tony, I'm telling you this because I trust you. And I'm telling you this because this very thing happened in California last year . . . I feel like I got my clothes off, but I didn't get in bed. So I feel, I can still go home to my husband and say, you know, 'I'm a virgin' . . . I trust that what was said between you and I was said between you and I."

"Exactly," I lied.

"But you need help. In techniques, approach, everything. And that's what I can give you, right now, is that knowledge. That if I had a gut check when I left, it happens to everybody that leaves that office. You need to know that."

It was a good tip. Obviously, Tony had come on too strong with Candy. We could have toned Tony down — Wall Street Tony? — and just let her take an illegal campaign contribution without the long speech, but that was only a misdemeanor. If the cops were going to spend a million dollars on a sting, they wanted more than a few misdemeanors. They wanted Brooklyn Tony, pinky-ring mobster Tony buying votes.

"Just so you know," I said. "I've followed sting operations throughout my life because I've lived on the fringe and they've tried to nail me a couple of times. Number one, they never let money walk. They just don't let the money walk. They swoop down like flies on you-know-what. People have gone out of here with ten to fifty."

Despite my argument, I could tell Candy's mind was made up.

"That's the only reason I'm telling you that," she reiterated. "Because of sleep and stomachache and all of that."

Just in case it was a bad burrito and not guilt that had her belly doing flip flops, I started working on her next visit. "The door is open. The door to my heart is always open. The door to my wallet is always open. What do you intend to do? Do you intend to totally fart me off in terms of everybody else?"

"No, no, no, no, no, no. I'm calling everybody else. I want them to talk to you. But I need you to know where I'm coming from . . ."

She explained exactly where she was coming from later on in the conversation. "If you lose your image, and I lose my image, we're both fucked and neither one of us get what we want."

Nagel wavered a bit, but remembering the prime directive, I let her walk. The cops weren't too upset. Ball contended that even in agreeing to sell her vote she was cooked, regardless of what happened the next day. He compared it to a police officer who had agreed to take a bribe, then changed his mind. Too late. They'd bury the officer under the building.

I had mixed feelings. I had worked hard to make the operation a success, and I wanted to score touchdowns for the team. On the other hand, it was nice, for once in my life, to see a functioning human conscience. Despite all her cursing, gossip, and bluster, she was a decent enough lady, and entertaining to boot.

Candy had danced with the devil but survived. Good for her.

But it wasn't good for us. My guess was that Candy talked it over with her husband and he told her she'd be a fool to take the money. Whether it was a sting or not, she was probably warned that it could blow up in her face. As far as we were concerned, if she just walked away quietly, that would be okay. Only that rarely happens — and it explains why, in the Mob, if you turn down an offer, you'd better get out of town, fast. Nagel was a prime example of this Mob creed. She was incapable of keeping her tongue holstered and could be the kiss of death for Operation Desert Sting. If she wasn't for us, she was going to alert everyone to be against us.

I called Kenney that evening and told him that Nagel had spooked. Before he had a chance to get crazy himself, I turned the tables. I said I suspected Nagel of running a sting on me. He said that was doubtful and suggested that we work through Nagel's campaign manager, a high school teacher named Gary Kaasa. He would help us get her comfort level back.

8

Ron Tapp was talking a mile a minute when he called the following morning. He informed me that Gary Bartlett was telling everyone that he [Tapp] was working for the Mafia. Tapp came in that afternoon to discuss what we were going to do about it. He wanted Bartlett roughed up to keep him quiet. I said I'd handle it.

The fourth room had decided that I had to talk with Ernie Hoffman, Representative English's bagman, to help English reach his comfort level. I had set a meeting between Hoffman, Tapp, and myself for 3 p.m. Hoffman was about five-eleven, lean, with sharp features and a crown of white hair. His most distinguishing characteristic was his booming voice. It sounded like he had a public address system built into his chest. The cops could have recorded him at the police station ten miles away.

Hoffman mentioned his big tobacco and insurance accounts, along with General Foods, Kraft, and Miller Brewing Company, and proceeded to educate me on the fine art of buying politicians. He warned me to be cautious because politicians gossip relentlessly among themselves, and such gossip could kill my bill before it got out of committee. He shared Kenney's opinion that most Arizona state legislators were unsophisticated and should be bought as cheaply as possible.

"So you say five [$5,000] for Bill [English] and five for Chuy [Higuera] . . ." I began.

"Five's too much for Chuy," he interrupted.

"Five's too much?"

"Way too much."

"What do you suggest for Chuy?"

"About two."

"Two thousand?"

"Ten checks."

Hoffman set the price of an Arizona legislator at $2,000 to $5,000. I got the impression that he didn't want me to inflate the market and ruin all the lobbyists' cheap action. He also advised me not to give them what they ask for in one lump. Instead, I should dole it out in smaller payments to keep them in line. This guy was slick.

The talk turned to the latest developments in the gubernatorial race. Tapp and Hoffman stepped all over themselves to spill a nugget of juicy gossip that they both had independently discovered. Seems the Goddard people got wind of the gay-bashing assault Mecham's forces were allegedly planning and had swung into action.

"If Mecham wins that primary, you're gonna hear more homosexual talk," Hoffman opened. "I won't be a bit surprised if some guy comes forward and says he's the boyfriend of Goddard."

"They'll smear him to death," I said.

"Oh yeah, and let me tell ya, the Democrats that talked to me personally, the Alan Stephens and all them guys on the inside, they're scared to death."

"Let me tell you something," Tapp cut in. "I had a conversation with Dave Hull. It was a private conversation. They have tracked that gal that [Goddard] brought in here as his girlfriend."

"That's the one from New York," Hoffman interjected.

"Yeah. They spent some money, and Hull's got the money to spend, and they established where she was, where she came from, the whole shot. They also tracked a bank account . . . She was paid."

"Oh, she was paid money," Hoffman confirmed. "When she came in for the [engagement] announcement."

"That's right," Tapp said. "Dumbest fuckin' thing he could've done . . ."

"I am shocked that you heard that . . . " Hoffman said. ". . . She gets good dollars for that."*

"Hull is a Mecham supporter from day one and they're gonna unload on [Goddard] like you won't believe," Tapp predicted.

"She's a charming gal," Hoffman continued. "Dresses New York style . . . She got five thousand bucks."

"Well, they have tracked this guy [Goddard]," Tapp said. "They

---

*This would appear to be a particularly spurious allegation. Goddard's girlfriend of five years is an accomplished New York banker and environmentalist. No evidence was ever presented to support these charges.

knew he was gonna run a long time before he ran. He made some trips to New York and I understand they got pictures."

". . . Yeah, and now [former California governor] Jerry Brown, you know what he did. He was with Linda Ronstadt . . ." Hoffman gossiped.

This was getting so good I had to cut in. "That's right. She was his 'beard.' The first law he passed was a consenting adult act."

"He, you know, he had Linda Ronstadt from Arizona, imported her to be with him during that campaign . . ." Hoffman went on. "Yeah, well, that is fascinating that you know about the [Goddard] gal. I didn't think anybody knew that."

We meandered from gay governors and phony fiancées back to the wild and wacko-filled Arizona State House. Hoffman said Higuera was so poor he drove from Tucson to Phoenix twice a week just to sign in and collect the $75 per diem stipend. Hoffman also said Chuy tried to hit him up for $40,000 to kick off his shrimp business.

Hoffman's specialty, however, was procuring studies. He insisted that I needed an ecomonic impact study and a research poll that could be used to help persuade legislators on the fence. Hitting them with a study helped feed their comfort level. These studies were known as "MAIs" — made as instructed. That means we tell the researchers what we want the conclusion to be, and they work ass-backwards and build a study around the desired result. Hoffman claimed to have a list of hired gun professors and Ph.D.s at Arizona State University (ASU) who would produce such slanted studies.

These unethical studies were a volatile financial commodity whose cost increased like a soaring stock during our conversation.

"How'd we get from $8,000 to $40,000?" I asked as the price grew before my eyes. "Where'd we jump $32,000?"

"We're talkin' about an economic study as well as a survey of a thousand people," Hoffman said. "To get those professors, you know, doctorates on that economic study, you're talkin' about $20,000, $25,000, at least that because you're gonna do more than just one person . . ."

"So I'm buying them in a sense, too?" I clarified.

"Yeah, buy 'em, just like I bought [ASU Professor Cliff] Bogart for $8,000 last week. I'm writin' the report. You know what the report says. 'We need a college.'"

"You're writin' a report and he's putting his name on it?" Tapp laughed.

"Oh yeah, he'll put it in his legalese."

"It's like an 'MAI' appraisal then?" I offered.

"You know exactly what I'm doin'," Hoffman said.

". . . Okay, now that's the survey of a thousand people, now back to the economic study. What does that do?" I wondered.

"We'll go after the same people who are starving to death out there at ASU who did the Fiscal 2000 report . . . For the Fiscal 2000 they paid them I think $80,000 and there must've been eight of them on it . . . You get four of 'em. You pick out all the Ph.D.s. You want impeccable results off it. You don't want one person because they're gonna figure you took a hit on one person . . . 'How much did they pay him to write that?'"

". . . So what would the four professors run us?"

"You know, as a ballpark . . . why don't you just even it out to $50,000 for the economic study and the survey."

Boy, I thought. I better close this deal fast. It just went up another $10,000!

"Okay, so $50,000 for an economic study . . . And that's guaranteed to come back my way?"

". . . You sign off on the language and the scope of the study . . ."

"And you sit with them, like we're sittin' today and say 'Hey . . .'"

"Oh yeah. Oh yeah . . . When I do political surveys, and that type of thing, I've never let a guy go out there and say, 'Well I hope it comes out right,' shit. You beard 'em' like I said before. You 'beard 'em' and everything and the guy doesn't even know."

It dawned on me, at this point, that this had to be probably one of the few conversations in which the word "beard" was used twice in its two most obscure slang derivatives. In business, entertainment, and politics, a "beard" is a closet homosexual's front girlfriend. In academia, I learned that a "bearded study" was one in which the real purpose is disguised. For example, a study on casino gambling could be skewed with "yes"-inducing questions about lowering taxes, pumping money into education, economic growth, increased tourist dollars, and healthy job markets.

This talk of dirty college professors hit me as hard as any other aspect of the sting. I knew politicians were thieves, and "lobbyist" is almost a synonym for "crook," but professors at our country's institutions of higher learning on the take? Nothing is sacred.

This job was supposed to be my introduction into life as a law-abiding citizen. Instead, I was learning that every stratum of society was as rotten as the wise guys on the streets. In fact, the wise guys had a greater sense of honor. They were what they were and they were up-front about it. In this sleazy world I now inhabited, everybody screwed everybody. Everybody back-stabbed everybody. Everybody and everything was for sale.

But who was I, Billy Graham? I wasn't qualified to start getting preachy. I mentally slapped myself and wandered back into the conversation. Hoffman was talking about the legislature in a bordering state.

". . . The New Mexico legislators aren't even bashful . . . They wanted all green. In paper bags. And, they didn't even want you to leave it inside the door. Just knock and leave it. I said, 'Bullshit!' . . . I said, 'I ain't gonna work here anymore!' That is absolutely crazy. The big thing, what happened in California is making everyone very sensitive. The sting operation that they had there with the FBI . . . What we do now in business in California, I do business and assume everyone's wired."

"That's the way you have to," I said.

"And you're crazy if you don't do it that way. So I'm extremely careful . . ."

After lecturing me about buying the legislators cheap, Hoffman hit me with his deal. He wanted a long-term arrangement that later worked out to $15,000 for the rest of 1990, four months, then about $90,000 for 1991. Those figures indicate who pulls the strings in American politics. The legislators make a scant $15,000 a year. The Ernie Hoffmans of the world get $90,000 a client and pull down a cool half-million a year. The entire system seems designed for bribes.

Hoffman's voice was starting to give me a pounding headache. I rubbed my brow and asked him how he funnels money to the legislators. He responded with a new twist on the now familiar "bundling" scam. In addition to using the names of family and friends, Hoffman was considering a move that would make the animal rights activists proud.

"I'm maxed out. So what I'm doin' I'm using all my kids now, and I'm one step away from using my dachshund."

Tapp rang that evening at home. He was more frantic than before and reported that Bartlett told an ex-judge that Tapp had bribed Kenney for $10,000. I tried to calm him.

"Remember, this guy [Bartlett] was screaming that Don Kenney was the biggest whore down there from day one and you could buy him for $200 and a broad . . . Incidentally, Candice Nagel told me his wife was real fat," I said, quickly switching subjects.

"Yeah, she is a little heavy," Tapp said, cooling. He didn't stay cool long.

"We don't need that [Bartlett] shit!"

"Well," I said. "We know the problem. What's the solution?"

"You know what the solution is."

"Are you talking about a Houston-type effect here?" I said, again referring to Tapp's alleged hit man.

"Yeah."

". . . So we're in Sinatra territory 'All the way'?" I said.

"Yep."

". . . Okay. I'll deal with that."

Just to be sure, I ran it by him again.

"So you decided breaks go out the window and 'all the way' comes in?"

"Yeah . . . All he's got to do is say one word to the wrong person, and here we go . . ."

"You want me to use my people or your people?" I asked.

"Your people."

"You got it."

"Okay."

"What else?"

"That's all."

We talked some more, then I ran it up the pole again, giving this bastard every opportunity to back off a murder conspiracy charge.

"Uh, you've given this enough thought with this pig that you're sure you wanna . . ."

"Can't have that," he interrupted, referring to Bartlett's blabbing. "Don't need that."

"Well, I thought you loved him?"

"No way."

"All right," I said, giving in. "We're gonna have to rent fucking pallbearers . . . nobody's gonna show up."

"Well, what can I tell you?"

In all my years with the Mob, I wasn't involved in a single hit, either doing or planning. I never even heard about one in advance. But here in Arizona, where I was dealing in politics, I had to set up three murders in less than thirty days.

I felt like getting out the state statutes, calling Tapp in, and saying, "All right, Coach! Look how far you've come! You started on page one, soliciting people for bribes. You worked your way through malicious slander, bribery, money laundering, and extortion conspiracies. Now you're way over here at the end of the book—conspiracy to commit first-degree murder. Congratulations!"

When Tapp hung up, I alerted the cops. They huddled and decided that we needed to get Tapp talking murder on videotape to further seal his fate. They also discussed Ernie Hoffman and his studies. To my surprise, they supported hiring him and paying for his bearded polls. That meant Desert Sting now had the unqualified support of the police and county attorney's office. They would spare no expense to keep the dirty politicians, lobbyists, judges, and cops coming to see me.

Back at the office on Friday, August 24, I decided to pull an old Mob move on Tapp and Bartlett. I told Tapp I was going to rehire Bartlett at $500 a week, let him do odd jobs to shut him up, and wait until he got comfortable. Then I'd send him on a one-way trip to the Bahamas and have him whacked there and dumped into the Atlantic. Tapp loved the plan. I called Bartlett and left a message that I had a job for him.

The next morning I picked up the *Scottsdale Progress* and was greeted by a front-page story reporting that Charlie Keating had resigned from American Continental, the company a federal judge said he used to loot two billion dollars from his savings and loan. Part of that money, it is believed, was used to fill the campaign coffers of five U.S. senators. As I was strumming through the paper, another article leaped out at me. Five state legislators in South Carolina had been snared in a sixteen-month FBI sting known as "Operation Lost Trust." More arrests were said to be pending.

Beautiful. Keating and a political sting, bunched together in the morning newspaper. The worst of the stories, by far, was news of the South Carolina sting. That was sure to run a hot poker through the comfort levels of all the legislators in Arizona.

Tapp called Monday morning and said he had planned a surprise for some kid who jumped bail on him.

"It's gonna cost me a case of Jack Daniels, but I'm gonna have his cellmate picked and the guy'll be about six-foot-eight with a ten-inch whopper, and he's gonna be callin' him 'honey' for the next twenty years!"

Tapp came by later that afternoon to pick up his salary and impart his latest police-political insight. He said the FBI was going local with political stings like in South Carolina and California to draw attention away from all the thieves in Washington. "What they're trying to do is make our federal legislators look like they're above and beyond that kind of shit. We have some out here on the take that are absolutely unreal. [U.S. Senator] Denny DeConcini . . . it wasn't the money, it was all the land he bought along the side of the Central Arizona [water] Project and some of it was right down the middle of that son-of-a-bitch that they had to purchase from him."

We sullied the reputations of several public officials, eventually arriving at Phoenix Police Chief Ruben Ortega. "I think he's a switch-hitter," Tapp said. "Yes. Old Ruben Ortega. Of course, you know, I've talked to people down there on Van Buren that knew him when he was a captain and he was prettier than shit then, in on the take!"

Tapp added that the Phoenix Police Department was running drugs and the only reason they had not been exposed as the River Cops in Miami had was because the operation was so widespread there was nobody in the force to investigate it.

"The only way that stays on the QT is because it goes clear to the top. Okay? In the other cities it probably doesn't go through to the top and that's why you have all of that problem."

Let's see. Tapp had called County Attorney Richard Romley a phony war hero, and now was accusing the chief of police of being a gay drug dealer. I think he was headed for some hard prison time. Someone with a "whopper" was going to be callin' him honey.

Ernie Hoffman mentioned the South Carolina sting when I spoke with him the next day. I brushed it off and said that I wanted to go forward with the studies. He was delighted and added that the studies were a test to see if I was legit. The police, he said, would never authorize $50,000 for studies in an undercover operation. Chalk one up to Romley, Ortega, Keppel, or whoever controled the operation's purse strings. Hoffman was right. The FBI wouldn't have gone for that. I was fortunate, extremely fortunate, that some back-room numbers cruncher wasn't playing with our budget.

Hoffman smelled the money and went into hyper-drive after that. Operation Desert Sting finally had a running back to help carry the ball.

Dave Horwitz dropped by that same afternoon and said he wanted $400 to finance a mailer for Candy Nagel and Sue Grace. I told him I'd get back to him. Candy and Susie weren't my players. They'd get squat. Kenney phoned the following day and pushed me to give Nagel and Grace the $400. I asked why they couldn't come get it themselves. He mentioned something about excessive donations being a felony. This from a guy who took $55,000. We huddled in the fourth room. The cops and prosecutors decided to let the legal $400 walk to bait the hook. That was interesting. Tony was now legitimately backing political candidates.

Fondia "Al" Hill ambushed me later that afternoon. I had first met Al, one of my neighbors in the office building, several weeks earlier. Al was a handsome, muscular black man, about thirty, who had once played professional football for the Arizona Wranglers of the old World Football League. He wore his hair slicked back into a ponytail, dressed hip, and drove a Porsche. Hill had some kind of one-man marketing and research business, but no one could get a handle on what it was he actually did. He was rarely in the office. I suspected that he was running a routine lease scam. He had signed a five-year lease, and was given the first fifteen months free. When the free ride was over, he'd probably disappear.

Hill kept trying to get close to me, running one hustle after another. His first was a movie he wanted to produce. Later he dropped off a script for a film titled *A Funny Thing Happened on the Way to Stuttgart*. It was pretty weak. Hill wanted me to invest $150,000 in the project. I told him the movie script was garbage and my partners weren't interested. However, I said if he could come up with some kiddie porn, I had a contact who'd be very interested. This wasn't something I pulled out of my ass. One of the maids had seen a video in Hill's office entitled *The Crayon Lady* and told my former secretary that she thought Hill was in the child sex business. I filed that away. Hill was trying to con me, so I set a particularly nasty trap for this slimeball.

Horwitz arrived the following day with R. T. Griffin, head of the Central Arizona Labor Council. Griffin was a big, heavy guy who resembled Roseanne Arnold's television husband, John Goodman. He half-laid in his chair. Ball later told me all they could see on the video was his stomach protruding from the chair like a humpback whale. If these two were any indication, union bosses were certainly well fed.

We talked briefly about my issue, then I peeled four $100s from my wad and handed them to Horwitz for Nagel and Grace. He grabbed it and said I needed to meet with Pat Cantelme, the firefighters' union boss. I flashed back to Nagel's comments about the firefighters owning Phoenix and told him to arrange a meet.

Before I bolted for the day, I casually flipped through the *Phoenix Gazette*. There was a picture of my wife, Gail, on the front page of the Community section. She was standing in our backyard beside a massive, multiheaded sunflower she had grown. It was such a botanical wonder that two local television stations had already visited. Wonderful. Here I was, the front man in a massive political sting, and my wife was giving press conferences with a mutant sunflower. Because of the sensitivity of the sting, the police had advised me not to tell Gail that the operation had emerged from the shadows of the gambling bars. That meant I had no compelling reason, from her perspective, to shut down her "Jackie and the Beanstalk" media activities. Instead, I was forced to hide in my bedroom every time the nosy reporters came around. I did manage to convince her to use her maiden name in the stories.

Gail's photo in the *Gazette* was right under a retrospective story about the explosion of the Hindenburg. I hoped that wasn't an omen.

9

By August's end, the chasm between Joe and Tony had widened so far that the characters began to take on different physiological identities. Joe was becoming stressed out. My hands shook. I broke out in cold sweats. I seemed to be on the verge of plunging back into the paralyzing darkness of agoraphobia—a debilitating panic disorder that imprisons people inside the safe confines of their home. I'd struggled with the illness periodically in the past, and was taking medication to control the sudden waves of crippling fear.

Tony Vincent had no symptoms at all. He was a rock under the most intense circumstances. His hands were steady as he doled out bribes to powerful politicians. He arranged murders without blinking. He loved cars, driving, juke and jiving, the great outdoors, and the wide open spaces of the desert. Tony had his act together.

It was the damnest thing.

I decided not to tell the boys in the fourth room that Joe was on the verge of coming unglued. No need. They hadn't talked to Joe in months. Nobody had talked to Joe but my wife, Gail, and I wasn't even sure about that anymore. Tony, the stronger personality, had taken over.

Although Gail handled the Joe/Tony transformation and the long days and late hours without complaint, the need to maintain my secret existence began to wear on her in other areas. She was discouraged from socializing with friends and neighbors and became lonely and isolated. When a neighbor's cat bit her on the hand, I couldn't even go inside the emergency room with her. I had to sit in a car outside the hospital for two hours in order not to risk running into someone who knew Tony.

The more Tony's world expanded, the tighter Joe's closed in.

Sue Laybe phoned the house at 10:35 a.m. on Thursday, August 30. She said she had to see me in fifteen minutes. I stalled her until 4 p.m. I had no idea what she wanted.

Gary Kaasa, Nagel's advisor, arrived at the office for a 12:30 meet. He was a short, mild-mannered man with thinning hair, a ruddy complexion, bad teeth, and Kmart clothes. He was also the most boring human being I've ever met. Despite these flaws, Kaasa was apparently an accomplished dirty trickster. He specialized in hit pieces and was said to have driven one legislator out of office with a particularly nasty mailer. He must have heard that there was this dumb Italian in town who was willing to pay big bucks for bad studies, because that's what he hit me with. He wanted to do a strategy plan for treating my issue as if it were a breathing candidate, sort of a study personified. This paper would only cost me the bargain basement price of $2,500. I told him I'd consult my partners.

Senator Alan Stephens called at 3:35 p.m. He wanted Gail and me to send $440 to James Henderson, Jr., an American Indian senator from northern Arizona who needed help with his primary. Stephens promised to bring the Chief in after the primary for a powwow. That wasn't the way Tony worked, but the fourth room approved. I asked Stephens where he wanted the money sent. He said to him made payable to Henderson. Nice move. Stephens wanted credit for the delivery. Tony was catching on.

Laybe came in at 4 p.m. and tried to sell me $1,740 in various fundraiser tickets. I said the magic words, counted out the cash, and handed her the money. She buried it in her purse and sped out the door. In the fourth room, Ball said they had sent some surveillance officers to scope out her house and discovered that she had contracted to build some additions. The police noted that the work stopped before she visited me, then started up again. It looked as if Big Tony was paying to remodel Sue's house.*

On Wednesday, September 5, I received a message from Marie that Senator Carolyn Walker had called. I'd been waiting to hear from her.

---

*Sue Laybe denies this and all subsequent charges that money from Tony Vincent was used to fund additions to her modest home.

Walker was pro-gambling and had tried to pass some bills in the previous sessions. I punched her buttons. She was friendly and said Alan Stephens had told her to call. We set a meet for the next day.

Senator Walker arrived at 2:15 p.m. on September 6. She was a tall, big-boned black woman who weighed a solid 180 pounds or more. Her hair was Afro-Sheen slick, her clothes were prime, and she deposited a smudge of lipstick on her Coke can with every sip. Sometimes, when she leaned forward, her big bosoms shook and nearly flopped out of her dress.

The Senator expressed a marked nervousness about Evan Mecham's Phoenix-like resurrection, and with good reason. Mecham had publicly referred to blacks as "pickaninnies," and was no feminist. In wicked irony, his impeachment hearing had come down to a black woman, Walker, casting the final vote: She bounced him.

That action, televised around the nation, lit the fuse of her political career. When the Martin Luther King holiday issue flared up, she again leaped to the forefront, receiving even more exposure. Walker had become a big name in Arizona politics. There was talk of her running for Congress.

All that was about to end.

We had hardly said hello when the senator cut right to the chase. She started by taking an initial $660, spread out as $220 contributions from me, my wife, and my secretary.

"You're my kinda guy, Tony. I like you."

"Well, you just tell it like it is."

"No shakin' and bakin'."

When the talk wandered to my alleged wife and girlfriend, she made a confession, "I like a variety of men."

The conversation shifted to another commodity she preferred in abundance. "What do you need for your campaign, Carolyn? What's the number you need?"

"Right now? Totally about $5,000 to get outta debt."

I took the cash from my drawer and placed it on the table. Walker let it lay there for a while like a big chocolate cake, then grabbed it.

"Call it a fund-raiser. Call it what you wanna call it. Just know Tony's your friend."

"Tony, you'll have me for a friend for the rest of your life!"

Senator Walker proved to be quite the ambitious woman.

"Well, you know, let me be truthful with you," she said. "I like the good life. I mean, I like helping, but I like the good life. And I'm tryin' to position myself that I can live the good life and have more money."

The talk turned to what the Reverend Ralph Abernathy wrote about Dr. King in his own controversial memoir.

"So Martin Luther King liked young broads, who don't," I said. "If he did, he did."

"I like young boys," Walker said.

This was an interesting lady.

"I gotta go, I hate to take your money and run."

I assured her that wasn't a problem.

There were no high fives in the fourth room after Walker left. Everyone was in shock. After haggling with Candy Nagel and the others, and wading through all the bullshit about bundled checks and studies and comfort levels, this barbecue went down so fast it caught us all off guard. And the funny part was, that nervous little weasel, Alan Stephens, had set it up. Stephens was still being evasive, but the legislators he pimped were swimming into our net.

Al Hill called on the cellular as I was driving home. He claimed to have found a source in Vancouver, British Columbia, that had sex tapes with chickens and dogs.

"What the hell do chickens do?" I wondered.

"Get fucked," he said.

Hill promised to come by the next day and discuss this further.

The following morning, Tapp called and said Hoffman changed a pending meet with Representative English to the Ritz Carlton Hotel. Ball told me to reserve adjacent suites, and they'd instruct the hardware boys to get busy wiring the room.

Al Hill arrived on schedule and immediately tried to squeeze me for the air fare to British Columbia. I wasn't about to finance this goofball's trip, not even with the police's confiscated drug money.

"I was thinking last night, what the fuck could a chicken do?" I asked again. "Is it with a broad or with a guy?"

"I don't know."

Hill promised to investigate further and get back to me. Tapp phoned and reported that the name we selected for our money-funneling corporation, Arizona Economic Resource Group, had already been taken. He promised to select another. I knew he'd stretch the process until the next week in order to justify his $1,000 weekly salary. He eventually selected Southwest Economic Research Development Group, Inc.

Al Hill interrupted my evening with the latest news from Vancouver.

"The guy says that everything is A-one quality stuff. It's under-underground . . . He said the minimum that he would want me to spend would be $2,500. And he said he would sell me two tapes."

"Is that munchkin land?"

"Munchkin land and animals . . ."

". . . Do you have the three to lay out?"

"Well, I don't have it right on me . . ."

Now how did I guess that.

". . . 'Cause I didn't go to the, you know, I didn't go to the bank. I didn't know if you have it around?"

I called the cops. They gave me the okay to front Al the money. However, Detective Ball said no "fuckin' chickens," which marked the first time I'd heard that expression used in the literal sense. I called Al back.

"Pass on the farm people and get three of the munchkins."

"Right. Well, that's gonna cost more than $2,500."

"So what do you need?"

"That'll be about $3,750."

I slapped on a body mike and met him at the Registry Resort at 10 p.m. He cruised up in a dark, 1984 Porsche Coupe license plate number FED-745.

FED!

Could this be a reverse sting? Could Al Hill really be a slick FBI agent instead of a dumb-ass conman? Naaaah. It had to be a bizarre coincidence. We decided to go for just two tapes at $2,750. I gave Al the money. He grabbed it and Porsched off into the moonlight. I figured we'd never see him again.

Gary Kaasa was unusually animated when he called me at home the next morning. An *Arizona Republic* columnist had burned Rep. Nagel in the newspaper. He referred to her as "lard" and said she was only enough lard to cover a small skillet. Nagel was beside herself. Kaasa wanted some money for a rebuttal. I told him to have her call me.

She called. She was steaming.

"Oh, is this lard?" I baited. "Hey, lard."

"You wouldn't believe it. I've lost ten pounds. How could they call me lard? . . . You know what, Tony, yesterday, I, you can't get me down. I mean you saw my personality. You cannot get me down. But I was. I was yesterday. Devastated . . . What it did to me is said, 'You did nothing for two years. You are incompetent.' So in fifteen minutes, these five assholes were able to strike a blow in two years' effort."

The "five assholes" were the *Arizona Republic*'s editorial board.

"See, the reporters are my friends and they actually warned me the night before," she said.

"They tipped you off?"

". . . They work with me every day. If I'm gonna get screwed, they call me ahead of time."

What Candy was saying was that the *Arizona Republic*, the state's largest newspaper, leaked advance information on upcoming stories and editorials to politicians.

"Yeah, it's a whole different rapport," she continued. "But the editorial, this [Bill] Cheshire guy comes from D.C. and he's a Moonie-type guy, real right-wing. He's pro-life. He has a litmus test."

"Gary said you had some issue or something that he wanted through, on a school bill, and you didn't vote for it?"

"Right, and so he really thinks that I'm dangerous, against his thinking . . . See I was actually able to kill, single-handedly in one movement, kill the most important bill to that man . . . I outmaneuvered him . . . I fucked him . . . But see, so that's 'incompetence' . . ."

"Well," I offered. "That's politics."

"But he buys his ink by the barrel . . . After the election, win, lose, or draw, I'll meet with the publisher and explain to him what he's doing to the economy of Arizona by telling everybody they're stupid and fat and we're all going broke."

We wandered off that subject for a while, then came back to it. Hell hath no fury like a woman told she is fat, even if it's only in a metaphorical sense.

"Well, the thing is, what happened to me was not because of competence. What happened to me was because of revenge! . . . I don't care how strong a man or a woman or anybody you are, you read that shit and you hear that shit and you even start to doubting yourself . . . I have never in my political life . . . you know, two years in the legislature, I have lived a charmed life. I have been loved. I have been revered . . . and I've never had a piece of, I didn't even have a rat turd thrown at me! . . ."

"Rat turd," for the politically unaware, means "a little shit," kind of a fleck of shit flung at a politician, rather than a whole smear campaign.

"I think he [Gary Kaasa] is more upset now," Candy went on, quickly losing her starch. "He's never seen me cry. He's never seen me shaken. He's never seen me down . . . You know what I told you about 'friends, assholes, and rubber men'? You know those rubber men are never there for you. From time to time, the assholes are, even though they're assholes. But your friends, Tony, I had probably seventy-five to a hundred calls yesterday. You know, I mean, people, I took my phone and put it on record. I couldn't stand it because every time somebody else would call me and say 'we love you' then I would start, you know, getting emotional again."

Candy was about to choke up. I felt like saying "Whoaaa, babe, it was an allegory. You're not fat. The story wasn't even intended to imply that you're fat. Dense and incompetent, maybe, but not fat. Get a grip! You dish it out. You can take it." Instead, I asked her if Tony's cash could make the pain go away. She responded that Eddie Basha, a big supermarket baron, told her he had $1,000 that he and his five sons were ready to bundle for her to strike back. I reiterated that I'd give her whatever else she needed.

Candy's man Kaasa called after she left and said all they wanted was a legal $440. I said I was maxed out, but I could get it to them in the name of my niece and her friend. He agreed and said he'd pick it up that afternoon. Kaasa called twenty minutes later and said never-mind. I could only guess that one of Nagel's other sources, one far less scary than me, had come through. Or, that she did the smart thing and just let the insult blow over.

Al Hill rang me from "Vancouver" on the following Monday, September 10. I was surprised to hear from him. He said he had met his source and had given him half the money twelve hours before and had not heard back. I couldn't determine if this was Hill's game, or someone was going to scam him. He called again at 10:35 p.m. and said he heard from the source. The guy, Hill claimed, wanted $10,000 for one tape and $3,000 for the other.

"That's way out of line," I said. "Tell them I have fifty tapes I'll sell them for $8,000 each."

Hill started whining about being burned for the money.

"Give me their names and addresses, and I'll take care of it," I said. Naturally, he didn't. We decided that he should buy the $3,000 tape and come home.

Tuesday, September 11, was primary day. My team spread out and attended various political functions around town. The Democrats converged at the Hyatt downtown and the Republicans settled in at the nearby Sheraton. I begged off everything and took Gail to see Itzhak Perlman at the Phoenix Symphony. I was about to dive into bed when the phone rang at 1:05 a.m. It was Tapp. He wasn't happy.

"I ran into the pig [Gary Bartlett]. We got a problem. We need to talk tomorrow."

"We're gonna be busy tomorrow. What's the problem?"

"Oh shit, this dumb motherfucker pulled something in public tonight that I couldn't believe he pulled."

"His joint?"

"No, well, he might as well have."

"What'd he do?"

"Well, I'd been watching him all evening. And I was talking to the county attorney [Romley] and was standing there shooting the shit with him . . . so Bartlett walked over and he said, 'You son-of-a-bitch, you better pay your bills you owe.' And he says, 'I got you by the balls. For bribing senators.'"

"Are you kidding me?"

"No sir. He did it right in public."

"Who heard this?"

"Romley did."

That was a break. Romley was my boss.

"And so anyway, when he walked away, Romley says, 'Who the fuck you been bribing?' I said, 'Well you I guess. I donated to you too.'"

I told Tapp to stay cool and I'd deal with it. Bartlett was a moron. I gambled that he was bluffing about taking his charges to the attorney general. However, I came away with a greater respect for Rick Romley. He got to play a little Tony Vincent and had passed his screen test.

I steered Tapp into other areas.

"So now Stragalas gotta take on West [for state treasurer]."

"That shouldn't be a big-time problem . . . West is a drunk."

"Hey, lay on that [Judge] Stump," I said a few minutes later. "He's avoiding us."

"He was out politicking."

"Yeah. For what? . . . He was unchallenged!"

"No, no, he was out helping the others."

The next day brought the news that all my legislature players, even the ones on the fringe, had survived their primaries. This included Candy Nagel, who kicked butt despite the *Arizona Republic*'s smear. None of this was a surprise. Incumbents rarely get knocked out within their own party. They'd all now have two months to campaign to keep their jobs. Since these would be head-to-head Democrat-Republican battles, the action was sure to heat up.

Big Jim Davis, however, lost his JP election and failed in his quest to become the first judge to perform a murder-for-hire assassination in between classes at judicial college in Reno.

The big news came from the gubernatorial race. Developer and savings and loan tycoon J. Fife Symington stomped Evan Mecham in the Republican primary. Everyone breathed a deep sigh of relief. That meant the feared homosexual bashing of Democratic candidate Terry

Goddard was thwarted. Symington would fight dirty, but not that dirty. Evan Mecham was finally laid to rest.

Or so we thought.

There wasn't time to celebrate the demise of Mecham or mourn the fate of my homicidal friend Jim Davis. I had arranged a big meeting at the Ritz Carlton between Tapp, Hoffman, Representative English, and myself. The police had three days to wire the place, so everything was a go when I arrived shortly after 11:30 a.m. The mini video camera had been planted in an old-fashioned desktop radio that mixed well with the standard decor of the room. Microphones were scattered about. My three guests appeared within the hour. We talked, ate, and drank for the next seven hours. Early in the conversation, when I mentioned my chat with the dog track folks, Hoffman jumped in.

"Let me do an ecomomic study . . . on the whole pari-mutuel take of the state . . ."

I just ignored him. Hoffman's take on brokering the slanted stats must have been phenomenal.

We talked straight politics for the first hour before getting to the important stuff.

"For years, the biggest fanny patter in the legislature was the Mormon bishop," English informed us.

"Remember Donna Carlton," Hoffman cut in. "She used to sit there at her desk, put her feet in the air."

Hoffman, English, and Tapp shifted from beaver shots to stings. They were preoccupied by the South Carolina and California operations. I received a call on my cellular phone from the boys in the second suite. "Get naked," Detective Ball said. I stood up, kicked off my shoes, peeled off my shirt and undershirt, and dropped my pants—all to prove I wasn't wired.

". . . I'm proud of my body," I said as the guys laughed uproariously. "I'm entitled to do this in a meeting."

I ate lunch and dessert, then continued the meeting with my butt hanging out. That ended the talk of stings. The tension in the room evaporated. Everyone loosened up.

Hoffman said he received a report on me from Chuy Higuera that explained why the senator took to me so fast. It had to do with my jewelry. "[Higuera] said, 'You ought to see what's around his neck.' He says, 'It's the Mexican flag!' He said, 'I'll play with a guy like him!'"

I was slick, but not that slick. It was the Italian flag. Same colors. Different design.

"Our trust has to be paramount with this group," I said. "I'm dead serious. I've been more scared of legislators than they've been of me because I know where I'm at. I can be picked up by the police and tortured, 'Do you know Bill English?' Take out another nail. 'Do you know Ernie Hoffman?' You don't talk outside of what we talk about amongst ourselves. It goes to the grave with us and that's the bottom line. This man [Tapp] and I have done some things together that are paramount toward what I'm tryin' to accomplish here and I think he knows as well as I do, none of it's provable. There's no trail back to us. We've covered our asses all the way . . ."

It was an effective speech. The presentation could have been better, however. I was still sitting there in my drawers.

"Can I put my pants back on?"

"Yeah, go ahead," Hoffman said.

After I dressed, we discussed the Martin Luther King holiday issue. Hoffman reported that his polls were showing it was favored by 64 percent, with 31 percent opposed—a substantial margin. There was, however, an ugly little cloud on the horizon.

"Now, what he'll have to do to get his pound of flesh, he has one thing left, to take MLK [Martin Luther King] down with him," Hoffman warned.

"He" was Evan Mecham. The guy was like a cockroach. You could swat him and step on him and spray the bastard with insecticide, but you couldn't kill him.

"So you're in the ugliness of another sixty days with this son-of-a-bitch out there sayin', 'Hey, I'm out . . . I didn't win the nomination, but I think I can do what's right,'" Hoffman said.

". . . He is the most stubborn son-of-a-bitch I have ever encountered in my life," English seconded.

There was another problem with the pending Martin Luther King Day fiasco. Instead of one simple issue on the ballot, there were two. One involved replacing Columbus Day with MLK Day, a stupid idea that merely enraged the Italians. The other was to keep Columbus and give King his own day. It sounds simple, but the twin issues were certain to brain-fry a large percentage of the voters.

The conversation wandered to my credentials. Tapp, who frequently fantasized that he was a former CIA agent, again claimed to have checked me and my partners with the "agency" and that we passed. Tony Vincent didn't exist before 1990. My partners didn't exist at all. Yet Tapp's CIA buddies had confirmed us all.

"I wanna tell you why we swept that office," Tapp babbled on. "This started at my insistence. I understand the operation of the attorney general's office better than most people . . ."

"And you're also telling me that Mecham is right about the lasers [bugs]?" English asked.

"They do have a laser," Tapp established.

"Is that why your blinds are drawn?" Hoffman asked.

"They're always . . . and they're changed," I mumbled incoherently.

"You could shoot a laser from here then, right?" he persisted.

"But they're changed every day to different directions," I maintained, explaining how a $12 miniblind can thwart a multimillion-dollar, state-of-the-art laser listening device.

"Right," Tapp agreed.

"Well, I'll be damned," Hoffman said.

I asked English what he needed for his campaign. He didn't state a specific figure, but mentioned bundling checks. That led us back to Hoffman's novel techniques in that area.

"[Hoffman] got relatives hangin' out the ass. He's gonna use his dog," I said.

"I think he already has," English laughed.

"His name's Angel. Angel Hoffman," Hoffman cracked.

English related that although he was serving his seventh two-year term, he was "scared to death" of being beaten this time around. He ordered another vodka on the rocks and set in for the long haul. We were at the four-hour mark in the meeting with no sign of breaking up. The boys in the second suite were getting antsy and started peppering me with calls demanding that I speed things along. That got to be a pain. English was going to take his sweet time. He wanted us to become family first. I couldn't explain that to the cops, so I had to parry with them on the phone just as much as I did with the guys in front of me.

It finally came time for the drop. I pulled $18,000 out of my briefcase and laid it on the table. Before anyone could take the money, there was a knock at the door. Hoffman scooped up the dough like the pro he was and stuffed it into his briefcase. The person at the door turned out to be a waitress bringing more vodka.

After the meet broke, Keppel, Mount, Ball, and Sergeant Davis came into the suite. Keppel was livid. They hadn't seen the drop. Since it was clear as day, I figured Sergeant Davis was goofing around as usual and they just missed it. I assured them it was on the video. Just to be sure, I agreed to double cover. I called English and told him I left home with $30,000 and was supposed to give them $18,000 and another guy $10,000. Since the figures didn't jell, I explained that I had either given them $20,000 or the first guy $12,000. English said Hoffman had the money at his hotel. I called and laid down the same story. Hoffman said the money was in his trunk and he'd go fetch it. He called back at 1:30 a.m. sounding exasperated.

"I've been counting over and over again . . ." he wailed. "I got it in piles, then the next thing I do, I go back to tens and everything else but . . . of course, I've never had this opportunity in my whole life even counting anything beyond a thousand."

Didn't matter. I had double sealed the deal with the calls. The cops and prosecutors met me at the apartment later that same afternoon. Keppel apologized for his outburst. Turned out the drop had come across loud and clear, literally, on the audio and video. Keppel was embarrassed, but his apology showed class.

Representative Sue Laybe came by on Friday, September 14, for another infusion of home-development funds. I plugged the cotton in my ears, cursed my pool again, and got down to business. Sue tried to sell more tickets, this time for everything under the desert sun: a Rose Mofford function; a dinner with Charlie Keating's pal, U.S. Senator Dennis DeConcini; a dinner with Phoenix Mayor Paul Johnson; some "battle of the sexes" event involving Fred DuVal, who was once former Governor Bruce Babbitt's presidential campaign manager; a bowl-off for Babbitt; and a dinner for the Democratic party, among others. Since I had already purchased her vote on the gambling issue, I dragged out my other concerns—private prisons, house arrest, and the election of judges.

Laybe started out against the private prisons idea but came around. She said as long as I used union labor to build them, she could jump on board.

After that, we discussed the reshaping of the legislature for the upcoming term, particularly whether Representative Brenda Burns had a shot at being chairman of the judiciary committee. "Reshaping" turned out to be the appropriate word.

"She doesn't look like that anymore," Laybe said, pointing to Burns' picture in the legislature book. "She got her boobs done . . . She took ten off the top [her nose] and put five on each side."

After that detour into the magic of plastic surgery, Laybe pimped more of her tickets. When she got to the Babbitt bowl-off, I told her to cut the shit and tell me what she really needed. She wasn't shy.

"Ten thousand dollars."

"You need another ten?"

"Uh huh."

We chatted for a few more minutes. The phone rang.

"Give her the ten," Detective Ball directed.

As I counted the money, Laybe talked bundling.

"I only have twenty names. You'll have to get me some . . ."

I ignored her comments and handed her the cash. She took it and launched into her count, snapping those bills like a baby being spanked.

"I'll need more names," she repeated.

"You'll need what?"

"More names."

I told her to call me after she figured out exactly how many names she needed, for both the $10,000 and Ticketron outlet she ran out of her purse. Laybe twisted a rubberband around the cash and dashed out the door.

Horwitz showed for the long-scheduled meet with Pat Cantelme, the firefighters' union leader. Cantelme was late so Horwitz had to bullshit until his buddy slid down the pole. When he arrived, I was disappointed. I had envisioned some aging but still tough *Backdraft* warrior. Instead, Cantelme was a small, mousy guy who, though a bigshot union leader, still seemed a wannabe. During the conversation, Cantelme related something interesting. I mentioned a petition drive we were considering that would seek to obtain 300,000 signatures from voters supporting casino gambling. That was to be used as a backup in case the campaign with the state legislature failed. We were going to do this as a ruse to bring more legislators into the fold. Cantelme informed me that once you obtain 87,000 signatures, the issue automatically goes on the ballot. That was a shock. None of the politicians or lobbyists in my pocket had explained that. I don't think the police or county attorneys even knew it. If we had gone forward with our plan, the damn thing would have gone on the ballot. The public may have instituted casino gambling in Arizona as an offshoot of a sting operation gone out of control. I could see the national headlines on that one—"Arizona Stung!: County Funds Used to Push a Public Referendum on Gambling." They'd have to clean house at the police department and county attorney's office. We'd all be lynched before we could get out of town.

Cantelme advised me to stop at 50,000 signatures.

The fireman was the first person to push me for the names of my associates. I rattled off some Italian names from the old neighborhood, the Marchese Brothers, Rulli, and DeVito. Cantelme joked that they sounded like members of his family. I explained that they were heavy "dis and dose" guys and wouldn't work well with the politicians, so that's why they chose me to front the operation. Cantelme then advised me not to hire another Phoenix lobbyist before consulting him. He must have had someone he wanted to plant on me for reasons that weren't clear. I dangled some bait, but the fireman wasn't biting. I wasn't sure why he was there in the first place. I thought of what my old Mob pals would say if the operation were real: "The guy's a fireman. Give him a hose and kick his ass out the door."

It was a short meet, less than an hour, but it proved educational and saved the good guys from a possible catastrophe.

I called Gary Kaasa after the fireman left and ordered him to hold off on his "my issue as a candidate" report. Neither he nor Candy Nagel had joined my team by taking a bribe. They just peppered me with requests and tiptoed around the fire. I wanted to cut off the trickle and let them decide if they were going to be in or out.

As the NFL's late game wound down on Sunday night, September 16, I was struck by a loose end that had been dangling out there for a week and had completely slipped my mind. What the hell happened to Fondia "Al" Hill and his magic chickens?

10

On September 17, 1990, Senator Chuy Higuera informed me that he had stopped his son from accepting a job at the Tucson dog track. He didn't want the greyhound people to feel that he was obligated to them. That meant Higuera had chosen sides. He was about to sign on with Team Tony. He set a meet for the following day in my office.

Senator Walker called and also set a meet for the next day.

George Stragalas reported that the long-awaited lunch with Sam Goddard had been penciled in for September 19. I would dine with the former governor at the ritzy Executive Park Hotel. Hoffman rang and said he wanted me to attend an upcoming political fund-raiser at ex-governor Bruce Babbitt's house dubbed the "Funds for Five Freshmen" affair. Tony was starting to travel in some heady circles.

Detective Ball filled my drawer with $25,000 prior to my sit-down with Higuera. It could all be his for the asking. The burly Tucson senator arrived at 3:30 p.m. He was nervous and fidgety, but still managed to tell me what he wanted.

"Yesterday I went for an interview, Canon Fax Machines. They want me to do some work for them. So if I can do that man, you know . . . everything relating."

Faxes! We don't need no stinking faxes! I thought.

"But I'll tell you what, you know, I don't have to tell people what the potential is," Higuera went on, waiting for me to swallow the worm.

"The fax machines and all, that's all open," I said, taking his bait. "I mean there's so many things open now. You are one of the ones in on the gound floor, Chuy. Just so you understand."

Higuera moved on to his problem of trying to serve two gambling masters.

"The dog track can't hurt me if I say, tell them right now I'm not with you. The thing is that until we get a final package from you, it'd be dumb for me to say, 'To hell with you, dog track, here I go Tony,' you know, you don't do things that way."

Not when you're trying to play both ends against the middle. "You don't have a problem voting for my issue?"

"No . . . I'll tell you what. I don't. I don't and I'm not waving. The thing is that if I make a commitment now and break it, I don't have to do it."

". . . You're with me?" I asked.

"Like I said right now, I can't say that, please don't say that because these guys are my friends, you know. And I still gotta work with 'em this year."

"You can't say that to them?"

"Yeah."

"But you can commit to me between me and you?"

"Yeah."

"That's it?"

"That's it."

Glad we finally straightened that out.

"I'll tell you what," Higuera said. "The last thing I need is crap or heat or something from somebody."

"You need heat? I don't need no fuckin' heat!"

"Yeah."

"The last thing I need is to look out that window and see twenty squad cars around here, forget about it!" I said.

It was time to get to the point.

"What am I gonna do for Chuy Higuera?"

"I'll tell you what. As far as the campaign, I'm gonna be doing a mailer and I'm gonna try to put up some signs here the last month."

"Okay."

"That's about it. That's what I'm gonna do with the campaign."

"Mailer and signs?"

"Yes sir."

"Okay, what do you need?"

"Well, I'll tell you what, any time we can get any kind of help if it's stamps, it's all right . . . I'm serious. Money to me [means] you buy stamps. But if someone wants to give me stamps, it's fine."

Stamps! Everyone told me Chuy would sell cheap, but this was ridiculous. For his own pride, I had to set his price higher. I didn't want the newspapers to write: "Tony Vincent bought the white Mormon representative for $55,000, and all the poor Mexican senator got was a sheet of 25-cent stamps."

"... What do you need Chuy, bottom line, what do you need?"

"I gotta do the mailer."

"[Hoffman] mentioned a number, about twenty-five hundred?" I offered.

"Twenty-five. I was gonna say thirteen."

Shrewd. In a few minutes, he'd owe me money.

"He said twenty-five hundred," I repeated.

The Senator squirmed and started talking about mailers and postage again.

"So what I have here is, I've got $1,540 in postal money orders," I said, pushing ahead.

"Okay."

"... Well, I'm gonna give you $1,540 here and then I'm gonna give you $1,000 in cash with names."

"Okay."

"... That's what makes you comfortable?"

Higuera mumbled something about a "finance committee." I didn't know what he was talking about, but played along.

"... Pay to?"

"Chuy Higuera Committee."

"'Chuy'?"

"Higuera Committee."

I ended up giving the senator a total of $2,545 in postal money orders and cash—a nice respectable bribe. When the case broke, he'd have his dignity.

"The shrimp is carved in stone," I assured him again before we parted. "If there's anything else you think of that you want on the back end, get back with me."

"I'll tell you what. Keep me in mind on the fax."

"The fax machines!" I said, having totally forgotten. "We're probably buying a couple hundred ..."

"Yeah, and copiers. So keep me in mind for that."

Senator Walker showed an hour later. She was in high spirits. The meeting was lively and boisterous. She knew about Higuera's shrimp deal, and had some back-end ideas of her own. After picking her brain about her interests, I awarded her the gift shops.

Although Walker poor-mouthed herself, she was actually doing pretty well. She pulled down $40,000 a year as a public relations executive for the telephone company, plus her $15,000 yearly legislative stipend, not counting her generous expense account. But it wasn't enough.

"... The least I want to do is die rich," she announced.

She later complained that the phone company didn't appreciate her.

"What do you do for them?" I asked.

"Public relations."

"Now me and you both know what that is."

"It's bullshit," she said.

"That's a token job," I said, egging her on.

"Yeah . . . 'cause they can't figure out what else to do with a senator."

"... They got things that they need down there so they put you on the payroll?" I speculated.

"Yeah, but they ain't willing to pay. So I ain't gonna do nothing."

"Well, if they ain't gonna pay, then you shouldn't do nothing."

"So now they're ready to get rid of me."

"Because you won't perform?"

"'Cause I won't perform. And they give me $40,000 a year," she said disdainfully.

"Chump change! And expect . . ."

"Expect miracles!"

"They want you in their pocket for forty K, that ain't the way it works," I said.

"Not to me it isn't."

"... I'm not U.S. West, but if I was, I'd know what your value is."

"Tony, you didn't get all that gold around your neck because you were dumb."

"... I'm not wearing nothing heavy. Next time you come in, I'm gonna put on some of the heavy pieces, just when I know I just got you that day. You'd freak out."

"I probably would, might try to rob you."

"No, you're allowed to!" I said. "You can stick me up without a gun."

"Okay! But I mean, I want a business of my own where I got, you know . . . I'd be happy if I had six figures . . . but I know I ain't never gonna make it big."

"Well, we got the back-end deal with me to start with. That's carved in stone. The gift shops, you got the first refusal."

"Okay."

"... Take it to the bank. I told you the shrimp's gone, the insurance is gone, the real estate is almost all gone, and I got hit today on the faxes. And that's it. Ain't nothing else gone. The gift shops are gone to you until you tell me you don't want them. You might want something else."

"And I can take it right now?"

"That's carved in stone. And if you need the money to start them, you don't have to go to the bank . . . You sit down and figure out what it's gonna take you to start off with. And you're gonna need, $700,000, $800,000 to operate six gift shops, if you want six of them. I'm gonna give you that money and you pay me back off the top but not all at once. With no interest, no juice. I ain't taking no juice from you 'cause you're the lady that's making me possible. How can I take juice from you? See what I'm saying. You take juice from a sucker. You don't take juice from people that take you to the well. And you're gonna stand up in the Senate and say 'I proudly introduce blah, blah.' I can't take no juice from you. That's carved in stone!"

I was sure doing a great deal of masonry with Senator Walker. "Carolyn, I don't believe there's anything such as what you would call an honest man."

"We all have our prices," she agreed.

"Exactly . . . I got my price. You got your price. My niece has her price. Everybody has their price. Think about it."

"Oh, I know it."

The conversation turned to the man who sent her in, Senator Alan Stephens.

"Alan cut himself into a deal at the airport. He's been real quiet about it . . . but he'll take and he'll turn around and screw you," Walker charged.

I smiled at that line. It reminded me of a famous quotation about honesty and politicians: "An honest politician is one who, when he is bought, will stay bought." According to Walker, Stephens wasn't even honest by that standard.

It was time for an honesty gut check with Ms. Walker.

". . . Anyway, this is our second meeting," I started. "I'm comfortable. I'm relaxed. I'm gonna sleep good tonight . . . What can I do for Carolyn. We're back to the question."

"Well, Carolyn needs money."

"Carolyn needs money. All right. How much money does Carolyn need?"

"I'm going through my head."

"I'm not pushing. Take your time. Take your time. 'Cause I need Carolyn."

"Ten thousand would get me out of financial difficulties."

"Okay. And that's your comfort level?"

"Actually, I'd really rather have fifteen, but ten would get me out of debt."

"Do you want ten or fifteen?"

"I'd like fifteen."

"That'll straighten you out?"

"That'll straighten me out."

"And you're committed to me? I have your support?"

"I was committed to you regardless."

Wrong answer. She spit out the hook. I tried again.

"Are you committed to me?"

"I said I was committed to you regardless."

Damn. She spit it out again.

"Are you committed to me?" I repeated.

"Yes I am."

Bingo!

"Do I have your support?"

"You do indeed."

Double bingo!

"When we get to the floor, you're gonna vote yes for me?"

"I'm gonna vote yes for you long before we get to the floor. If I don't vote yes for you before we get to the floor, you'll never get to the floor."

Triple bingo! But say what? "That's the other thing you gotta teach me. What you gotta do?"

"We gotta take a bill through committee first before we ever get to the floor. You don't get to the committee, you don't get to the floor. Okay."

"Yeah."

"Ernie will walk you through."

"Who?"

"Ernie."

It took a few beats for me to realize she was referring to Ernie Hoffman.

"How do I, uh, launder this much?" Walker asked.

She caught me off guard with that. I was there to give them money, not provide lessons in shady banking. "The best way to do it, is spend it on tangibles, I guess. If you don't have a way to . . . clean it up. What're you gonna do with it?"

"Well, they'll pay some bills. Finish paying my daughter's college tuition."

"You think about that and let's get together the first of the week,

before Friday . . . Let me think about a way for you to clean that up . . . "
I said as I handed her a stack of bills. "A hundred and fifty hundreds is
15,000, just count that and make sure there's 150 there."

"Do I have to count it?"

"Yeah, only because I'm not sure when I put it together this morning, I put it in bundles of fives and I didn't know."

"I'm gonna have to trust you for this."

"Let me count it then, 'cause I tell you why," I said, reaching for
her stash. As I counted, I gave her the rap I laid on Representative Bill
English about starting with $30,000, giving one guy $10,000 and
another $18,000, and having to determine who got the extra two. She
listened half-interested and then offered me another deal.

"Tony, would you like to own a TV station?"

"Yeah."

Walker explained that she had been involved in a license application deal in Tolleson. Her group managed to push through an application and get it approved by the Federal Communications Commission—a gargantuan task made considerably easier if the applicants are
minorities. Then, as often happens, the main players didn't have the
millions it took to build the station and kick it into operation. That
made it a big fat mouse waiting for some hawk to swoop down and
gobble up. Too bad Tony wasn't real. The hell with Tony. I made a note
to check that out for Joe—if Joe was still alive inside me somewhere.

There were spirited high fives and whoops of joy in the fourth
room after Walker dashed with her cash. It had been some afternoon.
Two senators toasted in as many hours. Desert Sting was now zipping
along like a roadrunner on mescaline. Where it would crash, nobody
knew. The only thing that was certain was that it would indeed crash.
There was no turning back, and no way to slow down.

Representative Kenney called that evening and advised me to stop
telling people the bundled bribe checks were from me. I figured that
was Representative Candy Nagel talking again. I turned it around and
said I was insulted that she took money from the supermarket tycoon,
Eddie Basha, and not Big Tony. Kenney advised me to keep sitting
with her man Gary Kaasa, who would eventually take the bait. Kenney
also asked me if I wanted to meet J. Fife Symington, the Republican
gubernatorial candidate. I most certainly did. He added that both he
and Ernie Hoffman were working on setting up a meet with Representative Jane Hull, the Speaker of the House.

The next day brought the big lunch meet with former governor
Sam Goddard. As I was leaving home, the phone rang. It was the long-
lost Al Hill.

"You're still alive?" I asked.

"Yeah. Man, I'm still in Vancouver, believe it or not."

"No. I find it hard to believe."

"Yeah. I'm still here. It's been, what do you call it? 'A roller coaster.' . . . And uh, so, I've gotta, ah, ah, videotape machine and [the video's] not quite what I thought it was. You know, it's, it's, it's, it's like for example, it says 'young boy and young girl' but you know. I don't think that, it's not, it's not the, you know. It's not the group. It's not quite as, as what we talked about. You know? I think maybe instead of . . . you know, the group that we talked about is just a little bit, trying to look that, that part. You know what I mean?"

Yeah, you got screwed.

Not to worry, Al continued. He had a bead on a new source. ". . . But, that would involve me taking a trip out of the country, to ah, Denmark and Copenhagen."

Before Al winged it to the cold countries, he pitched another tape he said he could get a lot closer than Denmark.

"They had some other wild stuff . . . it was in this crap . . . 'fisting.' You ever seen anything like that, man?"

"Fifting?" I asked, wondering what new perversion this bumbling moron had stumbled upon.

"Fisting."

"Say it again?"

"Fist. Like your fist."

"Fifth?"

"Fist. Like your hand."

"Oh yeah, yeah," I said. "I've seen that. That's old."

"Oh is it?"

"Yeah, and that's got to be with an older party anyway, for that to fit."

I instructed Al to use his fists to bring the tapes he had — the ones I paid $2,750 for — to my office first thing when he came back to town.

I hung up and ventured out to meet the governor. All I knew about Sam Goddard was some crazy story Stragalas had told me about Goddard once having taken a bribe from a union boss in the form of a shopping bag full of gold. I expected Goddard to be far too slick to hit me up during the first meeting, but I stuffed $20,000 in my pocket just in case the years had feebled his brain. Goddard strolled into the restaurant like he not only owned the place, but the whole state as well. He was a tall, lanky, balding man in his late sixties who had the smell of an old-time player about him. I switched to J. R. Ewing Tony to complement my cowboy outfit and bolo tie, and let fly a rapid-fire version of my "Casinos for Arizona" rap. Goddard sat there cold and aloof.

"You got a long way to go," he said.

His condescending tone pissed me off. Actually, it pissed Tony off. We touched upon the gubernatorial race. He appeared to be only slightly more interested. He finally came to life when we started talking about how loaded his son's opponent was. J. Fife Symington III, the Republican nominee, was an old-fashioned, blue-blood Republican.

". . . His mother-in-law is the daughter of Spencer Olan, who is Olan-Matheson Chemical Company, which is Remington and Winchester Arms," Goddard explained.

Don't look for Symington to come out in favor of gun control, I thought. Goddard added that the less handgun-happy Democrats had a "good chance . . . of pulling a complete switch," meaning his son would not only stomp rich boy J. Fife III, but enough Democratic representatives and senators would ride in on his coattails to gain the party complete control of the legislature.

The talk wandered back to gambling. Goddard began to thaw.

"You know, every motel over on the river is wired for slots," he said.

"Yes sir," I responded, realizing that he was referring to the stretch of the Colorado River near the casino mecca of Laughlin, Nevada.

"All of the river people have been tryin' to do something about this for years and years . . . Well, they've done nothing but talk for the last twenty years, believe me," Goddard drawled.

I fed him some lines about "Tony the Doer" and how determined my well-heeled partners were, but he drifted off. Stragalas redirected the conversation to my financial support of various politicians. Sam was pleased to learn that I was pumping money to Democrats even though Tony was supposedly a registered Republican.

"We have lots of those," Goddard said. "At least we're hoping we have lots of 'em . . . You know, we take all kinds of money, one way or another . . . the issue is that money drives these political campaigns, right?"

"Since history began," I said.

"And yeah, well it does more now than it had before . . ."

Sam mentioned his busy schedule, then disappeared like a thief in the night after a little more than an hour. That's when the conversation livened up. Stragalas and I were both ticked over his snooty behavior.

"See, let's say we were at the hard-line meeting and he came out and looked at me and looked arrogant Arizona old-time way," I said.

"I'd say, 'Hey, fuck you and your queer son, asshole, I'll go with a referendum!' But ya see, I stayed a gentleman. And I asked 'Would you be kind enough to give some thought about it?'"

". . . He wants money," Stragalas said.

". . . What I said to him without saying it coldly was, 'Hey, you motherfucker, I'll give you what you need, but what are you gonna do for me?'"

I didn't realize until later that I was angered by the way Goddard showed disrespect for Tony. Tony didn't exist, yet my blood was boiling over the insult. I remembered what Tapp said about undercover agents losing their identities when they're under for too long.

"One thing when you deal with Goddard . . . he doesn't even trust his own son. Do you hear what I'm saying? You'd never know, but see . . . I've been fucked once," Stragalas said.

"Yeah, you don't wanna get fucked again," I said, cooling down.

Stragalas was referring to the $90,000 he felt Goddard screwed him out of by not following through on a promised political appointment.

"I would never, ever do what he did to me," Stragalas whined.

". . . If he fucked me for $90,000, he wouldn't be walkin' around. He'd be history. We'd be sittin' here having a nice lunch, sayin' 'Remember Sam?'" The scary part was, Tony, who and whatever he was, wasn't kidding. ". . . If you don't know it by now, I trust a politician as much as I trust a roach. They're roaches! . . . You coulda raped him in front of me, if you wanted to. You could have said, 'Sam, he's here to give you a package. What are you, a stranger to packages?'"

The conversation turned to a Keating-DeConcini-Goddard connection.

"What happened was, Sam asked Dennis DeConcini—Dennis was his administrative assistant when he was governor . . . Dennis met with Sam and said, 'I'll raise between $50,000 and $75,000 because Terry's runnin' for mayor. It's big money, considering the limit is a quarter million. And Sam made the deal with Dennis. Dennis goes to Keating and Keating commits to the money and Keating says, 'I wanna meet with Terry.' Terry said, 'No meeting. Let him put the money on the table. If he wants me, he wants me, that's what he's getting. He's not getting anything in return.' So Keating says 'Fuck you!'

"Okay, now . . . Terry calls Dennis and says, 'Where's the money?' In Washington on the phone . . . three and a half hours on the phone this [U.S.] senator in his office talkin' to Terry, who's running for mayor. He [Terry Goddard] says, 'Where's the money?' Dennis said, you know, 'What kind of commitment' and so forth. [Terry said] 'No deals. This is a gift.' Well, Terry never got the money. The only politician that . . . stood up and said, 'I'll tell you what. I didn't take money from Keating.'"

Shiree Foster dropped by on September 21. She looked better, or worse, than ever, depending upon one's tastes for painted-lady types. I updated her on the lunacy that had befallen me since her last visit, and thanked her for the introduction to Higuera. We talked about who else she could send my way. That led to a discussion of the physical attributes of state treasurer candidate Tony West.

"He's a fat ass . . . let me tell you, his rear end is like this big," she said, spreading her arms apart like she was describing a marlin she'd just caught.

"What are you doing checking out his rear end?"

"He works across the hall from me and I can't help but look."

During a previous conversation, Shiree mentioned a problem she was having with her American Express account. She was a few grand light, and a telephone collection goon was riding her hard.

"Here's $500 you can send him," I offered.

"No, Tony," she protested. "There's no way. I'm not a legislator. You don't buy my vote."

"I didn't buy your vote," I protested, noting that Tony had gained a bad reputation.

"I'm your friend," she asserted. "Because I'm your friend, you don't ever . . ."

"I'm not buying nothing. I told you that . . . that's for helping me with Chuy."

Instead of taking the money, she reached for my legislators book and did the now familiar slam dance.

"[Representative] Jenny Norton, you talk about an airhead. She's an airhead! . . . There's one in here, let me find her. Oh, [Representative] Brenda Burns. She's the big whore of the House."

"What do you mean 'whore,'" I asked. It was a legitimate question. There were all kinds of whores in the state house—cheap whores, expensive whores, unsophisticated whores, extremely careful whores—one never knew with these people.

"I mean, she sleeps with everybody and anybody. That's what I hear . . . She's married to some old man . . . She lets everybody know he's a lot older than she is."

How refreshing. According to Shiree, Burns was just an old-fashioned sheet-dancing whore. I mentioned Sue Laybe's claim that Burns was no stranger to plastic surgery.

"That's her . . ." Shiree confirmed. "That's the truth."

I motioned for Shiree to continue down the directory.

". . . [Representative] Bill English. Let's go take him out and get him drunk and then send him home," she said. "He has about fifteen DWIs . . . Look at the goof [Senator] Alan Stephens! Have you talked to him?"

"Yeah, man. I maxed out with Alan."

"You know who he reminds me of? Meathead on 'All in the Family.'"

Shiree took a break to give her overall view of Arizona's lawmakers. "Have you ever seen so many goofy-looking people in your life? . . . I mean, these people decide our laws. It's scary. Okay? And I mean, not only, not looks-wise. I'm just talking their heads. I mean so many goofy ones."

"Well, what I like about them is the ones that are for sale. Because . . ."

"I think probably out of ninety, I'd imagine maybe 90 percent," she calculated.

The talk turned to back-end deals at my casinos. I mentioned that although the perks were quickly being spoken for, the mushroom concession was still open. "Your income would be somewhere in the neighborhood of $25,000 to $40,000 a day. Just in mushrooms. It's a monstrous business."

"How do you get into the mushrooms, Tony?"

"It's real easy. I used to wear a T-shirt that you'd love . . . On the front it said, 'Everyone must think I'm a mushroom.' And on the back it said, 'Because they keep me in the dark and feed me horseshit . . .'"

". . . Well, I want the mushrooms then if they're there."

The phone rang. It was Sergeant Davis.

"But Tony," he whined in a falsetto. "You promised me the mushrooms." I struggled to keep a straight face, mumbling something about needing my helicopter on Sunday. "Move her closer to the camera," Davis ordered before I hung up. Shiree and I returned to the book. We reached the picture of my skittish pal, Candy Nagel.

"She thinks she's the cutest thing walking in this town!"

"No, you are," I said.

"And she thinks she looks like Doris Day. Oh yeah, right. Not in her wildest dreams. Doris Day's beautiful. I'm sorry. Candice Nagel and her bleached-blonde, yellow hair . . . In her stupid Sears and Roebuck clothing or whatever it is."

I was loving this tit for tat. The slander queen raked over the coals by a lipstick-drenched gangster's moll. Was that poetic justic or what?

After Shiree ripped a few more politicians, I gave her some tips on how to pimp for me.

". . . Just tell me all you know about them before they come up so I don't embarrass you or myself . . . Your preconceived opinion of them. If a guy'll chase broads, he'll chase money . . . If I know that a guy's got a weakness for broads or a broad's got a weakness for broads or whatever it is, then I know they're a player."

As the meeting wound down and Shiree rose to leave, I noticed that the five hundreds were still on the desk.

"Take your stuff," I ordered.

"Tony, I can't take $500 from you, that's . . ."

"Take the $500."

"But Tony, I mean that's not . . . I'm not used to that. I can't . . ."

"You rendered a service unto Caesar. Caesar is now paying for the service."

She continued to protest. This wasn't a move to compromise her. I had no intention of that. She was a valuable fringe player, and I really wanted her to have the money.

"I'm paying the lobbyists $52,000 a year each," I explained. "And you did something that the lobbyists do, for $500. I saved money. Look at it that way."

"You're saving money on me? Boy."

"Yeah, think about that."

"I don't think I like that . . . Now watch me get mugged in the parking lot carrying this."

"Don't carry it in your hand!"

After Shiree left I walked into the fourth room. No smiles today. Ball told me that five more legislators had been indicted in South Carolina. That was sure to make the nervous Nagels out there even more paranoid.

Representative Kenney came to the apartment on Monday and tried to steal credit for the Bill English intro. That was okay by me. It would mean another felony count against him. He said he was working on Representative Jim Meredith, the House majority leader, and ripped Ernie Hoffman some more. Kenney wanted me to give him $5,000 to pump into Symington's campaign, a figure that would gain him access to the governor should Symington edge Goddard. That seemed a waste of money to me, but the cops and prosecutors said they'd consider it. Kenney also tore on Tapp, saying the crusty bail bondsman had no clout. He had enough clout to deliver you! I thought.

Much to my annoyance, Ernie Hoffman began instituting the tried and true P.R. tactic of papering me to death with junk mail. Anything vaguely relating to gambling or politics he dashed off in a letter. He even sent me his schedule. It was a slick move. It made him look like he was working on my case, when in reality, he was spending about five minutes a day stuffing manure into envelopes.

The cops and prosecutors decided that the "Funds for Five Freshmen" would be Tony Vincent's coming-out party. Not only that, my date would be that true-blue gangster's moll, Shiree Foster. I told Hoffman that I was planning to attend and directed Foster to buy a dress that covered her thighs. I didn't want her to sit down and cause all the horny politicians to get whiplash trying to look up her dress.

I ducked Tapp on his next payday. The operation was outgrowing him, and I didn't what to hear him rant and rave about Gary Bartlett. From that point on, I let Marie drop the ten C-notes on him each week. Better to have a real cop grease him anyway. It dug his grave even deeper.

Kenney came by the office to brief me prior to our scheduled introduction lunch with Majority Leader Jim Meredith at the Black Angus.

"Okay, Meredith is the majority leader. He's a weak sister, but he's got a few ins . . ." Kenney prepped. ". . . I think we need to play it by ear there . . . He's kind of a weenie . . ."

Instead of leaving right away for the restaurant, Kenney lingered in the reception area. I heard him talking.

"Well Marie, do you have a boyfriend yet? Naah? Pretty girl . . ."

Where's my gun, I thought, losing myself for a moment. I'm going to put this horny Mormon out of his misery. Nobody messes with a wise guy's niece.

The cops handed me the bugged cellular phone and sent me on my way. The travel squad—Detective Ball, Sergeant Duncan, and Detective Kerr—were stationed in the spy van near the steak house. When I arrived, Meredith was at the bar. He was a sharp-looking father of four, smartly dressed in a well-tailored suit. Meredith was about five-ten, with dark brown hair and a killer smile. He was also, as Kenney warned, a weenie. His weak personality destroyed the positive impression given by his appearance. I played Park Avenue Tony and went easy on him.

Kenney fed Meredith questions and information like an attorney leading a witness: "Jim, we want the best guy around. We don't want any second-string lobbyist and you're in the leadership. You can tell us who you feel, who's in the dog house down there; . . . Jim, if you were reelected majority leader, which we're all gonna work for, would you do anything to stop this program? . . . Jim, could we look at your list . . ."

Even when Jim spoke up, Kenney simply overpowered him.

"You know, if you really think about it, the problem's with the majority Democrats . . ." Meredith started.

"They have all the fun and we do all the work," Kenney cut in.

"That's right. That's right. They really do," Meredith said, again following Kenney's direction.

"That [Representatives] Phillip Hubbard and Mike Palmer get more ass than a toilet seat between them," Kenney said enviously.

Kenney reached over and snatched a spoonful of my ice cream. "I'm gonna blow my diet, that looks so good." I clutched my fork, fighting the urge to spike his hand to the table.

I finally picked up on why Meredith was reaching out for Tony. A rival Republican representative, Mark Killian, was making a run for Meredith's majority leadership seat. Meredith needed to feed the campaign coffers of his supporters in the House to keep them from backing Killian. Politicians, I discovered, are incestuous. They bribe each other.

Meredith ended the lunch by making an appointment to see me the following Thursday. That's when he'd inform Tony what he wanted.

It was a good meet. Kenney had primed this guy perfectly. If Meredith agreed to join our gang, he could use his leadership position to bring us more players. My QB had tossed a touchdown pass.

Al Hill started my day on October 2, 1990, with another of his maddening calls. He'd called the previous day to tell me he had four tapes, but that they were "probably not what you want." Now he had no tapes. Pretty soon he was going to have no life. I told him to cut the jive and come up with something or Tony was going to be real unhappy. He instantly produced "something." He wanted to sell a franchise for a fast-food spaghetti place called Pail O' Pasta. The franchise fee was $170,000. That no doubt broke down to $10,000 for the franchise and $160,000 commission for Al Hill. I blew him off.

George Stragalas was wound tighter than a chipmunk's ass when he arrived at the apartment a half hour later. He rambled about everything from Arizona Supreme Court justices padding their expense accounts to accusations that U.S. Senator Dennis DeConcini was a member of a Mafia family. He also reveled in his halcyon days in the 1970s flying around in Sam Goddard's private plane. I was now Dr. Tony, the therapist.

"At that time, James Duke Cameron became the chief justice," Stragalas began. ". . . There were a couple of occasions that he went to the Bar Association, went to New York City to an institute to teach, and then he'd want me to process a claim to reimburse him more than what the state allows . . . I said, 'I can't do that Judge. If you went to Café de Perusas and spent $200 for lunch and the per diem says $30, don't put me in a position to sign it . . . have your bookkeeper do it.' I refused to do it, Tony. Where's it put me? I'm a twenty-eight-year-old kid, okay. So that's how the tension began."

". . . The Chief Justice of the Arizona State Supreme Court at that time is coming to you to fraudulently do his expense account, reimburse him for monies he wasn't due? . . ." I said, clarifying for the cops and prosecutors. "I love it! This is as bad as Nevada. I'm loving this state more every day . . . So you think that this Cameron probably hates your guts to this day because you wouldn't play ball with him?"

"Well, it goes on more . . . one of the judges, Sandra O'Connor on the U.S. Supreme Court, I was on her staff for a year. I've got notes from her. I'll show you, you'll die. It says, 'Dear George, I'm in a hurry. Get those papers together, just sign my name and send it out—Sandra' . . . When I was executive director [of the Arizona Democratic party] the appointments on state commission and judgeships went through my office as a courtesy . . . James Duke Cameron was up for an appointment to the federal bench. I get a call from a federal investigator and the federal court system and the ethics committee of Congress. 'Do you know James Duke Cameron?' 'Yes, I do.' 'Tell us about him.' And I ripped him a new asshole!"

"Did they block him? Did they stop him?"

"He never got nominated."

Vengeance, thy name is Stragalas.

George gave me a quick version of his own rise and fall.

"Okay, Sam [Goddard] calls me up and said . . . 'We're looking for an executive director. I will pay you out of my pocket 'cause the party has no money. I'll pay you out of the law firm' . . . I talked to his son and my responsibility was to get the party financially stable, get it organized for Bruce Babbitt, Dennis DeConcini, Mo Udall, and Jim McNulty to get reelected in '82 . . . Raise the money and hire the staff and hire a headquarters to get them reelected, that's my job . . . After about eight months, the money started coming by my raising it . . . Nineteen eighty-two, everybody wins . . . Needless to say, they're ecstatic . . . 'George' now has an access to Gerry Ferraro, Walter Mondale, whoever's running . . . I love it. Power! A lot of access . . . I managed the convention in '84 for the Western floor of the thirteen Western states. I'm the manager of the floor for the convention in San Francisco!"

And then came the fall.

"I said to Sam, 'Sam, I need to talk to you seriously . . . I'm now . . . thirty-eight.' I said, 'I'm gonna get divorced. I'm very unhappy. My wife and family are heavy into alcohol. I have a daughter that I care for very much . . . I can't continue serving as executive director.' Of which he says to me with a tear in his eye, 'You can't leave me . . . What is the public gonna say?' 'But Sam, think of me. It's me. I'm getting beaten up at home. I haven't slept with my wife for a year and a half. I'm in the public arena. I've got to get out . . .' It went on for about three weeks. The whole thing was 'How's it gonna affect Terry and I? How are the papers gonna play it?—Stragalas leaves Goddard. Third one to leave him in three years.'"

The Goddard-Stragalas connection turned sour after that, and Stragalas felt the brunt of the spoiled relationship. Now he wanted his revenge à la James Duke.

". . . Sam had a very close relationship with a guy by the name of Darwin Aycock . . . He was Secretary Treasurer of the AFL/CIO for twenty years . . . On one occasion, Sam comes up to the office . . . It was 1981, had his shopping bag . . . I'm at Sam's law office . . . And it's [the bag] filled with bullion, coin, gold, silver, a lot of it. And he says to me, 'George, look what I've got!' I said, 'Where'd you get that?' He says our friend gave it to me on the street . . .' I said, 'Who?' He says, 'You know, Darwin, Darwin Aycock' . . . He put the shopping bag down next to his desk in the law office. I said, 'Where do you think Darwin got it?' He said, 'Oh, I don't know, maybe that North American Coin Company' . . . It was downtown in Phoenix [and] eventually was closed down by the government for apparently doing something wrong . . .

". . . I think probably the most damaging thing that Sam's ever done . . . is he tried to link Dennis DeConcini with the Mafia in Tucson . . . The whisper campaign, of you know, Dennis' father used to do business with [Mafia boss] Joe Bonanno. He used to do business with [Detroit mobster Pete] Licavoli. They're all 'retired,' ha, ha, in Tucson . . . From what Sam would say is that Evo [DeConcini] always did business with the Mob . . . Now when Sam was elected governor, he said Evo called him up and said, 'I want my son to be your chief of staff.' And Dennis was made the chief of staff for Sam . . . Sam said the reason why he lost the [1966] election is primarily because of Dennis DeConcini . . . Sam says the way Dennis approached him was you go to the lobbyist and you get the people that have something to gain and that's where you get the money. Don't bother with going to the public . . ."

"How about Terry when he was mayor? . . . Is he bisexual or is he just gay or do you know?" I asked, switching Goddards.

"I think he's asexual. I think he has no sexual drive . . . In other words, I'm saying with a man or a woman, he can't get it up . . . There was a guy that told me that he had pictures of Terry having sex with another man and the second time I saw him I asked him for it, he disappeared. And I know where he is. His name is Bob Knapp . . . He [Sam] wants one thing in life before he drops dead. He wants revenge on the people that beat him for the governorship and he's gonna be the governor when the kid's elected governor and he's gonna milk it for every dime and power they can get. That's what he wants . . . I just know that since 1966, twenty-five years later, his whole life has been geared toward revenge . . . His whole life is to get rid of the embarrassment of the only incumbent governor to lose . . . He was discredited as a liberal buffoon who didn't know his way out of a paper sack . . . I mean, this is almost like true confession to a psychiatrist for me . . . It's like you're the shrink, you're saying, 'What really bothers you? Is there anything in your life, professional life, political life that you'd really like to kick somebody in the face?'"

Before the meeting ended, I gave Stragalas another illegal $10,000 contribution for his sputtering state treasurer campaign to help sooth his festering wounds.

Tapp showed up afterward with an old friend in tow, Justice of the Peace Donald Stump. The judge, who was still running unopposed except for a last-minute write-in candidate, needed another $2,500 for his campaign. Stump's normally high spirits were dampened a bit by a movement afoot to replace all the elected JPs in the state with appointed attorneys.

"I don't have anything against them [attorneys]," he rationalized. "I do know that the same as you do, that . . . they have an unquenchable thirst for money. They would sell their own mother for fifty cents. They would steal the nickels off of dead Negro people's eyes as they lay in the dadgum coffin . . . They can't help theirselves. They make money the old-fashioned way — they rob it from their clients."

". . . What's the judge need?" I said, cutting to the chase. "What's the JP need? Don't look at him," I barked as Stump glanced at Tapp. "This cocksucker always puts additional numbers on it . . . He might put some more on and cut it up witcha later."

". . . I need to get out and do some mailing . . . now that I've got the guy [write-in candidate], so that people just don't think well . . . 'Stump has gone fizzily poo, 'cause he's not even concerned.'"

Judge Stump fizzled on for a few moments more before I steered the conversation to the long green. "Now Judge, back to the question. What do you need? . . . Don't look at him again, Judge!"

"All right, I'll just keep my eyes right straight, probably I need a whole chunk of money. I need more than I can walk outta here with, Tony."

"That ain't no problem with me."

"That ain't no problem? Probaby twenty-five, twenty-five hundred, but I won't say twenty-five Gs cause that's a bunch of bullshit. But I'll tell you what . . ."

"Twenty-five hundred will get you through it?"

"All right, it'll get me through it. If I have some left over, I can turn it back to ya, Tony. That's no problem."

"Now where the hell would you find [such] an honest judge?" Tapp cut in, laughing. "That would tell ya, Tony. That he'll give ya the money back if he doesn't need it . . ."

"He's gonna give me the change?" I marveled. "That's when elephants shoot out of my ass!"

"Come stampedin' outta there, Tony," Stump laughed.

"Live elephants! . . . Boy, I tell ya," I said. "I'll call the Guinness Book." I counted out $2,500, handed it to the judge, and asked him to count it again. He did, then stuffed the wad in his shirt pocket.

". . . In case it ever comes up, what did I give you?" I asked the judge.

"Twenty-five. Nothing."

"I can't give ya 2,500 fucking dollars . . . put us both in the penitentiary!" I exclaimed.

"Oh, yeah, yeah."

"What did I give ya?"

"Just wasn't, just was, well, I was gonna say 250 dollars is the max I can have."

"Two-twenty, Judge," Tapp corrected.

". . . Now how will that change be comin' to me?" I wondered. "Through the automatic teller? I'll be driving down the street. Past the bank and I'll hear a voice that says . . ."

"Yeah, a . . . still small voice," Stump laughed.

Senator Carolyn Walker came by on October 3 to hawk the tickets to the "Funds for Five Freshmen" affair at Bruce Babbitt's house. I bought ten for $1,200 and kicked three tickets back to her for herself. She bitched some more about her paltry $55,000-a-year combined salary and said she was trying to work out a deal with the phone company to have them dole out her retirement fund in a single lump sum, which she calculated to be $300,000. She asked me if I knew of any investment opportunities. I told her about Al Hill's Pail O' Pasta. I also mentioned Stragalas' problems with the Goddards and the Democratic party.

"They screwed him," she said.

"Pardon me?"

"They screwed him."

". . . You know that too, huh?"

"I ain't so dumb. I may be black, but I ain't dumb."

I told Walker that I had promised Stragalas that he could parachute into my operation if he lost the election.

"Can I come work for you too?" she piped up.

"Hell, yeah! . . . You got the gift shops. I told you that and I'm committed to loaning you the money to open them."

"Oh I believe that, Tony. I don't know why I trust you, I just trust you."

Ernie Hoffman brightened my evening with a call at 11:30 p.m. He had returned from Reno and wanted to relay the good news that he decided to have some University of Nevada–Reno professors do the study instead of the ASU team. He put a positive spin on it, but I couldn't help wondering why we were going from a major university—ASU's Walter Cronkite School of Journalism, no less—to some satellite campus of Nevada's state college-basketball system. Ernie said the Nevada profs knew more about gambling. My guess was he stumbled upon a study that was already done and got it cheap, thus fattening his cut.

Strip joint owner Jack Smyth woke me up the next morning to say that Representative Mike Palmer and his cohorts wanted to meet with me after the general election. He added that he knew I had an upcoming tête-à-tête scheduled with Representative Bobby Raymond.

"How'd you know that?"

"Hey, you think I'm just sitting here watchin' tits?"

"Yeah . . ." I said. "You got my office wired?"

"Got your house wired," he laughed. "John and Mike were talking to Bobby."

I wondered where these two pillars of the community, Palmer and Raymond, were when they had this little chat. Staring up at one of Jack's hard-bodied dancers? If half of what I'd been hearing about the proclivity of this pair was true, then they must have been burrowing through Smyth's silicon valley like gophers on a golf course.

Al Hill finally dropped off his tapes with Marie that day. She turned them over to Detective Ball. The big undercover cop called me a few hours later and said all the tapes were bogus. They were the type of run-of-the-mill, commercial porn one can buy at the local smut shop for $15. They even opened with the FBI warning about duplicating them. Ball started breaking my balls about paying $2,700 for a $10 tape.

"What a hotshot undercover agent you turned out to be," he digged. "Burned by the likes of Fondia Al Hill."

Not only had Hill pulled a fast one on Tony, but he hit on my "niece" Marie during the drop. Tony Vincent would have killed Hill, his dad, his uncles and brothers, children and grandchilden for that. As it was, no matter who I was, Joe or Tony, I wanted to beat Hill with a spiked billy club until the bastard turned white.

I called him.

"Al, we got a little problem."

"Okay."

"That's bunk. I can buy that on McDowell [Street] . . . One's got Traci Lords in it. She's five years younger than me and I'm fifty-three."

"Yeah."

"So here's what I want you to do . . . They're $50 apiece at any store in town. So rather than get aggravated, let's just stay friends. Deduct the $200 and you owe me $3,550 or you can get me the product you were supposed to get me originally." In my anger, I had accidentally added another thousand to the $2,750 I had originally given him. Hill didn't notice.

"Good. That's what I plan on doing . . ."

"I wanna resolve it by next Thursday at the latest. That gives you five days to put something together . . . Traci Lords was around as a porno star before you were born. She's a grandmother!"

Hill, damn his crooked soul, continued scamming.

". . . You know, I incurred some expenses myself. I paid for the flights and all that crap. You know, that was out of my pocket before I even, even . . ."

"All right, let's not hypothecate that you bought back the right product . . . You want me to carry you to send you to Canada to bring back a fifty-dollar item?"

"No, no, no."

"Nooooo shit!"

Al said he'd leave for Denmark on October 19—two weeks past my Thursday deadline—and promised to return by early November. I told him I'd get back to him on that plan. I was calmer, but I still wanted to plant the guy.

Representative Jim Meredith, the House majority leader, arrived on schedule for his toasting. The forty-four-year-old owner of a successful real estate firm started out nervous and edgy but relaxed as I played him soft and easy, kind of Park Avenue Tony on Quaaludes. The theme of this meeting, as the prior one at Black Angus, was Meredith's intense desire to hold on to his leadership seat in the House. His fear was that a band of wackos—ultra-conservatives—would make a move to secure all the positions of power.

"You're probably the most important person that I'm sitting with, based on your leadership seat down there," I flattered. "I would hate to see ya lose that."

"[Representative] Don Aldridge is one of the rumors going around for majority leader and Leslie Johnson for the whip," Meredith explained.

"Leslie Whiting Johnson?" I asked, incredulously.

"Yes."

"The dildo lady?"

"The dildo lady for whip."

Dildos and whips. What a kinky combination.

I set the hook early in the Meredith meeting for no particular reason. The opportunity arose and I seized it, even though the actual money drop wouldn't take place for nearly an hour.

"All I would ask you is that I have your promise that you'll vote yes on my issue and that you won't shelve it."

"Yeah, I won't shelve it . . . My promise to you basically is that I won't shelve it . . . It'll go as long as you've got the votes, it'll go."

After that, it was merely a matter of giving this fish a lot of time and patiently waiting for him to hit the bait. We discussed the needs of the incumbent legislators and candidates who he had recruited in his effort to maintain his powerful seat. Interestingly enough, when Bill English's name came up, Meredith designated him as a nonplayer.

"Bill's not gonna need you. I mean money, he's not gonna need your money."

That's because he already had $18,000 from me. I took Meredith's comment as a good sign that the gossip about Tony Vincent's open wallet policy was being kept to a minimum.

Meredith kicked off the trading action by hawking four tickets to a Symington dinner to the tune of $550 each. I handed him $2,200 in cash.

"Don't you have a checkbook? It's always money."

"See if there's $2,200 there," I said, ignoring him.

"Don't you have a checkbook? I'm running around with $2,200!"

I found his uneasiness at handling cash somewhat surprising. Meredith was said to pull down more than $100,000 a year from his real estate business.

"Fife will talk. We may or may not have a speaker, but I can tell ya Glen Campbell's gonna be there."

"Geez!" I said, feigning delight. "I never dreamed that twenty-five years ago when I was sitting in Reno listening to 'By the Time I Get to Phoenix' I'd be hearing Glen Campbell at Fife Symington's dinner!"

I called Shiree Foster during the meet to see if she'd be my date to the big Republican bash. As we spoke, Meredith instructed me to give her a message.

"Tell her Glen Campbell's gonna be there. She likes him."

I passed on relaying the big news. Foster's taste no doubt ran more toward Bruce Springsteen, Paula Abdul, or some other entertainer who'd had a hit in the current century. After Shiree accepted, Jimmy and I got down to some serious negotiations. During the first round, he requested only legal $220 donations for his team. After I indicated that more was available and that Tony wasn't afraid of crossing the legal lines, he upped the ante a few zeros.

"Okay, M.G. [Mike Gilbert], two thousand," I said, tallying up. "Fifteen hundred was [Representative] Patty Noland? Okay, fifteen hundred to John King . . . A thousand was to [Representative] Ruth Eskesen . . . Am I right?"

"Yes."

"Six hundred was to Benton?" I continued.

"Ben Benton."

"And the $440 was to Gary Richardson? Right?"

"Right."

"Okay, total mine up and see if you get $7,040 . . ."

"Yeah, seven forty, seven forty. Yeah, we just need names. I need names and addresses, let's put down $220 each," the majority leader said.

Now came the bundling ritual. The cops had provided me with a bunch of phony names and addresses of phantom donors, but not enough. I decided to use the much-mispronounced name of my moll, Shiree Foster, to clean a substantial amount of Meredith's dirty money. I phoned her and she agreed.

". . . Two-twenty, all right, and four, five, six-sixty. Okay, let's do another Shiree," I said, slick as a C.P.A. "Geez, we're gonna max Shiree out today."

"We are," Jimmy said with a big laugh.

". . . Understand," I said when the dealing was done, "I do expect you to vote yes and I do expect you to not shelve me . . ."

"Yeah."

Meredith took the cash and stuffed it in his pocket. There were no further complaints about my method of payment. Marie escorted the cash-laden majority leader out of the office and all the way down to his car. That was so she could make his car and take down the license number. Under the law, since Meredith had used the car to commit a crime, the cops could confiscate the sleek, bronze Lincoln when the indictments were announced.

All in all, it was a solid meet. Kenney had tenderized Meredith perfectly. It was, however, by far the most boring of the burns. Jim was too passive a personality to pump life, or even a good shot of anxiety, into the room. His low-key manner and altruistic attitude toward his fellow legislators paled in comparison to the energy created by the lusty greed of his more colorful peers. I much preferred Kenney's out-of-control passions, Candy Nagel's searing, machine-gun gossip, Sue Laybe's "no baloney, thank you Tony" hit-and-runs, or Carolyn Walker's pie-in-the-sky ambition. The only interesting part of the Meredith fry was a subtle sidelight. Among the candidates Tony's latest contribution aided was John King, Laybe's hard-charging opponent. Talk about hedging a bet.

Ernie Hoffman called after 10 p.m. and said he arranged it so that we would attend a private dinner with four or five senators following the "Funds for Five Freshmen" affair the next evening. I countered that I had bought Symington tickets from Meredith. He wasn't pleased. He wanted his man, Bill English, to snatch the Republican majority leader seat from Meredith and get credit for the Symington sale. That kind of intra-party back-stabbing didn't interest me, so I instead took the opportunity to confront Hoffman about a bill he sent me. The much-plugged poll, touted as costing $15,000, had suddenly risen to $24,600. He stuttered and mentioned something about expanding the scope to produce more respectable results. What a guy. Always looking out for my best interests — at any cost.

I had a few butterflies in my belly as I lay in bed that night. The next day would be Tony's coming-out party. I'd be attending a major league political bash at the home of a former governor and presidential candidate. Hoffman had sent out the word that I was a new force in Arizona politics, so I was sure to attract some attention. And, I'd be in the company of the saucy Shiree Foster. Since Gail knew nothing about what I was doing, I was conveniently compelled to keep her in the dark about Shiree. Even if Gail knew what I was doing, I would have shrouded that aspect of Desert Sting. Gail protected her turf like a mountain lion. One look at Shiree, and she'd go nuclear.

12

David Horwitz called on coming-out day to advise me that Representative Bobby Raymond had a family crisis and couldn't meet us that afternoon. I figured the family crisis must have been that one of Jack Smyth's lap dancers got the afternoon off. Instead of pimping Raymond, Horwitz came by and pushed a candidate named John Dougherty who he said needed an infusion of ten to twelve grand for the stretch run. I told him to bring Dougherty in, gave him four tickets for the "Funds for Five Freshmen" affair that evening, and $500 for his continuing help.

Shiree arrived in her evening finery at 4:15. She looked hot, almost classy. I was in my cowboy getup. No matter how often I wore it, I still felt like an extra in a bad Gene Autry movie.

My relationship with Shiree had taken on a new, deeper significance. The cops told me that Emil Vaci, the maitre d' and assistant manager of Sbrocca's restaurant, Ernesto's Backstreet, had been murdered gangland-style—shot in the back of the head and dumped in an irrigation canal—in June 1986. They wanted to know if I could find out anything about it. I queried both my Mob and FBI sources and learned that Vaci had been summoned to appear before a grand jury investigating the Mob's activities in Las Vegas, where Vaci had previously worked. The hit order came from a vicious Chicago mobster named Anthony "the Ant" Spilotro who looked out for the Mafia's interest in Las Vegas. The cops and I continued to view Shiree as Sbrocca's eyes and ears. None of us believed her story that she had cut her ties with him. I requested that they put a tail on her to determine one way or another, but the police felt it unnecessary. My initial behavior with Shiree was to feed her an exaggerated version of Brooklyn Tony, a very rich Brooklyn Tony, to set myself up for a shakedown. However, having learned of the murder, I decided to make our relationship more personal. Maybe through Shiree I could find out if Sbrocca knew anything about the murder of his employee. Shiree was displaying a keen interest in Tony. Even if it was an act, I didn't figure her to be the loyal type. She would hitch her wagon to the biggest, wealthiest, and most powerful man she could find. Tony Vincent was definitely a bigger catch than Romano Sbrocca. Since I was going to be looking for information about a hit ordered by "the Ant," I had to be ready for trouble. If the Mob found out what I was up to, it was possible they might send an enforcer to blow me away. If the hit did come without warning, we were ready. Marie was my first line of defense. She had a .38 snub-nosed revolver in her drawer and knew how to use it. If he got by her, I had a big .380 in my desk.

As the time grew closer to leave, Shiree became increasingly nervous. She paced the office like a caged bear.

"So tell me, Tony, just what do you want me to . . . what do I say? I mean, how do you want me to act? Just tell me what to do."

"I want you to just be Shiree," I rhymed.

"Okay, but I mean, if say somebody says, 'Oh, who are you here with?' I mean, I could say 'Tony Vincent'? . . . And they'll say, 'What company is he with?' Then they'll say, 'What's he do?' I mean, what . . . so I don't say anything wrong."

"Economic developer," I said.

We had some time to kill before the party so I peppered Shiree with some questions about her job.

"It's been hard lately," she began. "For a while I was goin' like gangbusters. Lately, I haven't done anything. And you know, Tony, I'm so stressed out . . . See, I hate my boss and there's another girl I just can't stand. And I'm doing about fifteen things at once constantly . . . and I'm, Tony, I go home so worn out. I mean, it's like the energy is just sucked out of me when I get home . . . Susan and I both, we decided we're tired of our situation."

To me, this sounded like a lady angling for a new Sugar Daddy. If Tony had dangled a grand a week plus a condo, she'd have bit. It might have been a good move, but the cops and prosecutors wanted to keep the taint of sex out of the operation.

We departed for Babbitt's house. The disappointment started from the moment I arrived. Instead of some high-line political Cinderella ball, this was a backyard barbecue at Babbitt's surprisingly modest home attended by twenty to thirty people, most of whom had probably been comped. A swarm of flies buzzed around the beans and mystery meat that I'd paid $1,200 to eat. I felt like sending out for a Pail O' Pasta. Shiree and I were talking with Carolyn Walker when Representative Bobby Raymond strolled up. I asked him about his family crisis.

"What family crisis? Horwitz told me the meeting was next Friday!" Raymond protested.

I noticed Raymond undressing Shiree with his eyes. I introduced them. He was on her like flies on $1,200 beans. If this guy "sucked a dick" like Gary Bartlett claimed, he was giving an Academy Award performance as a rutting pig. Raymond and Shiree were both from Texas and seemed to hit it off. Shiree cast off the gun moll posture and became a coquettish Southern belle. While Raymond drooled on my date, I glanced across the backyard and spotted Sam Goddard wandering around like a lost wino. He was wearing a ratty used-car salesman's jacket and high-water pants; the outfit was topped by a straw hat. I'd seen migrant workers with more style.

"Hey Bobby," I said, interrupting his lounge lizard rap. "I'm gonna give you $1,000 to go buy Sam Goddard some clothes that fit!"

He howled.

"I'm gonna have to throw a party to introduce his pants to his shoes. I don't think they've ever met," I cracked.

"There's a man who really fucked up this state," Raymond said.

When Shiree went to shoo the flies off the food and forage for something edible, Raymond made his move.

"Tony, what's the deal with you and Sherry?" he said, pronouncing her name the same way as his wife's.

"We're just friends," I said. "Do what you want to do."

Bobby informed me that his wife, Sheri, a former television reporter, was out of town. He was about to tell me what precisely he wanted to do with Shiree when an odd, somewhat lethargic man approached. We spoke for a while and then he wandered off.

"Who the hell was that?" I asked. Shiree punched my ribs.

"Babbitt," Raymond said. "Former governor. Ran for president."

"Oh."

"I can't take you anywhere," Shiree whispered.

Sue Laybe circled and paid her respects. I could see that she wasn't spending Tony's money on clothes. She was wearing another of her "Olive Oyl Collection" dresses, complete with the white doily around the neck. I glanced back to the buffet table and spotted the two union goons, Horwitz and R. T. Griffin, standing there like potbellied stoves sucking down beans and beer. I made a mental note to give them a wide berth as the night wore on, but not before I pulled Horwitz and Raymond aside to clarify the meeting snafu. As Raymond revealed the truth, Horwitz's face turned as red as Evan Mecham's neck.

The crowd thickened as the sun began to set. There were now more than a hundred people mingling about. It wasn't quite the bomb I thought it was going to be, but it wasn't close to the star-studded bash I'd been expecting. I'd attended better parties in prison.

I spotted Ernie Hoffman working the crowd by Babbitt's dirty swimming pool. He later introduced me to Senator Pete Rios, an upscale Chuy Higuera. Hoffman said Rios was one of the marks who was set to dine with us later.

"Don't fill up on the food here," Hoffman instructed.

"No chance of that," I assured. I looked back to where I'd been standing and saw Shiree on her tiptoes whispering into Raymond's ear. Alan Stephens interrupted my contemplation on the Texas two-some and paid his respects. He looked as weasely as ever and promised to call me soon. Horwitz lumbered by with another short guy in tow. He introduced him as Fred DuVal, a Wally Cox–type with glasses and undistinguished features. I noticed him earlier trying to shout through the noise of the crowd to make an announcement. DuVal tilted up his head, looked me in the eye, and squeaked, "I hope you're not trying to put casinos in Arizona. If you are, I'm going to have to fight you!"

"Do what you have to do," I responded. "I love a good fight." What I really wanted to do was grab the fly swatter and give him a good swat. I knew his move. Carolyn Walker had warned me that he lobbied for Circus Circus, the big Vegas casino. If that was true, he'd use me to talk them into a fatter retainer.

By 7 p.m. I had had enough of the big-time political fun and left with Shiree. Raymond followed us to our car.

"Don't worry about DuVal," Raymond said. "He can be dealt with. Believe me." My eyebrows raised. The handsome, hair-sprayed representative was talking like he was already part of Team Tony. That was peculiar. My only contact with him was allowing him to salivate all over my date.

We drove to the Ritz Carlton for our big dinner with the senators. As we gathered at our table, I noticed that there were no senators in attendance. It was just Shiree, Hoffman, and his date Judith Ross, the director of Arizona's motor vehicle department, and Bill English. This was not the A-list. The dinner turned out to be brutally boring. As I was about to stick a fork in my ear to end the agony, the cellular phone rang.

"This ain't going nowhere," Jim Keppel said. "Wrap it up."

I excused myself and drove Shiree back to her car at the office, then went home and gave my wife a great big kiss.

"What was that for?" she asked.

"Just for being you, baby," I said.

Bobby Raymond rang me at home the next afternoon, a Saturday. He wanted to rendezvous at a bar somewhere. I told him to meet me at the office instead and set it for 5 p.m.

"We can hit it off well as long as you understand when I talk business and I talk politics, I only know one way," Raymond said. "And that's straight and blunt."

"I'm glad to hear that because I'm tired of dancing. I've done more waltzing here than I did at my senior prom."

I phoned Ball after Raymond hung up.

"Get the crew in gear," I said. "Another one's about to bite the dust."

Shiree phoned a few minutes later complaining bitterly about a call she received.

"I just thought you might be interested in this. I checked messages a while ago."

"I know," I said.

"How'd you know?"

"He called here."

"Lookin' for me?" she assumed.

"You got it," I lied.

"What'd you say?"

"I don't know."

"He has nerve callin' you about that, doesn't he? . . ."

Shiree wanted me to repeat every word Raymond had said about her. I felt like telling her to read the police transcripts. She also wanted to know what I was going to do about it.

"I'll deal with that at five o'clock," I assured. "Let me get him in my pocket first. You understand?"

"Yeah . . . you know, I thought geez, it made me have a headache . . . And the thing is, I would help the guy 'cause I like him. I think he's a type of guy you could get somewhere with as far as if you needed something with the state legislature . . . I'll do whatever I can to help him out . . . I oughta be there sittin' on your lap, when he walks in and go, 'Bobby, you were looking for me? Yes, what did you need? A phone number or something? Did you need me to help with a mass mailing or something?'"

"How'd he know where to call," I asked.

"That's what I wanna know! Well, my name is listed under, it's my initial in the phone book. Do you think that . . ."

"There's no doubt in my mind that's how he got it," I lied again, playing along with this clever little she-devil.

". . . Well, I just thought he'd be a nice cool guy, you know, I wasn't . . . The thing is, I know most men are shits, got their weakness, but it's like, I have a lot of men friends . . . and it just bugged the heck out of me and I thought, I can't. The thing is what's wrong with the guy? How does he know? I mean, I'm with you last night. He saw me get in the same car. I mean, he's sure got a lot of nerve!"

"Well, in my circles, that's known as more nerve than a sore tooth," I said, adding that it was more important to recruit Raymond as a player than dwell on the perceived insult to her honor.

"Well, I'll just be nice and play it dumb. I'll play it really dumb . . ." Shiree decided.

I directed the talk from Raymond's lust to her evaluation of Babbitt's party.

"Oh man, what a bunch of low-class idiots," she said. ". . . Bill English is a nice guy, but come on Tony, he's just as sleazy as . . ."

". . . Next time you look at him just see $18,000 on his forehead; $18,000, that's all I see," I said. "I was looking around that party last night. I looked, I saw $20,000, $660, $21,000, $740. I knew exactly what I had given everybody . . . So that's all I see when I look at him, eighteen."

If Shiree was reporting all this to Sbrocca, I wanted to make sure she had the numbers right.

"Is Stephens your man, too?" she asked.

"Not yet."

"Not yet, but he will be . . . He was butterin', he was brownnosin' you last night . . . Another thing I wanted to tell you . . . I can't stand that Horwitz guy!"

"That makes two of us."

"He's so danged two-faced . . . Tony, do you have to be associated with him?"

"I need him . . . I pay him for bringin' me politicians . . . He's a necessary entity right now. And that's one of the things I learned early in life. Even if you don't like somebody and you gotta do business with 'em, you do it . . . I mean, I wanted to kick Sam Goddard right square in his ass last night."

"Could you believe that? . . . I think he is gone . . . He acts like a vegetable. I mean, the guy's off the deep end . . . This is such a fun thing, though, watchin' all this happening, listening to you do all this business."

I brought up my faux pas with Babbitt. "I honest to God didn't know who Bruce Babbitt was."

"I still laugh at that. I've laughed at that this morning."

"Was he drunk or just goofy?"

"Oh no, that's the way he is," Shiree insisted. ". . . And the water didn't work in his house for God's sakes! He didn't pay his water bill or somethin'? That was the ugliest home . . . I can't imagine my family havin' a big [party] like that, my parents, you know . . . there wouldn't have been a thing out of place. That pool would've been, I mean . . . it was just trash! It was embarrassing. Democrats are screwballs. I called my grandmother today and I told her, I say, 'Yeah, I was at Bruce Babbitt's last night' and I go, 'They served pinto beans!' And she goes, 'See, Democrats are poor, Shiree,' and I said, 'No, no, no, no, not the politician Democrats. They're not poor, they just play it.'"

"Well, we'll see what [Raymond] asks for today," I said. ". . . I'll take twenty large with me and see what he wants. On top of the seventeen I have, it's thirty-seven. He's only worth twenty, though. If he asks for more than twenty, he's in trouble."

"I think he's only worth about a hundred bucks."

"Yeah, well, unfortunately, that ain't gonna get his attention."

". . . Boy, I'm anxious about this meeting," Shiree said excitedly. "This is really gonna be a good one! . . . I'd like to be a fly on the wall. You've gotta remember everything and tell me."

"I will," I promised. ". . . I tell you what he might've thought, and don't get crazy with this, but this might've been part of what he was thinkin', that part of my proffer to him was, was . . ."

"Ooooh."

"Okay."

"Oooooh."

"And I gotta straighten that out real fast . . . I'm gonna tell him I had a call and that you don't wanna talk to him."

"Ooooh, Tony, that's kind of harsh. I don't wanna make an enemy of the guy."

"Okay . . . Tell me what you want me to tell him."

". . . I wanna pretend like I don't know, that I'm so stupid that I don't realize that's what he's doin'."

"Yeah, why don't I leave it alone then, until you decide what you wanna do."

What she wanted to do was hold all the cards. She was a clever one.

Mount, Sergeant Davis, Ball, Keppel, and Captain Black showed up at the office at 4 p.m. to man the fourth room for the meet with Shiree's new boyfriend. I gave the building's security guard $40 to sign the good guys in on a different sheet—an oversight everyone missed but me. The guard palmed the forty and buried the log. I returned downstairs shortly before 5 p.m. to await Raymond. He arrived a few minutes later, suited like an attorney going to trial, unusual for a Saturday. Raymond turned out to be a breath of fresh air, a no-holds-barred crooked politician. He was up-front about it, which I respected. He was like a wise guy who made no bones about being a gangster.

"What are you looking for?" he asked.

"Regulated casino gaming."

"Statewide?"

"Statewide."

". . . Understand where I'm comin' from," he announced. "I don't give a fuck about issues. There is not an issue in this world that I give a shit about. I do deals. That's what I do. I mean, I do deals. I mean, there's two or three issues that I'll fall on my sword over, and that's the people that got me here . . . Other than that, I don't give a fuck if school keeps tomorrow."

"If what?"

"If school keeps tomorrow. I don't care. I mean, I like the deals of the legislature."

I liked this guy!

"See, Terry [Goddard] is anti-gaming," I said, touching upon one of the problems I faced.

"Oh well, fuck him!" Representative Raymond said. So much for the Goddard problem.

". . . You be very careful with Laybe because she's a dangerous person. She doesn't know how to keep her mouth shut," Bobby warned before getting to his deal. ". . . Dave [Horwitz] . . . came to me two or three weeks ago. He said, 'Where are you financially?' I said, 'I'm kinda in a shit storm, Dave, because I'm trying, toying with a challenge for a leadership position' . . . So I've been busting my ass thinking that I didn't have any race at all. I've been busting my ass raising money for everybody else in the state . . . All of a sudden now I find out I've got all these fuckin' Jesus people chasing me!"

"The born-agains?"

"Yeah."

"Oh man, they're tough."

"And, you know, I mean, it's a little bit more serious than I thought . . . To answer your question, I was sitting there before I showed Dave my budget, I said, 'Shit man, I gotta raise about ten grand here between now and election day to pay for this sucker . . .'"

Raymond, like so many other politicos, was a package deal. He started pitching his favorite lobbyist.

"I'll tell you honestly and frankly, you not only need a Maricopa County lobbyist, you need a Democratic lobbyist . . . Ernie is a nice guy. I like him as a friend. Frankly, he has never done shit for me or anybody else in my party . . . The most successful lobbyist in this state is a guy by the name of Rich Scheffel."

". . . I had four names . . ." I said. "Scheffel was at the top of the list. Uh, Charlie Stevens?"

"Charlie Stevens is a useless motherfucker. He's garbage. In fact, he represents the Maricopa County Bar Association."

"Pass," I said. Anybody who pimps for attorneys has got to be, as Candy Nagel might say, "The King Asshole of the Assholes."

"If you look at Scheffel, he represents everything that's considered sleaze," Raymond went on. "I mean, his clients are R.J. Reynolds, Anheuser-Busch."

Scheffel sounded like my kind of guy. Raymond kept promoting, both himself and his bagman.

"Outta that twenty-two [Democratic House members], about fourteen of 'em are votes that I can pull."

"That's a lot of votes, Bobby. That makes you a key man to me."

"But you know, a lot of it is . . . I would suggest strongly that you talk to Scheffel."

That was telling. It was Scheffel, not Raymond, who pulled the strings on those fourteen votes.

". . . Well, you need to understand my angle in all this," Raymond continued. "I have a leadership position picked out and if it doesn't happen this time, it will happen next time . . . I mean, what's going on in the House, [Representative Art] Hamilton for years has pretty well ruled the Democratic caucus all alone, solo. I mean, he's the one in charge. His other two leaders have always, traditionally been very weak people. Whatever Hamilton wants, they never challenge him. I mean, people are terrified of him 'cause he's a big massive black guy that can cut you to shreds with his tongue. He is great. He is one of my close friends. I am close enough to Art Hamilton that I am the only Democrat in the House that will say, 'Fuck you! You're outta your mind! Go to hell. You're crazy!' I mean, I had brutal, brutal wars with Art Hamilton. But he knows when he's not around, I'm controlling his caucus because his other two leaders . . . [Representative Debbie] McCune and [Representative Jack] Brown have absolutely no respect . . . See, Art has been elected to a national office. He has been elected as vice president of the National Conference of State Legislators. Big, big office . . . The next four years of his life, it's all laid out. Next year, he's vice president. The following year he's president-elect. The following year, he's president. The following year, he's past-president. And then he's done. Art doesn't give a shit what's goin' on down here now. I mean, his new focus in life is the next four years. He will travel all over the world. I mean, he's not gonna be here. He knows it. I know it . . . And there's a lot of mischief that's gonna be played."

I'll bet.

"I look at it with just delight," Raymond bubbled like a mouse at the funeral of the house cat. "I think it's gonna be great the next four years — but I intend on being the one that replaces him as minority leader . . . Four years after that, I may run for a statewide office."

Why not, I thought. Raymond looked like U.S. Senator material to me. He had all the qualifications. Good looks. Slick rap. No ethics. An eagerness to accept bribes. An inability to keep his pants on. He'd be the perfect replacement for Arizona's embattled U.S. Senators, the "Keating Five"–tainted Dennis DeConcini and John McCain.

"What I'd like you to do, Tony, is you go out and ask a few people about me."

"Bobby, your name has come up to me without me askin' . . ." I stroked. "'Great guy.' 'Keeps his word.' 'Solid guy.' 'If he tells you somethin', it's carved in stone.' Nobody has knocked ya. I'm amazed to sit here and tell ya that . . . These union guys can't sing your praises high enough. They love ya."

"Well, they're part of the folks that brought me to this dance . . ."

Raymond had had enough of political discourse and switched to the important stuff.

"Tell me about your relationship with this Sherry [Shiree] and the Chamber? Where are they at in this?"

"They're nowhere . . . I joined. That's it. They're not involved at all. The girl took a likin' to me and I'm not interested in her sexually or romantically. Understand? I don't have any designs on her sexually . . ."

"I'd hire her if I was you."

"She wants to come to work with me."

"I wouldn't hire her away from her job at the Chamber. If anything, I would hire her to stay there . . . You want her there . . . If she works there, she knows some of the inner workings of the Chamber . . . She's

The Black Hats

(*Below*) Senator Jesus "Chuy" Higuera wanted the shrimp concession in my phantom casino hotels. (*Melanie Rook D'Anna*)

(*Above*) Senate Majority Whip Carolyn Walker at the Azscam arraignment. Walker wanted $750,000 from my alter ego Tony Vincent to start a record company. (*Melanie Rook D'Anna*)

(*Above*) Representative Bobby Raymond and his wife, Sheri. The Azscam tapes not only caught Raymond taking bribes, but recorded his lustful pursuit of Chamber of Commerce staffer Shiree Foster. The Raymonds divorced after the charismatic lawmaker was sent to prison. (*Melanie Rook D'Anna*)

(*Left*) Representative Sue Laybe spoke so softly I put cotton in my ears and faked an ear infection to get her to speak loud enough to be recorded. (*Melanie Rook D'Anna*)

Representative Bill English attended the marathon meeting where I did a striptease to prove I wasn't bugged.

Although Senate Majority Leader Jim Meredith accepted nearly $10,000 in illegal campaign contributions, he was talked into filing a complaint against Tony Vincent with the Arizona Attorney General.

(*Left*) "Judge" Gary Bartlett started it all with his boasts about being able to buy legislators. (*Melanie Rook D'Anna*)

(*Right*) After working his way through the criminal code, lobbyist Ron Tapp became a $1,000-a-week ghost. (*Melanie Rook D'Anna*)

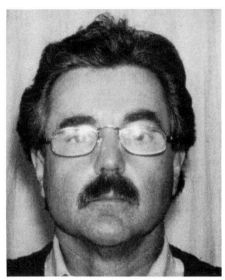

(*Above*) Shiree Foster, the Chamber of Commerce representative whose mug shot could pass as a pin-up photo. She once joked to Tony,"I'm coming over right now. And I'm undressing on the way!"

House Judiciary Chairman Don Kenney

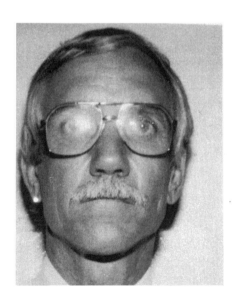

Representative Jim Hartdegen

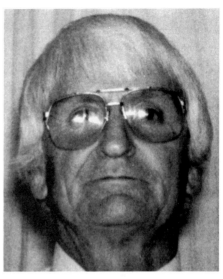

Former State Democratic party chief
George Stragalas

Lobbyist Ernie Hoffman

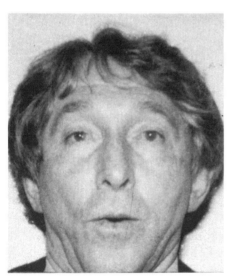

Justice of the Peace Donald Stump

Sheriff's extradition officer Jim Davis

Political consultant Rick DeGraw

County Democratic party head
David Manley

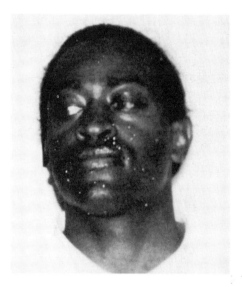

Accused kiddie pornographer Fondia
"Al" Hill

Union lobbyist David Horwitz

The Ones That Got Away

Representative Candice Nagel, the Rona Barrett of the Arizona legislature, agreed to take my money, then had a change of heart.

I handed Senate Majority Leader Alan Stephens an envelope containing more than $4,000 in "bundled" checks, but because the recording was bad and I didn't emphasize strongly enough that the money came from me, he skated.

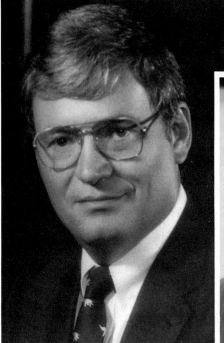

(*Left*) Senator Leo Corbet and Tony Vincent danced like Fred and Ginger, but Corbet never took the bait.

(*Right*) Lobbyists washed my $10,000 contribution to "The Big Kahuna," House Majority Leader Art Hamilton, through the Democratic party, thus shielding the powerful lawmaker from sub-sequent charges.

(*Right*) Gangster Tony Vincent contributed to both candidates in Arizona's razor-close 1990 governor's race, but could never arrange a sit-down with either Republican runoff winner J. Fife Symington . . .

(*Left*) . . . or former Phoenix Mayor Terry Goddard. However, the Azscam transcripts do provide a chilling look at the backbiting and vicious gossip that go on behind the scenes in gubernatorial elections. (*Melanie Rook D'Anna*)

The White Hats

(*Below*) House Majority Whip Jack Jewett was the only legislator to immediately file a complaint with the Attorney General after meeting with Tony Vincent.

(*Above*) State Treasurer Tony West grilled Tony Vincent like a cop interrogating a suspect, then ran to the Attorney General.

Speaker of the House Jane Hull admonished anyone who met with Tony Vincent to report to the Attorney General, and even agreed to wear a wire to sting me. Tough lady.

County Attorney Rick Romley approved Operation Desert Sting and kept it going while knowing the political backlash might destroy his own career.

(*Left*) Assistant County Attorney George Mount, a part-time pilot . . .

(*Right*) . . . and chief Deputy County Attorney Jim Keppel were part of the field unit behind the walls of the fourth room and second apartment.

Tony Vincent in action with Senator Carolyn Walker. (*Wide World Photos*)

Joe Stedino, pondering an uncertain future.

pretty personable. I think you'd probably get some mileage outta her."

". . . I'm fifty-three years old Bobby, and she's twenty-five. What am I gonna do? . . . She'd break my back . . ."

"Everybody's got to die."

". . . If she's looking for a boyfriend . . . if she's lookin' for a guy that's gonna be a lover and a paramour and if she sees me that way, that's not the way I am. I'm a sick old man with a bad back. Tryin' to get somethin' on and bustin' my ass to do it. She's seen me spend nine tons of money so that may be another reason why she's attracted."

". . . My call on her is she is somebody that wants to go someplace. And she is more than willing to play the game to get there."

Not unlike you, eh, Bob? This sounded like a match made in heaven. The conversation returned to more traditional politics.

"You do what you gotta do," I said. "You get your friends elected and reelected and you try to defeat your enemies. Isn't that what that [party] was all about last night? The Ds [Democrats] lookin' to knock out the Rs [Republicans], the Rs lookin' to knock out the Ds. I'm not into Rs and Ds. I'm into Mr. Green [money] and the green [yes] button. That's all I'm into . . . So anyway, Bobby, gettin' back to me and you now. Naturally, you're a right guy, you wanna do the right thing by me. Now I wanna do the right thing by you. What can I do for Bobby Raymond?"

"Well, if you want me to go out, number one . . ." he said, counting on his fingers.

"I like when people go like this, 'number one.'"

"Oh, there's gonna be more . . . Okay, let's just do it this way. I hafta raise about another $10,000. From a dollar to whatever you can help with, that's just fine."

"Is that all you need? . . . Now, you go ahead and finish with your points. That's number one. You gotta raise $10,000."

"For me. That's what I need to win my election."

"All right."

"On the fourteen votes, Tony, if I call you and I say, 'You need to direct some money to this candidate,' that will be a person that will vote for your issue."

"Okay."

". . . That's the way we passed the chiropractor's bill issue. The chiropractors had raised and contributed over $100,000 to the Democratic campaigns this year . . . There are two or three people in this state, Democrats, that could be in trouble and I will call them and I will say, 'Look, I know you're broke. I have some access to this money. What is your position on this issue? Understand, I can raise some money from this source. You will be committed to support this bill.' And if they say, 'Well, I don't know whether I can or not,' I will say, 'Well, thank you very much. When you decide, you call me.' I mean, that's the way I work with the caucus members. That's the way I work."

"That's two. What's number three?" I asked.

"Uh, that's about it."

"Two points? Take care of you, take care of your friends."

". . . You know, if I come in and say, 'Look, Tony, I got a problem. I need something taken care of.' You can do it. You say, 'I can do it.' If you can't do it . . ."

"We can do it," I cut in.

". . . Well, the other thing, I would strongly encourage you to do . . ."

"Number three!" I said, laughing. "Here we are."

"Well, this is not, you know, you do whatever the hell you want."

"I'm followin' your advice. Go ahead."

"I would strongly encourage you to talk to Scheffel."

"Okay."

"See, Scheffel's a dealer. Do you understand? He's a player."

"As you and I understand a player?"

"He's a player."

". . . There's something else I wanna throw at you Bob because it looks like you and I are gonna become close friends . . . If there's anything you want on the back end of this, let me know, but try to think of it quick. I'll tell you what's gone. The insurance is gone. The shrimp is gone. You didn't laugh when I said shrimp. You know it's big money. The mushrooms are gone."

"The mushrooms make me laugh because I eat mushrooms."

"It's big money, big money. Uh, the real estate is bein' cut up. The gift shops are gone. Everything else is still there. So be thinkin' about that . . . If there's somethin' on the back end, maybe you wanna put your wife or somebody else in?"

"Well, my wife owns her own public relations video production company."

"We're gonna do in-house video production . . . See what I'm sayin' how this could be a natural tie-in. We're gonna do that in-house promotion like they're doing now in Vegas, which was my concept twenty-five years ago. People can sit in their room and not be embarrassed and watch the TV and learn how to play blackjack, learn how to shoot craps, learn how to play roulette. We teach 'em that right in the room."

". . . And you'll hafta keep my wife away from the crap table."

"Hey forget about it."

"That's all I ask."

"You and I will have an understanding. I'm like you are, not only would I fall on the sword for those who have gone to bat for me, but if your wife had lost $5,000, the markers get torn up."

"Well, she's never got in quite that heavy, Tony."

At that point, I walked over and, without warning, dropped $10,000 in Raymond's lap.

"What is this now?"

"Ten thousand."

"A lot of money, Tony!" he said, pushing the cash on to the couch.

"That's what you asked for."

"Yeah, I didn't expect you to cover the whole thing."

"What'd you expect?"

"Well, I certainly didn't expect you to cover the whole thing."

"When Tony does business, he does business. I'm blunt and straight. That's the words you used. I'm more blunt and straight than you are. I try not to make as many enemies. I mean, you said you made enemies out there by doing that."

"Well, you know, there's a lotta different style politicians. Like Nagel. Nagel's really effective, but she's a kissy face, huggy bear. [Senator] Lela [Alston] is very effective because she hugs and kisses everybody. You know, I'm more, 'Fuck you! You give me what you want and I'll give you what I want.'"

"Exactly. Thank you."

"You know, my favorite line is, 'What's in it for me?'" Raymond said.

I took what was in it for him off the couch, counted it, and then handed a stack back to him.

"So you got a camera in here taping all this, Tony?" he said. "Are you gonna be like those people on TV?"

The phone rang before I could answer.

"You're on candid camera," I said before picking up the receiver. "'Hi. Call me back on 468–7816. Bye.' Tell her to hold on when she calls," I added, motioning for Raymond to answer the phone.

"Who is it?"

"Shiree."

The phone rang again. Raymond answered. "Hello. Guess what? No, this is Bobby. I'm doing okay. How are you?"

I handed a second stack of money to Raymond as he talked with Shiree. He stuffed it into the pocket of his jacket, which was laying on the couch.

"Oh, you're gonna put us on hold?"

"She's puttin' us on hold?" I laughed, realizing that Shiree no doubt was trying to regain her composure.

"Do you have time to go out for a drink?" Raymond asked me.

"No, I got my accountant in town," I said, remembering the cop's rule about fraternizing after a drop. Raymond could later claim he gave the money back at the bar. Shiree came back on the phone. I could hear only Raymond's side.

"I am offended," he said. "You coulda called me almost anything. I mean, that's worse than callin' me 'Stan Barnes.' You have very strange buddies . . . Oh, we're just talking a little business. Well, can you think of anything else better to do? Always. Always . . . Yeah, you're gonna hafta mess him around, break his legs. We found out that we're both very blunt people here. Yeah, well, we were gonna invite you out for a drink, but he can't go."

"Tell her I won't be upset if she meets you for a drink," I said, feverishly working the handle that stirred the shit. Raymond handed me the phone. "Hello, hold on a second."

"Do you care if I ask her out for a drink?" Raymond asked. I mouthed no.

"Shiree, I gotta run to the bathroom," I said. "I'll be right back." I handed the receiver back to my man Bobby.

"He just left," Raymond continued with Shiree. "Well, he'd never met anybody like me. I don't think I make him 'sick.' Oh well. About an hour. Yep. So you wanna go to dinner tonight or what? Okay. From what? Hard times. Yeah, right . . . So what are you going to do, like a minister or something? . . . I was all set to take you to dinner, since I'm not gonna do that, I don't know what I'm gonna do. Okay . . . I'll have him call you."

I looked forward to Shiree filling me in on her end of the conversation. She was probably steaming, loving it, but steaming.

Following that ill-timed diversion, Bobby brought up Rich Scheffel again.

"Can I just come out and say, 'Bobby told me that you're a player?' . . ."

"Rich and I have played at some bad shit."

"That's good."

The talk shifted to Alan Stephens. Raymond made a confession: "In all honesty, Alan is one of the people that told me to come sit down and talk to ya."

That was weird. Stephens had yet to sign up, but he was becoming my best pimp. He sent Walker and now Raymond—both quick burns.

Stephens was shrewd. He was sending his friends to the front line first to see if they would catch a bullet between the eyes.

Before he exited, Raymond left me with one final request.

"The only thing I don't do, Tony, is I don't discuss any business with my wife. Ever. Never discuss politics. Even though she runs my campaigns and does all my shit like that."

". . . You think like an Italian," I said. "You might be from Yo Shit, Texas, but I think you might be from Yo Shoo, Italy."

After Raymond left with the ten grand, I went into the fourth room. Mount and the cops were their usual happy, high-fiving selves.

"I'll make a prediction," I said. "When you guys drop the net, Bobby Raymond will be the first one to cut a deal. Mark my word." I noticed that Keppel wasn't sharing in the post-burn celebration. He appeared deeply concerned about something and later took me aside.

"Tony, Romley and Ortega are really disappointed in how many politicians are falling. They never expected this. They're afraid there's not going to be anyone left to run the state."

Keppel added that what was also keeping the county attorney and the police chief up nights was the fact that I'd been handing out bribes for seven months, and no one had turned me in. Even the so-called good guys were keeping me a secret. I understood Romley and Ortega's dismay. Honest people are always shocked to learn how dirty the world really is.

13

Shiree called me on the private line after I returned home.
"I feel like throwing, I'm so mad at you!" she steamed.

"What's the matter?"

"Don't even ask 'What's the matter?' I am mad at you. Seriously mad."

"I knew what you were gonna do," I said, referring to the phone stunt I pulled with Raymond at my office. "You had to handle that."

"Tony, I don't appreciate being caught off guard. I called YOU, damnit. Don't put that ass on the line any more. Don't ever do that to me."

"He was beggin' me to call you at that point, and you rang in," I lied.

". . . Tony, I'm pissed off, and then you never called back and now he's callin' me every five minutes practically . . . I don't know how to handle him . . . You know what people do to me."

Use you like a Kleenex and toss you in the wastebasket? I bit my tongue.

". . . I get the life sucked out of me because I'm a nice person," Shiree went on, her anger melting. "I don't wanna hurt anybody's feelings, okay? I like for people to like me . . . It's the story of my life. Either they get what they want from me, or they drop me. I can't ever have a relationship with people because either I play it their way or 'Screw you Shiree,' you know, 'I don't care if you were laying in traffic. I'm not gonna pull you out of there.'"

Not this again. "You're mad at him and you're taking it out on me," I suggested.

"No, I'm mad at you! I'm mad at you!"

"Oh, me too?"

"Yeah!"

"Okay."

". . . I'm drained of people suckin' the life out of me. I'm serious. And I just get to the point, Tony, where I think I just can't go on. I just don't think I can anymore."

"Sure you can."

"Tony, I can't. I'm tired."

"Sure you can."

"No, I can't!"

"Okay, no you can't."

"I'm tired. I'm worn out. I just, I feel like such a failure. I can't deal with people . . . I need to go to a class or somethin'. I'm a failure with people. That's all there is to it."

"Not really," I assured her. I shifted the conversation to the political part of my session with Raymond, thinking it might amuse her enough to forestall the razors-to-the-wrist act. ". . . We'll get together next week and I'll give you the dialogue. You'll love it. It was funny. You know, 'I wanna know what's in it for me?'"

"That's what he said?"

"Oh yeah, yeah," I laughed.

"He's such a creep . . . Give him the janitorial contract. Cleaning the toilets," she proposed. ". . . I'm a pretty tough cookie and I said 'I don't think you wanna mess with me.' That's what I said. And he goes, he kinda laughed about it. I go, 'I have some pretty "funny" friends and you know,' and I kinda made a joke about it, but yet there was some serious note, like 'don't mess with me.' And he, you know, he's wantin' to come over to my house . . . This guy is 100 percent, full-fledged pervert!"

". . . I think it'll pass," I said. "It's just the weekend. His wife's out of town and he's gettin' crazy."

". . . I'll just have to pay it cool. Oh, he wants me to go out with him tomorrow night . . . You know what I said? I go, 'I have someone I have to report to' . . ."

"Good for you," I said, knowing it was probably true.

"Sometimes I just wish I had someone to take care of me in that way . . . that I could just use that person. Not use 'em, but at least have a person that I didn't have to . . ."

"A beard!" I interrupted, leaping at the chance to use one of my favorite Desert Sting words. I advised Shiree that if she didn't want Raymond's advances, to be more assertive and tell him she didn't go out with married guys, or at least, lie and tell him she didn't go out with married men.

The fireman, Pat Cantelme, showed for a meet at 11 a.m. on October 8. As usual, he was loaded with suggestions. As he spoke, I was reminded of the old creed about advice: "A wise man don't need it and a fool won't heed it." He wanted me to hire a planning committee to work on the casino gambling project. The members would preferably consist of people close to Terry Goddard. It would have been a good idea—if Tony were real. But Tony was there to sting, and the cops wanted the fireman bad because they felt he beat a cocaine rap. I again dangled the bait, but Cantelme wouldn't bite. Either he was clean, or I was using the wrong lure.

Representative Jim Meredith called to thank me for the money. He said it would help keep him in power. That was nice of him. It also buried his butt a little deeper. Ernie Hoffman phoned and said Senator Corbet needed cash to salt the legislature to gain support for his run for president of the Senate. Hoffman wanted to handle the drop, but I vetoed it, as I already had a meet with Corbet set for that evening. Hoffman added that Senator Lela Alston needed financial help. I told him to bring her by.

I grabbed my bugged cellular phone and drove to Marie Callender's at four for another evening of fine microwaved dining and political babble with Kenney and Corbet. I had $10,000 in each of my front pockets, plus another $10,000 in my left jacket pocket and $7,000 in the right for a total of $37,000. It would all be Corbet's for the asking. My QB arrived early, as scheduled, and presented the game plan. He would make the intro, lead the initial conversation, and then make an excuse to leave. This would enable me to do my "What does Leo need?" routine in private. It was Kenney's belief that legislators wouldn't reach for the bucks if anyone else was around, even another crooked legislator. That would interfere with their comfort levels.

I had misgivings about meeting with Corbet. I was worried that the FBI, county police, state police, CIA, Interpol, "60 Minutes," or any of a half-dozen other investigative bodies might be following him. I didn't need Leo dumping his heat on me. He started out on a bad foot by arriving twenty minutes late. I was used to Mob time, which meant if a meeting was set for 2 p.m., you got there at 1:30. Corbet's tardiness forced me to listen to Kenney talk about one of his favorite, dinnertime subjects.

"About once every six months, I have a little hemorrhoid problem and it's been bothering me the last couple of days. Us assholes got to stick together."

I made the grave mistake of asking, "What, uh, what do you do for it? You go to the doctor or what?"

"Oh, he gives me some stuff that looks like toothpaste that you put on it . . . Well, let me brief you on Leo," Kenney said, mercifully changing subjects in mid-sentence. "I would suggest we treat Leo the same way we did Meredith . . . Leo's been strange. You know, he's usually the guy that you'd love to have at a party . . . He'll screw around, but he's dieting and . . . grumpy and bitchy . . . He apologized, 'Well, I been dieting and it's the shits. I gave up smoking. I don't drink. My girlfriend doesn't like me.' I said, 'Hey welcome to the club, bud.'"

"What's the story on [Representative] Brenda Burns?" I asked Kenney, having heard a lot of interesting things about her, including detailed accounts of her alleged forays into plastic surgery.

"Brenda would like to become chairman of the judiciary, too. She's a gal who's kind of cute, likes to swing her butt around there, and all the lobbyists and guys just kind of pant when she goes by. She's not that bad . . . She's ambitious but she's real into the right-wing church people . . . If we can get Leo on our team, whatever it takes, do it," Kenney said, U-turning back to his buddy. "Ten thousand dollars with Leo will be worth ten times $10,000 with Susan Laybe."

Corbet finally arrived at ten minutes to five. He was a short, heavy-set, fifty-three-year-old veteran politician with a round face and a cautiously arrogant demeanor. Kenney briefed me that Corbet had a rich lady on the line, but she refused to marry him until he got a real job. Corbet reminded me of an alley cat with one eye, no ears, and a tail gnawed in half. He had been in so many scrapes during his inglorious political career that he was teetering on the last of his nine lives. Like that battered alley cat, he was aware that his next scuffle could be his last. He wasn't going to dive in easily.

"Right now, if it went to the floor tommorrow, House and Senate combined I can count on eighteen votes," I boasted, updating Corbet on where I stood. "But that's split, that's House and Senate, that's not . . ."

"Last time I heard, that won't get you very far."

Ouch. Leo jabbed Tony! I felt my neck muscles tighten as Corbet downplayed my legislative efforts and pushed a public initiative referendum instead.

Kenney lightened the conversation with a bizarre report on how he had made sure "Tony Vincent" was okay. He said he had checked Tony out with U.S. Senator Harry Reid of Nevada. And Tony checked! Ron Tapp confirmed Tony with the CIA, and now Kenney checked with a U.S. senator. These guys were in Disneyland.

Corbet complimented me on my cellular phone. I handed it to him without pause, bug and all. He made some calls, which could only be recorded one way, that is, only his voice was recorded. As Kenney was reaching over and slicing off a chunk of my banana cream pie appetizer, I decided I wasn't going to deal with Corbet. He was talking referendums, pimping signatures, and babbling about how he wanted to make sure I knew how to "make it work" even though he didn't know anything about the casino gambling industry. My gut told me that recruiting him would be a bad move. He had the stench of political death about him.

"But you got to have your homework done, you know. I mean, this isn't the kind of thing that the president of the Senate shoves through in the middle of the night," the senator said.

I glanced at Kenney, remembering his "push it through at 4 a.m. on the last day of the session" speech. He shrugged. We broke the meeting without having dinner. Kenney had a baffled look on his banana cream pie–smeared face as I slapped a twenty on the table and left. I hadn't even given him a chance to leave me alone with Corbet as planned.

"Good move," Ball told me afterward. "That meeting was going nowhere."

Stragalas came to the office on October 9 to slam the Goddards some more. My mind began to drift. Stragalas downshifted from the Goddards to Don Bolles, the *Arizona Republic* investigative reporter who was blown up in his car in 1976 just as he was about to publish a massive story on corruption in the state. Stragalas said he was with Bolles shortly before his death and was shown parts of the article. According to Stragalas, the piece touched upon corruption in Phoenix City Hall, the judiciary, the State Supreme Court, and the legislature. That woke me up. Here I was, in a hundred miles deeper than Bolles, and he ended up eating his dashboard. That didn't bode well for Tony. If a Mafia goon didn't get me, some desperate politician's pyrotechnician might.

Kenney called on the ninth to tell me that Corbet liked me and would call to arrange another get-together. I told Kenney I didn't think we were getting anywhere with Corbet. He advised me not to fold my hand and added that he had set up a meeting for the following week with Jack Jewett, the House whip.

Detective Ball, Sergeant Davis, Captain Black, and Deputy Chief Click came by the undercover apartment to shoot the breeze. Click said an associate of his told him that Corbet was "the biggest crook in the legislature." Corbet called right after they left. He advised me that I could give unlimited amounts of money directly to the Republican party. That was the same jig Sam Goddard had tried to get me to do— just fill the party coffers with my money and let them dole it out. I wouldn't have operated that way even if I was legitimate. The money could end up in the pockets of those voting against you just as easily as those on your team. For the "biggest crook in the legislature," Corbet was sure playing this close to the vest.

Tapp phoned and said he lunched with Representative Nancy Wessel, a Phoenix Republican. He reported that she was skittish and worried that the organized crime cops were going to sweep in and take Tony down. I was scheduled to sit at the same table with her during the the J. Fife Symington fund-raiser and joked that I'd be sure to give her my best "dis, dem, and dose" Brooklyn Tony rap.

I called Shiree on the morning of October 10 to tell her that her "boyfriend," Bobby Raymond, was coming in later that afternoon.

"He called again?" she asked.

"Yeah."

"Don't tell me he wants more money . . . Oh, I'll kill him. That's terrible."

"Not only did he want my money, he wanted the girl I was with. 'Give me $10,000 and I wanna fuck your girlfriend.' Anything else? What else could I do for ya."

"That's terrible . . . Now don't get him started. He's leavin' me alone."

"How many times did he call ya?"

"Probably seven times."

"What do you think he wanted?"

"I don't know, he wanted me to go out to dinner with him."

"What do you think he wanted?"

"He goes, you can be home by nine. I just wanna talk to . . ."

"Bottom line. What did he want?"

"I don't know, Tony. I don't think like that so I don't know."

"What do you think he wanted?"

"He wanted to just take me out to dinner."

"What do you think he wanted?"

"He wanted to take me out to dinner."

"That's all?"

"Yep."

"... How long you been livin' in Disneyland?"

"Quite a while and I love it! And I don't plan to move out."

Sue Laybe was back on the horn requesting an immediate sit-down. I called Ball and suggested that he have someone drive by and see if the construction on her house had stopped again.

Laybe showed on time at 1 p.m. She came at me with a new move—the Catholic legislator wanted $2,500 for the extremely un-Catholic pro-choice abortion movement. I played pro-abortion Tony and handed her the dough. Sue would have to account to a higher authority for this transaction. We then discussed what Laybe wanted on the back end of my casino operation. She suggested restaurant management or the food and beverage manager slot in a big hotel. That was telling. Most people wanted easy money through open-ended, middleman jobs like brokering shrimp, mushrooms, faxes, etc. Laybe picked two bare-knuckled, salaried positions that would involve a considerable amount of labor. For all her faults brought to light by Tony—not to mention double-dealing God—she remained a solid, salt-of-the-earth lady.

The talk circled around to the "Funds for Five Freshmen" party and Bobby Raymond.

"I've never seen him drool over somebody so much as he was over me the other night," Laybe said.

That raised my eyebrows. I knew Raymond was drooling over Shiree Foster. But I couldn't imagine him drooling over Representative Olive Oyl unless he was the horniest Texan who ever lived. It finally sunk in that she wasn't referring to sexual drool à la Shiree. She was saying Raymond was drooling on her to get close to me and my money.

Raymond himself blew in at 2 p.m. He was in high spirits.

"Let me be blunt," he opened. "You have scared the fuck out of so many people, Tony."

"How? I haven't met that many people."

"Do you know a guy by the name of Bill Mundell?"

"Oh yeah," I said, remembering the Chandler representative who told me he needed $7,000 and then went bug-eyed when I asked him how he wanted it."

"You just totally horrified him ... I'll tell you where I figure you're at now. Everybody is trying to figure out who you are. Everybody is trying to figure out if you're some kind of a sting operation."

"... Who's everybody?"

"Nagel really likes you, but she's scared shitless."

"I'm scared of her," I countered, launching into my I-thought-she-was-going-to-sting-me counterrap.

"I was not stupid enough to walk up here Saturday without knowing a little about where you came from," Raymond said. ". . . You know, I mean you are a well-respected person from Reno, Nevada."

"Yep," I agreed.

"You have a spotless clean record with the gaming commission."

"That's right!" I seconded. A man that doesn't exist can't have many spots on his record.

"And the chairman of the tax committee in Nevada says Tony is a good guy."

"Good. Thank you. Thank you." What the hell was this guy talking about?

"Now that raised my comfort level about four hundred notches to come up here Saturday."

It was becoming eerie. Tony Vincent, a fictional character with no past, had somehow survived yet another background check. I knew the police hadn't planted anything other than a parking ticket in the Nevada police computer. The only explanation was that like Tapp and Kenney, Raymond had dazzled himself with his own bullshit.

"Well, right now, I believe you probably ought to slow up . . ." Bobby advised. "Mundell, I mean, he just freaked . . . You're right back to your 'unsophisticated whore.' He wanted the money. He didn't have the balls to do the deed . . . My concern is if you spread too much money, there's too much noise that goes on about it. You draw too much attention to yourself which ultimately will draw an investigation . . . This attorney general we have [Corbin] is a vicious son-of-a-bitch . . . A couple of things you don't wanna happen. You don't want these campaign expenditures showing that you have absolutely given over $2,200. If it all totals over that, you have violated the law. My other concern, Tony . . . people keeping their mouths shut and some of these guys, they're all well-meaning, nice people, but they like to be big shots . . . If somebody draws a circle around this thing and figures out all this money is coming from you, you're gonna get a whole lot of attention drawn on you all of a sudden that you don't need . . . What I'm scared of . . . Ernie [Hoffman] gets drunk and Ernie starts talkin' . . . This is you and me talking here but I figure now I'm in this thing right up to my ass . . . Laybe is another one. Tony, please. I know this woman. I know her well."

"She's a yakker," I acknowledged.

"Before you do much more, what I'd like to do for you is save your money."

Raymond's concern was heartwarming, but he didn't complete his sentence. What he wanted to do for me was "save your money" for himself! He was fencing up the trail, desperately trying to keep the goldmine for himself. Beautiful.

"Tony, I think you're gettin' stroked in several places."

"You mean a person would take twenty large from me and then not vote 'yes'?" I said, feigning shock.

". . . I wanna help you save some of your money . . . Frankly, if I help you save some of your money, you might hire me to do something one of these days."

"Exactly," I agreed. "How can I save money? I wanna hear it."

"You need a lobbyist. A local lobbyist."

That was interesting reasoning. My first lobbyist, Tapp, was costing me $1,000 a week. The next guy, Ernie Hoffman, was all set to dig close to $200,000 out of my pocket over the next fifteen months. I was dying to know how Raymond's boy, Rich Scheffel, was going to buck this trend and actually save me money.

"Rich Scheffel is not a cheap guy," Raymond said. ". . . He's not the highest priced, but he's probably the highest powered lobbyist in the state . . . He will not let you pass all this money out. He will be the first one to say 'Man, you're lettin' these people take your money.' He will sit down and work out a program how you get the money to the people, and he's the one that's doin' it."

Just what I needed. Another $100,000-a-year bagman. But think of all the money I could save!

"And you isolate yourself," Bobby continued. "That way, you go to these dinners and you don't have to sit down and talk to people about what you want. You don't need to do that. You're Tony that everybody likes . . . If I were you, I'd be real uncomfortable meetin' with 99 percent of these assholes in the legislature. I think you know, some of these guys are just jerking your chain . . . Tony, in this state man, people with money scare the shit out of legislators . . . Remember, they're unsophisticated whores. Most of these people, Bill English . . . If Bill gives ya a commitment, you got it. Kenney, I would assume when Kenney gave you a commitment, you got it. When Meredith gives you a commitment, it isn't worth the fuckin' air it took him to say it! . . . Let me tell ya about Laybe . . . They had this big fight, huge fight over changin' this credit card law . . . Security Bank came in here, spread some big money around . . . We had to change a statute. It had something to do with the way they charge fees . . . Then they would put this credit card center here, six hundred jobs. Okay, well, so the Security folks come in. They hire this lobbying firm. They all go around and pass out their 'two hundred' checks, everywhere. And they get all these votes . . . Laybe is a committed 'aye' vote. Took money from 'em. Went out to lunch with 'em. Good friends. Go to the floor. Huge fight. She votes against 'em. The bill dies. So a couple hours later, they bring this bill back again for reconsideration. They went around, gathered up a couple more votes, bill passes next time around . . . Up to the governor it goes. The next day the governor's gonna have a bill-signing ceremony. All the big shots from Security Pacific Bank are standing there. The governor's standing there. Here's Laybe standing in the picture."

"I love it!"

"True story."

"I love it. She jumped in the picture!"

"Seventy out of ninety assholes there, they're the same way. And I mean, it crosses party lines."

"That's why I'm staying bipartisan," I interjected.

". . . You gotta understand. Like a Jim Meredith, hates me. He would love to see the attorney general come after me. If he had to get you along the way to get me . . ."

"I'd go down with ya," I said.

". . . One of the legislators to call . . . [Representative] Jack Jackson. He's one of the Navajos from the reservation . . . Absolutely in no way, shape, or form do you offer him over $440 . . . See, there's no use in giving those guys a thousand, two thousand, three thousand dollars when you can get their vote for $440. I mean, I'll tell you what, Tony, let me pinch your dimes for ya and you can give me a bonus."

Underprice everybody else and give Raymond a bonus. Beautiful.

". . . What's this lady here cost," I asked facetiously, pointing at the picture of twenty-term House member Polly Rosenbaum.

"I don't think there's any way."

"God love her . . ." I said. "She's got forty years in the legislature . . . How would you feel if you give this broad $50,000 and you read the obits the next day and she's in there? She's gotta be ninety."

"She's ninety-three years old . . . She's the longest-serving, oldest state legislator in the United States."

Raymond asked me if I expected any trouble from the casino power elite in Vegas. I kicked into Street Warrior Tony. "That's the worst mistake they could make. I'm ready to deal with them. I'll put an army together in two days and then forget about it. But I'll hold that war in Nevada . . . I don't want to muddy up Arizona."

That little speech would do nothing to tone down Tony's "scary" image. Actually, Raymond's reaction to Tony, and everybody else's, reminded me of the great movie *Being There*, that starred Peter Sellers as a dimwit gardener who ends up being a political power broker and presidential candidate simply by inheriting a nice suit. When questioned, he mumbles some gardening nonsense that everyone mistakes for great pearls of wisdom. It was the same with Tony. Everybody was looking at me through their own prejudices, cultural backgrounds, or Hollywood "Godfather" fantasies.

Bobby didn't mention Shiree until he was just about to leave, and even that was only in passing. It was obvious that what really got him hard was politics. I, of course, had no intention of informing Shiree of this. From her perspective, the only thing worse than Raymond talking about her would be his not talking about her.

Raymond returned the next day with lobbyist Rich Scheffel. The big-time political fixer I'd been hearing about for months was a short, bald, bespectacled guy. He was smart, glib, and well-connected. Even his wife was tied in—she was the administrative assistant for Francis X. Gordon, the Chief Justice of the Arizona Supreme Court. Scheffel told me he represented the "sin" industries—cigarettes and beer. He hard-pimped himself for the job as my lobbyist, but didn't talk any real turkey. We agreed to meet again.

Detective Ball called afterward and nixed Tony's Second Coming, the J. Fife Symington affair. He said there was too much Mob talk going around. I agreed. Tony didn't fit at these boring political functions. I stood out like Madonna in a convent. I called my "girlfriend" Shiree, said I had a cold, gave her the bad news, and suggested she go without me. She jumped at the opportunity and went stag.

Gary Kaasa showed for a scheduled sit-down after Bobby and Richie departed. The high school teacher was toting the outline for his "my issue as a candidate" proposal. There were some solid ideas there, but the typing and spelling were atrocious. I felt like adding a new issue to Tony's backup arsenal, basic skills tests for Arizona teachers. Kaasa was better at keeping his ear to the ground. A lot of what he was hearing involved one Tony Vincent. The first rumor he heard was that I was paying a lot of people's ways into fund-raising parties.

"Another rumor, a lobbyist in a restaurant says that a legislator by the name of English took a bundle of money from you . . . And the next one was, not a rumor, it was a perception by a political type that had heard about you and the rumor was, and it goes back a long ways, but it was said . . . what's the word? What's the 'setup' word? Government tryin' to get you so they set up a . . ."

"The government's tryin' to get me?"

"The FBI is gonna set you up, uh . . ."

"They're gonna set me up?"

"Yeah, no, no, no, no. Look. I'm just lookin' for a word. That you're from the government. You're the FBI."

"Me?"

"I'm just tellin' you this. It's a bullshit rumor . . . What's the word . . . where they set somebody up and they come in an nail ya?"

"They nab ya?" I said, refusing to say the "S" word.

"You know, they did it to Marion Barry and the South Carolina legislators."

"Cocaine?"

"No, no, no, no."

"I don't fool with drugs."

"No, no, no, no, no. Shit. It's, it's a term for, let's say you were the FBI."

"Okay."

"And I'm the legislator."

"Right."

"You give me a thousand bucks. There's a TV camera. I take the thousand. I'm arrested as I go out the door. What's that called?"

"Violating the law."

"Well, I know, but what's that?"

"Bribery?"

"Yeah, it's like, a s —"

"Bribery?"

"Sting! Or is it, now, but then I'm arrested. Anyway, that was that word from this guy's mouth."

". . . Well, we gotta quash that."

"Well, we really do."

It was quite a dance, especially considering that most of the "sting" talk was coming from Kaasa's client, Candy "Nervous" Nagel. ". . . I didn't have a problem in this town until I met with her," I barked. "And then she went off half-cocked. She's gotta be calmed down, right? I would ask you to do that."

I pulled out $1,500 and handed it to Kaasa as a down payment for his study. All the talk of stings didn't keep him from taking the money, although the only crime he had committed was against the English language. Kaasa didn't have a vote to sell, and his gal Candy had yet to take the bait, so he couldn't be charged with conspiracy.

"People just talk because I think the whole political thing runs on rumors and speculation," Kaasa said. "That's what it's about."

Bill English and Ernie Hoffman arrived at my office after Kaasa fled with the fifteen hundred. The slippery duo were dressed to the teeth, ready for the big bash with Symington. I begged off because of my cold and handed them a ticket to drop on Shiree. Like Bob Raymond before him, Ernie advised me to ease up on the sit-downs and instead refer everyone to him. He'd then process the marks, tenderize them, and send the best ones to me. In his dreams, maybe. I countered by pulling out Kaasa's study, along with an outline Pat Cantelme had given me, and laid them on him, being sure to mention that Cantelme's cost nothing and Kaasa was doing his for a mere $2,500. That was a sharp contrast to the $60,000 paper hustle Hoffman was doing on me. The lobbyist glanced through the materials, faked some praise, and displayed no shame.

Instead of talking shit for two hours and then passing the cash, I decided to spice this gathering by dropping $24,600 on Hoffman right off the bat. The money was to cover that morning's purchase on the always volatile Arizona study and poll market.

Hoffman scooped up the pile. It wasn't until later that I realized I'd given him the wrong figure. The bill he sent was for $26,400. I had transposed the figures and shorted him $1,800. He didn't notice.

We meandered into a disturbing dialogue.

"... What I'm gonna hafta do with my own campaign is as we discussed before," Bill English began. "Those damn money orders or whatever it may be, names and addresses at $220 a shot. At this point in time, I'm twenty grand shy of that ... I don't give a shit what it costs and everything else, we'll do it."

"What did we do with the eighteen?" I wondered, using the Royal "we" as Tony was not amused. I was under the impression that I'd taken care of English's campaign needs when I dropped $18,000 on him at the Ritz Carlton marathon meet where I'd done my striptease.

"We got that, we still got that back there," Hoffman said.

Back there? Back where? What kind of move were these two goofballs pulling now?

"How are we gonna get that into his campaign?" I inquired.

"Well, see, that's the whole point," English said. "We can't in that sense. There are things that we can do to create a certain degree of friendship and cooperation ... In terms of leadership situation, but we cannot get that into my campaign. Period. There is simply no way ... Well, if we had names and addresses and you know. We could deal with that. With names and addresses."

"Do you need twenty on top of the ..."

"No, no, no," English said. "... And see, as far as I'm concerned the eighteen doesn't exist. Ernie's got an advance on his fees ... But that won't go into my campaign. That's gonna go against your other expenses. The things that you are doing, the very legitimate things that are being done."

What a pair of loaded dice these two were. Tony was ready to plant them right next to the freshly dug grave of Fondia Al Hill. Hoffman sensed my displeasure and like the oily P.R. man he was, began furiously backpedaling.

"I will translate it in some manner myself, how I'm gonna help Bill," he boomed in that grating voice of his, butchering verbs with abandon. What was he planning to do, "translate" the money into pesos? "Right now, I'm doing full credit for Bill. I'm paying for everything on it. I'm paying for his tabloid, $10,000. I've got another mailing of another seven. We just picked some bills for $400 worth of photos. I'm paying for everything now. My corporate set up . . ."

"I'm, I'll be real honest," English cut in. "I am very concerned that that cash, which I didn't know about until much later, obviously he's providing services, obviously he needs to bill you against that, and obviously it has to come into the corporate coffers, and the only thing I can deal with are those money orders and have you come to me very legitimately at 220 bucks a whack."

Say what? He didn't know about the cash until "much later?" He was sitting right there when Hoffman, his personal bagman, sucked it in at the Ritz. The bastard was drunk, but not that drunk. I suspected that English had gotten wind of the sting rumor that was sweeping the legislature and was frantically trying to cover his ass, just in case. Giving the $18,000 back, or refusing the $24,600 Hoffman had just swallowed, would seem to have been a more logical way to clean up, but it would snow in Phoenix in July before they gave a dime of the money back.

As with Bob Raymond, Bill and Ernie were suddenly worried about my financial well-being. They wanted me to shut off the faucets. It was touching. All my new friends were so deeply interested in saving my money. However, this concern always developed after they had taken their cut.

I lifted the conversation out of the quagmire and refocused on sweeping in more legislators. They brought up Leo Corbet.

"You know," English said. "I take him out and get him laid and he doesn't even know how to reciprocate . . . If Leo asks you for a big sackful, tell him Bill English said to kick you [Corbet] in the balls if you did that."

14

Senator Leo Corbet soloed in my office on October 12. He was the sitting chairman of the judiciary and was trying to leap to Senate president. Everybody told me he was coming for a package.

"When I get money from people or anything," he explained, setting the tone of the meet, "it's an ear and hopefully a reasonable solution to the problem. It is not a guaranteed vote one way or the other."

That wasn't what I heard from Deputy Chief Glick and all my legislator friends. The fourth room boys wanted me to push Corbet hard, so I persisted.

"Leo, what has Don told you about me?"

"Not much. He told me that his son's [daughter's] possible future father-in-law said that you were okay and that he was with the gaming commission."

"Oh Harry," I winged. "Harry Reid. He's a United States senator now." It was another in a long line of Tony Vincent confirmations. I had stopped even trying to figure out how they came about. Hell, even I was starting to believe that Tony existed. He had better references than Billy Graham.

Corbet loosened up enough to let me in on a secret that explained why he was so cautious. Apparently, my suspicions about him being targeted by other law enforcement agencies turned out to be well founded. He had passed through the heart of an FBI sting involving the teamsters and some shady land deals. He insisted he was clean, but feared the political ramifications if word got out.

"This guy comes to my office. I sold him a couple of casino sites in Laughlin . . . He comes to me and says he has some people . . . these lots that are now worth $18 million that were worth three then, I could've bought 'em for about four and a half . . . So anyway, he said, 'Well, why don't you borrow the money from the Teamsters?' I said, 'What? Shit, I don't want those guys with knuckles dragging the ground coming after me'. . . So I put a deal together and give it to him and he's gonna turn it into them . . . Anyway . . . it turns out that it's an FBI sting operation. This guy's just gotten out of jail. So they're coming after me . . . Ultimately it will come out, you know, what I did and what I said was okay, but in the meantime if the press really wants to give you a hammer job, they can do that."

With both the FBI and media itching to crush this guy, it was imperative to hook him with haste. The last thing the local cops and prosecutors wanted was to have some arrogant FBI suit breeze in, flash his badge, and snatch the senator away from us. Or worse, we didn't want to wait until the local newspaper slammed Corbet and turned him into a political pariah.

"Okay . . . would you have a problem with giving me your word that you . . . wouldn't shelve or kill my bill?" I began.

"Well, let me think about it . . . Let me tell you about me. The reason I don't give my word up-front as quick, you know, to get the money and run or do shit like that, is that when I give it, I'm not gonna back off on ya."

"I know who has the power to kill me and shelve me, and I don't want that to happen. And if you can promise me that, that you can live with that, then that's where I'm at with Leo Corbet."

"The other thing, Tony, is we're gonna have an inordinate amount of Mormons screwing around . . ."

No Leo, you're thinking of Don Kenney. We weren't talking about horny Mormons. The senator continued his verbal wanderings while I kept to the point. "We're talking about me getting killed or shelved before I can get anywhere, and you're in that position."

"The way I stay alive in this business and the way that I don't have a lot of people on my ass over stuff is that we understand things on the front side and that's why I'm glad we're talking like this . . ."

Corbet kept spitting out the hook. Undeterred, I continued to toss it back to him.

"Leo . . . it's not the vote so much as it is a man in your position, as chairman of the judiciary or Senate president, I know the power that office wields and if that guy says, 'Hey, I want to fuck him,' it goes into the drawer and it stays there and I'm dead. That's what I'm asking Leo Corbet to do, is promise me that won't happen."

"And I'm telling you that won't happen, you know, I can't imagine it happening. I cannot, you know, think that for some reason, now let me tell you this . . . you've got to understand if something happens and Tony Vincent all of a sudden becomes a persona non grata for some reason that you and I aren't talking about today, that maybe, you know, it's like if Charlie Keating had a bill to do anything. I don't care what it was, the minute the shit hit the fan on him everybody starts scurrying . . ."

A nibble, maybe, but no snag. Not even close. "Let me, let me rephrase the question," I opened.

"Just so we understand each other," Corbet laughed, well aware of the dance we were doing.

"Tony Vincent is a bona fide guy who can stand the scrutiny of licensure application. He's a guy that is committed to $10 to $20 million to get this project through. He has a five-year plan. He's not in a hurry. I've been here fourteen months . . . a legitimate clean bill comes up in front of the Senate . . . You look at it, and I know I have your word you're not gonna take my bill like a piece of candy, throw it in the drawer, and slam it shut."

"You have my word."

Okay! Finally! "That's the promise I'm looking for. If you can promise me you won't do that then I can promise you that I wanna do for you what I can do for you."

". . . You get your hearing. If it gets the votes to get out of there it will get scheduled for the floor."

That's perfectly legal. That's the way it's supposed to be done.

". . . I'll also tell you that, you know," he continued, "the only caveat I tell you about all this shit is if something hits the fan and you got legislators and politicians running for cover for some reason, then all bets are off."

I made another cast. "How can Tony Vincent, in return for your promise . . . help you get elected to the Senate presidency? What's that gonna take?"

"Well, first, my promise is to be fair with you and . . . to treat your bill like I would treat one of my own, okay? . . . And I assume I'll vote for it because I don't think my people are, I think my people are gonna say 'That's a fun deal' . . . The other thing you need to know, I'm not interested in anything for me. That sounds sort of like flag waving or something. The only thing I'm really interested in is seeing the state mature, develop, and prosper . . . I believe in business and, you know, so that's where it is for me . . . If it makes sense to do, without you ever doing anything for me or anybody else, 'cause it's just the thing to do . . . It's like the first time old Bruce Babbitt and I ever got together. I was minority leader and . . . he wants votes from us and I said, 'Fine. We'll give 'em to you.' And he said, 'Well, I got lots of chits.' I said, 'I don't need any chits. It's the right thing to do.'"

This old alley cat must have made me. His speech, complete with Kate Smith in the background singing "God Bless Arizona" was tailor-made for police video.

"If it's the right thing to do, I'll go down to see and make sure that it gets done, Tony," he reiterated. "If it turns out to be, for some reason, and I don't mean a moral reason 'cause I'm not, uh, morally, I don't think it's wrong to do, but if it turns out that it's not the right thing for this state to do, then, you know, I'm not gonna do it."

The door was slammed, but not locked. ". . . The bottom line is, when I'm one on one with somebody like I am with you today, I have to go back to the main focal point. What would, what reason would Leo Corbet have to keep his word to me?"

"What reason does anyone have at any time, Tony?"

I could think of about 150,000 reasons, and counting.

"I've survived in this fucking jungle, and I found out real big time when I lost the governor's race in '82, that you run into the same people on the way down that you saw on the way up," he explained, losing me on this point. "And if you haven't treated them with some degree of dignity and respect, then you're gonna get shit on."

Nice cliché, but wrong conversation. This was a cash deal, not a lesson on the Golden Rule. "Back to my initial question a few minutes ago . . . I need to know I'm not gonna get fucked or thrown into a drawer."

"I told you, you won't get screwed."

"Now if that's gonna happen, and I have your word on that, then I need to know what can I do for Leo Corbet to help him get the Senate presidency. 'Cause at that point it becomes paramount to me to see [you] in that seat because then I know I'm not going in here, see, I don't know who's in there now and I don't know who else is . . ."

"I think I'm gonna, if the Republicans are in, I think I'll be president or I'll be majority leader, one or the other. If I'm the majority leader, then the president's gonna be the weak link . . ."

I went on too long with my question and gave him a big hole to slip out. I was getting so dizzy from the cat and mouse game that my rap was starting to unravel.

"Why don't we do this today, Leo . . . Think about what I've asked you for. Think about what you want to do for me, what I can do for you. I see it as important to me and to you that you get the Senate presidency. If you don't get the Senate presidency and you're still chairman of the judiciary, which obviously you can hold that seat as long as you want to . . ."

"I'll be there for a while. 'Till we're both ninety."

I believed him. If he kept dancing like this, they'd never blast him out of there. After he left empty-handed, I entered the fourth room and shrugged.

"Damn nice try," Ball said. "You kept pounding him but he wouldn't bite. We'll get 'im next time."

"You watch," I said. "I bet the FBI ain't got nothing on him either. That's one wily mother."

Next on my agenda was a meet arranged by Dave Horwitz. Candidate John Dougherty was said to need $12,000 to keep his campaign going. He was one of the "Five Freshmen" whose party I graced. Dougherty was a big, Tip O'Neill–like guy in his sixties with a mane of white hair. He was a retired Air Force colonel and college professor. I didn't figure him for a player. The colonel, at least on paper, appeared to have too much on the ball.

"Well, what I wanted to ask you, Johnny, is when you're elected, when this comes up on my issue, do you foresee any problem with you hittin' the 'yes' button on it? 'Cause I wanna help those that are gonna help. That's where I'm at."

"I understand, but I think that before I could commit myself, I'd have to see a study that would indicate that this thing . . ."

Did he say study? I could certainly accommodate him there. Thanks to Ernie, I'd soon be up to my ears in studies. I outlined the polls, economic studies, and focus research I had in the works, not to mention the "my issue as a candidate" bible and the freebie outline the fireman gave me.

". . . See, I was told by [Horwitz] that you didn't have any problem with this and that I could count on your vote. Maybe he shouldn't have committed that."

"No, he shouldn't have. Nobody has the right to commit to my votes," he said icily. "Nobody can commit my vote!"

"Except you."

"Except me and I'm not committing any votes before I actually get into office. And it would be based on what I thought was the welfare of the state of Arizona, not on the money you might give me."

I could see that this man wasn't going to get anywhere in politics.

"I just can't make a commitment until I see what it's all about, and I'm not sure that a study that you promoted would meet my needs in any way. I think, what I was thinking about was a study that would be conducted by the state, authorized by the legislature . . . I think in order to sell it to the people of Arizona, we would have to have a piece of paper, a study that would be considered to be independent of you, who have a special interest."

Good point, and one Ernie Hoffman didn't mention when he was pushing $100,000 worth of polls and studies on me.

"... In any event, I'm not going to commit myself."

"Oh, that's clear John. We're past that."

"... I'm not hostile."

"No, I understand that . . . You and I are gonna stay friends no matter what," I lied.

"Well, of course, of course."

"... But, uh, I'll kiss your ass on a hot day in July if anybody can speak for my vote!"

That was one commitment I wished to avoid. After summarily rejecting my offer, Johnny Dougherty turned around and asked me to be on his finance committee so I could raise money for him. He wanted me to spend my money and bust my balls so he could beat a veteran politician whose vote I might be able to buy. Not on this planet. The phone rang. It was Ball.

"This guy's got us all standing and saluting the flag. He's clean. Get him outta here."

I validated his parking ticket and sent him on his way.

Dougherty strolled out of my office and ran smack into Bobby Raymond in the reception area.

"This guy's met me at least a dozen times and doesn't recognize me? He's got to be senile," Raymond cracked in the reception area as I ushered him into my lair. Once seated, Bobby launched into another pitch for Rich Scheffel.

"Tony, he can get done what you want to and he will not fuck you! . . . I mean Scheffel and I, absolutely, I will not lie to you, we do some deals together . . . Your deal and his deal, you know, your deal with him is your deal with him. Your deal with me is your deal with me. I don't wanna know anything about his deal. I don't want him knowing anything about mine.

"He knows where every button is, where every body is buried," Raymond continued. "He knows who to push and what button to get what . . . Probably the most controversial bill he ever got through was his chiropractor bill. You probably can't fathom how controversial that was. Every major insurance company in the United States came down in opposition to this bill. They hate chiropractors. They didn't wanna be forced to pay for chiropractic visits . . . This bill set chiropractors on the same playing fields as doctors . . . I mean, I watched him kill cigarette tax last year, I mean, the bill never even got up to committee, just boom, dead. The beer industry, Anheuser-Busch and all, they're all, you know, they're all constantly in . . . legislation and all that kinda shit . . .

"More of my concern though, Tony, and the reason I wanted to come by here is, I don't wanna cut my own moves off here to fight my case, okay? I mean, I see us having a long future together. Frankly, I wouldn't have taken the money from you the other night if I hadn't made up my mind that you were good people. You could help me get to where I wanna go and I can help you get to where you wanna go. Rich Scheffel to me is a tool. A very valuable tool to get there . . . I tried to keep you well-versed. I mean, I probably talked to you more this week than all the rest of these people put together."

"Exactly. I'm thinkin' of hiring you as a lobbyist," I joked.

". . . See [Scheffel] won't lay out studies and this and that. He will lay out, for instance, he's gonna say, 'I want you to let me go out and hire some people and put together a media package.'"

Don't blink, I thought. Here comes Bobby's next move.

"Now I'll tell you one of the people he's gonna recommend to you that he hire is my wife's company. Not because she's my wife. Because she's the best in town at doin' this shit . . . He said, 'First I'm gonna talk to Sheri and see if she'd do it.' My wife kinda sometimes gets off on these fuckin' moral tangents, but she loves to gamble and things. Thinks it would be wonderful to have casinos, but I gotta be real careful with my wife because she's very fuckin' high, whatever you call it, ethics."

I could see where Raymond would have a problem remembering that word. The conversation moved from his high-minded wife back to his low-minded lobbyist pal. "Can you endorse him that strong to where I could believe that the money is gonna go where he says it's goin'?"

"Let me answer it this way. Rich Scheffel and I have done enough business together to land both of us in jail for a long, long time."

I'm sure that popped open some eyes in the fourth room. ". . . How would I direct money through him? PACs? Super PACs? Finance committees?"

"Finance committees. He'll be on everybody's finance committee . . . For instance, the chiropractors, he had a $100,000 budget for 'em in campaign donations. I mean his organization is a flat 450 chiropractors. They had $100,000 and he directed every dime of it . . . this race, that race, and other races."

That was an intriguing revelation. If Rich gave everybody in the legislature a legitimate $220 from the chiropractors, that would total only $19,800. If they bundled checks with the chiropractors' husbands and wives, that's still only $39,600. The chiropractors must have done some serious legislative manipulation.

"And see, he knows, Tony, where [the money ends up]. Like I said yesterday. If you gave Meredith money, that's comin' after me."

"I'm well aware of that and I won't give Meredith money," I lied. I'd already given the majority leader nearly ten grand. I was also backing Sue Laybe's opponent. Tony was an equal opportunity briber.

"See, Rich knows all these little, I mean they're everywhere, all over town, there's little deals . . . He delivers his end . . . makes $450,000–$500,000 a year . . . in a legal way . . . I don't think there's probably but about two other people that Rich does the kinds of deals that he does with me. One's [House Majority Leader] Art Hamilton and he is a major key to this. Rich does business with Art. I mean, Art travels all over the United States and Rich takes care of it somehow. Art makes $20,000–$30,000 a year in speaking fees for R.J. Reynolds, for Anheuser-Busch."

David Horwitz interrupted our meeting with a call. I took it as he had hell to pay for sending me Honest John Dougherty.

"It wasn't the way you had thought it was," I lectured. "So I had to let him head back to Yuma or wherever he's from with his briefcase . . . The dialogue wasn't right, David, so I just had to do the right thing and tell him it was nice seein' him and go with God . . . Obviously, that ride you [two] took, you didn't drive far enough."

"I guess not," Horwitz conceded. What I didn't tell the union man was that if Honest John Dougherty did the right thing and ratted me out to the attorney general, Horwitz was cooked. Horwitz was cooked anyway, but now he was cooked either way, sting or no sting. I shook Horwitz off the line and returned to Bobby. We discussed all the commotion that I'd started by sending Shiree to the party with Ernie Hoffman. Bobby said everyone was buzzing about Hoffman waltzing through the Republican fund-raiser with a "gorgeous blonde" on his arm. As we spoke, the phone rang. It was Ernie. I took the call because I needed to chew him out for sending me Leo Corbet.

"I let [Leo] walk," I explained. "He walked on empty. I prefer he stay that way as far as I'm concerned."

After I hung up on Ernie, Raymond had some startling things to tell me about my expensive lobbyist.

"See, Ernie has a habit of showing up with these very young gorgeous women. Well, he rents them."

"He rents 'em?"

"Yeah."

"From where?"

"Some dating service around town."

"Are you serious?"

"Oh yeah . . . He showed up with one, Tony, swear to God. I mean, God strike me dead. Before the session was out. We were having this, I forget now, what the hell it was all about, but we were having this fight over some bill and it was some tax bill that Ernie was involved in. He shows up at the legislature with this probably twenty-one-, twenty-two-year-old. I mean absolute knockout. Miniskirt, you know . . . and she's sitting in the gallery. But see, I saw him a couple nights before with the same broad. I asked Hank the bartender . . . is it his daughter? He said, 'No, no, no, far from it.'"

"So now Shiree'll be classified," I said, loving that. Shiree strutted around at a big gubernatorial fund-raiser, proud as a peacock, oblivious to the fact that everyone there was whispering about her being from "Hot Blondes for You, Inc."

"Southwest Gas Corporation and Arizona Public Service is coming after my ass pretty hard," Raymond said, shifting to his own affairs.

"Really," I said, wondering what happened to the Jesus People he previously said were after his seat.

"And they're dropping some pretty big money into my opponent. They're gonna try to take me out. Over environmental shit. 'Cause I kicked Southwest Gas outta my office last year . . . We've identified these different corporations as polluters and we're startin' to go after 'em. Well, Southwest Gas came at me last year and said 'Look, we can't stand this! We're a good corporation. We're good people' . . . And I said, 'Yeah, you polluted the fuckin' groundwater in my district and the people don't like it!' 'Yeah, but we need to be taken off this list.' I said, 'Well fuck you! . . . Out!'"

Whoaaa. I was shattered. Bobby Raymond was a closet environmentalist? The man who said "there's not a single issue in this world I give a shit about" risking his political life to butt heads with some powerful and vengeful corporations determined to blot his name out of the legislature book? That was noble. That was heroic. That wasn't Bobby.

"They're all of a sudden putting big money into my opponent. I mean the president and the vice president and all the lobbyists and you know, are all writing personal checks. They're takin' a shot at me."

"What do you think Laybe's chances are?" I asked, too disillusioned to dwell on the concept of Hero Bob.

"She's in rough shape."

"I hope she hangs on . . . She's a nice person. I like Sue."

"Except she talks too much."

". . . With time," I suggested, "if she learns how to play the game, you see, she'll open her mouth in the wrong spot and then Art Hamilton or a Bobby Raymond or somebody'll bite her in the ass and she'll say, 'Whoa, I gotta stop talking.'"

"That's like an everyday occurrence for the last two years," Raymond said. "I mean, I bit on Sue's ass so many times it's like my teeth have dulled on her!"

Bobby and I discussed what to do about Candy Nagel's big mouth. He said not to worry, he'd talk to her. Everybody was talking to Candy. The problem was, nobody was keeping Candy from talking. That discussion led to Gary Kaasa, Candy's fixer.

"He's making me up like a bible," I said, describing his "my issue as a candidate" booklet. "And you talk about getting fucked, he charges $1,000 to candidates. He's charging me $2,500. So there's a case of what you're talking about . . . He's playin' a little hide the weenie with me, but it's all right. I can live with it."

Raymond advised me not to overestimate the intelligence of Arizona's legislators. ". . . There's a lot of stupid people. I mean, there are people, Tony, that you would sit down and they'll sit down and they'll talk to you, and you'll wonder, 'How did they ever get there?' It's absolutely frightening."

". . . Listen, we both agree on one thing, pal, and that's, I don't do issues either. I live for the deal," I said.

"I like it!"

"I live for the deal. The deal excites me. I'll get out of a sickbed, oh I love it. I wish I had a picture, I'd pay $5,000 today for a picture of Shiree walkin' around on Ernie's arm. Wouldn't you?"

Raymond left without any more cash, but with what he must have felt was the key to Tony's safe. His bagman, Rich Scheffel, was playing coy, but I had Scheffel pegged for a major player. I wanted to bring him on board. For the first time, the cops and prosecutors balked. They didn't think I needed another expensive lobbyist on the RICO funds dole. I knew that I'd have to bring Scheffel in and get him to spill some solid dirt before the cops would give me the okay to sign him up.

Detective Ball called Saturday and said the police transcribers were unable to keep up with the material I was producing. They were working full shifts typing the video and audio tapes, and were still fifteen video and fifty audio tapes behind. Ball encouraged me to take a day or two off to let them catch up. I gave him lip service, but there was no way I could slow down. This snowball was charging down the mountain on its own. I later learned that the transcribers had talked among themselves about taking out a contract on my life. I'm chatty, no question about that. Some of the transcripts were coming out with the politician saying "Yes," "Right," and "Ummm," and "Okay" while I talked for fifty pages. What they didn't realize was that I had to keep the conversation going until I hit the person's comfort level. Sometimes, like with Laybe, it would be a quick toast. Others times, like the Ritz Carlton meeting with Bill and Ernie, it could take seven hours.

Ron Tapp called on Monday, October 15, as he always did on payday. It was remarkable how far I had come in the six months since first hooking up with him. He was now virtually useless to me. I'd have long ago cut him loose, but the cops wanted me to keep giving him his weekly grand to buy his silence, even though he was doing absolutely nothing to earn it.

Ernie Hoffman was in town and delivered something like a hundred copies of a pre-study outline. I mentioned my meets with Rich Scheffel. As I expected, Ernie wasn't happy about it. He said he broke Scheffel into the business and then when he went on a trip to try and save his marriage, Scheffel stole all his best accounts. He said Scheffel would use my gambling issue to further his own ambition. Like Ernie wasn't? He added that with Scheffel aboard, he wouldn't be able to call the shots like he was doing now. I didn't recall awarding him that power. He seemed deflated so I stroked him by assuring him he was still my main man.

Jim Davis, a voice from the past, called late that afternoon. He apologized for losing the justice of the peace race and claimed that the ballot box had been stuffed.

"I was set up and sunk," he insisted. ". . . Right now, I'm just doing closet work, lookin' for skeletons."

". . . I just wanted to confirm with you, that 'situation' of mine'll be comin' up some time soon . . . so I wanna be sure that you're still with me," I asked, reconfirming the murder contract.

"I'm still with ya and I still got some other stuff that I'll just need to stop and talk to you about. Like the one you're lookin' for is available and there's options with it and so I need to explain the options."

My mind spun. What the hell was he talking about? What was I buying from this guy? There were two contract murders, I remembered that, but what else? "Options?" What would this guy be selling? Orphans! That was it. Unregistered guns. I'd forgotten. I told him to bring them on.

Detective Ball gave me some infuriating news at home that

evening. He said the police had decided upon a new procedure regarding the surveillance operation. Instead of gathering in the room prior to a meeting, Detective Ball would be the only one there. Then, after the politician or lobbyist entered my office, the rest of the surveillance team would be summoned. This was supposed to reduce the manpower load.

"Are you insane?" I raged. "That's a recipe for disaster! Laybe would be in and out with $20,000 before anybody made it to the room! She'd bump into Sergeant Davis and Keppel in the hallway."

"It's not a perfect world," Ball said. That was his standard tag line any time some garbage from above was sent down the line of command.

"Whose idea is this? Captain Black? He's the only one who would think of something like this."

"It's police business," Ball said, leaning on his other favorite line.

Representative Jack Jackson, the Navajo, called on the sixteenth to arrange a meet for the following day. Shiree strolled by at four in a corduroy skirt and white blouse, flashing flesh and steaming up the fourth room. So far, however, she was proving to be all sizzle and little sale. I hadn't heard word one from Sbrocca. I decided to turn up the heat.

"I need to get away," I said. "I need to find a nice girl and take her out of town for the weekend. Do you know any nice girls?"

"I know only one, honey. I'm the only nice girl I know."

"Do you know any nice girls?" I repeated.

"I know what you're saying 'cause I'm about to pull my hair out."

Actually, even if I'd been so inclined, a weekend romp with Shiree was out of the question. The cops and prosecutors expressly forbid me to be alone with her for even a second. A sheet dance between an undercover agent and one of the players would compromise the entire investigation. Shiree, it was quickly determined, was far too great a temptation to risk even a few stolen minutes of electronically unchaperoned time. So our activities were confined to double-entendres and mental masturbation.

"Bill English and I are like this," she said, crossing her fingers.

"... Who's on top?"

"You're sick, Tony ... I'd like to sit on that couch and watch you, you'd have to be invisible, and watch you conduct these meetings. I bet it's hysterical."

"It is," I confirmed. The meetings, as I went on to explain, could also be a drag. "The [football] game just starts to get good. Philadelphia's turning the game around. Guy calls me at 8:30 and keeps me on the phone for one hour. But he's an important candidate so I gotta listen to him, one hour! And I thought, 'Oh man, this is Shiree calling me and she's in heat. She's in season.'"

"You're sick," she squealed.

"She's calling me and she's gonna say, 'Come over and massage me and I'll massage you' . . . but it was a guy . . . I joke with you, remember that. I love you."

"I love you, too."

This was getting thick.

"I want the names of the bars where you hang out 'cause I'm gonna go out one night and find you and embarrass the shit out of you . . ." I said. "Come in and scream, 'You stole money off the dresser and you left after charging me $200!'"

". . . Only $200? Don't embarrass me about that."

Shiree sashayed to the ladies room. The phone rang.

"Get her to take her top off," one of fourth room boys joked.

"If she did, you guys would come through the wall."

"You know what I did," Shiree said when she returned. "I leaned up against the counter, got all wet."

". . . Well, take that skirt off and let me hang it up," I said as the dull thud of cops and prosecutors fainting from heart attacks vibrated through the room. Shiree laughed and declined.

Don Kenney had arranged a lunch intro on the seventeenth with Representative Jack Jewett of Tucson. We gathered at the Black Angus at 1 p.m. I was double bugged—a listening device was planted in the cellular phone and another inside my beeper. The game plan was the same as before. Kenney would lead the witness through lunch, eat my dessert, then excuse himself so Jewett and I could get to the illegal stuff. The skinny on Jewett was that he was making another run for House whip and needed to salt his supporters to gain their support. Jewett was a tall, lanky, Ivy League–type snotty rich kid with dark hair and no lips. We weren't five minutes into the conversation when I realized that Kenney had led us to the slaughter. The revelation came as Jewett ordered milk with his barbecued chicken.

"I'm personally not involved in gambling," he explained. "I never had, you know, that strong a feeling one way or the other. But I do have a strong feeling about the character of the state, and how that would change the character of the state. And that would be the essence of my reservation, and probably lead me toward not being, you know, one who would embrace your program."

This meeting was going nowhere. I ordered two pieces of cheesecake for dessert and pushed one on Kenney, despite his protests, to keep him from mooching mine.

"Well, I'm gonna let you two guys visit and thanks again for your time, Jack," Kenney said after dessert, breaking for the door. I couldn't believe he was sticking to the game plan even though the meeting was going down the crapper.

"Do you see this as something that might come across your desk, that you would be tempted to throw in the drawer?" I asked Jewett when we were alone.

"Yeah," he said. That got me steamed. He was telling me he would bury my bill. "On the other hand . . . if I'm personally opposed to something, but there's a great deal of support for it, it's gonna go. With me or without me . . . What bothers me, Tony, I think the opponents are going to be almost desperate. You know, that moral, religious thing that undoubtedly will be a factor."

It was a bad meet. Don Kenney had sealed his coffin six ways to Sunday. If Tony was a sting, he was done. If Tony was real, then Jewett's almost certain run to the attorney general would result in an investigation that would jackhammer Kenney from that angle. The wily, horny Mormon legislator had left himself no way out. I felt like kicking Kenney's hemorrhoids from his ass to his throat.

As I later learned, Jewett did exactly as I predicted. The next day, he ran right to Bob Corbin, the attorney general. Jewett reported that he suspected that I was bribing legislators. Corbin asked Jewett if he would wear a body bug to a future meeting. Jewett said he'd consider it. Jewett also ratted out Kenney as his contact, and added that Kenney told him that he would not be able to vote yes on my issue because of his religion. That was news to me. Fifty-five grand, and this dessert-mooching son-of-a-bitch Mormon was planning to double-cross me! Jewett's action kicked off an investigation into J. Anthony Vincent that was leaked to various legislators and thus spooked some of those dancing on the edge. Even so, I knew investigations of that nature were slow, painstaking processes. When and if it eventually reached the county attorney, the two agencies would have a sit-down and quash it. Plus, Corbin was a lame duck who would be history in a few months. His investigation probably wouldn't get anywhere before the change of command. Tony had been grievously injured, but not killed.

Bobby Raymond came by again that afternoon. He was getting to be a regular on my couch. As usual, he started hard pimping his man Rich Scheffel ad nauseam, along with his wife, Sheri. Raymond was playing three ends against the middle, taking his own money, then tripling it by pimping his team. Slick.

"Understand about these Indians," he opened, briefing me on the upcoming meet with Jack Jackson. "You can count on me to deliver his vote . . . I'll get him something like $2 million worth of fucking school buses or some kind of increased medical benefits or something like that in exchange for his vote . . . The only thing you need to say to him is, 'I'm sensitive about that [the reservation] issue, and when we put a bill out, it will be something that you'll like.' That's all you need to say . . . Give him $440. Legally, okay, because they're dumb people, Tony. And he could fuck things up."

Raymond shifted from how he hammers the Indian legislators to how he and his gang would control Terry Goddard if Goddard won the governorship as expected.

"Terry can be handled. He's got some lessons to be taught . . . It's like, [Art] Hamilton hates Terry Goddard. Absolutely hates his guts."

"But he supports him."

"As do most of us. You know, we don't like him, and we'll jerk his chain real hard. I mean, first year he's there . . . until he learns he's gotta deal with us. I mean, frankly, nobody down in our humble surroundings gives three shits about what he thinks. He's got to deal with us!"

"Can he veto your bills and fuck you back?"

"Well, he can, but it's just almost like written in the Bible that a Democratic governor does not veto a Democrat's bill . . . He's got to count on us to get his legislation passed. We killed some of Rose Mofford's shit last year. She didn't want to play with us, we killed some of her shit. That's just the way it works . . . Mike Sophy is the real power behind Terry Goddard. Mike Sophy is the guy who does the deals. I mean, Terry's got a campaign manager by the name of Jim Howard and another bimbo over here that is in charge of something else, and you know, ten other people over here in charge of other things, and then in the back of the building there's an office with no name on the door for . . . Sophy. He is the one that controls Terry Goddard and everything that goes on . . . One of the reasons he's always kept in the background is he was Bruce Babbitt's deal maker, and he got busted one night for soliciting a prostitute. He's Bruce Babbitt's chief of staff . . . the dumb shit pulled over and solicited a vice officer! And they busted him and shit, it made headlines . . . He resigned. I mean shit, it was headlines for days."

". . . Stragalas told me, and if it's true Terry's a shoo-in, told me Symington is $200 million in debt. If that's true, then he's finished," I interjected.

"Symington's in deep shit over this [building] project and several others," Raymond confirmed. "Yeah, he's in deep shit."

"How can he profess to the state that he, as a businessman, can pull them out of debt when he's got himself in $200 million?" I wondered. "Imagine what he'll do to the state?"

". . . You look at the latest polls, Goddard's pulling away from him."

To his credit, and my wonderment, Raymond had yet to say word one about the rumors of Goddard being gay, and how that might affect the pending election or the legislature's power over Goddard afterward. I knew that, like Laybe, Raymond had heavy support in the gay community. For all his myriad faults, Bobby was hip to "politically correct" thinking.

". . . When we start in on that bill, I'm gonna have to say, 'Okay, Tony, we're gonna get this through for you and then you're gonna have to give me a job in your organization, 'cause they're gonna kick my ass off next election' . . . You'll have to have a Gaming Commission, or whatever they call it . . . One of these mornings we're gonna sit down and talk about, down the road, how we grease this board or how we grease the appointments to the board 'cause you're not gonna want a major battle of the licenses . . . See, we control the fucking Liquor Board," he continued. "I mean, we put this asshole out of business a while back. Guy by the name of Jack Cox . . . Great Alaskan Bush Company, a titty bar out on Grand Avenue. He moved in here from Alaska . . . He hired the best liquor license attorney in town and you know, the guy had a lot of money and was going after the best and the brightest and he fucked up . . . He failed to list a conviction on his liquor application . . . It's automatic, you fail to list a conviction for something, I mean, you are denied, period, boom . . . I kinda tend to believe the guy when he said, 'It's a deal that happened years ago. I flat forgot about it' . . . He bopped some guy, beat the shit out of some guy in a bar, and got convicted for assault, whatever, anyway, he didn't put it down and they torpedoed his license. So he reapplied and then he proceeded to start a threatening process . . . He threatened me . . . [Senator] Lela Alston, and then he made the big mistake of threatening Art Hamilton. Art had him physically removed from the House by two DPS officers . . . We broke that fucking guy. We absolutely fucking broke him!"

After Raymond left, I phoned Kenney at his home and chewed him out for the Jewett intro. He countered that I needed to meet my enemies as well as friends, and claimed Jewett was only turned off because he didn't like Bill English and Ernie Hoffman.

"Don, I thought you were going to scrutinize these people a little bit . . . I mean, I had difficulty not puttin' my fork in his eye! . . . He's talkin' about the attitude of the state . . . This is the last guy in the world I shoulda sat with, he's the kiss of death for me!"

"Well, ya know, we need to find these guys out first and early so you know who your opposition is."

"... Better you find out than for me to sit with 'em!"

"... He knows about your issue now. You can't expect to get a close of sale in a six-dollar dinner every time, Tony. You knew that upfront."

"You're missing my point! ... This is a guy I'm supposed to meet after the general ... He's a frightening guy!"

"So he wouldn't even make any commitment to you about ..."

"Fuck no! He made a commitment that if he got a chance to shelve it, he would."

"He actually said that?"

"Yeah, there you go, now you're coming to life ... All I'm sayin' to you is, qualify these people a little better before I sit with them, so I don't have to get, I got raped. That's what he did, he raped me! ... If we were in Nevada, or if I was in my turf ... the paramedics would still be there trying to get the fork out of his eye!"

"... I'm sorry you were put through that, Tony. I thought he was more amenable."

As I drove home, I tried to figure out why I was starting to take everything so personally. It had been the roughest week by far, dancing with Corbet and getting slammed by Dougherty and Jewett. But why should I care? If these guys were honest, I should be happy, not furious. It didn't hit me until I was in bed that night. This had gone far beyond an investigation into dirty politics. I was fighting for Tony Vincent's life. The instant the investigation blew, Tony would be just as dead as if one of the Mob's gorillas blasted him with a clip of .45 slugs. Of course, the Mob's messenger would also be clipping Joe, but who the hell knew where Joe was anyway. Tony was the living being operating inside my body—and his existence was in grave danger.

15

My friend Johnny Rulli called from Vegas on October 18 to say that a paddy wagon full of our old Pittsburgh pals had been taken down by the FBI for everything from drugs to murder. They got nailed because a mobster's grandson got busted, entered the witness protection program, and then buried them all. I was glad I was out of that treacherous life.

Don Kenney materialized in my office with Representative Jim Hartdegen, a sixteen-year veteran Republican from Casa Grande. Hartdegen, the original "unsophisticated whore," Kenney had told me about, was a good ol' boy Will Rogers–type who had served some heavy combat duty in Vietnam. He was about five-eleven, with sandy gray hair and mustache, eyeglasses, and a laid-back manner. When he wasn't legislating, he worked as a safety inspector for a mining company.

Kenney got right to the point.

"I talked to my friend, Jim, and he needs to get another mailing out. He estimates it's gonna cost about $2,500 and I suggested he just run it to Ernie and let Ernie handle it."

". . . Yeah, I'll call Ernie and just let him do it," Hartdegen followed, swallowing the hook before I'd hardly said a word. "I'm being targeted by the Environmental Group of Life, the Sierra Club, Greenpeace . . . this ENSCO situation . . . kind of an unknown factor."

Environmental Systems Company (ENSCO) was a hazardous waste–burning facility in the early stages of construction in southwest Phoenix. The environmental groups and area residents were raising such a stink that the politicians responsible were ducking for cover.

Interestingly enough, one of the lobbyists who helped grease the ENSCO bill through the legislature was Ernie Hoffman. Hartdegen had supported ENSCO and found himself on the environmentalists' shit list.

". . . All right, so Jim, we definitely have a yes vote, I mean, I have a sponsor, and how do you want me to help you," I offered. "What can I do for you?"

"Well, I'll talk to Ernie . . ."

". . . Do you have any names?"

"Of what?"

"Names, just of people. I have money. I don't have names."

"Uh, yeah, I'm gonna hafta work on that . . ."

"Well, what do you think your bottom line is that you need to sponsor a vote? . . ."

"I don't think it would cost over $2,000 for this little mailing . . ."

He was cooked. The only thing left was to get him the money. I wasn't comfortable with running the money through Ernie. Although it would be a clean bust either way because Hartdegen was personally confirming the deal, too many things could go wrong when the cash starts taking detours. I took a stab at a direct buy.

"You prefer I just give the money to Ernie or you prefer I give it to you? What do you wanna do? Whatever you wanna do."

"Let me talk to Ernie and find out."

It was clear that Ernie was pulling Hartdegen's strings.

The long-lost Al Hill called during the meet and said he was on his way to Copenhagen to purchase kiddie porn. I bid him farewell and wished him luck. A few minutes later, Kenney made his move for the door so he could leave me alone with Hartdegen. Before he left, Kenney set his own hook.

"Okay, you will arrange to get him the $2,500 through Ernie?"

"Yeah," I confirmed.

"So that you pay for this?"

"No problem."

Out in the hall, Don Kenney ran smack into Deputy County Attorney Jim Keppel. The prosecutor was heading for the fourth room as per the new, after-they're-in-my-office decree. It didn't take long for that asinine directive to blow-up in our faces. Although Kenney and Keppel had met in the past, Kenney was preoccupied and showed no sign of recognition. Keppel waited until Kenney ducked into the bathroom before vanishing into the fourth room. Smooth.

Meanwhile, unaware of the potential disaster in the hallway, Hartdegen and I continued our chat. The conversation loosened after Kenney left, but Hartdegen remained convinced that the money should route through Ernie.

"Yesterday, I met the prize asshole of the legislation group . . .," I said, discussing one of the anti-casino legislators.

"Is he in the legislature now?"

"Total asshole, yes."

"Bobby Raymond?"

"No. Bobby's pro-gaming. Jack Jewett!"

"Oh Jack . . . Yeah, Jack's full of bullshit . . . We can neutralize him."

Jim left with no cash, just an agreement to work through Ernie. As I feared, the Tony-to-Ernie-to-Jim deal hit a snag and never came off. Hartdegen later decided he didn't need to waste money on the mailer. Without cash changing hands, there was no crime. He had slipped away—for now.

Rich Scheffel followed at three. He brought a strategic outline and made a big push for Bobby Raymond's wife and her video company. He also informed me that he had decided to accept me as a client. For that honor, he wanted a cool $20,000 for the remaining seventy days of 1990—some decent coin considering that the legislature wasn't in session and the period included big chunks of Thanksgiving and Christmas holiday time. After that, he wanted $90,000 for 1991—the combined salary of six state senators. Rich was talking big bucks, but still wasn't doing anything to incriminate himself. I said I'd get back to him.

The cops wanted to stall Scheffel until we dumped Ernie Hoffman in January. I argued in favor of hiring Scheffel earlier. Who knew how much longer Desert Sting was going to last? I wanted a fresh horse to carry me to the finish line. After arguing with Detective Ball, it was clear that the only way the cops were going to okay Scheffel in 1990 was if he spilled his guts about all those things Bobby Raymond said they did that could put them both in prison.

Jack Jackson appeared for his sit-down on the nineteenth. His appearance was quite an honor. Jackson would soon become the invisible legislator. He was in the process of preparing for the 1991 session, during which he would miss 231 roll call votes, or 37 percent. The newspapers lambasted him, but I was sympathetic. He represented the Navajo reservation in northern Arizona. I'm sure none of those 231 votes meant anything to the Indians. In fact, probably 99 percent of the votes he did show for had nothing to do with his people.

Jackson looked like the Indian in every cowboy movie ever filmed, only his hair was shorter and he was in a cowboy suit. I did my casino rap and he sat stonefaced. I handed him some of Ernie's outlines and he barely moved. He did say, however, that he thought he could support my issue.

"I know Bobby Raymond is a pretty levelheaded guy . . .," Jackson said. "I asked him for support on this bill that he helped me [with], and I in return, I'll help him with his . . ."

The meeting had to be cut short because Jackson had to get back to the Indian Rodeo at the state fair—where, interestingly enough, my wife's multiheaded sunflower was competing for a blue ribbon.

". . . Be thinking about if there's anything I can do for you," I offered.

"Well, I'm running again."

"Are you?" I bit.

"The only thing is, I have some financial problem there . . . trying to get back down here next term."

"Well, if you're gonna be a favorable friend of mine, then I certainly would wanna keep you in office, wouldn't I?"

"Sure . . . I'll be back down next week and I'll give you some kind of answer."

Jackson left for the rodeo, and I never heard from him again. I was glad. That was one prospective member of Tony's rainbow coalition that I wasn't keen on recruiting. The white man has backstabbed the Indians enough. We didn't need to ruin another one by snaring him in a police sting. That wouldn't be politically correct.

Bobby Raymond was back in his reserved seat within an hour of Jackson's departure. I started off by handing him two cashier's checks totaling $1,100 for Terry Goddard's campaign. Raymond said he would deliver the money to that hidden back office where Goddard's fixer, Mike Sophy, operated the controls of the Goddard political machine like the Wizard of Oz.

"You decide if I should meet this guy and when I should meet him," I said. "'Cause I do deals. He does deals. You do deals. The Dealmakers. Call it the 'Dealmakers Meeting.'"

Raymond revealed that the latest rumor about Tony going round the House was that I was an FBI agent. Someone claimed to have discovered that there was an agent named Frank Anthony Vincent based in San Francisco. I picked up the phone, called the San Francisco FBI's office and asked for Frank Vincent. They said they had no agent by that name.

"There you go," I said. "Tell whoever started that one, 'Misfire. Start again.'"

We meandered conversationally to the on-field performance of my quarterback, Don Kenney, particularly the rash of critical interceptions he had thrown. Representative Bill Mundell could be a problem. Nagel was trouble. And Jack Jewett was big trouble. All were Don Kenney productions.

"Fuckin' Kenney," Raymond said. "I'd tell him: 'You ever do that to me again, friend, I'm gonna pull your mustache out one hair at a time!'"

Bobby was starting to talk more like a gangster than me.

"You know Kenney, for all of his wearing his morals on his sleeve, he's as big a fucking sleazebag as I am," Raymond confessed. "Or bigger!"

". . . He's not as bright as you are," I flattered. "He doesn't know how to do deals. He wants to do them, but he doesn't know how."

Raymond said something during this meet that gave me and the fourth room crew considerable pause. In talking about how he quashed rumors with Nagel, he mentioned checking me out with Ralph Milstead, the former head of the Department of Public Safety. It wasn't clear whether he had actually tried to do that, or was just stroking Nagel. However, there was little doubt that Raymond knew Milstead and could get information. That was another crack in the Desert Sting dam.

"There's a lot of unsophisticated whores . . ." Raymond said, swinging back to his two favorite subjects, deals and the mental short-comings of his fellow lawmakers. "They don't know how to beeline. I mean when a deal walks up, somebody walks up and hands 'em a deal in their lap, it scares the living shit out of people!"

The phone rang. It was Shiree. She had an uncanny way of calling when Raymond was around.

"No, be careful," I said, playing to Bobby. "I don't want you fallin' in love with me. Remember what I told ya. I got a bad back and I'm an old man."

". . . I can't help myself, Tony," she said breathlessly. "I'm coming over right now. And I'm undressing on the way!"

Bobby left shortly thereafter with the twin $550s for Terry Goddard. Shiree didn't show, dressed or otherwise.

Carolyn Walker phoned early the following week and said she was going to the Virgin Islands for Thanksgiving. Glad to see Tony's money was going to good use. I then broke for a sit-down with the cops at the apartment. They said that they were nixing the Rich Scheffel hire because he mentioned that he would have to drop two conflicting clients, both racehorse breeders, if he came with me. They were worried about a lawsuit. I said that was bullshit and pointed out that if

I didn't hire him, it would anger Raymond and fuel more sting rumors. I argued that we needed to hire Scheffel to bring everybody back to their "comfort levels." It was a stalemate. When Scheffel called later that day, I stalled saying there might be problems with trying to blend him and Ernie on the same team. Scheffel suggested we all get together and sort things out.

Tapp stopped by with Tom Mason, a small, soft-spoken man who edited and produced a Republican party newspaper and was angling to become the Republican party state chairman, that is, another George Stragalas, only on the other side. I told him I didn't want any ink on my issue yet, and he agreed. He ran through the legislative directory, telling me who he felt would vote yea or nay, but failed to spice his comments with any decent gossip. We agreed to meet again.

Shiree called me with news that she was going to bring over the "next state treasurer." Instead of Stragalas, she was referring to his rival, Tony West.

"All right. I'll see this guy [West] at 2 p.m. tomorrow."

". . . You're gonna die when you see him," she laughed. "He's got the biggest butt I've ever seen! Oh, it's huge, Tony. Make sure you have a good chair that'll fit him! . . . It reminds me of the 'Saturday Night Live' skit with the big butt family."

Shiree called again later that evening to tell me that West was "very receptive" to meeting me, and that "his eyes tell me he's a player."

Tony West arrived on time at 2 p.m. for his sit-down. Shiree hadn't been exaggerating about his build. He was a short, rude, fat former senator with a huge rear end. As we said our hellos, I couldn't help focusing on his protruding belly. If he joined with Team Tony, just feeding him was certain to break our RICO budget. West plopped down and grilled me.

"Do you know [Stragalas]? . . . Let me ask you something, where's your background? You were born in Reno? . . . How long were you with them [Summa Corporation], twenty years? . . . Who are the four (associates)? . . . Be prepared for a full background check on yourself and your associates . . . Why open it statewide rather than along the river? . . . Have you talked to the political parties? . . . Did [Sam Goddard] want money for the party? . . . How old are your kids? . . . Boys or girls? . . . When are you comin' public and gonna take a high profile of yourself? . . . Who you got carrying the legislation, that's important? . . ."

Please stop it! No more! No more! I cried in my mind. I did it. I killed Jimmy Hoffa. Chopped him up and buried him under Goofy's House at Disney World. Please, Mr. West, no more!

"Do you see this [gaming] as somethin' you'd be able to maybe live with, Tony?" I parried, squeezing in one of my own questions.

"No."

"Do you have a problem with gaming?"

"Yeah. I have a problem with what I perceive it would do to our state . . ."

Then what the fuck are you doing here? I thought. West continued to hammer away, focusing his attention on my relationship with George Stragalas, his opponent for state treasurer. He had lots of information about our meetings, including the one with Sam Goddard. I told him I'd met Goddard alone, just to screw up his head.

"I have a high-level name," West bragged. "I have high name identification. See, I served sixteen years on the judiciary committee of the House and Senate. All the organized crime legislation introduced in Arizona, I was either the prime sponsor or cosponsor."

"Good for you," Brooklyn Tony cracked.

"Including all the narcotics legislation."

"Good for you . . . You know, what I admire about this state the most are the RICO statutes," I countered, praising the law that's the bane of every wise guy's existence.

"I helped put those in . . . Tony, where are you livin' at?" he went on, sticking the bamboo shoots under my fingernails. Sergeant Davis had called in a dozen or so questions back ordering me to "get this guy out of there. He's interrogating you! Get him out!" I had allowed West to continue a while longer partly because I fed on the mental duel and mostly because I loved annoying Davis. But I didn't want to push it too far. I escorted West out of my office.

Regardless of how long I kept him there, I knew West's next move would be a run to the attorney general. His sole intention in meeting me was to see who his opponent's benefactor was, and then burn us both. Shiree now joined Don Kenney and David Horwitz in performing the anatomical feat of cooking her own ass. She fed me a rat that turned and bit her. Unlike the others, however, I wasn't too mad at her because she was an amateur at this political intrigue stuff. Plus, if Shiree knew how to read a guy from peering into his eyes, as she had claimed with West, she wouldn't be constantly complaining about being screwed over by men. In any case, four days later, West rang the attorney general and dropped the quarter on Tony. The state treasurer hopeful covered for Shiree somewhat, identifying her only as a Chamber of Commerce employee who worked for Tony Vincent on the side. Some cover. It would take about five seconds to make her based on that description. West told George Weisz, the attorney general's investigator assigned to the case, that he knew of Vincent's meetings with George Stragalas, and added that he had contacted a reporter for the *Phoenix Gazette*. That last revelation was the most damaging. A newspaper story would spell sudden death for Tony and Operation Desert Sting.

I was feeling irritable when Raymond and Scheffel arrived separately for their sit-down. I wanted to hire Scheffel, and I needed him to stop playing Captain America. Raymond arrived early and briefed me on Tony West.

"He has been caught up in more land swindles and real estate schemes than I've got fingers on my hand. He is a dangerous son-of-a-bitch . . . He's crooked as a snake. But he will fuck his own mother, I mean, this is the kind of guy that will take a bag of money from ya in one hand, and go to the attorney general and blow the whistle on you with the other . . . All that freeway land . . . that's how the [Mecham] impeachment all came about. I mean, there's some heavy fuckers involved in this land fraud. Some of 'em were prominent folks in the Department of Public Safety . . . One of Tony West's best friends is a guy by the name of Ralph Milstead, . . . now one of Mofford's administrative assistants . . . They were all involved up to their ass in this thing. Mecham started to uncover this shit and started to expose it. That's when they went after Mecham. I mean, this is a dangerous son-of-a-bitch."

"What do you think the chances of Stragalas beatin' him are?"

"Zero."

Raymond displayed a renewed interested in the person who linked me with West—Shiree. This time, it had nothing to do with his wife leaving town. As I suspected, his interest in her was more than physical. He had gotten word that the Chamber's independent campaign committee, known as Vote PAC, was preparing a hit piece on him.

"If you told her to do something, you wanted it done, do you think she'd do it? . . ." he asked. "See, I don't know whether to trust her or not. You know her, I don't know her. I wanted to take her out to dinner so I could spend two hours talkin' to her and figure out whether I can trust her . . . Pussy's fine and it's fun, but it doesn't buy a thing with me. You know what I mean?"

"We do think alike," I said.

"If they're gonna do a piece, I need to know about it and I need to know what it is."

". . . No problem, buddy. I trust her."

"The opinion of Shiree is she's a very nice person, always seen in the company of high-rollers, has very expensive tastes and doesn't make anything working where she's working . . . I think she could be pretty valuable inside that Chamber. And that's why I want her, you know. That's why I wanted to have dinner with her. Frankly, it didn't have anything to do with pussy."

I rang Shiree and left a message for her to call. The talk turned to Art Hamilton, the powerful House minority leader who controlled dozens of votes.

"I would have to caution you, 'cause if you hand Hamilton ten grand and say, 'This buys your vote, and it buys X amount of other votes,' he will flip back over backwards. And he will say, 'Fuck you! I don't need your money!' He would go off."

According to Raymond, Hamilton's payments had to be washed through the Democratic party and everything had to be on an unspoken basis. I'd get my votes, and he'd stay insulated like an old Mob capo. That was fine if Tony was real. But as the front man for a police sting, it wouldn't do. In order to make a case against the "Big Kahuna" as Raymond called him, I had to hand him the money and get him to say the magic words. From everything I was hearing, that was going to be tough.

"The bottom line here is, without him here, I'm payin' a guy a lot of money to go take my money and buy the votes, but yet I don't have any control," I protested. "And he's the hero."

"He's the hero? Fuck bein' a hero! You get your law. You get your casinos. Fuck this hero shit. Heroes come and go."

Good point, Bobby. Still, I had to covertly sell my true agenda. "My point is, if they should decide to fuck me, he's still the hero with them guys 'cause he'd give 'em the money."

"I guarantee you, as big a scumbags as there are in that legislature, ain't nobody gonna commit and then run backwards . . . There are these things that we call laundry lists," Raymond tutored. "You want me to vote for this, I gotta have this. Art is the master at the laundry list. Somewhere on the laundry list will be your bill. He will trade people that you don't even know that are gonna support you. Like Jack 'The Fuckin' Weenie' Jewett. Jack 'the Weenie' Jewett wants some big transportation bill out. Art Hamilton goes to Jewett and says, 'Here's what I'll trade.' He doesn't produce five votes, he produces thirty-one votes! . . . It's the same theory like we got the chiropractor bill out this time . . . It was on a laundry list . . . Maybe I'm the one that puts it on the laundry list and I withhold my vote on any budget or any tax bill, until I get my gambling bill . . . And the better you are at getting your laundry ticket punched, the more successful you are down there. I got everything I wanted this session."

". . . The problem is, I don't know if I can live with this laundry ticket thing," I argued. "That's what's bothering me . . . I mean this could realistically, between [Hoffman and Scheffel], you're talking $200,000–$300,000!"

". . . You're not gettin' anything for $200,000–$300,000 that you couldn't get for twenty or thirty. That's what I keep trying to impress with you."

Bob was oblivious to the fact that most of the $200,000–$300,000 to which I was referring consisted of Hoffman and Scheffel's retainers, not the bribes. I guess that money didn't count.

Scheffel arrived and asked how I was feeling.

"Well, my back's hurtin' me," I answered truthfully.

"Is that right? I can recommend a good chiropractor."

I'll bet, Rich. About 450 of them! Each more crooked than a hockey player's teeth. Rich started into his rap. Bobby cut him off.

"All right guys . . . I've got two friends here. Cut the fuckin' bull-shit!"

". . . That's the greatest man I met in this state, sittin' right there," I said, pointing to Raymond. "That's the only honest man in this state!"

"Yeah, he talks pretty straight," Scheffel understated.

". . . We'll take him from lobbyin' to governor," I promised. "If Rose Mofford can make it, he can make it."

"Rose made it from spreadin' her legs to governor," Scheffel said, loosening up. "She took a good long time to, fifty years."

Shiree returned my call. I asked her to get us the hit piece on Bobby. She readily agreed.

"Carved in stone," I said to Bob. "She ain't sayin' a word."

"Good."

"She has a great ass," Scheffel cut in. "Oh I mean, she's got a great ass!"

Scheffel certainly was cutting the shit. In fact, we were all ready to get down and dirty. I pounded away on the bagman issue. "I'm gonna pump money in for this mommaluca and I'm not gonna have a commitment from him? What do I look, fuckin' goofy? Would you? If I took you guys right now to a high line whorehouse, would I pay the whores and you don't fuck 'em? Let me have some pussy."

"Fuck yeah, somebody's gotta have some," Scheffel agreed. ". . . When you give somethin' you make sure you get the credit for it. If you don't get the credit for it, why are you givin' it?"

"Rich, that's all I'm tryin' to say."

". . . I don't know where you've been swimming, but I'm in this pool here and it ain't ten thousand and twenty thousand per pop," Scheffel said. "[Representative] Jeff Hill needs the money, Bobby Raymond needs some money and I gotta list of people . . ."

"Let me cut to the quick. If this was you with Jeff . . . how would you handle that situation with me?"

". . . I'm gonna level with him. I'm gonna bring him up here. You're gonna have a nice social conversation, and we're gonna give him the thousand bucks. And he's gonna be grateful as hell . . ."

". . . All right, so I'll give the thousand bucks, and he's outta here. Does he know it's my money?"

"You bet your ass he knows."

"How does he know that?"

"What'd he come here for, to look at ya? You're not that cute. He came here to get your money."

". . . What have I bought for my $1,000? . . ."

"You bought a vote. You bought his support. Or what we like to say . . . you bought his ear."

Bingo! Conspiracy to bribe a politician. Another lobbyist bites the dust. The phone rang. It was the fourth room.

"Okay, you got your wish," Sergeant Davis said. "He's cooked. Hire him."

Scheffel went on to discuss bundling checks, buying legislators for less than Hoffman's price, and then went through the legislators directory and wrote prices besides the pictures of the targeted lawmakers. Among those designated to receive a bundle was Bobby Raymond — another bundle for Bobby! Scheffel laid out his master plan, which included bribing the legislative leaders and having them control their forces. I told Marie to get "Carmine." That was a sign for the cops to call. Sergeant Davis did, and I bullshitted for a while, making sure they definitely wanted to hire Scheffel. They did. I hung up and informed the lobbyist that my partners gave the word to bring him on board. Scheffel pulled a contract out of the air like David Copperfield.

"Holy shit! You already had this thing typed up. Boy, was he sure of me," I said to Raymond. "Well, I guess he shoulda been. All I wanted him to do was tell me the truth."

"Well, I'm tryin'," Scheffel said. ". . . Let me ask you a delicate question. Close your ears again [Bobby]. If we were to run payment of Sheri for the production services through my books, do you have any problem with that?"

"No . . . I was gonna pay her cash anyway. It don't matter."

"Yeah, I'd rather do that then. This is none of [Raymond's] business."

"Whatever you wanna do."

The talk turned to the anti-casino forces.

"Fred DuVal might be a snitch for some outfit in Vegas," I said. "We gotta keep an eye on him. He's an enemy."

"Oh, he's a good friend. We'll deal with him," Scheffel promised.

"Well, you'll like him better after I disfigure him. When his arm's up like this and he's a cripple sellin' papers out there, he'll realize you don't go up to a stranger and say, 'I'm gonna have to fight you.' Wrong. Bad move."

". . . Bobby and I were wonderin' if you had given thought to packaging legalized prostitution in this bill," Rich joked.

"Only in the sense that you and Bobby and I would have private stock. And first chance refusal."

Rich and Bobby said they'd be back the next day for the contracts. A couple of real eager beavers, these two.

16

When Representative Jack Jewett ran to the attorney general, he set off a wave that would quickly build to a crescendo. Within eight days, Tony West, Speaker of the House Jane Hull, and Majority Leader Jim Meredith would all follow in Jewett's path. On the surface, it appeared to be a bizarre coincidence. In the first eight months of bribing legislators, not a single politician or lobbyist had rolled on Tony. Then, in eight days, four went running. Upon closer inspection, it was business as usual. Politicians, like lemmings, tend to march together in crazed packs, even to their own destruction.

Of those who went to the attorney general, Hull and Meredith were the most surprising. I'd never laid eyes on Jane Hull. Kenney bandied her name around a few times, but she'd never come in. The Speaker, like a mother hen protecting her legislative flock, merely had to catch wind of the rumors to prompt her to reach out to Attorney General Bob Corbin. Corbin asked her if she was willing to meet Tony Vincent while wearing a wire. Hull said she'd be happy to. Corbin told her not to discuss the matter with anyone.

Meredith's visit was an even bigger mystery. Hull had learned that Meredith had met with me and suggested that he contact Corbin. Meredith meekly followed her order. The majority leader thus lifted the art of cooking one's own ass to new heights. He had walked out of my office with $9,300 for his promise not to shelve my bill, and here he was scurrying into the attorney general's office. Meredith gave state investigator George Weisz a version of our meet right out of *Alice in Wonderland*. He professed to have made no deals, denied taking any money other than the cash for the Symington fund-raiser, and even denied being "sympathetic towards Vincent's issue." When pressed on why he accepted $2,200 in cash for the Symington dinner, Meredith was described as becoming "visibly nervous." During this meeting, Meredith mentioned that he heard that the Capitol Police—whoever they are—were investigating George Stragalas' connection to Tony Vincent. He also tossed in that a reporter from the *Arizona Republic* was after him about something.

From all reports, it was a lousy performance. Meredith did little but heap suspicion upon himself. Most troubling, however, was the information regarding the Capitol Police investigation, and the news that a second journalist had been tipped off about Tony.

On Wednesday, October 24, Detective Ball gave Marie $19,000 to purchase a bevy of postal money orders and cashier's checks to spread around and help seal the fate of lobbyist Rich Scheffel. The bundles didn't include the $20,000 in cash I'd soon fork over for Scheffel's retainer, or the extra $1,000 Bobby Raymond wrangled.

Rich landed in my office at 3 p.m. I signed contracts and lobbyist forms, then doled out the $20,000 cash.

"I got names. We got some names. Bobby's got names. He wants to come over, if it's okay," Scheffel said as pocketed the money.

"This is not a state where you gotta go and hit people with twenty grand," he continued, speaking for everyone but himself. ". . . I'm glad I'm on board, Tony, I gotta tell you, you're a hell of a nice guy, but in this kinda business you gotta know how to deal with these guys. Leo's [Corbet] thought was, you wanted to buy his vote."

No shit.

". . . You don't say, 'Here's the money. Where's the vote?'" my new employee taught me. That technique had worked pretty well up to then, but I understood Scheffel's point. I had already nailed the "unsophisticated whores." Now we were going after the sophisticated ones.

To clean the checks designated as contributions, Scheffel jumped on my phone and began a series of calls asking people to let him use their names. Included were some of his chiropractor friends. Although it was illegal to allow ones name to be used to cloak someone else's political contributions, Scheffel didn't receive a single turndown. The Arizona system had been greased right down to the local shoemaker.

"These [legislators] care about one thing," Scheffel said. "They wanna get reelected. They wanna gain influence. And they wanna set themselves up if they can for some good. That's the agenda with most of 'em."

That sounded like three things to me.

Raymond showed at 3:50 p.m. and instantly enlivened the proceedings. I was becoming fond of the glib representative. His entertainment value was off the scale. He immediately wanted to know the latest on the alleged Chamber hit piece. I tried to explain that Shiree's espionage determined that it wasn't a smear. He wouldn't hear of it. Thinking that a little cash might soothe his anxiety, I handed him the $1,000 Scheffel had him down for, plus another five dollars to pay for the postal money orders. I wanted to give Marie a break and get him to do his own bundling. He grabbed the bills — both the grand and the fiver.

"Marie, is she tapped out?" Raymond inquired, hunting for names.

"She's maxed out more than I am. I used her cat on a few people," I said.

The chatter sank from politically conscious felines to Arizona's chiropractors.

". . . [The] two guys that went out and raised all this money for the chiros . . . they saved a little back for themselves . . . " Scheffel said. "You know who they gave all their money to this year? [U.S. Senator Paul] Simon and some of those . . ."

"Hey, that doesn't count," Raymond cut in, meaning that Simon's stash didn't count against the money the chiropractors could give him.

"It counts for them. It's been comin' outta their pocket. You know what kind of money they gave Simon? Ten big ones. He's hearing their bill in a subcommittee."

"Who's Simon?" I asked, seeking a clarification for the record.

"The Senator from Illinois . . ."

"They're into the big-time crooks," I laughed.

"Yeah," Scheffel confirmed.

Raymond steered us back to what was in it for him — info on the alleged Chamber hit piece.

"I've had a couple of real nasty people call [them] . . . Vern called and said, 'Y'all do a hit piece against Raymond . . . we might be inclined to pull our little fat ass right outta the Chamber!'"

"I could pull a couple out on that one," Scheffel seconded.

"And I'll cancel my membership!" I thirded. Boy, we were gonna show them Chamber of Commerce goons that they can't mess with our man Bobby! What power. We weren't gonna break legs and cut off horse heads, we were gonna pull our dance cards!

Despite my blind leap aboard the revenge bandwagon, I was confused. Shiree had insisted that the pristine Chamber didn't do hit jobs. Why was Bobby so perturbed?

"Do they do a hit list? Is that a lie?" I asked.

"Scumbags!" Raymond answered. That was short and to the point, but wasn't quite the informative response I was angling for.

"Is it a lie?"

"Yeah it is."

"By not endorsing you and praising your opponent?"

"That's the same as a hit," Scheffel explained.

"A hit piece, in the sense of, they put out a piece callin' me a child molester or something, no, maybe they wouldn't do that," Raymond elaborated. "But they do this piece: 'Well, Bobby Raymond screwed you on this, and screwed you on that, and voted for this and voted for that, which is Bad! Bad! Bad!' And then [they] expound the virtues, on the other page, of your opponent. To me, that's a hit piece! . . . If we can get our hands on it, by the weekend, if in fact they're gonna do it, I could do a piece to counter it. That's what I mean. And we got a printer and everything that's kinda like on standby."

Scheffel grabbed the phone to canvass for more names. This call was one smooth hustle, a textbook example of a master political bundler in action: "Hey, Terry, how you doing? Well, I'm doin' great. Hey, you remember what a great American you were when we needed some help with [ex-Representative] Burton Barr? And we had to make some extra contributions? I gotta make some extra contributions now to the state Democratic party and to about five or six legislators. Would you and Cindy be kind enough to allow me to use your names on those contributions? Well, I'll tell you what, they're goin' to the party and how they use those is beyond me. So, yeah. Now, what I'm gonna do is you don't have to pay anything. Yeah. A thousand from each, you and your wife, to the state Democratic party . . . Here's what I'm gonna do. I'm gonna tell ya who these people are just so you're at your comfort level . . ."

Everybody in the state seemed to have his or her own comfort levels.

". . . We're gonna do . . . [Senator] Jeff Hill," Scheffel continued in his pitch to Joe Citizen. "[Representative] Debbie McCune, [Candidate] Hershella Horton, [Representative] Karen English, and um, Jim Hartdegen. That's it . . . and you're the contributor . . ."

"Oh God, I feel better now," Raymond said. "We've all committed felonies."

Raymond's confession hit me like a slap. My mind spun. I was unprepared for his next salvo.

"Can I just ask one question? It's the only mystery I have left. What's behind this wall?" he asked, pointing in the direction of the fourth room. I had a whole rap planned for such a moment. The cover was that the fourth room was where I kept the confidential files of my overseas casinos. But all I could think of was Raymond's admission that he and Rich had committed felonies, and how that seemingly damning fact fed his comfort level.

"I have no idea," I ad-libbed brilliantly.

". . . And there's this door right out here and this is 'Private.'"

"That's part of the suite next door, I believe." Seven months of anticipating that question and all I could come up with was "the suite next door"? The "Private" door was right next to mine. The "suite next door" was down the hall. My story sucked. I had dropped the ball, and I hadn't even been hit! I was spending so much time with these addled politicians that I was starting to lose my street edge. I needed to get my teeth kicked in to keep me sharp. Thankfully, Scheffel finished pistol-whipping his friends and got off the phone. I directed Raymond's attention back to bundling.

"He's got a signed contract. He's paid, and everybody else is paid," I said. "That takes care of it."

"Time for us to rock 'n' roll," Raymond beamed.

Every once in a while, it was necessary to remind these guys who they were dealing with. The more Brooklyn Tony stories I wedged into the conversation, the better the bust would hold up in court.

"I shoulda been a lobbyist," I opened. "I'd've been great. Take the guy outside, put a gun to his head: 'How you gonna vote?' And he'd say, 'Well, how do you want me to vote?'"

As the talk wandered to shrimp, mushrooms, and back-end action, Raymond seized the moment to inform us that he had finally decided what job he wanted in Tony's casino hotel empire.

"I want the position of the number-one deal doer. The number-one fuck over!"

He was certainly qualified.

"Do me a favor," I said to Scheffel, growing serious. "I'm gonna ask you for a favor. With the people that I'm givin', like Art, we'll separate these checks and do what we gotta do. We'll have Art's package ready and it'll be presented to him like a gentleman . . . Let me give 'em the money when I meet with him."

"Yeah, sure. Absolutely."

"See, it's like, nobody wants to pay the whore after they fuck her. Think about that."

Before they exited, Scheffel said he set a lunch date with Leo Corbet for the upcoming Friday. It appeared that I was set to waltz a few more times around the floor with the master.

Detective Ball caught me at home on October 25 to give me the news that Corbet's land deal sting had hit the papers. The undercover detective who headed the operation was John Berentz, the same guy who had originally recommended me to the county attorney for the social gambling operation that started it all. Small world. Scheffel canceled the lunch date with Corbet. Although the wily senator would never be indicted, much less convicted — as I predicted — the newspaper slam made him too hot to handle. Ironically, the public revelation probably saved Corbet from the claws of Desert Sting. He may have been on the verge of taking a package from Tony. I had been wrong about the old alley cat. He was only up to his eighth life.

Ernie Hoffman was upset when he called next, and it wasn't about Leo. He said a friend of Bill English's had tipped him off that the attorney general was investigating me. That news hadn't taken long to spread. Ernie wanted an emergency meet later in the afternoon. I informed Ball and he gathered the forces at noon in the apartment. When I arrived, the whole cast of good guys were there, Ball, Keppel, Mount, Davis, and Black. They laid it out to me. After Jewett and Hull ran to Attorney General Corbin, Keppel and Black had a sit-down with Corbin and his chief investigator, George Weisz. They spilled the beans on Desert Sting. Although Corbin promised to keep it under wraps, the cops and prosecutors were seriously considering shutting the operation down. I felt the life, Tony's life, draining from my body. My hands began to shake and I became dizzy. I got a grip, dug into my soul, and pulled Tony back into the picture. Joe's fear was replaced by Tony's fury. I thought it was ill-advised to go to Corbin. He was a lame duck riding out his last months. His investigation would have gone nowhere. Leveling with him did nothing but open the door to leaks. Corbin would be out in the private sector in eight weeks with knowledge of the state's biggest sting. If everyone had just kept cool, it would have taken months for the new attorney general to acclimate to the job. And once he settled in, how long would it take an investigator to dig up information on a man who didn't exist? Desert Sting could go on another year before the attorney general's office made sense of it.

After softening them with that argument, I started throwing the big punches. To shut down the operation at that point, with so many new fish on the line, would constitute selective prosecution. We couldn't just toss Bobby Raymond and Don Kenney in jail, and arbitrarily allow Jim Hartdegen and Art Hamilton, Alan Stephens and all the others circling Tony to walk. The defense attorneys would have a field day. We'd lose everybody. As for Hull and Jewett, I reminded the cops and prosecutors that my forces were already at work "neutralizing" them.

"Okay, we'll go on. But we're going to monitor this very closely," Keppel announced.

Before we broke, Keppel took me aside and shook my hand.

"I don't know anybody on this planet that could be doing what you're doing," he said.

I welcomed the compliment, but I couldn't help feeling there was a lot of stroking involved. There could be a lot of trouble in Tony Vincent's future thanks to the sit-down with an outgoing attorney general and his chief investigator. In politics, everybody looks to gain favors. It would be a miracle if Desert Sting wasn't leaked to selected politicians. As it was, the investigation into Tony Vincent wasn't even a week old and it was already old news at the capitol.

What my white-hatted friends failed to tell me was that Jim Meredith had also run to the attorney general, and that Tony West would check in the following day. They had even sent Detective Ronald Sterrett to the session with Meredith. Why they only told me about Jewett and Hull remains a mystery. Whatever, I was steadfastly determined that Tony Vincent would have to be carried off the battle-field on his shield.

Don Kenney was flying high when I met him later that afternoon at the Black Angus. Speaker Jane Hull had assured him he would be chairman of the judiciary for the upcoming session. That was a powerful position, and the mustachioed Mormon was all but glowing. Oddly enough, Kenney knew nothing about the attorney general's investigations. I decided that there was no need to tell him and rain on his coronation. Kenney, flush with his new political duties, wanted to bench himself on Team Tony.

"I think we need to reassess our game plan and let Scheffel be the primary quarterback," he suggested.

Although I had grossly overbribed him, and probably should have demanded more for the $55,000, I let it slide. Replacing him with Scheffel was a good move. Plus, Kenney had thrown three devastating interceptions in the clutch and brought the attorney general down on me. He belonged on the bench.

During lunch, Kenney produced what would be a first in a series of hit lists on his political enemies. The lists grew nastier with each new generation. This forerunner contained six names and opened with the comment: "Tony: I think we need to do a thorough background check on the following individuals who are likely to be leaders of the opposition to your cause." The names followed: Representative Brenda Burns, "a righteous do-gooder" who "would step on her mother to get ahead"; Representative Kyle Hindman, "a real frightening wacko"; Representative Patricia Noland, "has been married three or four times, real emotional, has been sucked in by the right-wingers"; Representative Don Aldridge, "wishy washy"; Jack Jewett, "we need to neutralize his opposition"; Candice Nagel, "just in case." Along with the stinging adjectives, Kenney wrote the names of people who were either political enemies of, or merely hated, the targeted legislators. This included former opponents and ex-spouses. It was a mean list, and Kenney was just getting started. It was also strange that an attorney would put such a damning piece of evidence in writing.

". . . I think it's important for our cause to have a background on these people thoroughly investigated," he said. "I want to know who they have been sleeping with . . . This little bitch, Brenda Burns, she's the type, you know . . . She's married. She's had kind of a flashy life. If you had to set priorities, I would think hers is number one."

Burns was Kenney's chief rival for the judiciary chairman seat. He had been warned that she would go ballistic when she heard that he had gotten the plum appointment. The warning had obviously shaken him. I concluded that all the other names on the list were mostly a cover.

Kenney spoke on the perils of political ambition. I relayed an old wise-guy credo: "I can live with greed. I can live with corruption. I can live with bribery. I can live with whores. I can live with whatever. But an ambitious man is a dangerous man."

"Well, Brenda Burns and Jewett are both ambitious," he cautioned. Kenney went on to explain why he needed a hammer on his fellow legislators.

". . . The way we've done it before . . . These assholes say, 'Hey, you set up a meeting with Tony, you vote and we're gonna blow the whistle on you.' I wanna be prepared [to say] . . . 'Let's lay our hands on that business you have in Kansas. You want that to come out?' . . . I want to vote. I want to participate, but I don't wanna be put in a box with these assholes and caught with my pants down."

I informed Kenney that a P.I. in Reno named Denny Davis—D. P. Davis, as in the Sergeant—was my chief hatchet man. I promised to put Davis to work on his hit list, then left to meet with Ernie Hoffman at the apartment. I was anxious to squeeze Ernie for everything he knew about the leaks. He was pacing the parking lot when I arrived. We made our way to the apartment.

"[Leo Corbet's] dead for Senate president," Hoffman boomed, his thunderous voice even louder and more charged than usual. "You oughta hear the talk out there. They said over their dead body . . . The

Democrats . . . They're doing a hit piece. I mean, they're gettin' one out real, real quick."

"What would you do?"

"Oh, if I were out to win, I'd go right for his balls. Gotta do it."

Ernie downshifted to his other troubled politician.

"Bill [English] called in a panic . . . He said, 'I'm not 'spose to tell you I had this meeting. Bullshit. I gotta tell ya. It's the Speaker.' Now, the Speaker said this meeting never occurred and 'if I ever hear it back again, you're dead.' That's what she told Bill . . . Sat him down. Locked him up for an hour. 'I'm gonna talk to you about your friend, Tony Vincent. The AG's [attorney general] got it. Corbin has it and they're doing a complete investigation' . . . Somebody went to the AG that you had talked to . . . I'm tryin' to pinpoint who the hell would be an asshole to go over there and say, 'I wanna turn this thing in.' We're thinkin' about Jewett, it could be. We're thinkin' maybe even Meredith, in spite of him comin' into your office . . . And Bill said, 'What the hell could they do to me?' I said, 'Nothin'! Absolutely not a thing!' . . . Incidentally, and Bill told me that last time, the eighteen on advance of my fees hasn't been touched. I said, 'Bill, I'll tell you right now, that's an advance fee. I've got it and that's it.'"

I was impressed with how Hoffman had nailed the attorney general rats right on the button, especially Meredith's asinine move. I'd never have guessed that. I was ticked, however, over how he was frantically trying to rationalize taking my $18,000—even with me. In his mind, it had now officially become an advance on his fees. I had given the money for English's vote. You can't put the bullet back into the gun.

". . . We racked our brain. We talked, Bill and I talked, all night, back and forth," Hoffman said. "Bill was scared shitless. In fact, I kicked him out of Phoenix. I said you get down there and start hittin' the bushes. Be in every radio station, cuttin' spots, 'cause if they're gonna do a hit, it's gonna break, something's got to be done before the election."

It was becoming increasingly clear that Bill and Ernie didn't have the mental toughness to handle even a wade in this particular hot water. That was surprising. Of all the people snared in Desert Sting, I figured these two old war horses, with nearly a half-century of political maneuvering between them, would be the coolest of the bunch. I needed to pump some steel into their backbones.

"They're allegedly investigating me, is that it?"

"Yeah."

"Okay, I can live with that. I'm cleaner than a baby's ass."

Banking on the moves I just learned from Don Kenney, I asked Hoffman if he had any dirt on Speaker Jane Hull.

"She wants to be Speaker desperately again . . . What she's askin' me to do right now is go out there and bundle money, put it together, everything, and she said, 'I don't care how you do it.' I said, 'You wanna be Speaker?' And she says, 'Ernie, you taught me one thing, that's self-preservation.'"

". . . So she obviously has a comfort level . . ."

"Well, what I did to her, I said well, 'How would you want me to do it?' She says, 'Maybe we can work it through the party . . . Then you and I go down there and we tell 'em where to spend it' . . . See, we use the party to launder the thing, and then what I do, I go there and tell 'em where to spend it. That's illegal! That's against the law right there. You cannot earmark money like that."

"And she knows that."

"Oh yeah."

"You know what that tells me . . . that your comfort level with her is, you could just about leave her in the car while you rob the bank, and come out and give her the money, and she'd take it."

"Jane Hull probably would . . . I've always been like that with Jane."

"Is that illegal what she wants you to do?" I asked, after he related a few more stories.

"Well, what she wants me to do is go ahead and finance the campaign."

"Is that illegal?"

"Yeah, that's illegal."

"Then you own her."

Next up on Ernie's hit list was Tony West.

"I'll tell you who [went to the attorney general], it is Tony West. It's Tony West!" Ernie boomed, the light coming on upstairs. "There's no question in my mind now, because Jane inadvertently said West is right on top of it . . . I'll tell you what, if my name's involved in any way whatsoever, Tony would be the first guy to call and say, 'Hey partner,' 'cause we're very close. Tony's a millionaire. Are you aware of that? He's the number-one hog farmer in the entire Southwest. He grows more hogs than anybody. So he doesn't need money. He kept $35,000 when he ran for Senate and then retired. Instead of giving the money back to people like myself that have been knockin' our ass off, you know what he did? Kept it."

"That's legal . . . There's gotta be some skeletons in his closet."

"Oh hell yeah! . . . You know what he's done to me personally? While he was a legislator. He used to pound on me to rent the Tucson Country Club down there and bring in his personal clients and he'd pitch 'em for land deals and stock deals right in front of me. If the press ever got a hold of that son-of-a-bitch, he would've been in jail for some of the stuff he did down there. Using my facilities. I didn't know he was gonna do it. He says, 'Ernie, can you get me a little room?' I said, 'Yeah, the Tucson Country Club. I'm a charter member. Come on down and use my club.' I got the room and all these people show up and he comes in with this guy selling stock shares and what he did, he called up people that were doing capitol business out there. And I said, 'This is extortion, Tony. You're calling people out here to sell 'em this shit.' And he said, 'How else you gonna do these things?' I said, 'You can't use my club anymore for this. I'm not gonna be part of this. If one guy goes to the press, I'm in deep shit trouble by providing a place for you!' . . . This guy scared me to death."

"Now that tells me somethin' about his character."

"He went to your office the other day, and he went and saw Corbin . . . I'm puttin' the scenario together."

". . . Now you're telling me that while he was a state senator, he met with people at the Tucson Country Club and offered land deals?"

"Chiropractors, who he got a bill passed for. He called in all the doctors down there and made 'em show up. Gave 'em literature and then they were selling shares right there in the Country Club! . . . What's his name . . . showed up at the club and I had known him before 'cause he's a pretty big shot around the Republicans. I said, 'What the hell you doin' out here?' And he says, 'Well, Tony's tryin' to get started. I'm tryin' to help him on how to sell this.' I said, 'Yeah, but what you're doing, you're squeezing Tony's people that work at the capitol!'

"After Tony left the capitol, he got a deal . . . for private prisons. He went out there without registering as a lobbyist and went back to all his colleagues . . . and it hit the editorials, front page, 'Tony West lobbying without registering and has been asked to cease and desist.' It didn't come from the AG. It came from some other people. So Tony got his fingers burned."

"What were the deals he was tryin' to do at the Tucson Country Club?"

"You buy a big parcel of land, then you buy shares in that land as a syndicate. You're part of a syndicate . . . I'm a good friend of the guy, calls me in and pounds me then for ten shares . . . he said, 'If you do it in front of the rest of the people, they'll see it as a good deal.' I said, 'But I don't want your land!' He said, 'You cancel the order later' . . . That's like Tupperware parties. I said, 'Tony, I can't do that.'"

"He was using you as a Judas goat."

"Oh yeah."

"Now what's illegal about that?"

"The fact that he was using the people that he works for at the capitol, the people that he's getting bills either passed or otherwise. It was actually extortion. He was calling them up and saying, 'You gotta be here' and then he had the secretarial staff at the office doing it . . . He was very good to them on some bills coming before the capitol, so they owed Tony something . . . He tried to get the Department of Transportation to route the freeway so it would have an access [to the land] and so he went and intervened to the Department of Transportation. Got himself slapped on the wrist for that one . . . This guy's been involved, it's one deal after another and has gotten by with it, over and over again, 'cause his buddy is the AG. The attorney general would never press."*

"You're giving me some excitement because the possibility exists that the attorney general may come and talk to me," I said. "I love it! You know why? I'm pretty sure of my people. Number one, Don Kenney ain't gonna open his mouth. Carolyn Walker, Bobby Raymond, Chuy [Higuera], Bill [English]. Who am I forgettin'? I'm forgettin' someone."

"Sue."

"Sue Laybe. They ain't gonna chirp. I ain't worried about it. I'm so isolated and protected that it's frightening."

Ernie was becoming less anxious but remained pumped with adrenaline, which kept his lip loose and his voice booming.

"There are whores out there in the worst, worst way," he said. "I mean, it's a jungle the way they earn money . . . There is, like Alan Stephens right now, he calls me all the time. 'I need money.' Needs money all the time . . . Lela Alston chasin' me up and down the hall-ways today. She said, 'You got an extra two-twenty?' 'Yeah.' And that's all she said, so happy, she ran away. That was it. But people go for their own money. Now the only thing that Alan can do, he can call in lobbyists and say, 'Hey, I need some help 'cause I wanna knock off that Republican.' You know what we do in the lobby court? 'Fuck you! He's

*"That's all an unmitigated lie!" West says. "Ernie Hoffman is just puffing himself to Tony Vincent. All my business ventures are perfectly legitimate!"

already in and you're tryin' to tell me that you wanna help an opponent?'"

I understood that last statement to mean that lobbyists and their deep-pocket, corporate clients don't differentiate between Republicans and Democrats. They only care about the buttons being pushed on their issues. Thus, they'd rather keep an incumbent in office that they've already greased than help a party leader bring in new faces to shift the power his way. Of course, if a bill is divided along party lines, as some are, then the lobbyist will go after an incumbent in order to replace a nay with a yea. But that move could just as well come from within the party, that is, they'll flood the primary coffers of a rival Democrat looking to knock out a fellow Democrat. If that fails, then they'll back the Republican or Independent in the general election. Thus, the special interests get to take two shots at their enemies.

"Bill takes a lot of pressure," Ernie said, suddenly talking tough. "Shit, he's gone through shit, land sales, hell, they had the guy for soliciting prostitutes on Van Buren. Front-page picture! He don't give a shit. He's a trooper."

Before he left, I assured Ernie that I had a handle on all our problems and there was nothing for him to worry about.

I spoke with Scheffel that evening to get another view on the events of the day. He confirmed that there was a wave of panic washing over the state legislature because of the Corbet sting. The only one who wasn't panicked, according to Scheffel, was Alan Stephens.

"He just wants to meet you again . . . He wants some financial help on his own. And he is enthusiastic that you're gonna do something with the party."

Once again, the enigmatic Senator Stephens was going against the grain. When other legislators were enthusiastically approaching me, he was cautious and distant. Now that all hell was breaking loose, he was relaxed and ready for another sit-down. Strange little man.

17

By late October, Operation Desert Sting appeared to be drowning in a sea of rumors and conflicting leaks. The legislature was buzzing with the news that the attorney general was going to grab Tony, turn him upside down, and shake all the politicians and lobbyists out of his pockets. The truth was just as threatening. The out-going attorney general—an elected official—had been briefed on the sting. Could this lame-duck lawman and his staff be depended on to keep their mouths shut, or would they whisper words of warning to favored politicians statewide? My money was on the whispers.

And what about the sleeping dogs in the media? They had been tipped at least twice about Tony. No question, the *Arizona Republic* and *Phoenix Gazette* were blinded by their own sense of self-importance and stripped of their competitive fire by a merger. But even running on pilot lights, how long could the newspapers ignore the frantic wails of the legislators?

The assassins, real, figurative, or imagined, were coming after Tony Vincent from a dozen different angles—and still I motored on.

George Stragalas stopped by the apartment on October 26 to talk about his race, ask for more money, and feed me the latest, preelection dirt on Terry Goddard. Interestingly, I had not heard one word about Goddard's alleged homosexuality since Evan Mecham got bounced from the primary in September. Symington was thrashing Goddard on assorted other issues, but, as predicted, the Republican stayed away from the sexual mud. My pal George had no such qualms. He shoveled the biggest pile since Tapp and Hoffman got together and smeared Goddard over his so-called beard fiancée. But first, George wanted to revisit the case of Don Bolles, the Arizona journalist who was blown up in his car before he could publish an investigative article on land fraud.

"Besides Bolles, twelve persons associated with some of the land-fraud scandals have died over the past six years, all before they could testify. Five died in two separate plane crashes. One jumped off a cliff. Another succumbed to carbon monoxide in his automobile. Three separate fatal heart attacks. Another died of cancer. One was gunned down twenty-four hours before he was to testify before the grand jury . . . That's the story."

Some story. Welcome to the wild, wild West. Nice to know the tradition of sooners, claim jumpers, and bloody land battles would continue into the twenty-first century. After that trip down mortality lane, it was time to play smear-the-Goddards.

". . . There's a guy who says that he has pictures of Terry in sexual, uh, engagement with males."

"How do you sit with him?" I asked, eager to break a blackmail ring.

"I can't find him . . . Sam [Goddard] gave him money."

"The photographer?"

"No, he wasn't a photographer . . ."

"Who's the guy that allegedly has the pictures?"

"Bob Knapp . . . And there's another guy, Frank McGinn. Lives in Phoenix still . . . I'll tell you what happened. Terry gets on his bill some 900 calls where you call the 900, you can talk dirty, except it was to the males. So when it came in, [Sam Goddard] confronted Frank McGinn, who was Terry's administrative assistant, and said, 'What's these?' And he said, 'Terry made those.' He [Sam] says, 'Fuck, Terry didn't make those calls. You did, Frank!' And he tried to make Frank into a homosexual."

". . . And [McGinn] took the heat for the 900 calls?"

"Yeah . . . Terry fired 'im. And nobody saw Frank for about a year. Frank shows up at a Christmas party at Terry's office. At the law office. And Sam about shit and Terry about shit. And he was drunk, and he said, 'I'm just here to wish you a happy holidays' . . . He disappeared for like a year because he got a job. He tried to make some money. He got fired again. So he was angry at the whole world. So he figured, 'Well, I'll go in there and take my frustrations out. It's a holiday. I'm drunk.' He walks in and Sam said, 'Oh these families here and all these kids' and everything and he said, 'I wish Terry would find some woman.' And Frank said to Sam, he said, 'The kind of "woman" that

Terry would bring home, Sam, would not please you very much.' And [Sam] said, 'Those words are explosive.'"

That was an ugly one. If Stragalas is to be believed, this poor man was falsely painted as a 1-900-BOY-TOYS freak and then forced to take a nasty fall. And instead of crumbling into dust, he haunts them on Christmas Eve.

Stragalas left Terry's bedroom long enough to speculate on the latest major development in the gubernatorial race. President Bush had been scheduled to fly into Phoenix and spend the day talking up Symington. There was much speculation that Bush's visit would knock all the undecideds into Symington's camp. But, at the last minute, Bush stood him up.

"What do you think it did to Symington with Bush not coming in here?" I wondered.

"I think it killed him," Stragalas speculated. "Particularly, the next day he goes to California . . . I think they figured Goddard's gonna win . . . Pete Wilson is more important 'cause Feinstein in California might beat him and then if California goes Democratic, it'll go Democratic in the presidential . . . Symington's just an expendable thing . . . Symington hasn't been sharp . . . Terry's manipulated him around. And he's got a shitty staff."

Getting to his own little acre, Stragalas said he needed yet another infusion of Tony's cash to help him finish the state treasurer's race. He hit me for $5,000. The cops called and gave the okay. I told Stragalas I'd have it the next day.

Ernie Hoffman showed first at the apartment for the big confrontation with his arch rival, Rich Scheffel. Ernie wanted me to expand my office suite to include some offices for him and a staff. Scheffel arrived and I naturally offered him a phantom office also. He thought it was a swell idea. We had hardly finished our introductions and I'd already achieved my goal in uniting the lobbyists. They were united in their desire to lighten Tony Vincent's wallet.

I wandered into the fourth room after the lobbyists left and asked Keppel how things were going. Keppel looked at the floor and said they were again comtemplating shutting me down. Speaker Jane Hull had called an ex-legislator turned lobbyist named Joe Lane and bent his ear about Tony Vincent. Lane called Deputy Chief Benny Click and asked him if the operation was a sting. Click assured him it wasn't. We had narrowly dodged yet another bullet.

"We'll get through this," I said. "Don't fold our hand yet. It'll blow over."

Keppel suggested that I sew up the murder-for-hire cases with Jim

Davis and Ron Tapp. That was another nail in Tony's coffin. If they wanted me to "sew up" the loose ends, that meant they were looking to put a bow on this operation.

I heard from Al Hill that Sunday, October 28. He said he was back from Copenhagen, complained about the cross-continental flying, and claimed he had the goods—a tape with four, ten- to twenty-minute kiddie porn segments. The only trouble was that the tape was recorded in the European PAL system and had to be converted before it could be played on American VCRs. Al said I owed him $6,000 for the tapes, and wanted to know what his royalties would be. I told him to get the tape converted and we'd talk.

The sit-down with the Big Kahuna, House Minority Leader Art Hamilton, was switched from the Black Angus to the office of a political consultant. It was a move worthy of a veteran wise guy—always change the location at the last minute. I could deal with that. However, if part of the move was to get me to hire yet another lobbyist or consultant, I was going to be ticked. Scheffel arrived and collected $8,480 in bundled postal money orders that he said were for Hamilton to spread among his supporters. We then drove to Roots Development, a consulting company owned and operated by a guy named Rick DeGraw. I was instructed by Scheffel and Raymond, and the cops and prosecutors, to play this scene easy in order not to spook Hamilton. The cops decided to let the money walk without a hook in order to build goodwill and set the stage for a future relationship with Hamilton. Besides, there would be too many people around to try and say the magic words and drop some cash. In deference to his power, Art would be allowed to take the money and run.

Bobby Raymond was among those present when I entered the room. That was good. If Raymond could draw Hamilton into talking turkey, we'd be in business.

Art Hamilton was a hefty six-footer who reminded me of comedian George Kirby. I saw the eighteen-year House veteran in action on the floor of the legislature the day I visited the capitol with Gary Bartlett and had come away impressed. He combined eloquence with an imposing physical presence. It was easy to see why his fellow representatives held him in such awe.

When Hamilton wasn't running Arizona, he worked as a public affairs officer for the Salt River Project, one of Phoenix's two electric companies. It was probably a nice, cushy, Carolyn Walker–type job, only the power company, unlike Walker's phone company, no doubt knew how to use an employee in such an influential political position.

Hamilton's fixer, DeGraw, was a pleasant-looking man, about five-ten, with a dark hair and mustache. He was a political junkie of the first order. One of the walls in his office was covered with a collection of campaign buttons.

I wore a sportscoat and alternated between Brooklyn and Park Avenue Tony, eventually settling upon Brooklyn Tony because Art knew the streets. I gave him the Reader's Digest condensed version of my casino rap. Hamilton responded that the economics were promising, but politically, it would be a tough fight. He quoted an ethics professor he once had.

". . . The first thing he tells you . . . is politicians almost always overestimate the cost of doing the right thing."

The Kahuna offered other words of wisdom: ". . . We are lost in terms of where we wanna go as a state and frankly, it is clear to me, and I think to most folks now, that if we wanna do what we think this state wants to do, we probably don't have the economic base to do that. I think if there's anything that would give me hope if I were where you're sitting, it's simply in terms of we're flat on our ass . . . Bruce Babbitt was very much opposed to the lottery. But when the people passed the lottery, he was very big on how to spend the money . . . I think someplace down deep in our psyche there really is a realization that all that bullshit we talk about gambling being bad, we don't really believe it 'cause we gamble ourselves . . . It is as clean and as viable as any other industry . . . I'll tell you what I want to do . . . I'll be chairman of the Gaming Commission!"

Bobby Raymond didn't say six words during the entire hour-long give and take. Scheffel and DeGraw barely said more than Raymond. Their respect, or fear, of Hamilton was obvious. Meanwhile, I'd hit it off with him. He vigorously shook my hand and complimented me on my straightforward presentation. Although I hadn't snared him, I felt strangely satisfied. I had played it as if I was on the level and had won Hamilton's vote honestly. That wasn't my job, but what the hell, it felt good.

Scheffel chose not to present Art with the checks during the meeting. He said he mailed them instead, assuring me that the Big Kahuna would know it was Tony's money. As far as the law was concerned, that didn't count. Hamilton could easily claim that the checks were legal contributions from multiple donors.

The session broke in time for me to attend a mid-afternoon meeting with Al Hill at the apartment. Hill's latest move was as insanely inspired as his previous ones. He claimed to have contacted a company in Florida that was sending him a machine that could convert PAL tapes to NTSC, the American system. The special duplicating recorder would arrive the next day COD—$4,500 worth of COD.

Al also wanted to know about his back-end action. I told him that my people worked from an exclusive mailing list of ten thousand sickos who would pay $500 to $1,000 for a good, half-hour kiddie porn tape. Hill would get a generous 25 percent royalty on each tape, or a total of $500 to $750,000 within two months depending upon the quality. Hill's eyes nearly popped out of his head.

"Okay, what do you intend to give me, three finished products or one?" I asked.

"Three tapes."

"There's not four on there, there's three?"

"There's, what I think is on there is a series of like nine or ten different segments, okay."

"You done lost me, Al."

"In other words, the total tapes, I believe it's between forty-five and ninety minutes, I'm not sure on the total length. But each one has a ten- to fifteen-minute sequence, you know, story. So you maybe, you've got ten different stories. I mean nine different stories on one tape."

It had been like that for months with this guy. Every time he opened his mouth, a new story drooled out. Now he made his pitch for the money he'd need for the alleged COD package from Florida.

"Well, the only other thing I was gonna ask you that with the, I might need some immediate help though. For the . . ."

"Let me see the tape."

"No, I'm talking about for tomorrow though."

"Let me see the tape."

"Well, you can't see the tape 'til I buy the machine."

"Exactly. And you can't see the green 'til I see the tape."

"I know, but what I'm asking you now is that tomorrow . . ."

"I want the finished product. That's all I want to know."

". . . What I'm sayin' is that I actually . . . I'm out a lot more than that because I did the Vancouver trip. I paid for myself."

"How'd you pay for it? You still got my thirty-seven fifty!"

Al kept coming at me as if I didn't quite understand what he was saying.

"The only thing I'm having a problem with right now is that . . . I've spent a lot of cash these last couple of weeks, right. I'm tryin' to figure out if I've got the $4,500 for tomorrow . . . Now there might be a possibility that I might need some help with that, gettin' that machine paid for tomorrow COD."

"Al."

"It's a done deal at this point. I mean, I got the product here and it's good!"

"It ain't a done deal 'til I pop the tape in the machine and sit and look at it and say, 'yeah, yeah, yeah.' Then it's a done deal. To that point, it's up to you. Deal with it."

Sue Laybe interrupted our haggling with a call requesting that I dump a grand into a dinner for Richard Gephart.

"What's he running for?"

"No, no, no, he's majority leader, back in Congress."

"Oh, in Washington," I said, suddenly remembering the man with no eyebrows who ran for president in 1988. I explained that I'd just given Rich Scheffel $10,000 for the Democratic party. Sue asked if I wanted to give another grand so she could make the points with the Big Boys. I told her no, but added that I'd be happy to give her more for her campaign. She said that wasn't necessary. I guess her home renovations were completed.

"On the 4,800 bucks, I'm stretched for cash," Al continued when I hung up. He had tacked another $300 on the cost of the mystery machine. "I've got about a grand . . ."

". . . I ain't gonna buy no machine, Al . . . That's it . . . If you can't get it dubbed then bring it to me and I'll ship it to Australia. That's all I can do because I ain't buying no machine . . . See, if you would have come to me up front before you ordered that machine I woulda told you don't order no fuckin' machine."

Al asked to borrow my phone. He dialed a number and made arrangements for a local video company to convert the tape at six the next morning on the promise that they would do it without viewing the confidential material. The employee told Al that they receive requests like that all the time because big corporations do profit and stock presentations that must be kept secret.

"I'll tell him I'm involved with a diamond dealer and it's information about some diamonds for the, for the U.S.S.R!"

To cap off the meeting, Al told me the Danish tapes cost him 14,000 "yodas." May the force be with you, Al.

At Jim Keppel's direction, I then called Ron Tapp and said I had some serious business to take care of and needed to reach out for his hit men in Houston and Flagstaff. He said he'd get on it.

Stragalas was next on the horn. He said he'd been receiving obscene phone calls, which he attributed to his opponent, Tony West. If a monsoon destroyed Phoenix, Stragalas would attribute it to Tony West. He explained that he had aired some hit commercials — probably financed with my money — attacking West for his land deals.

He feared West's revenge to the point of paranoia. Stragalas was starting to lose it.

Tapp phoned later that evening to let me know that his enforcer from Flagstaff would be in town on Thursday. He would bring him by.

Al Hill rocked me out of bed the next morning wanting to set up a meet to deliver the goods. I told him to call me back later. He waited ninety minutes and rang again. I tried to stall until Friday, but he claimed he was leaving town and needed to drop off the goods and collect his "yodas." I thumbed through my appointment book. Stragalas was coming in for another $5,000 shortly before noon, and I had a critical lunch date with Alan Stephens. I told Hill I could squeeze him in at the apartment late that afternoon. He said he'd be there, smut in hand.

George Stragalas shot by for his next infusion of cash, then I got ready for my lunch with Stephens. Following Rich Scheffel's directive, the cops and I had prepared $4,180 in bundled postal money orders to take with me—$660 for Stephens' campaign and the rest for him to spread around to fellow legislators Representatives Karan English (no relation to Bill English) and Cindy Resnick, Senator Gus Arzberger, and candidates Catherine Jacobson and Stan Furman. The five were expected to support Stephens in his quest to hold his Senate leadership post. (Resnick and English were running for Senate seats.) I knew the staging at the Black Angus was bad the moment I sat down. We were given a table next to the busboys' station, probably the noisiest place in the crowded restaurant. Plus, there was a group of five women loudly celebrating a birthday at the next table. I had a bug in the cellular phone, so I plowed ahead, hoping that technology would prevail.

Stephens was so jittery when he arrived I suspected that he was wearing a wire and had been sent in by the FBI. Stephens attributed his anxiety to pressure over his campaign.

After some routine political chatter, I pulled the envelope containing the checks from my pocket and handed it to him. I explained that despite the elaborate bundling, it was my money and it was given to assure that he wouldn't shelve my issue. However, because he was so nervous, I said the words fast, low, and to the point. If you blinked, you missed it. I can't even swear that Stephens comprehended what I said or even heard it. He merely took the envelope, folded it in half with a shaky hand, and buried it in one of his pockets.

"Now he's maxed out. I'm maxed out, so you may recognize some of the names on there as other people," Scheffel said, explaining the need for bundling.

"Perfectly," Stephens said, nodding.

"Don't lose your race because of money, please," I said.

"So you're talking about the mailing, like I need to do. Just do it?" Stephens asked.

"Don't lose your race because of money," I repeated with a wink.

"Okay."

Finally, after eight months of dancing, Stephens was cooked—maybe. There were no high fives in the parking lot across the street after Stephens and Scheffel left. I knew the instant I saw the big frown on Detective Ball's face that something had gone wrong in the surveillance van.

"The transmitter screwed up," Ball said. "The tape may not be good. We won't know until we do a transcript. Don't worry about it."

Damn, I thought. Eight months with this guy down the drain. If the magic words I'd said so quickly weren't on the tape, he was free. If Scheffel played dumb—which he would if there was any chance that Stephens would survive—then it would come down to my word against his. Nobody would believe me. The senator would walk.

"Don't get down," Ball said. "Let's wait for the transcripts. Maybe it's there."

"Did you hear it?"

"No," he said. "But that doesn't . . ."

"If you didn't hear it, it ain't there."

Stephens was one charmed individual. The last time he called, when he requested $440 for Senator James Henderson, Jr., the tap on the phone malfunctioned. There was nothing illegal about that request, so no one sweated it. But twice in a row under widely varying circumstances?

I was in a rotten mood when I pulled up in the apartment parking lot for the video session with Al Hill. The con man was lingering in the lot, leaning against his maroon Porsche, eating some greasy fast-food and sucking on a Coke. He carried a white plastic bag in his left hand that contained four videotapes, the original PAL master, a full-length converted copy, and two edited copies of about forty minutes each. He was smiling like he'd just signed with the Raiders. I escorted Al to the apartment and popped one of the tapes into the VCR. For the next hour, I had to watch some of the most revolting images I have ever seen. There were little girls, known as "Lolitas," having graphic sex with little boys whose erect penises were the size of my pinky; little girls and little boys in the "69" position; little girls going down on little girls; little girls ramming their hands and arms inside big girls; little girls being worked over by grown men in every manner imaginable; little girls having sex with people identified as their mother and father; and little girls and little boys urinating on each other.

The titles said it all: "Teaching Lolita Sex," "Masturbating Lolita," "School Boys Sex Orgy," "Lolita's Examination," "Family Sex," "Lesbian Lolitas," "Brother and Sister," "Lolita Mix," "Lolita's Auntie," "School Girl and Boy," "Child Love," "Incest Family," "Virgin Masturbation," "Children's Sex Party," and "Sucking Daddy."

Through all this vile filth I had to hide my revulsion and feign fascination while Al Hill ate his burgers and gave a running commentary:

"Wild thing! Wild thing! . . . I've never seen anything like this before in my life man! . . . Real deal! . . . Yeah, that one, she's about ten . . . I aim to please, man . . . This'll sell good . . . Dig this shit man, this wild! . . . You not no cop are you? . . . They're gettin' at it! . . . That one girl is suckin' both of 'em off . . . She can't be a day over nine . . . Boy, if you were a cop, I'd be shit up a creek, wouldn't I? . . . There they go. He gets it in! . . . She's about nine . . . He's got it in her! . . . She's suckin' the little kid off! . . . Look at that! . . . How long before I see my money?"

When it was over, I gave Hill $6,500 and told him they were premium quality and that he would make $1 to $1.5 million in royalties. After he left, Keppel, Black, Davis, and Ball came into the apartment. All were fathers. I showed them a few of the videos. It was like a cloud of death hung over the room. Ball gathered the tapes, and we all silently trudged out of the apartment, each haunted by visions of tortured little girls who were somewhere, at that very moment, being forced to make more movies like the ones we had just seen.

Bobby Raymond phoned me at home that evening and asked why I was so "grouchy." I couldn't tell him the truth. As we talked, I thought of how the crimes Raymond and the others had committed would explode in the media when the indictments were announced. Al Hill would just be a footnote. Raymond would no doubt come to symbolize Arizona's dirty politicians, and the public would be led to think that he was the ultimate sleazeball. They would be wrong. Raymond's bluster about deals, and his taking money for a tough race were nothing compared to the child pornographers. In fact, if Raymond embarrassed the corporate polluters by tossing them out of his office, one wonders how he would have treated a child pornographer.

I was "grouchy" all right. It had been one of the worst days of my life. Stephens would probably skate because of an equipment failure, and that bumbling idiot, Al Hill, had delivered some horrifying scenes that I would be unable to shake from my brain for months.

18

Desert Sting was supposedly on its deathbed, yet my schedule remained full of hit men, child pornographers, gun molls, wheeling-and-dealing lobbyists, and power-hungry politicians — bedfellows that were becoming increasingly less strange. The dramatic shifts in real-life method acting needed to communicate with such a diverse mix of characters was starting to take a toll. After the bungled Stephens drop, my brain short-circuited and I failed to do what had become standard procedure — call him on the phone under some pretense and get him to confirm that he knew it was my money. I had done that in the past with Kenney and English, and Ernie Hoffman. But because I was struggling mentally to erase the kiddie porn images from my head, I blanked out everything that happened that day and forgot about making a follow-up call to Stephens. And no one, not the cops or prosecutors, jogged my memory. We all snoozed it.

Pat Cantelme, the fireman bedfellow, tossed his hat back into the ring on the eve of Halloween. He wanted to do another strategy outline and said he could work through Rick DeGraw and Phil Gordon. I'd just met DeGraw, Hamilton's fixer. I didn't have a clue who Gordon was. There was some kind of move afoot, but I couldn't get a cross hair on just what it was.

"Rick has identified eighteen people, eighteen legislators who he thinks will support this . . ." Cantelme said. "I'm not so sure that I would be doing that much at all, but what I would do is get Rick and Phil Gordon involved and lay out a plan for you that would take it from here all the way to an election. And show you how that would happen each step of the way. My involvement would be on the periphery through Rick and Phil."

". . . Okay Pat, what would you charge me to do that?"

"Nothing. Nothing."

So what's the angle, I wondered. What's the point?

"If I, if you used them, then industries would be built into whatever the date proposed to you, in terms of what I'm doing there, you know. I'm not gonna charge you anything."

That was it. But what was it? What language was that? Firespeak? I was missing something, but for some reason, my instincts told me to let it drop for now. I'd get a better feel for the big picture at the next session scheduled the following week.

Detective Ball greeted me early Halloween morning with some good news. The Organized Crime Racketeers Unit had authorized another $100,000 in confiscated cash to keep Desert Sting going. With all the talk about shutting down, that was especially significant. The Grim Reaper would have to back off Tony a bit.

I was just dozing off again when Al Hill called. He wanted to know what my partner thought of his tapes, and when he'd get his money. I looked at the clock by the bed. It was 8:30 a.m. It hadn't been twenty-four hours since he dropped them off, and he was already bugging me about his money. Al was going to be a problem.

Assistant County Attorney Jim Keppel was standing in my parking spot when I arrived at the office. He was steaming. He had gone upstairs to the fourth room and couldn't get inside because Sergeant Davis was late. When he opened the door to my office to get the key, he locked eyes with Rich Scheffel. The lobbyist was waiting to ambush me for a quick, unscheduled conference. Keppel mumbled "whoops, wrong office" and ducked back out. The prosecutor said he had met Scheffel in the past and was sure the lobbyist recognized him. He was angry at Davis for not being in the fourth room as arranged. I told him not to worry. I'd handle it.

I met Scheffel in the hallway. He had come by to pick up three $220 checks for Jim Hartdegen. He said nothing about Keppel and gave no indication that he had made the assistant county attorney. False alarm.

Scheffel reappeared that afternoon at the apartment with a tall, stern women in her thirties with shoulder-length brown hair. He introduced her as Sheri Raymond, Bobby's wife. Scheffel also brought his own television and VCR, two items I already had at the apartment. Because I'd been told that Mrs. Raymond was a former television reporter, and because she was Bobby's wife, I expected her to be much prettier. They set up the machines and popped in a tape Sheri's company had done on mental health. It was professionally filmed, but was a real downer filled with scenes of derelicts and mentally ill street people. I complimented her on her talents, cut the viewing short, and promised to hook her up with my P.R. people in Vegas. It was a stall. I wasn't sure if the cops would go for funding a video.

The whole meeting depressed me. Sheri Raymond was cool and unfriendly, and I was disappointed in Bobby for sicking his wife on me. In the wise-guy world, you never involved wives. That's bad business. I had to remind myself that these weren't gangsters, burglars, and thieves I was dealing with. They were worse.

Mr. Excitement, Gary Kaasa, dropped by the apartment to deliver the final version of his "my issue as a candidate" ministudy. After the paper and cash exchange, he asked if he could stay on as a consultant. I explained that I was up to my eyeballs in lobbyists and consultants. The phone rang. It was Detective Ball in the next apartment.

"If you don't get this boring son-of-a-bitch out of there in five minutes, you better duck 'cause we're gonna start shooting through the door!"

I muffled a laugh, made an excuse, and showed the schoolteacher the door.

Shiree Foster, a considerably more interesting person, phoned and confirmed that they were about to let fly the hit piece on her favorite legislator, Bobby Raymond. I told her if the stuff got lost on the way to the post office, I'd be a happy mobster. I was only half serious, but the cops and prosecutors threw a fit. They said I couldn't interfere in the election. That was another fine example of police thinking: What about the $200,000 we pumped into people's campaigns? There was no sense arguing the point. I rang Shiree and explained that I was just trick-or-treating.

When I arrived home that evening, my house was covered with huge spiderwebs and giant spiders. Gail greeted me wearing a hat, trenchcoat, and one of those Groucho Marx nose, eyeglasses, and eyebrows disguises. There were plastic pumpkins full of candy by the door. I kissed her, grabbed a handful of Toostie Rolls, then vanished into my room. I couldn't face seeing any little mermaids or princesses that evening. I kept wondering what kind of Halloween Al Hill's Lolitas might be having.

November opened with a call to Bobby Raymond to inform him that his long-feared Chamber hit piece would soon be falling like rain on his district. He hated to hear that. I said Shiree had faxed a copy and it was no big deal, just an endorsement of his opponent. That made little difference to him. He was ready to nuke the Chamber. I told him not to sweat it.

I went to the apartment early to prepare for the sit-down with Tapp and the hired killer. There was an air of tension in the surveillance apartment where a full force—Keppel, Mount, Ball, Black, and Davis—had gathered. For the first time, I noticed the cops checking to make sure their weapons were loaded. We were all expecting Tapp to stroll in with some gorilla. I stashed a .357 Magnum under the couch just in case the negotiations snagged. You never know with these psycho killers.

Tapp arrived with—Ward Cleaver! That scared me even more. Man, I thought, this character must be one hell of a hit man. Who'd suspect such a straight-arrow? Tapp excused himself so we could get down to the dirty deed. I launched into my Brooklyn Tony-needs-someone-wasted rap. However, instead of presenting the victim as a soft touch as with Jim Davis, I painted this guy as a tough player who'd be sure to put up a fight.

"He will open the door. He will let you in. He will think you're from me, which you are. What he won't know is why you're there. And I want him taken out. All the way . . . He's not a punk. He ain't gonna go down easy . . . He's gonna put up a beef . . . So do you think you can?"

As I spoke, I could see Ward's eyes getting wider and wider. He looked terrified.

"I'm not comfortable."

A hit man with a comfort level?

"I didn't have, I didn't have enough information when I came down here," he said, gulping.

"Okay, what did you think it was?"

"I had no idea."

"He just brought you in blind?"

"Well, you see, different words have different meanings depending on the context you're, that you take in the particular time. The word 'contracting' means a lot of things to a lot of different people."

"Yes."

"And I'm a contractor."

". . . You're a builder?"

"Yeah."

"I apologize. And Ron owes you an apology," I said.

"No he doesn't, no, because Ron and I have had a lot of discussions over, you know, doin' different things, uh, covert type of operations."

Translation: Ron was laying his bogus CIA rap on Ward Cleaver here, and Ward decided to one-up him by claiming to secretly be a Mafia hit man. Cute game. Trouble was, if Tony was real, he'd have to kill them both. You don't accidentally lay out a murder request to a building contractor, then let him skip through the door.

". . . I would never tell anybody anything," Ward promised, his voice quavering.

"Okay, but you're outta the business. So that's history," I said, giving the poor schmuck a way out. If he was a retired pro, then I could let him live. Honor among thieves and all that.

"Yeah, I really am."

The guy recovered enough to pitch me on financing a million-dollar condo project he wanted to construct in Flagstaff. That's why he had come. Unreal. I said I'd get back to him. The phone rang. Ball was laughing so hard he could hardly talk. "Get this guy outta there before he has a heart attack!"

The second apartment boys were literally rolling on the floor when I ventured next door. Even stone-faced Captain Black was overcome by laughter.

"Where'd you find this guy?" I asked Tapp later. ". . . He sits here and says, 'What can I do for you?' I tell him, 'I'll put the guy where you want him, no problem. I need you to bop, bop, bop, understand you're good with your hands.' He thinks I'm talking about building buildings! He misunderstood you, he said. Is that possible?"

"No," Tapp said, sticking to his guns.

"Huh?"

"No, it was just his way of saying 'I pass.'"

No Ron, it was his way of saying, "Ron and I are complete jackoffs who make up phony secret lives." There was no sense hitting Tapp with the ugly truth. He'd never admit to it. Tapp was another in the growing list of Desert Sting characters who were extremely fortunate that they were merely going to jail.

Al Hill, another extremely fortunate character, nailed me on the cellular on November 5 and said he was back in Holland getting new product. I told him to call me when he got back. Another big scam was in the making.

Scheffel dropped off a bill for Sheri Raymond's proposed promotional video on casino gambling. The final cost was listed as "$45,500–$53,500." It included such expenses as $3,000 for "script development," $2,000–$5,000 for "concept development," and another $3,000 for the "final script." They must have ran out of synonyms for the word "story" or they would have tacked on another $10,000. There was also $7,500 for Sheri's "retainer." I now had a video consultant on retainer. And the kicker—the payments were to be washed through Scheffel's company to distance Sheri Raymond from the finished video in order to protect Bobby from a conflict of interest. The moves were starting to come fast and furious, like a surreal shell game. And I was losing sight of the pea.

Out in the reception area, I heard Sergeant Davis tell Marie that Captain Black wanted her to start typing transcripts. I went berserk.

"Are you out of your mind! You want her to transcribe meetings right here in front of everybody! Is there no end to the nonsense with you idiots? Keppel bumped into Kenney in the hall, then walked in on Scheffel, and you guys don't learn a thing?"

"That's the Captain's orders," Davis said. "I do what he tells me."

"I got a better idea," I said. "Why don't you let Marie wear her police uniform? She can sit here typing transcripts in her blues! If you weren't such a wimp, you'd tell Captain Black that he was a moron!"

I disappeared into my office, slamming the door.

That night Ball told me that they were preparing to bring the case before the grand jury. He assured me that such juries are airtight, and it wouldn't compromise the operation. I didn't see it that way. A grand jury meant twelve to twenty-five average citizens would be let in on our secret. If one of them knew a politician, we were dead.

Tuesday, November 6, was destined to become an election day of infamy in Arizona history. But the results of the public's lunacy wouldn't be known until the wee hours of the following morning. As far as I was concerned, it was business as usual. I called Ball in the morning and told him that if we were in Desert Sting's final count-down, the best move would be to arrest Scheffel, roll him, wire him, and put him back out on the streets. Scheffel could then reel in a few big fish before we turned the boat toward shore. I calculated that Scheffel would go for it in order to protect the $400,000-a-year lobby-ing life he had carved out for himself. Of course, ratting out legislators wouldn't be good for future lobbying business, but it beat going to prison. Ball said he'd take it up with the gang during the next meeting. I also told Ball about my run-in with Sergeant Davis over Captain Black's latest bright idea.

"I have no comment. I wasn't at the meeting."

"Yeah, and it's also 'police business,'" I snapped, sarcastically.

I met Scheffel and Don Kenney at the Black Angus for lunch.

Scheffel wanted to discuss who to put on Kenney's critical judiciary committee. They mentioned possible candidates, leaning toward those who would be favorable toward my issue, while excluding the wackos.

Sergeant Davis was waiting when I drove across the street to check in and return the beeper bug. I asked Sergeant Duncan, one of the van crew, to wire the conference room at my office because Marie was now going to come to work in her uniform and type transcripts.

"Why don't you go back to work with the Feds where they do things right," Davis screamed.

It was the strangest jibe I'd ever heard. Was he insulting me, himself, or his employers? I pointed out that Marie was not allowed to type her supplemental reports or overtime slips at my office, but they wanted her to put on headphones and type transcripts. Bobby Raymond could walk right behind her without her knowing it and watch while she typed him saying, "My favorite line is, 'What's in it for me?'"

Davis just stormed to the back of the van. Duncan took me aside and said that in his twenty years in law enforcement, he'd never seen or heard of an operation like this one. It had been far more successful and had gone on longer than anyone had dreamed.

"And we've only fried half the fish," he said. "Imagine what we could do if we got someone on the inside?"

Davis returned, baited for bear.

"Who do you think you are? You're not Ruben Ortega. You're not Rick Romley. You're nothing but a snitch!"

The "snitch" accusation pushed my hot button and he knew it. I was an employee of the county hired to do a job that was too dangerous for the police. Police Chief Ruben Ortega himself would say that repeatedly. A "snitch" is a little creep who rats out his friends for personal gain, usually a drug fix. I didn't know any of these politicians when I signed on. Davis' words stung like a desert wasp. I went nuts.

"You wimp! You're too cowardly to stand up to that idiot captain!"

"You're a snitch!" he screamed, red-faced with hysteria. "You're a snitch!"

"You're a wimp!" I yelled back, thundering toward him in a black rage. Sting or no sting, I was gonna strangle him. Davis had the good sense to jump into his car — a seized Mercedes 450 SL — and speed off.

Both Davis and I were on a razor's edge. I don't know what was bugging him, probably the fact that a felon was spearheading a successful operation. I knew why I was uptight. Aside from seeing the end of Tony Vincent in sight, Detective Ball had been transferred to transcript duty to prepare to bring the case before the grand jury. From day one, Ball had been my lifeline. He was an unquestionably honest supercop who couldn't be corrupted if you kidnapped his wife and kids. He was my security net. Just knowing he was in the next room gave me the strength to go on. If anybody came at me, I could count on Ball's instincts to sense the hit and come out with his guns blazing. He was the guy I wanted to go to war with. The others were good men in their own way, even Sergeant Davis and Captain Black, but when the bullets started flying, I wanted Ball there. Plus, no matter how insane the police thinking got, I could count on Ball to be the voice of reason. If anybody was gonna stuff the idea of Marie typing transcripts in the office, it would be Ball.

Only Ball was buried in the transcript room while I headed into the most dangerous months of the operation. That made Tony nervous.

There was little time to mourn the loss of Detective Ball or dwell on my mental state. Al Hill phoned at 6:20 p.m. and said he was on his way from Sky Harbor International Airport and wanted an immediate meet to drop his latest cache of tapes. I suspected that Hill had held back some tapes from his original trip to Denmark and was planning to pawn them off as new product, complete with a bill for phantom airfare. His passport would later confirm my theory. Ball advised me to phase out Hill because he was cooked as thoroughly as he could be. It's a mandatory prison sentence just to own kiddie porn. With dealers, they throw away the key. I stalled Hill by saying I had a slate of election parties to attend.

The vote returns in Arizona must come in by donkey because the late news had nothing but single-digit percentages. It would be well into Wednesday before anything started to make sense. Screw that. I went to bed.

Tapp called early the next morning and described an electoral holocaust. Bill English and Leo Corbet had been voted out of office. If Tony had been real, that would have been $18,000 down the old crapper for English. Honest John Dougherty, the colonel who angrily told me that "Nobody can commit my vote!" beat Jeff Hill before I ever got the opportunity to meet the senator—bad for Tony, but good for Arizona. Sue Laybe squeaked by on a margin of eight hundred votes; the gays once again pushed her over the top. In the state treasurer's race, Tony West stomped George Stragalas. More money down the drain, and that wasn't good for Arizona. However, the real damage came in the statewide elections. The winner of the governor's race was—Evan Mecham! Not really, but in a way. In an extremely dramatic race, Goddard led Symington most of the night by a few percentage points. Then, around 2 a.m., the ultra-conservative vote from Mesa started pouring in.

Symington took the lead and ended up on top by about four thousand votes. However, eight write-in candidates chipped off 1.1 percent of the vote. That meant Symington was denied the newly decreed 50 percent "Mecham wall" majority needed to win. After Mecham had slithered into office with less than 50 percent of the vote due to a three-party race, the legislature enacted a law in 1986 that said the governor had to win by one vote more than 50 percent. That was to keep another prized wacko, or Mecham himself, from riding into office on a wave of united yahoos while the remaining two candidates split the sane vote. Since Symington didn't top 50 percent, that meant a runoff. Trouble was, the legislators forgot to specify the details of a runoff, so nobody knew what the hell to do. When? How? Where? Who would pay for it? Bottom line: Arizona didn't have a governor, and nobody knew what to do about it.

But that was only half of the Arizona's election lunacy. The Martin Luther King Day issue mirrored the Goddard-Symington race. The holiday led most of the night, sending everyone to bed secure in the belief that the state had avoided becoming a national laughingstock. Then when the Mesa vote, and the votes from the outlying counties, came in, King's memory was overtaken at the wire. Hello national embarrassment. Good-bye 1993 Super Bowl. Good-bye 1994 NBC All-Star Weekend. Good-bye to any good football teams coming to the 1991 Fiesta Bowl. Good-bye to about five hundred conventions. Good-bye to $2 billion.

Ironically, it's doubtful any state would have passed the Martin Luther King Day if it had been put before the voters. Most states had the good sense to legislate it into effect in order to keep their racists and rednecks under wraps. Not so with Arizona. Arizona wears them on its sleeve.

Carolyn Walker sounded drained and devastated when she called. She had been a leader in the King holiday movement, and seemed to be almost in shock. She put off a scheduled get-together for the following week.

Not everyone was bewailing the election day disaster. The Democrats had picked up enough seats in the Senate to become the majority. That meant Walker was now the majority whip, and Alan Stephens was the majority leader.

The election results combined with everything else I'd been going though to knock me into a deep funk. If I was nothing but a snitch to the cops and prosecutors, then screw them. When Ball called at noon, I told him I wanted to pack it in. Ball wanted to know my reason.

"I'm tired of fighting the bad guys and the cops. I'm alone out there."

Ball said he'd tell the county attorney. Keppel called an hour later. I aired my grievances about Ball and Mount and him moving on to the grand jury proceedings and leaving me on the front lines with Davis and Black.

"You knew this would happen going in," Keppel argued.

"Yeah, but I never considered the constant struggle I'd have with the cops. From my first secretary on down, it's been one battle after another with them. Here I am, going after dirty politicians, and the cops have been my biggest obstacle and have provided the most danger. The police! Who woulda figured that?"

Keppel suggested that we all gather at the undercover apartment. When I arrived, Ball, Davis, Keppel, and Mount were there. No sign of Captain Black. Keppel praised me to the hilt, calling me the best undercover agent he'd ever seen. He was stroking me big time, but it was working. Keppel added that this was the first time the county attorney's office and the police had worked together on an operation from the beginning, and it was important that it played out to a smooth ending. That brought up an interesting question. Sergeant Davis had said that if his chief, Ortega, ordered the operation closed, it was over. I turned to Keppel.

"If the police shut down, could we go on using our own people?" I asked.

"Yes."

He went on to say that they had plans for me that extended beyond Desert Sting, and that I could count on a job with them for as long as I wanted it. They pushed the right button. With Tony's grave being dug, I was starting to worry about what would happen to Joe.

My tantrum worked some reverse psychology. The more I fought to keep the operation going, the more they threatened to shut it down. Then, when I was ready to throw in the towel, they fought to keep Desert Sting alive. It appeared we were now dug in for the long haul.

19

It had been a bad week for George Stragalas. Not only had he been thoroughly rejected by the populace and crushed by a bitter rival, but the consensus was that his love/hate pal, Terry Goddard, was finished. J. Fife Symington had the momentum, and the Republicans were expected to be better able to finance a runoff than the Democrats. President Bush was hinting that he would make amends by winging in to shake some hands with Symington. Stragalas was already talking about Goddard licking his wounds and resurfacing in the next congressional or U.S. Senate race.

Al Hill kept hammering me to set the second tape drop. He said the latest batch he had acquired—or held back—was better quality. Hill was eager to collect the $14,000 he claimed I owed him. That included $2,500 in bogus airfare. I wasn't eager to see any more of his haunting filth. I stalled.

Rich Scheffel was upbeat when he phoned. Why not? Some of his old friends may have been tossed out of the legislature, but that just meant there were raw rookies to wine, dine, and corrupt. Nothing had really changed. For lobbyists, the game is always the same. They slink around in dark corridors, making deals, pulling strings, never having to worry about facing the public or getting reelected. And the good ones make $300,000 to $500,000.

Scheffel wanted me to give former Senator Jeff Hill $1,000 even though he lost and I'd never met him. That was like betting on a lame horse after the race was over, but the cops gave the okay. Scheffel had illegally bundled Hill's checks and they wanted that count on the lobbyist's mounting tab. (Since Hill would have received the money indirectly, he would not be charged.)

Sergeant Davis wandered by the office and made a crack about Chris Petti, my Mafia boss friend from San Diego. That meant Davis had been digging around for dirt on me. To what end? Probably just to let me know that he knew that no matter how well I was doing, deep down, I was nothing but a gangster. Instead of being drawn together by the success of the sting, we were starting to tear each other apart.

Detective Ball said he didn't know what was eating Davis and advised me to lay low for a while. He also said they were only authorizing $6,000 for Al Hill's new tapes, and they'd place Detective Jack Ballentine at the meet to act as my muscle in case Hill beefed. Ballentine was an enormous body builder whose specialty was infiltrating motorcycle gangs. That was comforting, but I had already developed my own plan for dealing with Hill. If he got violent, I was going to push him into the kitchen where the cameras couldn't see, jump back, scream "Don't Shoot!" pump six slugs into him, then do the old cop trick of sticking a fork in his hand and saying, "It looked like a gun!"

The more I thought about it, the more I didn't like the Ballentine appearance. I figured Hill would accept the $6,000 on the promise of the massive profits to come. Besides, it was just a cheap hustle anyway. And it was out of character for Tony to show muscle this early. Tony would be expected to take care of the Al Hills of the world on his own.

"You don't think Tony would stand for Hill's $14,000 demand?" Ball asked.

"You kidding? Tony would stick a gun in Hill's mouth and steal the tapes."

The education went both ways.

Just in case, we came up with a signal. If I felt Hill was going to get crazy, I'd say, "The guy from Reno is due in fifteen minutes." That meant I wanted Ballentine and crew knocking on my door within fifteen seconds.

Hill arrived on schedule with the tapes. He was right. He had held back the "best" material. These had better color, better sound, better stories, and a bit of dialogue here and there. Unfortunately, they contained the same revolting subject matter.

"To be honest, I can live with just getting the money that I spent, back," Hill said, letting the lies fly. ". . . When I went up there this time I spent twelve grand . . . That has nothing to do with the $2,500 bucks I spent to fly out there . . . They check you through Customs, at the airports. It's brutal. So, I'm constantly walking around sweating. There's a lot of risks involved, you know. It's serious shit, I mean, it's a serious crime . . . I'm talking real bad."

After we finished the nightmarish viewing, Hill took a dishcloth and began wiping his fingerprints off the tapes—right in front of the police cameras. We haggled some over the price, and eventually agreed on an even $10,000. That was four grand more than the cops wanted to pay, but four less than Hill felt he deserved. Seemed like a fair compromise.

Ball phoned that evening with the kicker on a bad day. He was planning to bring me stacks of transcripts that I needed to review before they were brought to the Maricopa County grand jury. I was already working twelve hours a day. I guess they figured I didn't need to sleep.

Scheffel and Hoffman came to the apartment on November 13 to collect and confer. I gave Hoffman $24,600 cash as another payment on the casino gambling impact studies, and gave Scheffel $7,500 for Sheri Raymond's retainer as my video consultant. The lobbyists said the mess with the gubernatorial race altered our plans. They wanted me to keep a low profile until the election was settled. They still feared casino gambling becoming an issue in that ugly battle. The speculation was that the runoff would be sometime in late February—nearly four months away. Meanwhile, Marge Simpson's grandmother, Rose Mofford, would reluctantly continue to run the state in the style she had grown accustomed to. According to the political wags, that meant by blowing gaping holes in the ozone with her hair spray and going on frequent shopping excursions to San Diego.

Scheffel's latest brainstorm was to hire a front man for my operation. He wanted a clean-looking newscaster type to be our spokesman once we came out of the closet. I guess they considered Tony too scary for public consumption.

Ernie Hoffman continued to try and clean up the $18,000 payment to ex-Representative English. As always, simply giving it back was not an option. He said it would become a credit on a future service and claimed to be taking a loss. The only thing he'd ever be losing was the four seconds it took to type the figure on the next padded bill he sent me.

I had labored under the belief that once the elections were over, it would be two years before the politicians would need to grub for money again. This was certain to slow the rush to my door. I was wrong. Scheffel presented a list of candidates who needed money to erase their campaign deficits. He said the beer folks, chiropractors, and eye doctors were already opening their wallets to help out. In politics, the need for cash is never-ending. I was entering a new phase of the operation—Deficit Bribing.

Hoffman phoned on the fourteenth to let me know that he was having some trouble with the studies. Seems the good professors had included a crime section that confronted the issues of hookers, pick-pockets, and loan sharks, three factions of society that go hand-in-hand with legalized gambling. Hoffman preferred to delete that portion of the study and the professors agreed.

Representative Sue Laybe arrived in my office on the fifteenth flush with victory—but still sporting Olive Oyl's discarded wardrobe.

"We kicked the Republican's butt and I drug two Democrats with me . . . I told Art I wanted a coat for Christmas with two long tails on it," she beamed. Susie added that she had chatted with Senator Nancy Hill, the woman who had snuffed Leo Corbet, and that Hill might be receptive to coming in and having me erase some of her campaign deficit. That was fine with me. The conversation turned to my meeting with the Big Kahuna, Minority Leader Art Hamilton.

"Well, I'll tell you, after your appearance, he came to me and said, 'Is this guy setting you up or is he legit?' " Laybe relayed. "I said, 'I think he's legit.'"

"Boy, that pisses me off," I countered.

"Well, I'm always worried about what's in the other door in the hallway but . . ."

As with Raymond, the question came without warning. This time, I didn't blink. "That is where my accountant works and that's where the records are kept for six casinos."

"Whose, which six?"

"Uh, are you goin' back to Vegas?" I said, hanging a verbal U-turn. She went with the new conversational flow and never mentioned the fourth room again. She did, however, mention money. Sue hit me for $3,000 for something she called "my public information account." She explained it as having to do with mailing letters to constituents. Whatever, I gave it to her.

Stragalas came to the apartment for another session with Dr. Tony. Hearing him out, however, was generally educational. He knew where the political bodies were buried in Arizona—and across America.

"He had me tailed. I know he had me tailed," Stragalas ranted, referring to his opponent, Tony West. Instead of trying to cure him of his delusions, I fed the paranoia.

"I believe that!"

Marie interrupted our lunch to say that a peeved Ernie Hoffman was on the line. He had learned about the lady doing my video and was upset that Rich Scheffel had stepped into his territory. Ernie had planned a slide presentation. Flaming his hypersensitivity was the double whammy of losing his long-term puppets, English and Corbet, and the fact that he knew his influence with me was slipping. I told him not to worry. The video lady was Bobby Raymond's wife.

"Well, that's different then. It's totally different," he said, catching on. ". . . That's no problem. I have no problem with that."

"It's a shakedown for a few extra dollars. It goes to Bobby through her and that's the end of the story," I explained, adding that I didn't care what Mrs. Raymond came up with. It was all part of the game. Hoffman's mood lifted. He knew the game well.

I scratched Hoffman off the telephone and turned my attention back to Stragalas. I sensed that he needed a new direction in life and was happy to oblige.

"How do you feel about being 'Vice President in Charge of Bribery'?"

"It sounds good," he said without hesitation. I was serious and so was he. I quickly brought my V.P. up to speed on the status of the legalized casino gambling drive.

"So now I'm running an ad in the paper for a 'Dynamic P.R. Type!' to get up and speak and do all this shit . . . I know they [Scheffel and Hoffman] are gonna sandbag me with somebody that they probably talked about over lunch. They want $75,000 a year for this asshole . . . It's always a move. Sheri Raymond? I need Sheri Raymond like I need another hole in my ass."

". . . I hafta make a decision as to whether I'm ever gonna run again," Stragalas said, still consumed by electoral politics. "If I run for governor in four years, or if I run for senator in two years."

". . . Stay outta politics," I advised. "You know what you're lackin'? You don't have the kill factor . . . You don't have the knockout punch. You shoulda beat this guy . . . You already knew what I found out. You had the most vulnerable candidate of all. And you didn't rip his balls off . . . A little investigation, sittin' with a few people. You know everybody in the world. You coulda had all the dirt in the world on this guy . . . The man's a crook. He's a bigger crook than you and I will ever be. And I am a crook. I'm a gangster. I don't pretend to be nothin' else . . . He is a crook and he will fuck this state!"

"Oh yeah," Stragalas confirmed.

". . . If he stole while he's a senator, what's he gonna do now that he has access to billions? What kinda way to get some money!" I marveled.

"Oh, sure he will."

After we ripped and tore on the treasurer, we set our sights on lobbyists.

"I don't understand the function of lobbyists . . ." Stragalas said. "What's the difference between the lobbyist and you givin' money to a legislator? . . ."

Damn good question. If a veteran political insider like Stragalas didn't know the answer, then who does? "I'm payin' these guys big money," I said, offering what little I knew. "I'm supposed to be a pimp. I'm windin' up bein' the whore . . . When this is over, if a guy votes 'no' that's taken $50,000, $20,000, I have the right to break his fingers. If a guy comes at me through a lobbyist, I got no finger-breakin' rights. I don't like that."

Stragalas nodded, sighed deeply, then dipped into his weathered bag of political war stories. ". . . I had a party for John Glenn at the Granada Royale, ten grand is on my American Express card. Ten grand he charged . . . John Glenn, Senator, Keating Five. What's he do? He rents the penthouse suite . . . He brings in his son, his wife, the boyfriend of his girl, and they order room service and cocktails. It was on my card . . . I mean, how can I say, because Terry [Goddard] says, 'Turn the election over to Gary Hart,' and I'm hangin' out there with John Glenn? . . . Sure, I could have gone after Tony's [West] throat, okay, he lives right across the street from somebody that'd make sure he never got up in the morning. That's not the point . . . I know the way I've been brought up. I know what's important. And I know the difference between the gangster and the guy who deals with the attache case . . ."

"They're all gangsters."

"Okay, and I know the corporations, the spies in corporations that get paid to go see this product and that product, and what the hell's the difference, okay? The point is though . . . when I asked you a question about the lobbyist and I hear DeGraw and Cantelme, they're all in it together and what their agenda is . . . They don't give a fuck about Tony Vincent . . . As a matter of fact, here's what they would prefer . . . They work hard on gambling and they put on the best show they can for Tony . . ."

"And it fails."

"And it fails."

George's spleen venting was contagious. I had a few beefs of my own to get off Tony Vincent's chest. ". . . This Hoffman, I don't know what he's cost me to date . . . Somewhere around $76,000. This asshole here, this Scheffel, he cost me about $68,000 and then he brings Bobby Raymond's old lady. I give Bobby $10,000. These are the things I gotta share with you if you're gonna come on board as Executive Vice President in Charge of Bribery. You gotta know who I done bribed."

"Right."

"I'm lobbyist-heavy and you ain't got the bullshit in ya to be a lobbyist. 'Cause see, you gotta be a lyin', cunning mother to do that and you ain't got that in ya . . . We'd develop a bullshit relationship, and you ain't gonna do that with me . . . If we tried to tie Scheffel to R.J. Reynolds and Anheuser-Busch, forget about it. No way . . . He's probably coming back from St. Louis, in fact, I'm thinking of having two guys waiting for him at the airport to grab his briefcase. He's probably gonna bring in $100,000 from Anheuser-Busch that he'll bury and he'll dole it out over the coming year . . . That's how the system works . . . The cocksucker might even be double-bangin'. Supposin' Art Hamilton said to him, 'I need $28,000 for these people.' Now [Scheffel] takes that list to R.J. Reynolds' people and they give him the $30,000. Then he comes to me and I give him the thirty. Then he goes to Anheuser-Busch. He puts sixty away and still got the thirty from me. And he still has the same access, only I paid for it and he picked up sixty goin' in."

"I don't think I have the stomach for it," Stragalas decided.

"From the day I met you, you made a statement, 'Politicians are whores' . . . These are the pimps, Scheffel, Hoffman . . . the lobbyists . . . The whore tells the pimp, 'Honey, I need new pearls so I can go out and sell my pussy.' And they get the new pearls. 'Honey, I wanna go on a trip.' You go on a trip. It might not always be cash . . . 'I wanna sixteen-, seventeen-year-old girl,' 'I want some cocaine.' They go out and get what it takes to keep their whore happy . . . You shoulda seen [Scheffel's] face when he reached in his briefcase and he shows me this list and he says, 'I got all these [legislators] to clean up, but I'm not gonna use you' . . . Here I see this long list of names . . . and on top of that, 'Chiropractors.' Then I see another list, on top of that, 'The Optometry Doctors.'"

"Rick DeGraw has a list . . ." Stragalas said. "'These are the people I tap to retire debt' and so forth . . . See, he's pimpin', too . . . What Rick gets is 17½ percent from the printers, 15 percent from the radio, 15 percent from the TV . . ."

"If he could get a kickback from the post office, he would," I joked.

"They do!" Stragalas blurted. "You know how they do it? There's a mail order [office] in South Phoenix . . . I go down there to make out a check for . . . the U.S. Post Office . . . six hundred bucks to handle a one-hour mailing . . . Then they bring me to the Teamsters printer up here, S & H Printing. And she's very nice . . . and she says 'We have to take care of Mike Crusa.' I said, 'Take care of?' She said, 'Well, you know.' Of course I know. Mike Crusa is Dennis DeConcini's state [director]. He gets his, I'm sure, 15 percent."

Stragalas' knowledge of dirty politics appeared limitless. He moved easily from Arizona to Tennessee, home of U.S. Congressman Bart Gordon.

"He's slated to be the chairman of the Congressional Campaign Committee, which means that all congressional races up in '92 have to go through him for funding . . . He wants to be the governor of Tennessee . . . We manufactured him a paternity suit. They say he's gay. So in order to diffuse [that] the first time he ran, we filed a paternity suit."

"I love it," I said. A legally orchestrated beard! The more George told his stories, the blacker his mood became.

"So, it was good enough when Terry [Goddard] took $150,000 from his dad to finance his campaign. It was okay to have Mike Sophy bringin' him money by the handfuls when he was elected as mayor in '83. It was okay for Sam to take bags of money and say, 'George, what do I do with it?' Some of it gold and silver . . . You're damn right! Why wouldn't I say it? I couldn't say it as a politician . . . That's why I'm makin' the decision here . . . I'm outta politics . . . They'd never support me!"

"No, they didn't support you when you needed 'em."

"Exactly. That's what I'm sayin'. So as far as politics, fuck 'em! . . . The other thing I wanna know is, did Babbitt take the million bucks not to run for governor this time? That's what I'd like to know . . . I've heard it more than once. He took a sizable amount of money not to run."

"From the Goddards? Or from Symington?" I asked.

"From somebody, not to run . . ." Stragalas said.

That was the second time I'd heard that Babbitt was paid to walk away from an election. Previously, it was the U.S. Senate race that DeConcini won. Both times the figure was a cool million. If this was true, Bruce Babbitt has based a cottage industry upon not running for office.

"It's extremely critical right now in terms of this runoff," Stragalas continued. "I think we could have a major influence as to who's gonna be the governor in this state. I will cut Goddard's balls off if you want me to . . . to where he will not win. I think I could ensure that . . . What I could [also] do is have lunch with [Senator] Nancy Hill . . . Nancy loves me. Nancy would go to bed with me in two seconds. You know what I'm saying?"

Certainly. I started my new V.P. out at $5,000 a month. It was well worth the money to have a man on board who could singlehandedly choose the next governor of Arizona!

"You wanna go to Fife Symington and unload?" I asked, tossing more bloody meat to the famished shark.

"Yeah! Yeah! . . . You think from a newspaper standpoint, from a public standpoint . . . They're not gonna believe Terry. They're gonna believe me! . . . Sometimes, I get high about the fact I got this guy by the balls . . . Babbitt and Goddard, and they're such experts on ripping things off. They're crooks . . . worse than anybody else I've ever imagined, except they use the state's money!"

Hell hath no fury like a politician scorned. Stragalas was going to be a fine addition to Team Tony.

Bobby Raymond appeared in the Ed McMahon seat on Friday, November 16. He was charged and eager to begin doing deals in the 1991 legislative session. Bobby was chock-full of new ideas, most involving sexual blackmail.

"All right . . . I first started thinking about how to fuck [Representative] Brenda Burns when I thought she was gonna wind up as chair of judiciary. Well, Burns is havin' an affair, you know, it gets a little nasty."

Do tell, Bobby. Do tell. "Is she married?"

"Oh hell, yeah! Married with four kids and plays this God's holy person. She's fucking a TV reporter and she's also fucking a lobbyist . . . I play for broke, Tony, and I assume you do too. I mean, I live on the edge and I play for broke and if we need to quiet Brenda Burns, then we'll quiet Brenda Burns."

Bobby had a second prime target on his personal smear list.

"The other one is [Representative] Stan Barnes."

"What's Stan up to?"

"Stan's fucking this little staff person from the House."

". . . Stan? Ken of 'Ken and Barbie' fame?"

"Yeah."

"I love it! Where does he take her?"

"I don't know. I've caught 'em two or three times. I caught 'em kissing in the parking lot one day. Barnes just about shit."

". . . All right, so what do you wanna do? You want me to get this [private investigator] down here. You want to sit down with him?"

"If you want . . . Barnes is gonna be, you know, nobody pays any attention to Barnes anyway. But Burns is gonna be a major problem."

"So?"

"You know, you kill your fuckin' enemies and that's the reason your friends stay friends."

What a great line. "So she's fucking two guys and got a husband. Now we hand her the pictures of her coming out of the motel . . . What does that tell her at that point? I don't know the Arizona structure. I know in Nevada, that guy shuts up immediately or that woman shuts up. What does she do at that point? I don't wanna rip her into goin' to the cops."

"Nah, I don't think she'd do that because she has too much to lose."

Ball called from the fourth room. "Keep riding with this. That's extortion." I was way ahead of him.

"Please, this stuff, man, it has to stay between the two of us," Raymond continued.

"I don't have a problem with that."

I wanted to start the sex, blackmail, and votes racket immediately, but Bobby said it wasn't the right time.

". . . The opening of session creates much opportunity for people to fuck around because you have parties every night and you have lots of opportunity . . . The week of the [January] eighteenth would be a good weekend."

". . . All right, so let's surmise that we're now into February and I've got the stuff . . . pictures of them . . . How do we use that to our advantage?" I asked, drawing out the extortion conspiracy.

". . . Somebody would just have to sit down and have a little talk with Miss Burns . . . You hafta sit down and say, 'Look, what we need out of you is the fact that you keep your mouth shut. You know how I would like you to vote.' See, she's got a husband who makes $250,000, $300,000 a year. She's never had to work a day in her life . . . They have four kids. She's a real, real active member of the church and tries to paint [herself as] this very religious type . . . You can destroy her, absolutely destroy her with that. Burns is smart. Smart like a fox . . . She's not gonna let what she has be destroyed."

". . . How about Stan?"

". . . He's just kind of a kid that's there and he runs his mouth a lot and nobody listens to him."

"How do you think he'd react to those pictures?"

"He'd shit. I mean, he's got this congressional career laid out for himself."

". . . So that would neutralize him?"

"Yeah, that would neutralize him. I mean, we're not out to destroy, we're just out to be accommodating."

Bob reiterated that it was the sexy and extremely dangerous Brenda Burns who really needed to be brought to her knees.

"She will be the person on that [judiciary] committee that would lead the charge of the opposition. Brenda Burns will go to any length to get what she wants. Any length! . . . I mean it's hardball. It's hard, hardball!"

As he talked, I couldn't help feeling bad. I loved this guy. He was so alive, pumped, and colorful. There was nothing malicious about what he conspired to do. To twist the old Mob phrase, it wasn't personal, it was just business—political business. You force somebody to vote your way, and nobody's hurt. Unfortunately, the wilder his schemes, the deeper he dug his grave. Raymond was quickly gaining on Ron Tapp, and Tapp had burrowed halfway to China. But there was nothing I could do aside from tipping off Raymond and blowing the operation.

"Now see, the reporter, I don't know how hot that is these days. The reporter's not married. He's got a place of his own," Bob went on, shoveling away.

"Well, it doesn't matter if he's single. She's married."

"Oh yeah, we don't give a shit about him."

"If he's fucking her at his house, that makes it great," I said.

". . . Hard shit, but that's life in this business," Raymond explained.

". . . How about Stan? Would he be vocal? Would you use that on him for a 'yes' vote or just as a neutralizing factor?"

"Using it for a 'yes' vote."

". . . And this girl works right at the legislature, the one he's fucking around with?"

"And she's a good-lookin' son-of-a-bitch. I'll give ya credit for that."

"He's married as I recall?"

"Oh hell, yeah. His wife was the former Miss Louisiana. I mean, she's one of these stay-at-home good little girls who was brought up in the Mormon church, or the Baptist, and she stays at home and is the beautiful wife."

"I think he's a Mormon?"

"Yeah. He's a Mormon."

". . . What do you know about this guy [Jack] Jewett, anything?"

"Yeah, divorced, has congressional ambitions, is mean as a snake, but is a very top-notch politician. He could be problems . . . The reality is Art can deal with Jewett."

"Jewett is my only major concern that I know of," I said. "Like

Burns, I wasn't aware that she could be [a 'yes'] vote. Barnes, I wasn't aware he could be twisted to a 'yes' vote. I love it!"

"Shit, I lay awake nights thinking about this shit," Raymond said.

"Well, you got it together," I laughed. "I was just sitting home thinking last night about [Speaker] Jane Hull. All these hit pieces that come out on you folks . . . that's Chuck Shipley [Chamber lobbyist] who is her son-in-law . . . What better way for her to neutralize or get rid of someone who doesn't think like she does than to use the Chamber of Commerce's money and their Votepak?"

". . . Stephens is out for revenge and I think Hull is gonna have to be real careful with her little conflicts of interest . . ." Raymond warned. "They came after me and they came after him with a vengeance . . . They'll pay a price."

"I would hope so. I would hate to see her just get away with it."

"Oh, she won't get away with it. Neither will the Chamber," Raymond vowed. "Right now, I got our staff people looking at every state budget to find every dollar of grants that we give the Arizona Chamber of Commerce and I would just about imagine that those grants are cut out of the budget."

Bobby saw another major hurdle in my casino drive, one that could poison us from within. "Hoffman worries me. That fucker and his mouth man . . . He's gonna get our nuts in a vise before this is over with . . . He's crazy. Trust me, brother, he's crazy . . . This shit's gonna get real hot and heavy the next six months."

There was absolutely no doubt about that.

David Horwitz followed Raymond and offered his recap of the recent election. "I shut the phones down at six o'clock 'cause there's no use callin' at six, but we had people out on the streets with walkin' around money, whole nine yards, gettin' 'em out [to vote]."

I asked Horwitz about the gubernatorial mess.

"I don't know if I played both sides of the fence, but every once in a while, I play both political parties. But in this situation, Symington's a greedy little fucker. And he might want a piece of the action."

"Did you do anything with this Brenda Burns at all?" I fished.

"I tried to go after her in the primary, but I didn't have enough stroke to go out there and do anything . . . She's a cunt from the word 'go.' She thinks she's very attractive and goes to the surgeon every time there's a flaw to make sure that she is okay. The uplifts and the tummy tucks . . . And she's had rumored affairs with several lobbyists and various other folks and what not . . . She hates the Speaker. Um, she's, she's a bitch."

And not a very discreet one at that. Was there anyone in Arizona who didn't know about Burns' alleged cosmetic surgery and affairs?

"What we've got is, 20 percent of the people in this state are genuine wackos," Horwitz continued, laying out Arizona's voting demographics. "They live back in the eighteenth century. They don't know where the hell they're goin' . . . Anything that government wants, anything that downtown Phoenix wants or anything that any other state wants is somethin' they don't want. And they don't care what the reason is. They don't have a brain between their ears."

Horwitz added that John Dougherty, now Senator John Dougherty, spooked during our meet because he thought it was a sting. The closed blinds made him nervous. Those thwart-the-state-attorney's-laserbeam blinds beat me again! If Horwitz was telling the truth, Colonel Dougherty wasn't such an honest man after all. He just didn't want to get caught.

Al Hill returned from a golfing trek to the Bahamas and immediately started pressing me for another $10,000. He claimed to need the money because his wife was pregnant. Suddenly, he had a wife and baby on the way, which was news to me. Doc Al explained that "They just scraped some of the cervix and just kind of sped up the process." I'm no obstetrician, but I don't think that's the preferred method of inducing labor.

On Sunday, November 18, I phoned Jim Hartdegen to set the hook for the $660 he had gotten through Scheffel.

" . . . Rich came to me and said I need, I can't remember, it was $660 or $880? He had the names and I got the money orders," I dangled.

"Yeah. And I appreciated that. That helped out a lot. 'Cause I did put out another limited mailing. And I bought some newspaper time that I wouldn't't've had," Hartdegen responded.

" . . . But Scheffel did let you know that was my money?"

"Yes he did . . . I pretty well know where it came from," Hartdegen went on, swallowing the hook and worm down into his belly. "He let me know where it came from. But if you need to know the names or so, I could . . ."

"No. I don't need them."

" . . . I have a sneaky suspicion . . . I'll be appointed Speaker pro tem."

" . . . That's good. I can still count on you for your sponsorship and your vote?"

"Yes. No problem."

20

Detective Ball greeted the third week of November with a proclamation that would test my ability to bullshit.

"No more money for Al Hill. Not another dime."

It was the right move. Al was done. Besides, he was just a sidelight to the political investigation, a fluke that enabled me to stretch my undercover acting ability. Unfortunately, I had filled his conniving brain with visions of greenbacks. He wasn't going to back off.

Carolyn Walker, the newly crowned majority whip, popped in on November 19. Walker's high ambitions had again taken flight. This time, she wanted me to lend her $750,000 to start a record company designed to nurture and promote rap groups.

". . . I wanna look at what I wanna do to take care of Carolyn when the legislative career's over . . ." she announced.

"You're gonna get some money out of the private prison issue," I said, referring to my backup project. "That's called somethin' for somethin'. That ain't got nothin' to do with loans."

"Tony, how am I gonna pimp you?"

"Honey, I've been pimped since I got here. Pimped for over $800,000. It ain't nothin'."

". . . I need some money, no use in me lyin' or anything, but I don't wanna pimp."

"Just don't hard pimp me . . . Just don't put me out on the street on Saturday night on Van Buren. In a wig."

"Shit . . ."

". . . Back to the private prison thing . . . I'm gonna take care of you on that."

"Yeah, well, could you make me a small advance . . . about four or five thousand?"

That, Tony could do.

"God bless you," Walker said, leaning over to grab the cash. I told Carolyn that I'd get back to her on the $750,000 for the record company.

"Can't I have a hug?" she said as she stood to leave.

"You kiddin' me? Can you have a hug?"

"Yeah."

"Of course you can have a hug, sweetheart," I said, pressing tight against her big body. When I withdrew, I discreetly checked to make sure she hadn't lifted another $10,000 from my pocket during our moving show of affection.

"I'm on board with ya. Let me tell ya," she cooed.

Ball advised me later that afternoon that they had decided to award the job of Reno private dick Dennis Davis to Detective Mark Stribling. I had wanted Sergeant Davis to play the gumshoe to test his mettle under fire and give him a feel for what I was going through undercover. Maybe then he would understand the tension and give me some respect, or at the least, lay off me. But Davis passed and Stribling quickly volunteered. He was a solid, low-keyed detective in his mid-thirties doing hard time in the transcript room. He would be set free long enough to attend the upcoming blackmail strategy sessions with Kenney and Raymond.

Al Hill polluted my home phone that evening with his incessant begging. I punched the record button and battled him lie for lie. Hill was beginning to tax my mental faculties. He was like a black hole of bullshit. No matter how much I tossed out, he swallowed it.

I caught my breath over the Thanksgiving break, then plunged back into the mire. George Stragalas collected his $1,250 salary in advance and began his first week in my employ. The cash must have made him feel obligated because he laid a whopper of a story on me that he had been holding back.

"We have a lever on [Terry] Goddard, let's put it that way . . . You'll have the hammer . . . He's a queer."

Big deal. Goddard's alleged alternative life-style was not only old news, it was politically incorrect to mention it. I needed better dirt. "Yeah, but see, we can shout to the world that he's a queer, but we never had sex with him," I explained.

"What if I did?"

That piqued my interest. I had sat through a relentless onslaught of malicious, slanderous, cruel, cold-hearted schemes during my nine-month foray into the filthy depths of American politics, but here was something altogether new. A man so vengeful he was willing to publicly debase himself in order to bring down an enemy. It was disgusting. It was sick. It was twisted. I needed to hear more.

"What if I did?" Stragalas repeated. "What if he tried?"

"That'd be wonderful."

"Albuquerque, New Mexico . . . Walter Mondale's running for president. 1984. Terry's . . . the first-term mayor. High ambition. Sam's all excited about how Terry won all this leadership . . . There's a debate in Albuquerque between Gary Hart, Walter Mondale, Jesse Jackson, John Glenn . . . Sam calls me up. He says, 'You are going with Terry to Albuquerque . . . You're gonna fly over there in the governor's plane. Bruce Babbitt's not going, but he's sending his wife Hattie' . . . And so we get to Albuquerque. We get to the Ramada Inn. I go to the desk and Lonnie Lopez, who's Bruce Babbitt's right-hand guy . . . Hispanic Godfather here . . . he says . . . 'You both can room together' . . . Lonnie says, 'I want you two to get along.' It was a weird conversation . . . [Terry] . . . has like five bottles of Maalox for some reason. He's having some tremendous stomach problems. He's walking around in his old-man shorts . . . At two o'clock in the morning . . ."

"You're hangin' on the bed naked with a rose in your mouth?" I interrupted.

"No . . . I feel this [slapping sound] you know, as I'm under the covers."

"He's pattin' you on the leg?"

"Yeah, on the leg and on the ass and stuff. I looked up, sleeping, 'What are you doing, man? Come on. Do what? Get the fuck outta here!'. . . He's going, 'What are you here for? You're not here to introduce [me around]. What are you here for?' I said, 'Not what you fuckin' think I'm here about!'. . ."

". . . What do you think that means?"

"What do you think? He wanted me to go to bed with him! Give him a blow job! . . ."*

". . . Just think, if you'da had sex with him, we'd own the governor for sure. You mighta had a kid with him."

"Maybe my memory serves me right and we did have sex. It's his word against mine, isn't it?"

*Terry Goddard says this incident is a figment of George Stragalas' imagination.

This was too sleazy for me. I hastily changed the subject.

"... You know where I am with the legislature? I've told you everybody I own," I said.

"No, you haven't."

"I own Don Kenney. I own Sue Laybe. I own Carolyn Walker. I own Jim Meredith. He was knocked out of leadership ... Who else did I buy ... Oh, Chuy Higuera, in my pocket. Jim Hartdegen, in my pocket. Alan [Stephens] and Art Hamilton, I own through Scheffel 'cause Scheffel took the money to them ... Bill English, I owned, he's out so I lose one there. Do I own anybody else? ... Bobby Raymond! I own Bobby ... Kenney's a Republican. He's chairman of the judiciary this year ... That was a good buy!"

"... Alan Stephens stands up in front of the tube every night now, talking about their [the Democrats'] program, he's a little pip-squeak! ..." Strag went on, still trashing the winners. "Alan says one night, I'm downtown and we're talkin', having drinks or whatever and he said, 'Let's go do some fund-raising.' I said, 'Where?' 'I'm gonna show you where.' You know where he takes me? To a topless bar on East Thomas Road! He sits down and he said ... 'There's a lot of cash around here.' ... He has a drink and his tongue is hangin' out of his mouth. So Alan, what his psyche is, 'There's a lotta cash around. Somebody has money. These people exist. I'm a legislator and they need me. I can't figure out how to get there, but George's maybe able to figure out how to get there.' I was waiting for him to say, 'Well George, where's the money?'..."

"... Did he make any money that night?"

"No, not a dime. What am I gonna do, go up to a topless dancer and say, 'Hey, there's ten dollars in your G-string. Can I have five of them?'..."

"He probably just wanted to see some titties," I guessed.

Ernie and Rich, the unlovable lobbyists, double-teamed me on November 29. Ernie reported that Team Tony had received 162 résumés and applications for the P.R. job fronting my issue. Another pound of worthless paper. When Ernie left early, Scheffel opened up.

"I'm goin' to Disneyland tomorrow morning. I'm gonna take nine legislators over to the Southern California School of Optometry in the morning, spend the day with them there, take them over to the Marriott and bed 'em down, feed 'em, get 'em up Saturday morning, traipse over to Disneyland, spend the day with them there. Some of them bring their girlfriends and wives ..."

"Now how do you do that? Is that legal?"

"Sure. I will give each of them a breakdown to the penny as to how much the association spent on their trips. It will probably be in the reporting range if, if the reporting range is five hundred bucks."

Sounded kosher to me. A little optometry and a lot of Mickey Mouse. Perfect political weekend.

Scheffel reported that Representative Stan Barnes was among those who had applied to be my P.R. spokesperson.

"You're kidding me."

"Nope . . ."

I never read Ernie's ad, but suspected that if Barnes applied, it must not have spelled out that the person was needed to front a casino gambling drive.

". . . Stan is screwin' an analyst for the governor," Scheffel added at my prompting. "Cute little Mormon girl. In fact, just had a baby. She's a couple of years younger than Stan. They went to high school together and they ran around like lovesick puppies last session. It was pretty obvious that he was dickin' her. Uh, Brenda [Burns], married to an optometrist . . . husband is a lush."

"Is that girl married?"

"Yeah."

"Whew."

"They're both married."

"And who's fuckin' Brenda?" my inquiring mind wanted to know.

"Couple of people . . ."

". . . I got a legislator that came to me that wants some information . . . and may want me to invest in having them [photographed] coming out of the motel room . . ."

"Bobby wouldn't do that, would he?"

"You know about it?" I said, surprised that Scheffel nailed the name of my accomplice.

"Oh shit, he hates her guts."

". . . I may have to put somebody on 'em."

"Yeah, well, I wish it was, I wish the situation was a little different and it was four or five years ago. Could follow the Speaker around a little bit."

"Jane?"

"Yeah."

"Who was she fuckin'?"

"Oh there, I don't know anybody in particular."

"The hell you don't . . . I don't know her . . . If she knocked on this door and said, 'I'm Jane Hull.' I'd say, 'Show me your driver's license.'"

"No, you can just look at the road map on her face and say, 'Yeah, I recognize you right away.'"

"I'll tell you what sucks about her," I said. "Chuck Shipley works for the Commerce. And they do hit pieces. What's wrong with that picture?"

"Chuck Shipley is dead meat," Scheffel decreed. "He can't go down to the legislators anymore, there wouldn't be any point . . . Those dipshits tried to take Alan out!"

After Scheffel left, Shiree breezed in to brighten my day—and that of the boys in the fourth room.

"I miss you," she drawled.

"You don't miss me . . . Why'd you have lunch with Bobby?"

That cooled her off for a moment. After throwing a tantrum about Raymond's lusty pursuit, I'd learned that she agreed to a lunch date. She quickly recovered and adroitly brushed it off as Chamber business.

"What's up?" I asked, letting the Bobby issue slide. "You said you wanted to see me about something personal? The rabbit died?"

"No. Why? Did you think you were in trouble?"

"Not me. I figured I gotta help you out."

"Why? Would you marry me?"

"If you were with child? No. But I'd make whoever's child it was marry you."

"Would you marry me if I wasn't with, if I asked you would you marry me? Of course, I would make you. You would have to become a Mormon or something, wouldn't ya?"

"Yep . . . Now get into what's bothering you. Get it off your chest."

". . . It's about to drive me crazy! . . . American Express . . . They want their payment of sixteen whatever. They want it in full! If you could help me out I would pay you back each month like a hundred bucks a month . . . They won't leave me alone, Tony . . . I need some help . . . I don't know what else to do . . . It's like they don't care! They want the whole thing!"

Shiree's plea was significant. I knew then that she was on her own and her professed breakup with Romano Sbrocca was real. A guy like Sbrocca wouldn't allow his girlfriend to get hysterical over a $1,600 credit card bill. Shiree's American Express problem meant she wasn't feeding Sbrocca information. The line was severed and with it all hope of getting any clue from Sbrocca about the death of the Mob-connected maitre d´.

"Do they have garnishee laws in this state?" I asked.

"I don't know if they do or not," she said. "I would hate to go through that."

The phone rang. The boys said to stall Shiree until they could get clearance on giving her the sixteen hundred. Since there was no crime involved, they needed approval from the top. I bearded my conversation with them by mentioning a friend's "sixteen-year-old" son who was taken to the Mustang Ranch on his birthday. Of the scores of fourth room calls I received, Shiree was the only one who ever paid any attention to the coded nonsense I babbled while talking to the cops. She often quizzed me on what I had been talking about. This time, she accused me of being "sick" for taking the youth to the notorious Nevada whorehouse. Here I was, trying to help her out, and I get slammed for a bullshit story.

"Tony, it seems like we could use Tony West . . . 'cause he was a crook," she said. "I mean, why don't we use 'em up? Why don't we take advantage? I know him and you met him. He thinks I'm a little sweetheart. He doesn't think I know diddly about anything. If we could just somehow figure out a way to use that guy . . . He's got a lot of power . . . Have you met with [Representative] Patricia Noland? That might be a good one . . . Now who's she having an affair with? . . . [A lobbyist who is] also doing Brenda Burns."

"How do you know that shit?"

"I know all the gossip."

". . . So [he is] servicing her and Noland? He's a hell of a man," I marveled.

"Yeah. I'm shocked . . ." she said. "He looks like a Ken doll."

". . . Speaking of Ken dolls, who's Stan [Representative Barns] fooling around with," I baited.

". . . He's clean. Oh shoot, who was it. Oh, I'm thinking of [U.S.] Congressman [Bob] Stump messing around with Nancy Weir. They're not together anymore . . . Brenda Burns . . . she has a nose job and a boob job . . ."

The fourth room called. "Okay, give the money to the honey." I smiled and reached for my stash.

". . . What do you need, $1,600?" I said, laying the cash on the table. This time there was no hesitation. Shiree grabbed it.

"Now you can get [American Express] off your back, get on to better things. Things are bad here. Hooker came up to me the other day, asked me to loan her fifty 'til she got back on her back."

"You're terrible! . . . Do you know what Tony, should I have angles? Tony, I want you to help me. I want you to do something for me. I want you to teach me. Teach me what to do. Tell me what to do."

"If you don't know by your age honey, you ain't never gonna know."

". . . Am I just a dummy, you mean?"

"No . . . I think you just tie in with the wrong people."

"Who are the right people, Tony. You. You're the right people, aren't you?"

"Yes. But you fucked around with that idiot [Sbrocca] and that wasn't in your best interest."

"I know it. And believe me, it's not the first idiot . . . What do I do, Tony . . . Help me."

"Just find a nice guy that's a for real guy, that's got some money put away and you latch onto him and you're loyal to him. Don't get mixed in with the Sbroccas of the world . . . That's for shortstops . . . Try to get more out of a relationship than you put in it."

" . . . You know I respect you very much and number two, I look up to you. In fact, if you probably said . . . 'You got to go stand in that street nude for an hour' I'd probably do it."

With that image swimming in everyone's mind, I ended the meet. It wasn't going to get better than that, and the cops and prosecutors had been teased enough.

Rich Scheffel had a little side business he wanted to conduct with Tony on December 2. The lobbyist said a pal was looking to put $250 on the upcoming Monday Night Football game pitting the New York Giants against the San Francisco 49ers. The friend wanted to bet the Giants to cover.

"Take the bet. We'll handle it," Ball said in his best Guido the Bookmaker voice. This was a new wrinkle. The county attorney's office was now making book on football games. If the Giants won or covered, we'd be obligated to pay. It turned out that the 49ers edged the Giants 7–3, enough to both win and cover the three-point spread. My fictional bookmaker buddy "R.R." (for Rick Romley) got to swallow the $250, plus $25 in juice. When he paid, Scheffel identified Representative Jim Skelly as the mystery man who reached out to lay down the illegal bet.

Don Kenney contacted me on December 4 and said he wanted $5,000 for Symington's campaign. The donation would give him access to the governor's office after Symington beat Goddard in the runoff. Ron Tapp, who was now nothing more than a $1,000-a-week ghost, followed and advised me that his "Mossad" agent, anti-espionage buddy, the little nerd who originally swept my office, was going for a job with the attorney general. He was probably going to operate the alleged laser listening device everybody in the state seemed to fear. According to Tapp, the guy wanted to know if I would supplement his income by hiring him as my attorney general's office spy. If he got the job, I was game. You never know when you need an inside man at the attorney general's office. Besides, I was getting sick of having to yank on the string all the time to fan my laser-shielding miniblinds in different directions.

Stragalas showed for a bull session on December 5. As usual, he rambled around, occasionally hitting upon some solid dirt.

". . . Now [Mike] Sophy got his start with Bruce Babbitt . . . was his chief deputy. When Sophy was busted on East Van Buren for soliciting a blow job from a prostitute, Babbitt fired him. Goddard picked him up immediately and put him on the law firm . . . This is significant. Sam [Goddard] is sittin' on a Federal Home Loan bank Board in San Francisco . . . A senior member of the board . . . Sam said to me, 'I know what's happening on the board. Things are bad in the S and L industry and they just fired Finerman [chairman of the board]' . . . So I think Sam has known all along about the S and L industry. I think he's known all along about Charles Keating. I think he tried with every ounce of strength to get Keating's support and money, and I think he tried to get Dennis [DeConcini] to do it and Dennis offered to do it. And when it came down to it, Keating couldn't stand Terry Goddard and he didn't give him any money and he didn't like him and he thought he was a fraud . . . I mean, DeConcini's being crucified in the media because of Keating. He's being destroyed publicly. He's gonna probably take the fall for all five [U.S.] senators. They all took Keating's money through Dennis when they wanted it . . ."

After Stragalas left, I huddled with the fourth room gang to discuss the Al Hill problem. We agreed that it was time to show our muscle. I was instructed to set up a meet at the apartment that would be attended by two bruiser undercover cops. If Hill tried to do anything stupid, he'd be busted on the spot.

Shiree and Hill both dropped in the office unannounced later that afternoon. Interestingly enough, they knew each other. I stood and watched in wonder as they chatted about old times in the reception area. When Shiree noticed me, her face flushed crimson red. So where had the kiddie pornographer and the discarded gun moll met? At church! They both attended the same Baptist church. I shook my head and bounced them both out of there.

Detectives Jack Ballentine and Mark Loftus jumped out of the pages of *Muscle* magazine and appeared at the apartment for Al Hill's meeting. I made them both take off their suit jackets so Hill could get the full measure of the men. I also wanted them to look less like the clean-cut cops they were. The detectives were instructed to stand around and look tough, but leave the talking to Tony.

Hill arrived ten minutes late at 4:10 p.m. I sat on the couch and yelled for him to come in. He took one step inside the doorway, spotted Ballentine, and froze like a rat caught in the beam of a cop's flashlight. I told Hill my friends were there for the next meeting, not him. Made no difference. Hill didn't budge. I spoke to him from the couch, fifteen feet away, and explained, firmly, that the money wouldn't arrive in late January and there wouldn't be any loans or advances. He was agreeable. At that point, he was agreeable to anything. He asked for a soda. I told him to help himself to one in the kitchen where Loftus was prowling around like the Incredible Hulk. Hill's thirst vanished and he quickly left.

It was a successful show all the way around. I scared the bullshit out of Hill without a direct threat. By claiming that the gorillas were for my next meeting, I was able to make my point and allow Hill to keep his dignity.

He phoned the next day and said the two brutes looked like cops. No wonder he was so scared. That's the trouble with using cops as undercover agents. After a few years on the force, they have "cop" written all over them. You can smell them from a doorway. I quickly cleaned it up.

"They've been with us for years. They live in the gym . . . That's good they look that way, it gets them access to a lot of places . . . They hang out in the casino . . . They're gonna stay down here and help me out with some of this shit that I got spread off into . . ."

To drive the message home, I gave Hill a rundown on what supposedly had happened at the next meeting. "The one bookie, he went to the hospital. He's seen the light. They took his car and his jewelry and just beat the fuck out of him and that's what you gotta do sometimes . . . They're here for 'educational' purposes . . . I had to buy a new top for my table. They put that mother over the table, busted the tabletop."

"They busted your table?" Hill said, gulping. "That table in your living room?"

"Yeah, they just threw his ass right on that table. And he [said], 'Please man.' I said, 'Please my ass. I been tryin' to reason with you for two months. All that "please" shit's out the window.'"

"He's been fucking with you for two months?" Hill asked.

"I just ain't had time to chase him . . . So I pulled him up yesterday and just said, 'Come on, let's have a talk.' And he walked into the trap."

"How much, how much did he owe you?"

"He owed thirty-seven before yesterday," I said, naming the total amount I had given Hill, plus the money he was trying to squeeze out of me. "We took his car, a '90 T-Bird. We took his jewelry. And took, he had about six thousand in his pocket. So we're pretty close to even.'"

I didn't hear from Fondia Al Hill again for a month.

Rich Scheffel came for a long sit-down two days later, on the tenth. He said Alan Stephens was ready to take another $4,000, this time to retire his campaign deficit. It was another opportunity to meet with the elusive majority leader. Once again, we had to bundle the money extensively to make it look legal.

"What I want to do is I'll give you seven names," Scheffel said. "Including mine, and my wife's and my daughter, my son, my son-in-law, my secretary, and one of the other gals in the office . . . I don't want money orders, I want them to write a personal check . . . A money order, Tony . . . doesn't send the right message. A personal check sends the right message . . . You don't have any problem with that, do you?"

I didn't. I wasn't going to let anything interfere with the magic words this time. I'd shout them through a megaphone.

". . . Soon as I have all of Stephens' things together, we'll take it to the lunch meeting we have and we'll give him a little envelope," Scheffel said. "You can hand it to him."

"He knows it's from me?"

"Yeah. And they're all, they're my family . . ."

". . . What do you need today?"

"I just want you to give me the money so I can give the money to people who can write the checks."

After taking $2,640, Scheffel again started working on saving my money. Ernie Hoffman had been squeezing me to hire Bill English's old secretary, a rescue mission Scheffel vetoed.

"Tony, you already got too many people on your payroll. I sat down today with a notebook and I wrote down names, and I wrote down seven names. You got me. You got Ernie. You got Stragalas."

"Tapp."

"You got Tapp. You got Kaasa or whatever his name. You got Sherry."

"Shiree."

"And you got Sheri."

". . . That's not counting my niece . . ." I said, playing along. "And see, the only money that I ever spend that I honest-to-God go home without feeling, 'Did I make a mistake' is the money that I spend with you. I'm telling you the truth," I lied. ". . . Hey, starting next month, I got to hand you seventy-five hundred a month . . ."

"That's our deal. Uh, I got expenses."

Naturally. And you're gonna have some hell to pay.

Ex-representative Bill English finally got the nerve to call—nearly six weeks after fumbling the election. He blamed his defeat on the anti-incumbent "throw the bums out" movement of 1990. If that was truly the reason, English and Corbet were among a handful of incumbents nationwide nailed by that hapless movement. Like the good politician he was, English was already planning his comeback. He had his sights set on the Pima County Supervisor position in 1992.

I told him Tony would be behind him all the way.

21

House Judiciary Chairman Don Kenney was toting another sex-smear hit list when he arrived at the apartment on December 14. He came to huddle with Reno P.I. Mike Harris, a.k.a. Detective Mark Stribling. Kenney was supposed to unload to Reno P.I. Denny Davis, a.k.a. Sergeant Davis, but the cops decided not only to switch to Stribling, but to change the name of the imaginary detective as well. That made no sense, but I'd long stopped trying to understand police thinking. Either way, Kenney didn't notice.

Extortion hit-list number II was shorter and more to the point, but just as damning as its predecessor. Targeted were the usual suspects—Terry Goddard and Representatives Brenda Burns, Candice Nagel, and Stan Barnes—along with some new players: Representative Don Aldridge, "Divorced. Lots of girlfriends. Real estate deals in Lake Havasu"; Representative Jack Jewett, "Likes the girls"; Representative Mark Killian, "Majority leader. Likes horse racing. Mormon"; Grant Woods, "Attorney General. Sexual preference. Didn't want to marry"; Senator Pete Rios, "President of the Senate. Bank accounts"; Senator David Bartlett, "Finances. Married. May be screwing around"; Representative Karen Mills, "Sex life. Finances. Right-wing Mormon wacko"; Representative Jane Hull, "Speaker of the House. Possibly screwing around. Husband is Dr. Terry Hull."

Kenney explained the need for this type of political muscle to Stribling.

"These people are people that may, at some point, become a stumbling block for Tony's goals. These people are the type that you can't go to and persuade with campaign contributions . . . They're just assholes and we want to find out whatever you can that we might use as a persuasion factor at a later point . . . Whatever hammer you can get. Preferably a sledgehammer . . . Killian, for example . . . I don't think he's been slipping and sliding. I don't think he knows what it's for other than to pee with . . . Candice Nagel . . . I don't think she screws around, but that's a possibility. But she sure does like to squeeze her body up against guys . . . Jan Brewer, Senator, District 19 . . . Gosh, this is the type of gal you get anything at all on her and I can get her to fold in a minute. She's El Foldo . . . Might check out [Attorney General] Grant Woods if I were you . . . He lived with this gal for a couple of years, got her pregnant, wasn't gonna marry her until they raised so much hell about it . . . He's gonna have a strong impact on testifying for or against ya. I'd put a star by that."

The last one caught my attention. The "gal" Kenney said Attorney General Woods knocked up and tried to duck was a beautiful, Latina television anchor named Marlene Galan. Since Woods would never be mistaken for Warren Beatty, he should be so lucky to get a wife like that. If he was going around the capitol bad-mouthing that babe, then he deserved to be extorted.

"He didn't wanna marry this girl?" I asked.

"No."

"But did he marry her?"

"Yeah, he finally did."*

The second apartment boys had advised me to draw Kenney out on how he would use such information. If he explained it, he was cooked.

"I'm visualizing here, the middle of June, the last week or two weeks of the session," he said. "They've expressed . . . what their position is and we'll just say, 'Hey Kyle, I'm tellin' you this just as a friend. We don't agree on this issue, but I like you and this issue is important to some people and they've checked you out and they found out that you've been screwin' goats. They've got pictures of it and I hate to have this come out' . . ."

Flip him over and serve him. Kenney was done. After that, it was just a matter of allowing the representative to ring up the "conspiracy" counts like bells on a pinball machine.

"Tony, all these guys are vicious. All these guys are gonna be run-

---

*Woods' press secretary, Steve Tseffos, relates that Woods was "very happy" to marry his wife and emphasized that the television anchor was not pregnant when they wed. "They were married in March 1990 and their son was born in April 1991. I don't know what the hell Don Kenney is talking about! It's important that the people know the truth."

ning again. Some of them wanna run for Congress. Some of them wanna become judges. Anything like that is embarrassing."

". . . You didn't give me any names of lobbyists that you think [Brenda] Burns is fuckin' around with," I said, expecting to hear the same, well-worn names.

"Uh, Chuck Shipley . . . He's the lobbyist for the Arizona Chamber of Commerce . . . Marty Shultz."

". . . What's he do?"

"He's the lobbyist for Arizona Public Service."

". . . Who else?"

"Mike Palmer, possibly . . . You might put down Tom Patterson. You get two for one. He's a State Senator. Minority leader."

". . . You gave me Shipley, Shultz, Palmer, you gave me three more," I said. "That's six guys she's fuckin' plus her husband. If she's fuckin' one of the six, we got her."

". . . If you can get her . . . you got half your battle won," Kenney said. ". . . She's one of these guys that are very bright and very articulate and you just have to neutralize to keep them quiet."

"And you don't have any problem with hittin' her with the pictures and tellin' her this is gonna be in the paper?" I asked, setting the hook deeper.

"I'd love to! I would love to! . . . 'Cause she has shit on me so many times! . . . And she's the one that's gonna torpedo you the most. She'd screw her mother to promote her own ends."

"That'd be a good picture," Stribling chirped.

"She's the type that would call a press conference on you, big exposé," Kenney continued. "She'd get all the reporters there and say, 'There's gambling in River City!' "

When we finished the hit list, I gave Kenney $5,000 to donate to Symington to buy some future influence.

"That'll open the door," he said, sweeping up the cash.

"I always remember the movie *The Godfather, Part II* where they caught that United States senator in the whorehouse . . ." Kenney recalled, relishing the thought. "Wasn't that a great scene?"

". . . My favorite part's where the guy wakes up in bed with the horse," I said, harking back to *The Godfather*.

". . . That's what we have to do with Brenda Burns . . ." Kenney suggested.

"Well, I'll tell you one thing I can't do. Be impossible to put all the heads of the guys she's fuckin' in her bed. It ain't big enough!"

* * *

Tapp tipped me off on December 17 that Ernie Hoffman had approached him for a private sit-down to discuss all things Tony. That was unsettling. I felt that Ernie was about to bail out on us. I called them all in, Hoffman, Tapp, and Scheffel, for a State-of-the-Tony session.

Scheffel arrived early and took fifteen minutes to outline the plans Sheri Raymond had for my video. Her concept was creative and loaded with effective visuals. It was obvious that she knew her stuff and had worked hard. It was still a shakedown to Scheffel and Bobby, but Sheri Raymond was apparently unaware and was taking the job seriously.

Rich followed that with a report on the latest troublesome leak in the Team Tony dam. Senator Pete Corpstein's wife, Alice, a muckety-muck in the tourism and travel industry, had gotten wind of Tony Vincent and was going around talking about the Mafia invading Arizona. Scheffel confronted her at some function.

". . . I said, 'You used the term "Mafia" and that's just not acceptable, Alice . . . You could be open for any kind of libel.' She finally said, 'If you're trying to intimidate me, it won't work' . . . I hope that little pinhead she's married to, Mr. Potato Head, gives me a call, 'cause I would love to tell him what I think! . . . I said, 'Tony is not a member of the Mafia and if you don't keep your mouth shut Alice, he's gonna blow your house up.'"

That last line was just a joke. A little Mob humor. My lobbyists were getting into the life. Another few months and I'd have them all in silk suits, pointy shoes, and diamond pinky rings. Or in coffins.

Hoffman arrived late and empty-handed. The long-awaited—and already paid for—economic studies and polls were nearly a month behind schedule and still nowhere in sight. Instead, what I kept receiving from him were waves of padded bills. Ernie was playing Tony for a sucker. RICO money or not, it didn't sit well with me. He billed $1,412 for airfare from Tucson to Reno. You can fly from Tucson to Moscow for that. Ernie said it was for two trips. I checked with America West Airlines. Round trip, without any specials or discounts, was $288. Southwest Airlines charges less, sometimes as little as $49 round trip to Vegas. Ernie also billed $1,768 in hotel and meeting expenses. Vegas and Reno have some of the cheapest hotel rates in the world. You can live in a casino hotel in Reno for a couple of months on that kind of money. Ernie claimed he had to entertain the professors doing the study.

What Ernie was trying to do was a little paper shuffle to hack away at the $18,000 "credit" he kept blithering about. He was closing in on Al Hill as the most irritating sleazeball in the entire Desert Sting operation. Tony didn't mind people robbing him. But this kind of thievery showed no respect.

I let Ernie squirm a while, then pretended to accept his explanations. The dialogue shifted to yet another mind-boggling aspect of Arizona politics—the media's alliance with the politicians. And I wasn't just referring to rumors about Brenda Burns and her buddy the television reporter, or the attorney general and the spicy anchorwoman. I had learned that the *Arizona Republic's* highly influential political columnist, a youthful-looking woman named Keven Willey, was married to a lobbyist named Mike Braun who worked for a big firm called Quarles & Brady & Fannin. One of the firm's clients was American Greyhound Racing, a staunch anti-casino force.

"I'm just picturing if my wife were a political columnist, and I were a lobbyist," I speculated, trying to elicit some comments. "And I need Jim Splivens to vote on my issue, and I go home that night and say, 'Honey, whatever you do. Don't knock Jim Splivens.' I mean, am I outta line?"

". . . Well, let me tell you what he's involved in," Ernie said. "[Braun] represents insurance, along with me. [Bob] Fannin does and Fannin hired him so we're both in the insurance business. We're both in the tobacco business. He represents the smokeless account as well as beer and you have never seen anything [in Willey's column] contrary to our clients . . . So you know, it does, it makes a difference. It flat ass makes a difference . . . And we're bad. We in the insurance thing, we're rippin' people and we've never had a bad article in that column. Smokeless tobacco, you know, the kids getting cancer of the mouth and everything else. I gave 'em that account and what happens, you've never seen anything in there about tobacco."*

I contemplated this as my employees continued to talk. I had the sinking feeling that when the dam burst, the local media wasn't going to view Tony as a good guy. He was stepping on their toes as well as on the politicians'. They'd slap around the county attorney and the police, but they'd save the sledgehammer for Tony. I was the most vulnerable. And this moment of nontruth had to be just around the corner. I was spread-eagle on the dam, with all my fingers and toes trying to plug the leaks, but the water was still spurting through. It reminded me of something a wise-guy friend from Pittsburgh once said. He was awaiting trial for armed robbery and was bitterly complaining about the justice system.

---

*Both Keven Willey and her husband deny that his career affects her columns in any way.

"They got fourteen witnesses against me, Joe. Two or three I could kill, but if I kill fourteen, they'll get suspicious."

He was dead serious. That was the way I felt. I could patch up two or three holes, but if I patched fourteen, they'd get suspicious.

Then again, I'd have given ten-to-one odds that Operation Desert Sting was going to collapse before Halloween. Here we were, closing in on Christmas, and Tony Vincent was still alive and well.

Chuy Higuera ended a long period of silence by ringing Tony on December 18. He was set to be chairman of the government committee and turned out to be another excellent purchase. Chuy needed to pay an attorney $3,600, and he only had $4,000 in his kitty, so by his logic, he needed $1,500 from me. I didn't even bother trying to make sense of it and offered him the entire $3,600. He declined, saying he required only $1,500. Unfortunately, Chuy didn't have any names to bundle the money. He suggested I reach out for Rich Scheffel to supply the names.

Bobby Raymond was next on Tony's hotline. He was peeved because I'd missed a sit-down he'd set with the Miller beer people. He wanted to know if Scheffel had orchestrated my no-show because Scheffel pimps for Budweiser. These guys were something. They came to me together but stood ready to knife each other in the back at the drop of a Bud Light. I told Bobby that Rich might have said something about the Miller people meet not being critical. Nothing like fueling the fires.

Carolyn Walker buzzed me at home to say that Sue Laybe put the move on Senator Nancy Hill regarding my issue and scared her senseless. Hill ran to Walker and Walker calmed her down. Such are the benefits of having a full pocket of politicians. They careen into each other for damage control.

David Manley, chairman of the Maricopa County Democratic party, dropped in on the nineteenth for an introduction. He was a college professor–type, about five-feet-nine, with brown hair and a thick mustache. When he wasn't dabbling in politics, Manley worked as an aide to C. Diane Bishop, State Superintendent of Public Instruction. (Bishop stirred some controversy in 1991 when the newspapers reported that her husband ripped her clothes off on the front lawn of their condo during a marital spat.) Manley sat crossed-legged on my couch and dangled one of his loafers in the air. That posture revealed that the sole of his shoe had almost peeled completely off. That was about all he revealed. Manley was cautious and evasive. I wearied of the game and ended the meeting.

George Stragalas and Sue Laybe skipped in as a team to discuss the gubernatorial runoff. Sue wanted me to pump $50,000 into Goddard's famished coffers. No problem, I said, just bring him in, put him in the Ed McMahon seat, and let me get him to say the magic words. If he played ball, he'd walk with the fifty.

Scheffel phoned during the meeting and relayed Stephens' latest move. He said Alan wanted to change our lunch date from my conference room to Monti's Steak House in Tempe near Arizona State University. That was not unexpected, but it still pissed me off. The police had spent the weekend wiring the conference room, and I had already ordered more than a $100 worth of food. The cops decided that I wasn't going anywhere. Either Stephens came into our lair, or he could forget the money.

I layed down Tony's law that night to Scheffel. "He's not trusting my good nature and my hand of friendship that I've extended to him. I have doled out well over $25,000 to him and Art. I didn't get a phone call. I didn't get a Christmas card. I didn't get a little thank-you note. I got nothing . . . I got it from people I don't even know. The Furmans and Jacobsons and whoever it went to . . . I got notes. I looked at 'em, I said, 'That's nice' . . . But this guy, this guy has pulled my joint to the point where my joint is sore. I'm tired of fuckin' with him. I'm tired of his attitude. He's treating me like a rank sucker . . . What he has to remember, he can say or do whatever he wants to do, but the sun don't shine on the same dog's ass every day. And if I have to teach him that, I will teach him . . ."

Scheffel meekly mentioned that he'd already given Stephens some of the checks. That really pissed me off because it enabled Stephens to stand his ground. Stephens reportedly took the money and got away clean—for the third time! The man was amazing. If I had gone along with the location switch, Stephens might have agreed to the magic words and taken the rest of the checks in the restaurant. Now, because of Scheffel's haste and Tony's new tough stand, the majority leader wouldn't even face the temptation.

Higuera was pumped full of piss and vinegar when he dropped by for his bundle on December 20. He grabbed a cold beer from Marie and explained that he had devised a new wrinkle that eliminated the need for lobbyists bearing names. Higuera was having a raffle for a gold chain, and I would have the honor of buying tickets—$1,500 worth of tickets for what was probably a $50 gold chain that may have been ripped from someone's neck that afternoon. That was a shrewd investment. No matter. It was votes I was buying. The rest was window dressing.

". . . I need to retire that debt that I have with the lawyer. And I need to keep a little bit in my kitty," Higuera said.

"Okay. What do you need?"

"The people, not you . . . I can't get it all from you."

"*Cuanto costo?* What do you need? I told you on the phone. I can take care of the whole thing if you want me to."

"No. I don't want the whole thing."

"What do you want me to do? It's $3,600. What do you need?"

"That's too much. That's too much."

It was the same old Higuera, negotiating down, selling himself short. "All right, what do you need?"

". . . I'm not able to say. I'm not used to this."

"Two grand? Yeah, you're not used to money. I know."

". . . Oh, maybe two grand is too much. I'm serious man, you know."

"Fifteen hundred?" Going once. Going twice.

"Fifteen hundred . . . I'll tell you what, I'm gonna drop some tickets, okay? . . . This is what I'm raffling," he said, handing me the chain. The jewelry turned out to be better than I expected, a chunk of gold worth about $800 wholesale. Chuy said he paid $2,000.

"Who's gonna win it," I inquired.

"Well, we'll put the numbers and we'll see who the lucky guy is, but . . ."

"Who's gonna win it?"

"The guy that buys the most tickets has a better chance."

Right. ". . . Between me and you, I don't need no fuckin' raffle tickets."

"Well, no, between me and you, it's only fair."

"I'm your friend. What do I need with that?"

Higuera took the $1,500 and kept the tickets. I like to keep my bribes clean.

Scheffel surprised me with a Christmas gift—an expensive statue of St. Francis of Assisi, the patron saint of animals. It had to have cost $100 or more. I had been giving everybody giant Hickory Farms gift baskets, but until then, nobody had given Tony anything. I didn't know if that meant Scheffel had a bigger heart, or was just a slicker player.

Of course, Desert Sting's money had bought the statue, and a lot more in its nine months. We had spent $751,000, including about $300,000 in bribes. It was all confiscated RICO money, mostly from drug busts. Easy come, easy go.

Tony closed shop for the Christmas holidays. Joe even visited the homestead for a while, but not for long. I was in miles too deep for Joe's panicky blood.

By whatever miracle, Operation Desert Sting made it into 1991. January marked the opening of a new legislative session. The lawmakers would be gathered together, gossiping, fornicating, preening, posturing, and pontificating. Tony would have to call upon all his wits just to survive to the end of the month.

22

The New Year started off with an uppercut to Tony's chin. Rich Scheffel informed me that Ernie Hoffman had hired a private detective to investigate Tony Vincent. The detective reported that Tony was a bookmaker operating out of Ernesto's Backstreet. The only shards of truth in that report were fourteen months old and hearkened to the long-forgotten social gambling investigation. Ernie was also said to have met with the big shots at Harvey's casino in Reno to try and talk them into hiring him to promote casino gambling in Arizona. He met with Harvey during a trip that I paid for. Cute. There was no limit to the double-dealing depths that these lobbyists would sink to. Since Ernie already had the fresh polls and studies, he must have figured he could hawk them again and pick up another $100,000. Whatever his angle, the implications were that Ernie had turned traitor.

". . . You need to be very careful on how we deal with this because he will screw me and he will screw you, but he will screw me permanently out there . . ." Rich said, twitching nervously. ". . . He wanted me to fly up with him the week between Christmas and New Year's, to Reno, to meet these people [Harvey's] . . . He told me how we can get a hell of a deal here. Tony, I'll do a lot of things, but I wouldn't ever do that to anybody . . . What you want out of Ernie Hoffman, besides what you paid for, is you want him to know that your record is completely clean and that if he says or babbles one more of these innuendos to anyone, and especially anyone at the legislature or remotely connected with the legislature, it won't be a fork, it'll be the ice pick in the ear . . . He's tellin' me he's tryin' to protect me . . . That son-of-a-bitch would fuck me in two seconds!"

I handed Rich $11,700 cash to calm him down. That broke down to $7,500 as the first installment on his 1991 retainer, and another $4,200 for Sheri Raymond's video extravaganza.

"I can't let this cockroach step on me. I gotta stomp on him real quick," I postured.

". . . I hate like hell havin' Ernie walkin' the halls at the legislature. He can kill a vote in a hurry . . ."

"I can fix it to where he can't walk the halls," I offered.

"I won't ask you how, but that'd be great."

It never ceased to amaze me how quick these political types were to suggest that I maim and murder their rivals. If lobbyists and politicians really did have access to the Mob's power, there would be bloodbaths in every state legislature in the country. Washington, D.C.? Forget it. They'd run out of body bags.

David Manley breezed in on January 3 with a new attitude. The Maricopa County Democratic party chairman said he could funnel cash through the party to individuals of my choice. That was against the law. In Arizona, you can give as much money as you want to a political party, but you can't designate who you want the money to go to.

"If I need to channel monies into these campaigns, Dave, can you handle it?"

"Yes."

"If I wanna give $100,000 into four campaigns, five campaigns, and I get that money to you, can you get it into the party and get it out to the people? . . . If we did it over a period of time, ten, ten, ten, ten. Can you do that?"

"Yes."

"Will you do that?"

"Yes."

". . . Sometimes we have to reach a little bit outside the laws to do what we gotta do," I said, making it perfectly clear.

"Okay."

The cops called, said he was a goner, and gave the okay to pay him off. This is where the deal stalled. It wasn't that Manley didn't want his share, he just didn't know what he was worth. I had to ask him seven times to set his price.

"What do you want in exchange for your services?"

". . . You know, some type of service for your endeavors, separate from that [the money to the party]," Manley said.

"Of course, you mean for your pocket."

"Yeah, right."

"... Now what do you want?"

"... What I, I'm tryin' to say is yes, I do want something and I also want to do something beyond my position as county chair to, um, justify anything that comes to me."

"Say that again?"

"Well, I wanna, in addition to the stuff that I'll do as county chairman for you ... this is my comfort level."

Silly me. I forgot that we needed to establish a comfort level first. Manley said he would be comfortable doing booklets and printing stuff. I explained I was up to my eyeballs in booklet people.

"See, I would think it would be best if you worked for me in a covert sense. Kind of a CIA operation ... What do you need for Dave? What's it gonna take to keep Dave happy? You must have some ballpark idea what you're looking for," I said.

"Basically, what I'm looking for is, I need a car and haven't got any credit to buy one."

"... So what do you think you're gonna need and how do you want it? ..."

"... I guess the first question that comes to my mind, uh, is what do you feel, you know, I mean like what, I know this brings a lot of value to you."

"... What do you think that you can live with? I gotta know what you think. I can't set your price, too ... I can tell ya what I want, but you gotta tell me what you're looking for to do it ... What's a comfortable starting figure for you? ... So what do you think you could live with today, David?"

He sat there stone quiet. I recalled Don Kenney's statement about Arizona politicians being "unsophisticated whores" who didn't know that they were beautiful.

"Okay," I sighed, breaking the silence. "By the month, and meet in three months ... to reevaluate." This payment schedule gave him an out in case he felt he sold too cheap.

"Well, life would be a lot easier for me if I had an extra $1,000 a month to ..."

Okay! "A grand a month," I said, cutting him off and reaching into my pocket. All that haggling for a lousy grand a month? "... I can live with that."

I flipped $3,000 to my new player for the upcoming ninety days.

"... That'll help you with your car and everything."

"It sure will!" he said, gleefully.

* * *

I drove to Sky Harbor International Airport on January 8—a beautiful winter day—and picked up my old boyhood friend, Johnny Rulli. Ernie Hoffman had been pressing to meet my other partners, and I'd suggested to the cops and prosecutors that Rulli would be perfect. I'd warned Hoffman and Scheffel that my partners were "dem and dose" guys who wouldn't stand for any grief, but Hoffman still pushed. Rulli said he normally would have nothing to do with helping cops and prosecutors, but since he hated politicians worse, he agreed to go along. I stashed him at the Registry Resort until the meet the next day.

Bobby Raymond moseyed by that afternoon to discuss the Ernie problem.

"... I'm gonna tell you who I get this from, but man, don't tell anybody, because if this comes back around, this fucker in DPS is gonna get bit in the ass and I'm gonna get bit in the ass ... It's Milstead ... Former director of DPS, now works in the governor's office overseeing DPS, the attorney general, the Department of Corrections ... He's come around and he said, 'We're lettin' some of you folks know that knows Mr. Vincent that DPS has been kinda looking into you and they think he's a bookie.'"

Raymond's report posed an intriguing question. Why was Milstead tipping off favored legislators about an ongoing police investigation into Tony Vincent?

"Anyway, [Milstead] said, '... We're not wanting to blow up the fucking world here. DPS is very sensitive that this could wind up in the newspaper. But we want you all to kind of pass the word quietly among yourselves that this guy is being watched because they think he's a bookie' ... Somebody brought it up in a [Goddard] campaign meeting the other day ... Sophy calls Stephens, Stephens just fucking shit all over himself! ... Stephens has gone nuts ... I call Stephens, I said, 'What's goin' on with you?' 'Well, I got this call from Sophy and blah, blah, woof, woof.' I said, 'Oh fuck him! You know, why don't you just relax' ... I said, 'What the fuck do you expect, Alan? So the guy's a professional gambler. Would you expect the minister from the First Baptist Church come in from Nevada and wanna legalize gambling? Use your fuckin' head, friend!'"

Good point, Bob.

"[Milstead] came to see me again this morning ... He said, 'I understand your wife's doing a video for Tony Vincent' ... He said, 'There's been some fairly heavy money passed around ... some pretty heavy contributions' ... I said, 'My wife does videos for a lot of people ... Are you tellin' me there's some kind of conflict of interest here?

Because if there's a conflict of interest, it's all the way around me.' He said, 'No, I'm not sayin' that at all . . . I want you to know this is out there and the people know this.' I said, 'I don't give a fuck! It's no secret. I mean, she's not doin' it in the dark of night!' . . . I said, 'What are you telling me, Ralph? Is this guy a real bad actor?' . . . All of a sudden, one of these days, are you all gonna come out with some big long criminal history and tell us 'This is a gangster and you're all caught up with him!' . . . He said, 'No, on the contrary, the biggest problem DPS is finding, they can't find out anything in this guy's past' . . . So anyway, I sat there . . . and I got to thinkin' what was this fuckin' Milstead tryin' to tell me? Was he tryin' to tell me to 'Get your fuckin' wife out of the middle of this.' Or what, what exactly? So I called the fucker back. I said, 'Ralph, I've been sitting here contemplating my navel on what you said a while ago and I wanna ask you something real straight. In a roundabout way, were you tryin' to tell me to get Sheri the hell out of this picture?' And he said, 'No, not at all. I honestly don't think there's gonna be anything wrong' . . . He let me know in no uncertain terms that this information did come from Ernie Hoffman . . . And you know, my only worry, Tony, is that fuckin' Hoffman!"

"What do you suggest I do?"

". . . I think you just tell him to go away and, if it were me — I mean, I'm not sure it ain't gonna be me — if he doesn't believe you, I'll kill that motherfucker! . . ." Raymond threatened.

"You think it might come to that?"

"No, I don't . . . Hoffman, he doesn't have any nerve . . . I would be more inclined to tell him, 'Hoffman, you go home to Tucson and if I ever hear a fucking peep! You better pray that nobody even runs a rumor that you're talking, 'cause I'll stick a fucking ice pick right straight up your nose!'"

For a desert town, Phoenix sure had a lot of ice picks. Scheffel was gonna stick one in Hoffman's ear. Now Raymond had staked out Ernie's nose.

"Hoffman's running around tellin' people that you gave me ten grand, too," Bobby continued.

"He's guessin'. He just guessed a good number," I bluffed, not wanting him to know I'd blabbed to Ernie.

". . . There's a lot of talk and a lot of speculation that if you send Hoffman back to Tucson and he shuts up, I think given two or three weeks, it'll all blow over. Because comin' into [the 1991] session next week . . . the focus is gonna be in nine thousand directions."

When I pressed the fourth room boys about the Milstead revelations, they went cold. It was obvious they wanted no part of an investigation into the activities of the former DPS chief. Instead, the Raymond-Milstead connection spurred more talk about sticking the ice pick up Tony Vincent's nose and shutting down. I was so concerned about Milstead that I checked in with my "Deep Throat" advisor in Miami, Gerald Arenberg of the American Federation of Police. His warning was stronger than ever.

"As I've said all along, be careful with the cops. They'll betray you in the end worse than anybody."

Ernie Hoffman dispatched an interesting fax at 4:20 p.m. He wrote that he wouldn't be able to make the Johnny Rulli showdown meeting the next day, and promised that a letter of explanation would follow. He also said he would send the economic report by Fed Ex later in the week. Scheffel phoned a few minutes before midnight with the latest on Ernie's moves.

"He's fuckin' us to death, my friend," Scheffel said. "He's talked to a lot of people . . . He's tellin' the world about this thing . . . The people he was talking to told him to create a paper trail, distance himself from you immediately . . . I think he keeps pressing the press. My gut feeling is he's dumped this thing on the press already and they're ready to nail us . . . This cocksucker is a crazy man. I know you have other ways you would have dealt with this guy in the old times, but you know, really, we need to get his mouth shut. I mean just totally shut!"

No one could figure Ernie's motives. He was accomplishing little aside from drawing attention to himself. If it was a sting, he was long cooked and no amount of revisionist history could clean him up. If it was real and he was trying to destroy Tony Vincent, he'd end up dead, or in jail with him. There was no method to his madness.

The next morning, Johnny Rulli climbed into a crisp, pinstriped suit, wrapped his $100 silk "John Gotti" tie around his neck, combed his wavy hair, and transformed himself from a Hilton crap table supervisor into Johnny D, grade-A gangster. He would have been the perfect prop for the sit-down with Hoffman had the frantic Tucson lobbyist made the mistake of appearing. As it was, we were going ahead with the show for Scheffel even though it was no longer really necessary. After a quick introduction, Scheffel opened the meet with more bad news, including additional accounts of the increasingly odd behavior of the rival Maricopa County police forces that operate on the highways and outside Phoenix city limits.

". . . The legislative liaison from DPS went to [Peter] Rios, the new president of the Senate, went to Hull, went to Hamilton, went to Patterson, and Patterson's the minority leader, and told them they're investigating you. And that they should tell their members to keep their distance."

"So he's tippin' them off to stay away from me?"

"He is telling them to tell their members to stay away from you."

All this was started, of course, because of Ernie Hoffman.

"That's the dirty motherfucker that took the money and went down to Reno and tried to solicit somebody else?" Rulli growled like Sonny Corleone. "And so he's gonna send you a letter sayin' what? Well this low-life fuckin' worm, motherfuckin' cocksucker. And I gotta sit here and listen to this shit?"

Rulli was getting so deeply into his character he was starting to scare me. Ernie would have had a heart attack. Scheffel coughed nervously, then continued outlining the decline and fall of Tony Vincent.

". . . They've got an investigator . . . They get the files from the state legislature and they see money orders and they're consecutive numbers . . . It'll cost me my career, but it's only six months in jail and a fine . . . My prayer right now is that we shut down this investigation . . . I value [Rick] DeGraw's advice. He feels you're gonna get hit real quickly by an investigative reporter . . . They're gonna love this story. This story can be filled with intrigue. It's gonna be filled with innuendo, political contributions, under-the-table money, you name it. It's all gonna be in there 'cause if Ernie's talked to ten people, he's talked to a hundred people."

Rich said the way to diffuse the snowballing investigation was to release my polls and economic impact studies, come forward publicly, and announce that I was going with a public initiative referendum.

". . . What this does is immediately remove the whole issue of campaign contributions and anything else," he explained. "All you're doing is comin' in here to do an initiative."

It wasn't a bad plan. No way could Tony come out of the shadows like that, but I had to give Scheffel credit. His other solution was for me to quickly hire a spokesman of his choice, and hire Rick DeGraw to clean me up. This from the guy who chastised me for spending too much money, and jumped on me for having too many people on my payroll. DeGraw, he explained, was real tight with the two major powers in the legislature, the skittish Senate Majority Leader Alan Stephens and the forceful House Minority Leader Art Hamilton.

". . . The problem is that Alan got some of those money orders . . ." Scheffel said. "His butt's on the line, too. He knew where they came from. You know that. If my butt ever gets on the line, I'm gonna say he knew where they came from. Even more important . . . I got two clients on there, you know, and these are people who wheel and deal in the legislature. Chiropractors, they get nailed with that they're dead meat . . . [Terry] Rondberg and [Alan] Immerman. They did it [lent their names to bundled checks] as a favor . . . We gotta close the loop of information . . . We hafta control the information . . ."

". . . Those people you gave me the names of, they're existing people . . ." I asked, thinking we were in the clear. "You called them all and told them up-front . . . that they were givin' 220 or whatever."

"Oh yeah, they know they gave the money."

"So, we don't have a problem."

"Well, Tony, how is it that twelve people who don't know each other, all went down to the bank and bought forty money orders in consecutive series and sent them to legislators?"

"Got a point," Rulli said with a wink. He was loving this.

". . . We did this for Art and Alan," Scheffel said. "They named the people they wanted the money to go to. They haven't forgotten that. I mean, let's be honest here. They don't want this investigation to go very far either . . . What I'm suggesting is they know that there's a problem and Art's gonna figure out a way to try to deal with the problem. Not Alan, Art . . . That's the way I see it . . . I'll tell you what . . . I'm a wimp. You know, shit, I've got a $250,000-, $300,000-a-year business. I'm not getting rich, but I do okay. I get nailed with one campaign violation and I'm history. I mean, I'm history! Hell, I got a wife and kids . . . But listen, listen. I'm not here to cry. I'm here to tell ya we need to get this damage control in place and make that thing work."

". . . I was nervous until you said that Art is gonna get involved," I said. "That calmed me down . . . We did right by him."

"Yeah, and he knows we did it. You know we did it. That's why he's gonna be involved," Scheffel insisted.

On the surface, this meeting on the downfall of the nonexistent Tony Vincent seemed like much ado about nothing. However, weaved into Scheffel's angst were some critical confirmations. He repeatedly maintained that Stephens and Hamilton knew the money they accepted came from me, and that they knew that it was dirty. Dirty enough, in fact, that the two legislative leaders allegedly would use their influence to stave off a police investigation into Tony Vincent that could explode in their political faces.

After the meeting, I went to the second apartment and told the gang that it was time to bust Scheffel, roll him, and put him back on the street. At 7:30 p.m. that evening, I received a rare call from Captain Black. They wanted Scheffel at the apartment at 2 p.m. on Friday. They were going to take him down.

The mail on January 16 brought Ernie Hoffman's long-awaited resignation. It was a model of furious backpedaling: "My participation with your company was solely dedicated to these studies and they are now all completed. If there were any lobbying activities prior to January 1, 1991, I did not participate in that process nor have I been present when any legislation has been discussed with any legislators."

Nice try. I searched the envelope for the $18,000 that he didn't take at a meeting he never attended to discuss legislative matters he never discussed. Not so much as a dime slid out. Apparently, a lobbyist can only backpedal as far as his wallet.

The postman also brought news that J. Fife Symington had ordered his Information Systems Manager, David K. Borg, to return $1,100 of the $2,200 I contributed for the Glen Campbell dinner I never attended. There was no explanation for the rebound, nor was there any sign of the other $1,100 or the $5,000 I had given Kenney for Symington—money that was apparently at work helping him become governor. The second $1,100 was in Marie's name, and Kenney had scrubbed the $5,000 through his family, so it was possible Symington didn't know that the money came from me.

Scheffel continued to press me to hire Rick DeGraw—at $5,000 a month—to clean myself up. Aside from his friendships with Stephens and Hamilton, DeGraw was said to be more skilled at the art of "crisis" public relations, a branch of the P.R. dodge I was told I now desperately needed. Whatever the P.R. nuances, DeGraw was just another mark to me. I told Scheffel to set a meet.

On January 10, Detective Ball instructed me to inform Jim Davis that his hit victim was coming to town and Davis' rubout skills, which I had partially paid for nearly six months before, were now in demand. The cops wanted to take Davis down before the operation blew. After that business was set, Ball mentioned that Speaker Jane Hull told the attorney general that a DPS major had leaked the information to Milstead that was being funneled to Raymond and others. That ticked Ball off, but he repeated that it wasn't something the higher ups wanted to pursue. When I persisted, he said it was "police business."

Jim Davis phoned at 2:15 p.m. and gave me his three preferred murder sites: the Fountain Suites, the Sheraton Greenway Inn, and the Marriott Residence Inn. No Motel 6s for this cowboy. He was gonna clip 'em in style.

". . . Give me two days, if possible," he said, responding to my question regarding advance notice. "If not, you give me as much time as you possibly can . . . And if an emergency comes up, you can call the sheriff's department. I'll leave there and call you on a land line."

That was neat. Whenever I needed someone killed, all I had to do was ring up the sheriff's department.

Rich Scheffel arrived in time to hear my side of the conversation with Davis. I bearded it enough to keep him from catching on. It was, however, a fitting beginning to what would soon be the most shocking meeting of Rich's life. We started it as usual, speaking one-on-one for a little more than a half hour. Rich was steaming over a confrontation he had had with Alan Stephens.

". . . Here's the majority leader telling me that if an attorney general investigation starts, he will not associate with me because you are my client . . . He's a fuckin' wuss! He's just a wuss . . . You see, he knows nothing any more . . . He got $440 from ya, and Jim Henderson got $440 from ya. I gave him those money orders, but he didn't know who those were from. He thought those were from my other clients. He recognized the names on them. Give me a break! . . . In other words, Alan knows nothing . . . Poor little Alan Stephens. Let me tell ya something, Tony. If it got right down to push comes to shove, I'll say, 'Yes . . . I did give Senator Stephens a number of checks that were bundled. Yes, they were money orders. Yes, he knew who they were from.' And he's . . . dead meat!"

". . . Did he know that was my money?"

"Oh, you bet your ass he did! . . . I told Rick [DeGraw] down there, 'Rick, you gotta get him calmed down . . . [Stephens] wants to run for Congress.' A guy running for Congress, you know, he's painted the headline for me today . . . He said, 'I can see it now, "Suspected Bookie . . . Makes Major Contributions to State Legislator'" . . . He didn't know that the envelope you handed him was from you."

". . . Well, who's it from?" I asked.

"Uh, it came from God, I guess. . . . If you're investigated, I'm investigated . . ." Scheffel railed. "His career is too important for him to deal with me. In other words, he'll cut off access . . . I'm persona non grata. That's it."

". . . Have you helped this guy over the years?"

"Oh, over the years, major."

"Has R. J. Reynolds helped him?"

"Everybody, everybody has. I've helped the guy like you can't believe!"

"Has Anheuser-Busch helped him?"

"Yes."

"The chiropractors?"

"Yes. Everybody's helped him."

"The eye doctors?"

"Oh he's been helped."

"How much help would you say that he . . ."

"A lot. Thousands. Thousands. Big time."

Scheffel explained that the big corporations have so many employees they can give politicians like Stephens lots of money in numerous $220 lumps to make it legal.

"In your case . . . we need to find names to match your contributions," he said. "That's the illegal part. That's it right there. In a nutshell. Tony Vincent's got no employees."

". . . So what would happen if you actually said to somebody, 'Yeah, I bundled checks and gave them to him.' What's that do to him?"

"It makes him as guilty of whatever campaign violation there was as I am."

That was Rich Scheffel's last line as an unknowing participant in Operation Desert Sting. At 2:55 p.m., there was a knock on the door. I answered it and ushered in Jim Keppel, Deputy Police Chief Ben Click, Captain Black, and Detective Ball. All the color drained from Rich's face as the good guys swarmed inside. Click badged Scheffel and went into his prepared opening line, an introduction of Keppel.

"This is Chief Deputy with the Maricopa County Sheriff's Office, Jim Keppel."

Wrong line, Chief. I glanced at Ball and stifled a laugh.

"County attorney's office," Keppel corrected.

"Uh, I, uh, don't want you to panic," Click said, about to panic himself from the thick tension in the room. "I'm gonna ask you to stand up in a moment, because Detective Ball is gonna pat you down. Make sure you're not, uh, carrying any weapons."

"Okay," Scheffel gulped. I went next door to allow the good guys to do their thing. As I looked at the monitors, I noticed that Deputy Chief Click was standing in front of the camera obscuring the view. Click wasn't having a good day. He handed off to Keppel and allowed the prosecutor to take command.

"Okay, I can tell you, first of all, that you and a lot of other people . . . have been under investigation . . . You can rest assured that basically every conversation you've had, every meeting you've had with Mr. Vincent has been tape recorded or videotaped."

"Okay," Scheffel whispered, catching his breath.

"Please try to relax. As I said before, and as Chief Click said and as Captain Black said, you are not under arrest. We would like to show you today some of the things we've been doin' . . . You were here on Wednesday, and you indicated at that time that . . . the most you could be charged with in the situation is a class one misdemeanor and perhaps spend six months in the slammer. I think those were your words. I'm here to tell you today that's completely wrong. It's much more serious than that and I think, sir, that you realize that."

Ball set up a video monitor and proceeded to play damning excerpts from Scheffel's previous conversations. Scheffel watched and sunk lower into his chair.

". . . We're not gonna use anything you say here today against you," Keppel said. "I want you to understand that. We're not trying to pull anything out of you today. We have plenty, believe me."

"I know," Scheffel confessed. ". . . I just, I gotta ask why I got, someone sent me into this?"

"Let Mr. Keppel finish," Ball ordered.

"I think your comments about Alan Stephens today were very timely and very appropriate. Alan is scared to death . . . I think Alan, and you probably think so too, would give you up in a New York minute . . . There are a few loose ends out there we'd like to tie up. Now quite frankly Rich, you're somebody that could help us do that. And in the process of doing that, you could help yourself in this situation. When I say you can help yourself, I'm talking about minimizing some of the charges against you . . . Let me tell you some of the things I'm prepared to seek as charges against you. First of all, this is an overall conspiracy that began back in January of 1990 that involves a conspiracy to, number one, illegally conduct an enterprise through racketeering, bribe public officials, offer to exert improper influence on public officials, fraudulent scheme, money laundering, hindering prosecution, and filing false campaign disclosures. Second . . . since your involvement in this case you participated in a criminal syndicate, which is a class two felony, you participated in the bribery of Bobby Raymond, a bribery of Art Hamilton, the bribery of Alan Stephens, the bribery of Jim Hartdegen, money laundering every time you received a salary in this case . . . So basically, what we have . . . is a class three felony . . . a class two felony . . . a class four . . . a class three . . . a class five. . . . Technically, a judge could stack those sentences if you were convicted of these crimes . . ."

Keppel's speech was so frighteningly effective it made me squirm. I had no idea the crimes went that deep. I could only imagine how Rich was feeling.

"What we're prepared to do today is tell you that if you are willing to cooperate with us, and I'll go into more detail about what we expect in that regard, we're willing to work with you and try to resolve your situation to the advantage of both parties in this thing. So with that in mind, I'll just throw the ball back to you . . ."

"I just wonder why people sought me out."

". . . Bobby recommended you at great length," Ball reminded. "Pushed very hard."

". . . He was beatin' the door down with Tony to get you on board," Keppel added. ". . . A lot of people aren't going to be talking to Tony any more, but they might talk to you, and that's where you come in. And we'd like your cooperation in return for some consideration from us on these charges. To have you work with us and basically, the deal would be that you cooperate fully by recording conversations with these individuals, and number two, testifying when called upon to do so. I've gotten a proposed written agreement in here to show you as to the details of what we'd expect from you for your cooperation. In return for that, I'm also prepared to make you an offer. A plea offer to a charge in this case to take care of the various counts against you. I would add one caveat as I said before, the timing of this thing is very important. It's crucial. Delay is not gonna help us. To us, the decision has to be made today. If it goes beyond that, I can't promise you anything."

"I understand."

"I don't wanna pressure you," Keppel continued, turning up the voltage. "I'm not trying to do that. I just want you to understand our dilemma . . ."

". . . I mean, can I just sit for a couple sec . . ." Scheffel stuttered. "I'm just kinda . . . I know how, how much you know about me. I, I, I've not been in trouble before. I . . ."

"Believe me, Rich, we've been through this hundreds of times. We understand how you feel. Just take your time and relax . . . Do you want to get a towel or something and wipe your face?"

"No. I'm, I'm just, I'm not sweating . . . Uh, I guess the first question I should ask you, would it be advisable for me to get some legal counsel?"

Rich should have said those words the moment Ben Click flubbed the opening line. As the law dictates, that request puts a stop to the conversation. However, Keppel was right on top of that, too. He had gleaned the name of a defense attorney Scheffel had recommended to me from the transcripts. Keppel had the guy, Tom Henze, waiting by the phone on standby. The prosecutor made arrangements to reconvene the meeting at the police station with Henze.

"You, you just listed all those [crimes] off there," Scheffel said. "None of those things ever, ever occurred to me that I was doin' anything like that."

Me neither.

"It's clear they fit the statute and the conspiracy," Ball said.

As I expected, Scheffel rolled. But just in case, he was kept under guard at the Embassy Suites Hotel that night, and at the undercover apartment the rest of the weekend. They wouldn't even let him go home for a change of clothes.

After Rich cut his deal, I phoned Bobby Raymond. Despite the leaking dam, he was as buoyant as ever.

". . . I know if I go in and tell Art, 'Look, I fucked up here brother and I fucked up big time and here's what I've done and I need you to help me protect my ass,' I don't have to worry about him goin' to the attorney general and sayin', 'He fucked up.' Republicans don't have that. They don't trust [Speaker Hull], and with good reason . . . So what else is going on, anything?"

"No, no. Everything's quiet with me," I lied. Your buddy Rich Scheffel just did a deal and will be coming after you first, but everything's just fine. ". . . As the session starts and things happen, it'll die down."

". . . I agree, Tony. We start droppin' bombs next week in the Mideast and the session starts here and the governor's campaign heats up and all that shit. Did you hear where Corbet sued Hill today? He filed a suit against Hill today for defamation of character . . . Nancy Hill, that woman that beat Leo Corbet. 'Cause of the campaign brochure they sent out on him . . . I mean, we start suin' each other over the lies we tell about candidates . . . for telling lies in campaign elections, boy, we're gonna have one hell of a bunch of lawsuits around here every year!"

I asked Bobby about the mettle of his friend, Rich. "Is he a pretty strong guy?"

"Yeah, yeah. Every once in a while he's gotta be propped up a little . . . Shit, like I told you before . . . he could clean out half of this legislature . . . if he wanted to."

"Half?"

"Or more!"

That was encouraging. Still, I had mixed feelings. Either Scheffel was going to go full force and bring Desert Sting to new heights, or he'd find it hard to deceive his old pals. If he picked door number two, he'd start double-dealing, become evasive, lose his memory, and end up hammering the final nails into Tony Vincent's coffin.

23

Detective Ball phoned Saturday morning, January 12, 1991, and related that Rich Scheffel had a hard time sleeping the previous night. "He kept seeing cameras." The lobbyist was reported to be "in shock," but coming along.

"Go ahead and hire DeGraw," Ball instructed. "We're gonna keep going."

Rich made his first phone call as an undercover agent late Saturday afternoon. It was, as predicted, to Bobby Raymond. The only significant aspect of the conversation was a jab Raymond took at me.

"If Tony woulda kept his big mouth shut and not talked about his business to everybody we wouldn't have this problem."

That was true—if Tony was real. But Tony was being paid to spread the news in order to entice more flies into his web.

Keppel, Mount, and Ball caravaned to the apartment on Sunday to squeeze Scheffel some more. The lobbyist talked for fifteen minutes short of four hours—and gave them squat. It was a virtuoso performance. Listening to him, you'd think he was the most honest, Boy Scout lobbyist in history. All he admitted was: Anheuser-Busch's checking account might be a few hundred dollars overdrawn; the chiropractors forgot to put specific legislators' names on a few insignificant checks; R. J. Reynolds paid the greens fees for some lawmakers during a convention at Pebble Beach; a few representatives received $500 honorariums for giving speeches; and, in Rich's most damning revelation, he confessed that he and five lobbyist pals had pooled their money to buy golf clubs as presents for a handful of politicians. Among those that got a set was Speaker Jane Hull.

The single result of the interrogation was that Ed Pastor, the Maricopa County supervisor, was embarrassed into giving his golf clubs back. They were a nice set too, $1,000 Pings. The supervisor cleaned himself of the sticky clubs in the nick of time. After shedding that political baggage, he successfully ran for Morris Udall's vacated congressional seat.

Whenever the talk turned to Art Hamilton or Alan Stephens, Scheffel suddenly got amnesia.

"There was a comment made that 'we do deals' and you asked me the other day what it means to cut a deal," Scheffel said. "I don't have any clandestine thought as to what 'cutting a deal' is . . . I've thought real hard about cutting the deal and I'm, I'm working on that. But [Raymond] said we'd done a lot of dirty things together and I'm sitting thinkin' about what dirty things we've done? . . ."

Keppel tried to jog his memory.

"Raymond says, 'Let me answer it this way, Rich Scheffel and I have done enough business together to land both of us in jail for a long, long time.'"

"That's prophetic!" Scheffel evaded, oblivious to the difference between past and future tenses.

"That was done before all this had even happened," Keppel clarified.

"Well, it, it, supposedly. Uh, uh, let me go on here now 'cause that hasn't jarred anything loose. I read that and that hasn't jarred anything loose."

They should have let me do the interrogation. I'd have jarred something loose. But these were the good guys and they had to be civil.

Scheffel saved his last dance for Stephens.

". . . He very clearly no longer felt that was Tony's money. He did feel it was Tony's money when he did ask to get contributions, but he didn't feel it was Tony's money anymore."

I met with Scheffel for the first time since the takedown on Monday, January 14. He professed to have no hard feelings. Instead, he seemed to be focusing his anger on Bobby Raymond. Scheffel said that on top of everything else, Raymond had tried to put the arm on him for a percentage of the $90,000 lobbying fee he was getting from me.

After three days on ice, the cops finally let Scheffel go home. He was free and on his own. He could either play along, or run to the first telephone and warn his friends and clients. If he ran, we would never know. If someone decided to take care of their problem by legislating a .45 caliber hollow point into my forehead, we wouldn't know that until my bleeding, lifeless body hit the carpet. Not too comforting a thought. Whatever he was up to, Rich returned to my office as scheduled for a noon sit-down with Rick DeGraw, the crisis P.R. expert. Before DeGraw arrived, Scheffel told me that every time he and Bobby Raymond walked by the "Private" door to the fourth room, Raymond would crack, "The FBI is probably behind that door taping everything we do."

Scheffel was visibly nervous during the meeting with DeGraw, which worked because he was supposed to be freaking over the investigation into Tony Vincent.

"You got a bunch of problems," DeGraw opened, addressing me. "For whatever reason, your reputation has gotten trashed . . . You have, over the last five weeks, gotten screwed dramatically by mainly one person. It's almost all traceable back to Ernie Hoffman . . . The feeling of the people who've come to me is 'He's either the heat,' or 'He's the Mob,' or 'He's got bad money behind him,' or 'I've had an investigator out,' or 'I've had two investigators out and you need to stay away from this guy.'"

DeGraw deserved an A for being in the know. The question was, what could he do to clean up Tony's image?

". . . It might be easier to go through your checkbook. And for you to tell me all campaign contributions that have been written in the name of you or your wife since you got to the state."

"Can I interrupt," Scheffel said, chuckling for the first time since he was pinched. "There are no checks."

We jumped that hurdle and kept running.

"What's Alan's problem," I asked, referring to the jittery Senate majority leader.

"Alan's problem is he got visited by DPS. And when you have a backbone that will sway, you get worried about things like that. I mean, as soon as DPS gets in on this, everybody starts to get antsy because they've just seen Leo Corbet take a fall . . . They see what's going on with DeConcini and McCain in Washington . . . They're afraid of the public perception . . ."

It was this "public perception" that DeGraw was going to work his P.R. magic on regarding me. "I wanna make this legal . . . Even if that means that you have to write letters to these people requesting that they send money back to you."

That would certainly make Tony a popular guy.

". . . Do you know a lawyer in Nevada, in Las Vegas, named Greg Jensen?" DeGraw asked.

"No."

"Okay, he says he knows you."

". . . He knows me?"

". . . He doesn't like you either."

This was the fifth confirmation of Tony Vincent's prior existence. On this bizarre note, I excused myself to make a phone call. My exit was staged to give Rich a chance to talk alone with DeGraw. Since it was all being taped and videoed, there was little risk.

". . . If there's stuff goin' on, this is gonna come back and it's gonna bite Art [Hamilton] right on the butt. Does he know that?" Rich baited.

"Yes," DeGraw confirmed.

". . . These are gross violations," Scheffel emphasized, making another cast. ". . . And Alan talked to me like he doesn't even know they exist anymore."

"I know. That's Alan's style," DeGraw said.

". . . You know where the Milstead thing came from, don't ya," Rich pitched.

"I know exactly where it came from. It came from Bobby . . . There had been a request to DPS . . ."

"How do you know that?"

"I know that from Milstead."

Scheffel scored a solid point with the Milstead revelation. That was yet another confirmation that the former DPS chief was leaking news of the DPS investigation all over town. Only trouble was, the cops and prosecutors didn't want Milstead.

DeGraw greeted my return with a move of his own. Aside from the five grand a month I was to pay for his services, he had some back-end action in mind.

"Now the other thing, Tony, I've probably done more initiatives in the state than anybody else. And it's my assumption that is the direction we will probably wind up going."

To each his own deal. I gave the Reputation Doctor $5,000, cash, for his retainer. He cleaned it right into his pocket.

". . . There's no bugs. There's no way of getting a device in here," I said. "That blind is closed because that's the only angle that anybody could shoot a laser in here."

"Right, I noticed that when I came in . . . 'Cause I have the same thing in my office," DeGraw said.

". . . They can set up, and if I just turn the blind, it takes them three days to get back on the frequency," I improvised. This laser stuff was the biggest bunch of hokum in the whole Desert Sting operation, but damn if the rumor didn't have a life of its own.

"Right!" DeGraw confirmed.

DeGraw went on to explain why Alan Stephens had balked at meeting me at my office. "The first rule was that you were the front of a sting operation. And that . . . you wanted to meet here . . . because everything was being taped . . . Alan trusts me to the point that Alan will shut up . . . I'm the one that's putting together the reapportionment for him so we can draw a district where he can run for Congress."

A congressional district made to order for Alan. However, the strangest aspect of my assocation with DeGraw wasn't anything he said or planned. It was the fact that even though both sides of my operation had jumped the track—Tony Vincent's fictional legalized casino gambling drive and the factual police sting—DeGraw didn't hesitate to hop on the wildly careening gravy train.

Ernie Hoffman's long-awaited economic study arrived in the mail later that afternoon. Instead of the 150 professionally bound copies I was expecting, there was a single stack of pages held together by a paper clip. I didn't bother reading it. Along with the study came the news that Ernie had sent a copy of his fantasy resignation letter to the attorney general and to the DPS. The guy had to be stone-cold nuts.

Fondia Al Hill phoned that evening ready to appear the next day and collect a million in cash I had promised to have for him. Unfortunately, Tony had some bad news.

". . . I heard from the old man's son. He's down. He went down . . ."

"The old man? What do you mean?"

"He'd down. He's sick . . ."

The old man's health problems, of course, had thrown a snag into the delivery of Al's millions. I promised to keep him apprised. Hill called back at 10:55 p.m. for an update. No word yet, I said. At 11:50 p.m., I called Hill with the terrible news.

"He's gone."

"He's what?"

"He's gone . . . I think they gave him a hot shot . . . I'm leavin' tonight . . . I'm gonna have 'em take the body to Cleveland to a doctor we have. I want an autopsy done in Cleveland . . ."

Hill called twice the next day. I was supposed to be out of town with the old man's body, so we ducked him. Instead, I fielded a barrage of calls from increasingly nervous politicians. Bobby Raymond relayed the latest from the capitol. The word was that Terry Goddard's brain trust was thinking of exposing Tony Vincent's campaign contributions to Symington and using them as an issue. We both agreed that would be a mistake on Goddard's part, especially when they discovered I had also contributed to Terry. Shiree Foster followed with the latest from her end. She reported that Chamber lobbyist Chuck Shipley had been asking questions about Tony Vincent.

Despite all the heat on Tony, Raymond came to the apartment as scheduled on January 16 to do his sex-smear tango with Reno P.I. Mike Harris. He marched through my door even after spotting Jim Keppel's car parked near the entrance. The prosecutor's gray Ford came complete with a police radio, multiple antennas, a county license plate — and the unmistakable odor of cops. We went out to take a look. Sure enough, there it was, right near the entrance. I ordered Harris/Stribling to get a make on it right away. Fortunately, the car did little to spook Raymond.

". . . Hey, I got Sheri's bill here," I said, referring to the $13,206 I owed his wife. "Can I settle with you?"

"No, go ahead and settle that with Rich."

"You're sure?"

"Yeah. You and her and Rich need to do your own fuckin'."

Most of Raymond's dirt was the same ground covered by Kenney — Brenda Burns' alleged torrid love life, Stan Barnes' parking lot frolics, etc. However, there was one notable exception.

"I think your money could be better spent looking at Fred DuVal," Raymond advised.

". . . Okay, tell me about DuVal."

"Well, he's gay."

"Oh, not another one!"

"Now this is a very closely guarded secret."

"He didn't even look cheerful to me."

"He is also one of Grant Woods' best friends . . ." Bobby continued, ignoring my mirth. "I mean, they go back years and years and years . . . I know at some point in the next week or two, I'm gonna have a visit from the AG [attorney general] . . . because they're looking at this video now . . . I will tell you, if the attorney general [investigator] comes to see me about [Sheri's] fuckin' video, I mean my intention is to take it as an affront and ask him, 'How dare you motherfucker come in here and question my integrity when Grant Woods' best fuckin' friend is representing the interest in Las Vegas and he's their hired gun to come down here and kill this fuckin' thing! Now if you want to fight this fucker out, friend, we'll fight it out!' . . . Grant Woods has got way too much in his past to get involved in somethin' like this."

"I like this, Bobby. I like this! I like your approach here on DuVal. 'Cause they'll go to Grant and report back . . . They'll tell him what you said and that should neutralize him real quick . . . You're smarter than you look."

"Well, I think about shit like this a lot. This is my game."

". . . Do you have a rapport with DuVal?"

"Oh yeah, very good rapport."

"How do you think he'd react if you walked up to him and showed him pictures? . . ."

"He would absolutely shit . . . His stepdad owns a little corporation called Empire Machinery. Caterpillar dealer, huge. I mean, this guy is big, big, big potatoes . . . I don't think Grant Woods, for nickels and dimes, would burn him. I really don't."

"What's their association other than school chums?"

"Best friends . . . I don't know Grant Woods . . . People say he's a really decent guy and he's not gonna be like dealing with the last attorney general. So I don't know."

"Do you know if he knows that DuVal is gay or not?"

"I wouldn't have any idea."

It was clear that even if DuVal was gay, which was by no means certain, the pair weren't lovers. Woods, according to Kenney, had just been shotgunned into marrying his beautiful television anchorwoman girlfriend. I had heard nothing about her being the attorney general's beard. Plus, I recalled that Gary Bartlett tried to tell me Raymond would gnaw a weenie. Raymond was a lot of things, but gay wasn't one of them.

"All right, if I spend the money and I get the proof, you're willing to confront him with it?"

"I will, certainly," Raymond said. ". . . We come up with that, then that could all but just absolutely make our current problem go away."

". . . If you got the balls to walk in there with it, I got the balls to get the picture," I challenged.

"Oh, I got the balls to walk in with it . . . I'm gonna say, 'Fred . . . you motherfucker got this AG involved in this . . . You wanted to play this fuckin' game nasty so we'll play this fuckin' game nasty. 'Cause this is live or die!'"

". . . I got no wind of that from him, you know, when I talked to him. That's such a shocker to me . . ." I admitted truthfully.

"You know, frankly Tony, he's a decent sort. He's a good kid. He really is . . . I would bet my life that he doesn't have a thing to do with any of this shit goin' on. Nothin' . . . But since he is the best friend of the attorney general, and he does represent . . . Nevada interest to kill the project, it's lookin' bad for him. He's got a little shit in his own closet that may have to roll out . . ."

Translation: He isn't guilty, and he's a great guy, but it doesn't matter. Fred was a pawn in the big political game, and he was going to receive a thrashing.* I turned to Stribling.

". . . Start with DuVal and stay with DuVal."

". . . In Phoenix, you got your closet gays, and you got your gays that don't give a damn," Bobby elaborated. "He is not only in the closet, but he's got it padlocked . . . Fred was . . . one of Babbitt's whiz kids. And he was one of the top guys in Babbitt's presidential campaign. And that's where the shit came outta, Washington. Because they go to Washington to play."

"Bruce ain't one of them, too, is he?"

"No, no, but he sure had a staff load of 'em."

". . . I don't care if this kid's pitchin' or catchin', I want the pictures of 'em in bed," I told Stribling. ". . . Either way, it ain't good."

"Especially if he's smiling," Stribling cracked.

". . . Mean shit, man," Raymond understated.

The phone rang. It was Keppel. "Quit talking about sucking dicks and move on," he barked. No doubt, we were getting pretty raunchy, but the call, and Keppel's angry tone, was totally out of character. An extortion conspiracy like this was serious business. Even the offensive jokes were part of the takedown. I surmised that Keppel was being ridden by the second apartment gang because of his latest faux pas with the car. That was Keppel's third, although he wasn't always at fault. Previously, he had bumped into Don Kenney in the hallway, and then was eyeballed by Rich Scheffel in my waiting room. Still, it pissed me off that the deputy county attorney would take his anger out on me while I was in the middle of a tense, undercover operation. I felt like telling Raymond, "That was Jim Keppel from next door. He wants you to stop tellin' gay jokes and start committing some other crimes." Besides, Detective Stribling started it with his "smiling" remark. It was official "police business."

". . . Who's the most panicky?" I asked a few moments later, moving away from the topic of DuVal.

"Stephens, by no short stretch of the imagination . . . He's really panicked . . . He's not frustrated over this shit flyin' around, he's frustrated because he's in a position [where] he can't make any moves.

---

*Fred DuVal responds: "I am not gay. Obviously this sad and desperate plot would have failed. What makes this particularly sad and hurtful is that Bobby knows me well and Bobby and Sheri have socialized with my fiancée and myself. Remarkably, both of us were donors to his last campaign."
Raymond later wrote DuVal a letter apologizing for the "untrue" allegations.

Alan is constantly moving, jockeying . . . It's just all a big chess game . . . But he feels like he's in a box where he can't move . . . He is, Tony, and I'll tell you why . . . See, he's fuckin' stupid. I mean, Art said, 'This is where I need the money to go, you take care of it Rich and mail these checks.' Well, Alan is so power-hungry that he couldn't have 'em mailed . . . He had to give everybody the checks so he was sure they knew he was the one that raised the money. Well, a couple of those people are nitwits and if they found out those checks they got from him came from you, and the AG was lookin' at all this shit, they'd run right straight to the attorney general with it . . . That's where he feels like his nuts are really in a vice . . . Both Rick [DeGraw] and Rich [Scheffel] have done a good job of convincing him just to 'Go about your business of running the state Senate. Don't say anything. Quit talking about this. Leave it alone. We'll take care of it. Go away.'"

". . . What did Rick tell ya he's doin' for me?"

"He is spending all day Saturday in the secretary of state's office. He's going to go through every financial . . ."

"How's he gonna get in on a Saturday?"

"Well, he's got access to it."

". . . So then he'll get me cleaned up?"

"Yeah, ain't nobody better than Rick at this shit. He knows it. He understand it. And he knows how to get around it . . . Do you know that Rick handles all of Art's accounts? . . . Art has a campaign account, a public information account. He has another thing called Leadership Foundation. He has five or six different slush funds. And he gets money. I mean, money just drops out of the sky . . . Art doesn't know anything about those accounts. Rick handles them all."

The talk turned to the Goddard campaign, the unions, and how Goddard's back-room fixer, Mike Sophy, was spreading rumors about Tony Vincent and his pocketful of politicians. As we spoke, there was a knock on the door. That was highly unusual. I looked at Stribling. He looked wide-eyed back at me.

"Who the fuck is this, now?" I wondered. "You expecting anybody?"

"No," Bobby said, ready to jump through the ceiling.

I walked haltingly to the door. Had Rich Scheffel chirped? Was this someone's assassin? As I reached for the doorknob, my mind flashed a childhood story about a schmuck in some ancient arena forced to confront a lady or a tiger. At least that guy had two doors to choose, and one contained a beautiful woman. My fate was behind Door Number One. It opened. I looked out and saw nothing. That wasn't good. I tensed. Then I looked down. Standing there was a little kid with a big smile.

"Hi! Do you get the newspaper?"

"No. No, thank you."

"Would you like to get it?" the kid persisted.

"No, thanks."

The kid's smile evaporated. "Okay."

"I don't need a newspaper," I said, calming myself and returning to the living room. "I got Mike Sophy callin' people."

". . . I mean, it just pissed me off for Mike Sophy to call [Dave Horwitz] in and say, 'Raymond's caught up in it. Laybe's caught up in it. Hamilton. Walker,'" Raymond said, quickly recovering from the scare. "Named all kinds of fuckin' names and 'They're carryin' out sacks of cash' and this and shit . . . This is what Sophy says to Horwitz, who comes and tells me . . . So I went and told Laybe, and said, 'You know, your fuckin' friend Sophy, let me tell you what he just told Horwitz about you, dear.' So I told her this stuff. Boy, she was fuckin' ripped. She called Sophy and said, 'I'm gonna tell you something motherfucker! I'm gonna be down there at one o'clock to see you. I don't give a shit if you're available or not. You fuckin' well better get DeGraw.'"

"DeGraw?"

"He told me Laybe went in and she lit into fuckin' Sophy. And he said she just ripped him to shreds. She said, 'You better keep your mouth shut until you discover how deep the Democrats and the party and this campaign is involved!' . . . DeGraw said she was just great . . . So I called this fucker yesterday afternoon and I said, 'Sophy.' And he said, 'Bobby, I already know what you're calling about. I have been beat up by Laybe and I have been taken apart, bone by bone, by Rick. Rest assured it won't happen again.' I said, 'Mike, let me tell you something, you motherfucker, how this game is played. You better hope you didn't tell anybody that's gonna tell somebody else that comes and tells me this again 'cause frankly friend, I've heard this from three different people in two days, and all three of them tell me it came from you' . . . I said, 'Mike, I'm gonna tell ya, the first fuckin' thing that you're gonna have to try and figure out, if you all keep playin' with this issue, is what the hell Samuel P. Goddard II was doin' having lunch with Tony. Now you think you're so fuckin' lily-white, just try me, motherfucker!' And he just shit. See, they don't know. They didn't know you had lunch with Sam . . . I don't think we'll hear any more problems outta the Goddard people."

No, I didn't think so either. ". . . I can't picture Sue Laybe goin' off on anybody."

"I can't either, but DeGraw told me, he said, 'Man, she was mad. And she just ripped him to shreds.'"

Before he left, Bobby had one last angle.

"Would you work out a deal with me? To advance me a fair amount of money and figure out a way for me to work it off . . . $20,000 . . . I'll tell you what I want to do with it. I want to filter $10,000 into my campaign account this year . . . and I wanna put $5,000 in my public information account, and I wanna quietly pay off a fuckin' tax lien with the other $5,000."

"And what would you do for me?"

"Whatever you need done, I guess. Short of, I, I, don't stick ice picks up people's nose or things like that. I can't stand the sight of blood . . . I don't believe that you're gonna ask me to do anything that, uh . . ."

"That's illegal, immoral, or fattening . . . No, I understand . . ."

I made an excuse and dialed the second apartment to see if they would front Bob the bucks. I felt he deserved it. Give the guy a few more good times before he goes into the cage.

"What do you want me to do about that situation in Reno?" I said, cloaking my request.

"No more money for Bobby. That's a negative," D. P. Davis answered. That was telling. A month before, they'd have given Bobby $50,000 without blinking. This was the death knell for Desert Sting. I hung up, forced myself into good cheer, and ran a laundry list of my other issues past Bobby — private prisons, changing the Draconian RICO law to give crooks like me a break, house arrest, a concealed weapons bill, and the election of state judges. Bobby promised to support the ones he personally supported and pass on those he didn't. That didn't sound like "I do deals!" Bob to me. It almost sounded like integrity. Whatever, it was just a stall, so we agreed to discuss it later.

It was a good meet, but I came away pretty depressed. Keppel ripped me, and the tightening of the purse strings meant Tony Vincent was doomed.

DeGraw phoned on January 17 and said Stephens had heard from the DPS that he had signed on with me. That was a bad leak, and a quick one at that. The bullets were starting to dig into Tony's flesh.

Al Hill caught me at noon. I fed him more bullshit about the dead old man and his son.

"My prayers are with you, brother," he said. Just what I needed. The prayers of a kiddie pornographer.

The action was now coming at full tilt. Tony Vincent's lifeblood was spilling out like money through a politician's fingers. I ignored the hemorrhaging and motored on.

Bobby Raymond dropped off a picture of Fred DuVal for P.I. Mike

Harris as promised. Hill called again and said he needed his money because he borrowed "quite a large sum of money" from a bank based upon what he had coming, and the loan was due. I wondered what bank would loan a nickel to someone who said they had a big score coming from a kiddie porn deal.

By then, it wasn't just my world that was spinning out of control. The whole planet was in an uproar. The F-16s had started leveling Iraq, and the cable television coverage on CNN was chilling.

"This is insane," I told Hill. "Absolutely insane on top of everything else . . . I keep comin' back to it. It's like you're drawn to it like a magnet."

Hill didn't care about the war. He wanted his money. I promised to bring it up with my associates.

Sergeant D. P. Davis wanted me to move a scheduled meet with Sue Laybe from Saturday to Friday. That set me off. "Criminals don't commit crimes from nine to five, Monday through Friday, to suit the cops! The meet stays as scheduled." He groused, but relented.

Hill was back trying to hustle an advance the next day. "Did the old man have a chance to even collect anything?"

". . . Couldn't ask him . . . Dead men don't talk."

I advised Hill that my two musclebound goons were back in town — on other business — and held him off.

Raymond called and said Hoffman was in bed with the DPS. He warned me that if Hoffman called a meet, the Tucson lobbyist better get naked to prove he wasn't wearing a wire. Ball phoned afterward and said if we arranged a meet with Hoffman and Scheffel, everybody would have to get naked.

"If the DPS comes in to grab you, Tony, I'll be right behind to grab them," Ball promised.

That sounded like fun. If any of us survived the hail of bullets, what a story we'd have to tell.

Sergeant Davis instructed me to try to lure Ernie Hoffman in on Monday. I called Ernie for the first time since he'd turned rat. He talked like we were still buddies and gave no indication of what he had been doing. He said he was busy on Monday, but promised to come by on Wednesday. Raymond phoned and said Milstead had uncovered a picture of Tony Vincent from the cops in Vegas. That was interesting. They said I was clean. Sergeant Davis speculated that there might be another J. Anthony Vincent. I countered that I was Giuseppe Anthony Vincent, there wasn't another, and it had to be the heat or the water 'cause this state was full of fruitcakes. Davis laughed and added that Scheffel told the cops that Ernie Hoffman had determined that I didn't have an Arizona driver's license. Ernie's word on that carried a lot of weight since he dated the lady who ran the Department of Motor Vehicles. Only trouble was, J. Anthony Vincent did have an Arizona driver's license. Had it since day one. These people found stuff that didn't exist, and couldn't locate the things that did. Amazing.

Sue Laybe drove to the apartment for her Saturday meet. She was dressed casually, like Olive Oyl on a weekend picnic. She bummed another of my unfiltered Camels and took me through her showdown with Mike Sophy.

"... I said, 'From all I know this guy is clean. He lives in my district and quite frankly, if I find out that some state agency is harassing a constituent of mine, I'll get on their ass.' And I said, when DeGraw was there ... 'The issue is that this shit is coming from a Democrat about other Democrats' ... I said, 'Okay, well, what about the other side of the issue? I hear you accepted money from Don Laughlin [a Nevada casino owner]. Has Terry committed to the other side of the issue?' ... Well, he was really backpedaling ... And I said ... 'I came close to askin' Terry Goddard if he'd take a walk, not that he'd sign it [the gambling bill], not that he'd veto it, but if this ever came across his desk, would he take a walk?' He goes, 'Yeah, he could take a walk. I'm sure he could take a walk ...'"

Raymond had advised me to ask Laybe what dirt she had on the attorney general, Grant Woods.

"Well, I heard that ... an independent campaign committee on behalf of Georgia Staton [Woods' opponent] was putting out this mailer about Grant Woods and all of his Mafia ties," she responded. "So I just put out my feeler that I need to know what that stuff was ... I wouldn't put it out unsubstantiated."

"So they never put it out?"

"I don't know if it went out or not."

Sue added that the $10,000 I'd given her for the Democratic party was funneled into the party's national coffers instead of the state or county as I'd assumed. That meant Sue had some top dog in the national party doing her laundry. She had hinted about this before, but the name wasn't forthcoming — yet.

24

My benched quarterback, Don Kenney, had been the first recruit to sign with Team Tony. Details of his involvement with the shady gangster were now being openly discussed among his legislative peers. Yet he appeared to be the last to hear about it. He was finally enlightened in late January when Speaker Jane Hull called him in for a chat. Hull showed him Ernie's Hoffman's inane resignation letter and warned him that Tony Vincent was under investigation. Kenney didn't appear overly concerned.

"... Jane says that ... she has talked to Hartdegen and that he's gonna back off [and] not sponsor the bill in the House ..." Kenney told me. "She said ... 'I trust you a hell of a lot more than I do half the people around here and I just don't want this blowing up in your face.'"

On Tuesday, January 22, Rick DeGraw warned me that the *Arizona Republic* had awakened and was hot on Tony's trail. DeGraw speculated that Ernie Hoffman had pestered a reporter, and the reporter was intrigued enough to phone Alan Stephens. DeGraw came by the office that afternoon to meet with Scheffel and myself to plan a counterstrategy.

"... In the picture that DPS is circulating of you, you're a lot heavier," DeGraw opened.

"... When ya lose weight, you can't specify where you lose it," I offered, playing along. The fourth room boys had yet to get hold of a copy of this mysterious picture, so I still didn't know what he was talking about.

DeGraw had determined during his Saturday research session at the attorney general's office that Tony Vincent had given only $2,090 in traceable political contributions in his name—$110 under the limit. That was a surprise. None of us had paid attention to whether I'd maxed out in that area. At the time, it wasn't important. Now, however, with the DPS on the trail, it was a lucky break. They'd waste time traveling that road and come up empty. Sparks of hope flew through my mind. Maybe Desert Sting could survive this attack and go on.

"In terms of meeting the restrictions of Prop 200 [the law limiting campaign contributions], I don't believe that investigation will continue," DeGraw affirmed. ". . . In terms of Don Kenney and Sheri Raymond, it's my understanding that they see nothing illegal, immoral, or unethical. You can hire a lawyer any time you want, and anybody can hire a video production . . . My concern right now is George Stragalas . . . I believe what George does is do medical billings for doctors and hospitals and things like that?"

"He sold it," I said.

"What's he do?"

"Works for me."

"He does? Well, good, I was gonna suggest that you hire him," DeGraw laughed. ". . . What's he doing?"

"Nothing."

"What's he supposed to be doing?" DeGraw said, laughing harder.

"Do you wanna know his title? . . . He's the Executive Vice President in Charge of Bribery. He accepted that position at $1,250 a week."

". . . Oh, shit."

Oh, shit indeed. How would the Reputation Doctor clean that one up? DeGraw didn't even venture a suggestion. He sidestepped it and informed me that Alan Stephens had deep-sixed a consulting contract DeGraw had with the Senate because of our association. "They're not going to pay me the other four thousand bucks. But hey, everything has a cost to it, that's the way life goes."

Yeah, and not just for Doc DeGraw. His "clean Tony" strategy would cost me far more than $4,000. He wanted me to free five of my pocket politicians from their commitments and toss them back into the stream.

"These are votes that are bought and paid for!" I protested. "I hate to give 'em up 'cause you're talkin' about over $200,000 I just pissed out the window . . . My understanding with some of these people that you named was cut-and-dried, 'The money is for your vote.' That's the deal. The quid pro quo—something for something.' What? Do I just give the money away? Do I look like Santa Claus?"

"Yeah, you do a little bit," DeGraw grinned. "It is my feeling that you've gotta make that call, but I'm not nervous about it . . . Tony, if there's one thing I've discovered in two decades of working with folks, is that most politicians are not self-destructive individuals. And there is no way that they can open the door on you without bringing themselves down at the same time. It's not like somebody can give 'em immunity, 'cause the voters make the decision on these folks, not some prosecutor."

DeGraw went on to say that Ernie Hoffman had more hell to pay than just from me.

". . . If I were Ernie, I'd be more worried about turning on Bill English than I would be about turning on you. I mean, Bill English is not somebody to screw around with . . . Let's see, he's had at least four suits of personal attack against him. He's had several defamation of character suits against him. He's had a variety of DWIs, [and was] picked up for soliciting a prostitute. Bill runs in a variety of circles."

Sounded like a typical politician to me.

"I think that we have to go back to living a normal life," DeGraw advised. "I mean, if in Israel they can go back to work carrying gas masks, we can go back to living a normal life."

After DeGraw bolted, Scheffel phoned Ernie Hoffman to see if he could get a bead on what the lunatic was doing.

". . . Everyone's just goosier than hell, Rich," Hoffman said. "I mean, just dynamite goosey! . . . I felt good until I talked to Alan. He scared the shit out of me, Rich . . . Anthony Vincent . . . is gonna hafta mention who he is. Jane knew all his aliases, so she's been briefed right up to speed."

Aliases? Tony Vincent now had aliases? First multiple confirmations, then a photo, and now aliases. Unbelievable.

"Alan seems to be concerned about something," Hoffman understated. ". . . He says, 'Ernie, I told you at that time I was concerned about whether or not it's a sting,' or this and that and then he suggested, 'Maybe you and Rich should have taken care of him better and made sure he didn't go this far.' I said, 'Wait a minute! Whoa! . . . We had no control whatsoever over him!'"

Ernie added that he was "shocked that the DPS had briefed the leadership in both chambers. I mean, all of them were in. Killian knows about it. Jewett, all of 'em."

The boys in the fourth room shared this shock. Unfortunately, professional police courtesy stopped them from pursuing it. It was "a police thing."

Don Kenney called from a pay phone to inform me that Attorney

General Grant Woods knew about the investigation from his carryover investigator, George Weisz. The Phoenix Police had alerted Woods about the sting, so that leak had been sealed.

Dave Manley phoned that evening to say he had a package of dirt on Woods involving alleged shenanigans surrounding a hotel deal in Mesa that went sour. Manley said he'd bring it by on Monday.

"One guy I know thinks that Woods is the most crooked son-of-a-bitch he's ever met in his life!" Manley exclaimed.

DeGraw phoned at 9:45 p.m. to warn me that a call from the *Arizona Republic* might be forthcoming.

". . . You need to be careful if you're gonna be dealing with the press at all."

". . . So you mean I shouldn't tell him that [Stragalas] is Executive Vice President in Charge of Bribery?"

"No, I don't think that's a real good idea . . . I don't know if you have a press person?"

"I did. I had Ernie."

DeGraw laughed, then sighed deeply. What a Hitchcock ending that was, sold out by my own P.R. man.

"This guy's turned on me like a snake and I wasn't gonna meet with him to hire him back," I said, dispelling the latest rumor. "I was gonna sit with him and motherfuck him until his eyes fell out!"

I called Stragalas at 10 a.m. on January 23 to see how he was weathering the storm. He was doing fine, so much so he was deeply involved in monitoring the nearly forgotten gubernatorial runoff.

". . . You oughta pick up a copy of the *New Times* this morning . . . There's a four-page article about Symington's land deals and the Esplanade and the syndication . . . He's on the verge of bankruptcy. They're holding off the investigation on Symington 'til February 26. The investigation being that he has not paid off investors, that he inflated certain things and whatever . . . It's gonna be very brutal over the next thirty days."

In more ways than one, George. Since Stragalas was the most politically experienced of my advisors, I asked his opinion on something that had been bothering me.

" . . . See, here's the move. [State Treasurer] Tony West goes to [Speaker] Jane Hull and gets her to go to the AG [attorney general] on me. Then she tips off two or three of the legislators. She launches the investigation, and then tips off her own people. Now, what's wrong with that picture?"

He just sighed and said that's the way the political game is played.

Detective Ball phoned after Stragalas to let me know that he would be finished with the grand jury the following Monday, January 28. The first wave of indictments would be sealed to allow the operation to continue.

"If we're still going by the twenty-eighth, it will be a miracle," I said.

"That's what you said about Halloween," he reminded me.

That was true. However, the leaks back in October were pinholes compared to the gushers that were coming through the dike now.

Al Hill followed Ball on the Tony Hotline and whined that his banker was breathing down his neck. ". . . He said if I didn't get in there by Thursday with some kind of deposit I was gonna have some problems."

I assured him the meeting with my partners was on schedule for that evening and I'd get right to him as soon as we broke.

Rich spoke with Ernie Hoffman again the afternoon of the twenty-third. Ernie reported that the *Arizona Republic* reporters were going down the list of Tony's players and peppering them with calls. Senators Higuera and Walker were the latest to be touched.

"You know, the last thing you wanna do is bein' quoted for somethin', then all of a sudden have three dots . . ." Ernie said.

Although Ernie was off the payroll, he was still dispensing advice. ". . . It'd be nice if Tony could sit down with himself and come up with some kind of plan—'I moved into town and this is what I did and this is what I'd like to see for the State of Arizona.'"

Sit down with myself?

DeGraw rang the cellular as I was driving home and gave the news that Randy Collier of the *Arizona Republic* had contacted Senate president Pete Rios along with Senator Walker and Speaker Hull.

"I talked to Alan and Alan had already written a check back to you," DeGraw said. "I'm not kidding."

"For how much?"

"He didn't tell me, but I assume it was for $440."

"How about the other four or eight thousand?"

"Everybody knows, I mean, they know what the truth is," DeGraw said. "Right now what they're tryin' to do is give themselves some distance."

". . . [Stephens] waited 'til the last minute and then, when he saw the smoke comin' over the hill, he said, 'Well, I better fire a Patriot Missile at this Scud comin' in,'" I said, deftly interchanging the lingo of Operation Desert Sting with Operation Desert Storm.

Scheffel called Stephens at 7:19 p.m., as directed, and said he had been summoned to a sit-down with a Sergeant Davis of the Phoenix Police Department's Organized Crime Unit. The cops designed this ruse to see if the wily Senate majority leader would panic and drop his guard. Stephens set a breakfast meet for early the next morning. Scheffel then dialed DeGraw and laid the same rap on him. DeGraw said he'd check and see if Sergeant Davis existed and get back to him. Within the hour, DeGraw reported that he spoke with Phoenix Mayor Paul Johnson and had confirmed the existence of Sergeant D. P. Davis. DeGraw took it in stride.

"... Anything dealing with gambling would be Organized Crime."

"Are they any good?"

"No," DeGraw said, skewering D. P. and the cops. "I mean, they haven't done much. They're not a sophisticated unit and they're just basically detectives that are assigned to that section. See, what I don't like is [Police Chief] Ruben Ortega. Ruben Ortega has Republican leanings ... Ruben is out for himself. He wants to eventually run for office as a Republican."

Ah, the plot thickens. Was Tony Vincent merely a tool of a politically ambitious county attorney and police chief? I doubted it, but there was no doubt that this theory would be touted far and wide when the operation was made public.

Sue Laybe phoned to advise me that she had received her call from the *Arizona Republic*. Someone must have drawn the newsmen a map because they were nailing all the right players. Laybe said she pushed the reporter off until the following morning when he was scheduled to materialize, pencil sharpened, at her office.

"What would you like me to say about you?"

"Whatever you want to say," I laughed. "I'll leave myself in your capable hands."

Laybe didn't appear too shaken. In fact, she changed subjects and hit me for a pair of tickets to Frank Sinatra's upcoming show at the Riviera Hotel in Las Vegas. She wanted it to be her mother's birthday present that March.

"No problem," I said, advising her to double check to make sure it wasn't Frank Jr. instead of the old man. Sometimes the ads "inadvertently" leave out the word "Jr." Even big hotels have their angles.

Rich conferred with Stephens at 10:15 that evening. Seems the *Republic* had called Stephens again.

"Did any reporters before ever talk to you about this?" Scheffel asked.

"No."

"Then why are you worried about it?"

"... 'Cause it's an unsavory story," Stephens understated.

The following morning, Scheffel and Stephens met at the out-of-the-way Grace Inn. Scheffel wore a wire and was instructed to get Stephens to admit he knew the $4,000-plus I handed him came from me. Was Rich able to get this critical admission? Who knows? The tape didn't work again. Senator Stephens' overburdened guardian angel had sprinkled his magic dust for the fourth time. This was getting scary. I was convinced Stephens' luck would carry him to the presidency.

Oddly, this time the angel may have been overzealous. Scheffel had to file a written account as to what was said. He reported that the senator stayed firm in his insistence that he didn't know the money was from me. Had the tape worked, it would have been exhibit number one in Stephens' defense.

Rich broke from the breakfast and was on the line with Bobby Raymond at 9:20 a.m. Bobby said his "Deep Throat" source, ex-DPS Director Ralph Milstead, had shown him a photocopy of the mysterious Tony Vincent photo.

". . . For the life of me, I couldn't positively identify that, 'That's Tony' . . . In all honesty, I do think it was," Bobby said.

Scheffel updated Raymond on his breakfast with Stephens. Despite Stephens' insistence that he thought the checks were legit, the spooked majority leader still believed his neck was on the line.

". . . He said that this could be a major scandal," Scheffel relayed. "He even told me that if something like this breaks, he'd have to resign. He couldn't be the leader under these circumstances."

". . . You probably oughta have Rick explain to Alan that since in fact he was the one that delivered all those checks, he's gonna have a hard time sayin' he didn't know anything about it," Raymond said. "I mean, can you imagine how that would look?"

Twenty minutes later, Rich phoned DeGraw.

"The investigative reporter has called twelve people," DeGraw reported. "He's asked every person for the phone number of J. Anthony Vincent. Now J. Anthony Vincent is in the phone book. This reporter is fishing 'cause he's heard a rumor somewhere."

While this conversation was going on, I was feeding Al Hill bull by the shovelful. I couldn't make the big meet with my partners because of a tail, I lied. That played into Mob rule number one: Never bring a tail to a sit-down. We'd try again later, I promised.

I hung up and phoned Hill's churchmate, Shiree Foster, to see if Tony Vincent hysteria had struck the Chamber. She said things were quiet on her front.

"I can't believe Ernie Hoffman turned out to be such a jackass," she said. ". . . It's probably all a greed thing. Greed makes people do weird stuff."

Sue Laybe updated me on her morning meet with the men from the *Republic*. The newspaper had sent a tag team to work her over in her office. She was firm and evasive and revealed nothing. Sue told them she knew me, I lived in her district, I'd donated a legal $220 to her campaign, and that everything was on the up and up.

". . . They wanted to know if I thought there was any underworld stuff and I said 'No.'"

Scheffel phoned Art Hamilton at 3:25 p.m. and talked for two minutes, fifteen seconds about Art's VIP passes to some auto race in Sacramento. Rich didn't even try to compromise Art. He wasn't going to dance with that devil, threat of prison or not.

An hour later, Stragalas called with some illuminating things to say about why a certain ex-police honcho was leaking the DPS's every move to the legislators.

". . . The previous [DPS] head, Ralph Milstead, who's workin' for the governor . . . apparently is putting a lot of pressure on the legislature to get him appointed as the Department of Corrections head," Stragalas asserted.

". . . Now I see why he's doin' all the favors for them," I said. "He's runnin' to them with everything that DPS is doin' on me . . . That fits into the puzzle here."

". . . Milstead . . . was the star witness against Mecham," Stragalas recalled. "He was the one that actually got on TV and said, 'I have information that the governor . . . extorted somebody and also threatened to murder one of the staff people in the governor's office' . . . And the only thing Mecham fought back with is that Milstead has had a series of girlfriends . . . Apparently one of the women came forth and said, 'Yeah, while he was married we were going out and sometimes we used a credit card from the state' . . . Milstead withstood the storm. When his term was up last year or two years ago, it wasn't renewed . . . So Mofford takes him in as some sort of job, an aide."

I returned a call from Bobby Raymond at 5:05 p.m. The *Republic's* hound's had tagged him.

"I found it pretty milquetoasty," Raymond critiqued. "He's just doing nothing but chasing a rumor . . . I mean, there were no pointed questions or no tryin' to put me in a little bucket or a box or something . . . It'll blow over . . . I'm relaxed. Rick's relaxed. Stephens is nervous . . . Scheffel's like a one-legged man in an ass kickin' contest . . . He's nervous! . . . I'm gonna go home and go to sleep. That's about how nervous I am."

At 6:45 p.m. on January 24, Sergeant D. P. Davis hammered the first serious stake into Tony Vincent's heart. He ordered me to funnel all my office and apartment phone calls to an answering machine that advised all callers to reach me on my pager. The pager would display the number of the caller. I was instructed to keep a personal phone directory with me at all times and return only those calls whose numbers I could identify. This step was taken to thwart both the *Arizona Republic* and the DPS. The up side of the pager strategy was that I'd never, ever have to talk to Fondia Al Hill again as long as I lived.

Davis also said they were worried about stringing along the DPS too long before letting them in on the sting. The problem was, the Phoenix Police didn't trust the rival county force and wanted to keep the operation secret at all costs. However, that left them open to bitter DPS charges that they had been lured into wasting time, manpower, and taxpayers' money investigating another police force's undercover operation. The police versus police conflict was headed for a messy showdown. I got the strong impression that their distrust of the DPS was so strong, the Phoenix Police would yank the plug on Desert Sting before exposing it to the highway cowboys. If Milstead's activities were any indication, their suspicion was justified.

Bobby Raymond met Scheffel on Friday at 2:20 at the Les Jardin's Hotel Lounge to relay some "surprising news." They had solved the mystery of the Tony Vincent picture.

". . . It's the wrong picture," Raymond laughed. "[Milstead] said nobody could identify the fuckin' picture."

"You said you could. You thought you could."

"What I kept sayin' was the face, right in here, looked like him . . ."

Raymond insisted that the right picture was on its way from Vegas as they spoke. That one could be of Vincent Price for all I knew.

"He'll give you a copy of it, won't he?" Scheffel asked.

"I don't know . . . I mean, you get right to the letter of the law, they're breakin' the law by givin' it to him."

"Who is? DPS?"

"Yeah. [Milstead's] not a law enforcement officer. They can't tell him anything. He's a private citizen."

"Well, they've been tellin' him plenty."

"Well, fuck yeah, they have."

They had indeed.

At 2:30 p.m., a number flashed on my pager that I thought I recognized. I dialed. It turned out to be a reporter from the *Arizona Republic*. Although I didn't identify myself, the guy took a stab.

"Mr. Vincent. Let me ask you a few questions."

I launched into a Spanish accent and said he had the wrong number. The guy paged me five times over the next hour.

A county attorney's office investigator came by and said he was in the process of getting a driver's license for Tony's new identity. He might as well have been a priest reading Tony his last rights. Tony Vincent was becoming Frank Pietro, my new undercover identity. I immediately started the psychological process of downloading Tony's mind and soul into Frank Pietro. If that task could be accomplished, Joe might not have to surface at all. That was critical. If Tony died and the stress and pressure of Operation Desert Sting fell, without warning, upon Joe's agoraphobic shoulders, it would squash him like an ant.

I recognized Don Kenney's number on the pager and rang the House judiciary chairman. As usual, he was ten steps behind everyone else. He said the *Arizona Republic* was on to us.

"I told [the reporter] we had a meeting at Marie Callender's, we visited, and I told him that I would probably be drummed out of the Mormon church if I supported this issue . . . I referred him to a couple members of the legislature. Meredith and Jewett and Hartdegen and other friends of mine."

Jewett? He turned the press on to Jack Jewett? The man who ran to the attorney general right after our meet? Was Kenney nuts? My QB had not only lost a few steps, he'd completely lost his mind.

" . . . So anyway, I just played innocent and dumb, which is not too hard for me to do."

No kidding.

The work week ended with a call late Friday from Ball. He said the grand jury hearings hit a routine snag and wouldn't be completed until February 5.

"We're not going to make it," I said. This time, Ball offered no argument.

"We're okay," Ball responded. "Whatever happens, we've got it covered."

I lay in bed wide-eyed that evening, my mind and body a mishmash of the dying Tony Vincent, the deeply suppressed Joe Stedino, and the infant Frank Pietro. My thoughts turned to the Good Guys. When the operation collapsed, it would be two men I hardly knew, County Attorney Rick Romley and Police Chief Ruben Ortega, who would feel the brunt of the intense political backlash. I'd talked only briefly with Romley a few times, and had never laid eyes on Ortega. Yet their lives and careers would be altered by my past and future actions.

25

The morning brought a renewed spirit and no small measure of hope. The biggest threat to the operation appeared to be the *Arizona Republic*. Upon analysis, that danger seemed overstated. Their reporters wouldn't be able to piece together a story based upon the dribs and drabs of information they were getting. Tony Vincent didn't exist. Any investigative story would have too many gaping holes to survive the scrutiny of a competent editor. Plus, if the reporters did stumble upon the sting, they'd be ethically and morally obligated to hold the story until the operation played out. To do otherwise, to expose an undercover operation without warning, would risk the lives of those involved. That kind of journalistic behavior would be considered unconscionable.

Maybe Bobby Raymond was right. Maybe it would blow over. Tony was seriously wounded, but wasn't dead.

My undercover home phone rang all day Saturday, January 26, but no one took the next step of calling the pager and leaving their number. Part of the reason was that doing so takes a small amount of knowledge. After dialing, the caller must punch the pound button on the telephone and then enter their own number. It's like setting the clock on a VCR. It's a simple process, but few know how to do it.

January 27 was Super Bowl Sunday. Sue Laybe phoned and punched the right buttons to leave her number. I called. She invited me to her house to watch the game with Bobby Raymond, David Manley, and some other Democrats. I thanked her and made the excuse that I was laying low because of the media. She said that she could relate to that. Like pro-gaming Don Kenney skipping around his anti-gaming Mormon faith, she was having a problem aligning her own political and religious views.

". . . That's why I've shut up about abortion," Laybe said. "My daughter's First Communion is coming up in April."

As the war raged in the Persian Gulf, the New York Giants beat the Buffalo Bills by a single point in the closest Super Bowl in the event's twenty-five-year history. After the game ended—dramatically with a missed Buffalo field goal—Detective Ball phoned and said that Rich Scheffel was having more memory lapses, especially when it came to Stephens. I suggested that they pull his plea, put him on ice until the operation ended, and then prosecute. That, Ball said, was a possibility.

The *Arizona Republic*'s Keven Willey had culled a timely joke from a Tennessee paper and plugged it into her column that Sunday morning. She wrote that the recession was so bad, a Tennessee lobbyist had to lay off five legislators. In Arizona, it was no joke. Tony was about to lay off eight legislators, four lobbyists, and a fistful of other political types. And the layoff was coming soon. Willey's industrious coworker, Randy Collier, had not taken Super Bowl Sunday off, which was a bad sign. The reporter phoned Rich Scheffel at 9:15 p.m. trying to locate me.

"Do you know of anything he's done that might have been irregular or illegal or anything like that?" Collier asked. It was hard to imagine anyone divulging any significant information in response to such a vague question.

"Absolutely not," Scheffel responded. "The man, as far as I know, is clean as a whistle."

Carolyn Walker and Rick DeGraw both paged me on Monday, January 28. I couldn't connect with Walker, but reached Doc DeGraw. He said Collier had followed the trail to him. He portrayed the reporter as being easygoing and nonaggressive. That didn't sound like a guy working on Super Bowl Sunday to me. Collier's questions might not be as focused as one might expect, but he was dogged. My pals were underestimating him, which is always dangerous.

Manley arrived at the apartment at 1 p.m. to drop off the dossier he'd amassed on Attorney General Grant Woods. The four-inch-thick stack of allegedly damning material on the attorney general's land deals was dense reading. It would take a trained real estate investigator to make sense of it. I preferred the simple, sexier stuff, like Woods' wedding with the TV anchor. I passed the stack over to the fourth room boys with nary a glance—and never heard another word about it.

After the drop, Sergeant Davis and I launched into another bitter argument. This time it was over his instructions regarding the Jim

Davis murder contract. The sergeant wanted me to reserve a room for the victim in Tony Vincent's name. That was insane. I was supposed to register in my name, deposit my fantasy associate there, then dispatch an assassin to clip him? Even a dim bulb like Jim Davis would smell a set-up. The trail would lead back to me from three different directions. The cops would have the murder solved before the body got stiff. I called Sergeant Davis a "wimp" for even issuing or relaying such a directive. He screamed that I was a "snitch." It was same waltz as before, only to a different tune. We both had to be physically restrained. The real problem was that we were all stressed by the effort of trying to hold Desert Sting together and our tempers were on a hair trigger. Still, there was no excuse for that order.

When we cooled, I confronted the cops about a second detail of the Davis hit. They wanted to take him at the hotel when he arrived, armed for the kill. I said that was an unnecessary risk that could result in a deadly shootout. I suggested they take him at the apartment when he came for the cash and photos of the victim. It wouldn't be as dramatic, but it was a hell of a lot safer. They agreed. The drop and bust was set for the following Tuesday, February 5. As an added bonus, they were going to grab Fondia Al Hill the same day.

I spent the next day covering Tony Vincent's footsteps. I was given a new cellular phone, a backup pager, and a new automobile.

Shiree Foster paged me at 9:15 a.m. on Thursday, January 31. Randy Collier had just phoned her. He was leaving no blonde unturned.

". . . What do you suggest? Just dodge him?" she asked.

"Whatever you wanna do."

"Tony, I don't know, dadgum it! That's what I'm calling to ask you. I don't know what to do . . . Believe me, I can play dumb. I cannot be reached, or you give me a script, I'll memorize it 'til I know it backwards and forwards and just repeat it. Name, rank, and serial number."

". . . I can't expect you to lie and get yourself jackpotted . . ."

"I can lie and be as dumb as I wanna be . . . You know what I oughta say? . . . He'll call me back and he'll say . . . 'What is your association with him?' 'Well, I met him through Chamber recruitment and then we fell in love and we were having sex every day and . . .'"

"Don't lie! Don't lie!" I said, flashing the image of my wife, Gail, standing over my prone body, blasting another round of number twelve buckshot into my groin.

"Well, then why couldn't I just say, 'Yeah, I met him through the Chamber. He and I have been dating. It's not as serious as I want it to be,' and just kinda go off into this love deal and never come back to where he wants me. Start crying, 'Well, he doesn't love me. He won't leave his wife for me.'"

I was glad she was reacting with humor rather than panic, but I couldn't let her go on thinking it was a game. I reminded her that she steered Stan Barnes, Chuy Higuera, and State Treasurer Tony West to me. The reporter could spot an opening there, and catch her with her lace panties down.

"Oh," she said, the playfulness draining from her voice. "... I forgot about that ... What's the right response?"

"Well, what was goin' through your mind when you sent 'em up?"

"To help you. To make you a contact."

"Well, that kinda flies, doesn't it? ... Many years ago when I was a boy, I was down in a small town in Texas ... in a guy's office ... he had a sign behind his desk ... 'Tell the truth and you don't have to remember what you said.'"

"Right ... But see, I don't wanna get in anything hot and stirred up ..."

Me neither. But Shiree seemed destined to spend her life getting into stuff that was "hot and stirred up," with or without my help.

"Geez, I'm sorry I put you in this position," I said sincerely.

"No, Tony, that's not your fault. You know what, it's some jackass, it's probably that dumb fat ass!"

"Tony [West]?"

"Mmm hmm."

Preparing her for every possible question, I pointed out that she allowed me to use her name to bundle some checks. Problem was, neither of us remembered who they went to. If the reporter came at her with a contribution list, she'd be caught with her panties all the way down.

"I gave $220 to [candidate] King and $220 to [Representative Jim] Meredith, is that what you're saying?"

"I don't know," I said. "I didn't even know King."

"... What are you saying? I gave $440 to Jim Meredith?"

"No. I'm saying I'm not sure what you gave ... The $220 from King is all I'm sure of because you got the [thank-you] letter."

It was purely unintentional on my part, but this conversation cooked Shiree. Nothing she'd done up to then was a clear-cut prosecutable crime. Her admission that she'd knowingly lent her name to illegal political contributions did her in.

Ron Tapp's number flashed on the pager at 11:05 a.m. He wanted to come by with Tom Mason, the new state chairman of the Republican party. We arranged it for Monday. If I could get in one last deal before the pin was pulled, that would be Desert Sting's coup de grace. Better yet, if politicians were still beating a path to Tony's door, the good guys might think twice about shutting down.

Tapp and I eventually got around to discussing the media closing in on Tony's heels. "Don [Kenney] told me that he told them that he'd known me through some mutual political friends in Nevada," I related. "Don's told that lie so many times, I think he's convinced himself . . . I've heard him tell me [so often] I go, 'Shit, yeah, that is how I met him.' Sometimes I forget that you introduced me."

I then asked Tapp what he knew about Ralph Milstead.

". . . I got my information from a retired sergeant at P.P.D. that knew him . . . He said, 'Everything that you've ever read about that son-of-a-bitch, and ever heard, triple it.' He said he's a 'first-class scum bag' . . . This sergeant told me . . . 'You do not take that son-of-a-bitch on.' And I said, 'Why? . . . I'm clean. There's nothin' he can do to me. Screw him!' He said, 'That ain't the point.' He said, 'Sam Lewis [Department of Corrections chief] is his hit man and you take that fuckin' literally.'"

"How do you read that?"

". . . I know there's a lot of hits that come out of that damn penitentiary. And that all it takes is a slip with a computer."

"They send somebody out to kill somebody?"

"You got it. And then guess who the hell takes that individual down when they discover they've got a mistake? DPS. And guess what happens to the individual? They usually don't make it back to the penitentiary . . . See, I tracked one. I tracked one through the penitentiary that way . . . When he was dead, I got a hold of the coroner's report. And guess what? He had marks on his wrists that would indicate handcuffs . . . Now this was before he went through a plate-glass window and died of a coronary from an overdose of drugs."

That was certainly something for the fourth rooms boys to chew on.

Shiree paged me at 2:20 p.m., right after she talked with the reporter. Among the questions he rained upon her was whether I'd ever paid her for making introductions. Someone was feeding this guy prime cuts of information. Shiree denied everything except for making the intro to Tony West, the man she now felt had ratted her out.

". . . I hung up, and about an hour [later] Tony West parks his car and comes in the door, " she said. "And I'm sittin' out here and I saw it and it just shook me up! And I saw him and I thought, 'I'm not gonna be shook up' and I saw him and I waved at him and blew him a big kiss. And he blew me one back. So you know, I'm just playin' it as dumb as I can be . . . So, did I do you, was that cool?"

"That's fine. I don't see a problem with that."

Buoyed by what she felt was a good performance, Shiree's mood lifted.

". . . If you're clean, who gives a rip? It kinda makes it fun to play with, you know . . . I can be an actress when I want to, trust me . . . I'm pretty good at times, darlin'."

Don Kenney paged at 3:40 p.m. and said Randy Collier called him a second time. Kenney offered a new theory on what was happening.

". . . I don't know if you've made peace with your friends from Circus Circus, but [Representatives] Jack Jewett and Jane Hull . . . they are very close with Joe Lane, and Joe Lane was the former Speaker, and also represents Circus Circus . . . Jack Jewett and Jane Hull don't go to the bathroom without touching base with Joe on how to do it . . ."

To his credit, Kenney appeared to be riding out the storm with his nerves intact. ". . . Everything's cool down here . . ." he assured, claiming to be successfully holding his Republican teammates together. "I said, 'Just play dumb, Meredith.' I thought to myself, 'That's not hard for him to do.'"

". . . I was worried about Jim sayin' something about the ninety-four hundred," I countered, fearing that the 1990 majority leader would crack at the first sign of a police badge.

"No, he didn't. He may be a little slow, but he's not that slow."

Kenney's speculation about Joe Lane and Circus Circus rocked me back to my senses. I'd been so caught up in trying to stop the snowball from rolling down the hill, I'd lost sight of the fact that I still had no idea who had originally pushed it—or why. It was definitely more involved than Ernie Hoffman or the three legislators who had originally run to the attorney general in October. The reporter's information was too detailed. At that point, everyone was a leak suspect—within or without, cop or prosecutor, from the top down.

Sergeant Davis and prosecutor George Mount admitted that Collier had contacted Romley, Deputy Chief Click, and former attorney general Bob Corbin, but insisted that the bigwigs all denied it was a sting. They also said the reporter claimed to know "what the deal was with Tony Vincent." I found the denials hard to believe. I couldn't see Rick Romley lying to a reporter or anybody else.

The best move at that point would have been to summon the *Republic*'s editor, explain what was going on, compliment the reporter for his skill and diligence, then order the newspaper to back off until the operation was officially ended. When I suggested this, I was told the Arizona media couldn't be trusted. That was bullshit. Reporters have no immunity to commit crimes, and interfering with an ongoing police investigation is a serious crime. The cops and prosecutors had it in their power to ground the newspaper's activities.

Such a meeting was never called and Randy Collier continued to plug away. He connected with Tapp next. The bail bondsman had initially dodged the inquiries, but this time decided to field them. The reporter asked Tapp if he had ever been in a room when a substantial amount of cash was put on a table, and if Don Kenney received a large contribution from me. Collier's information was so precise he might as well have been in the fourth room. Tapp had been at the "get naked" hotel meeting where I dropped $18,000 on the table for Bill English, and he had introduced me to Kenney, who took a very large $55,000.

Tapp denied it all. He even denied that he was working for me. There was no reason for the stonewall, unless Tapp wasn't telling the tax man about the ten C-notes Marie handed him each week.

Tapp paged again at 7 p.m. A friend of his had been at the Phoenix police station and overheard a *Republic* reporter checking to see if he and Gary Bartlett had private detective licenses. That meant they were on to Bartlett, who wasn't going to be friendly.

"You know, I brought you English," Tapp said. "Who brought the bagman [Hoffman] with him . . . Let's have one thing that we'd never do again. If we think the guy's a drunk, we don't deal. We should've known goin' through the front door, you just don't deal with a drunk."

At 11 p.m., a ten-digit number scrolled across my pager's screen. That meant someone wanted me to call them on a cellular phone. I checked my book. The number matched Rick DeGraw's mobile phone except for a single digit. It had to be DeGraw. I dialed.

"Rick?"

"Yeah."

"What are you doin'?"

"How's it goin'?"

It wasn't DeGraw. I couldn't recognize the voice.

"Where are ya?" the caller asked.

"Where am I?"

"Yeah, is everything all right?"

A bulb exploded in my brain. It wasn't DeGraw, it was Fondia Al Hill! By cruel fate, I'd been suckered into phoning him.

"I was gonna get hold of you tomorrow," I bluffed, clearing my head.

"My banker's been all over me."

"Wednesday at 12:30 p.m., your problems are over," I announced. What I really meant was Wednesday at 12:30 p.m. *my* problems were over. That's when the cops were dropping the net on Fondia Al.

". . . So what am I lookin' at Wednesday?"

"Probably around somewhere between three and four-fifty," I promised. Al thought I meant hundreds of thousands. I was talking years.

I woke up on Friday, February 1 feeling beaten and bloody, but Tony was still standing. I was so elated over that small feat that when Al Hill paged, I called him back. He had a new deal. He wanted $1.2 million in cash to open a nightclub in Scottsdale called Ice on Fifth.

"The way it goes, the investment would be returned in 180 days with a 35 percent profit on it," Hill wrangled.

"Well, bring it with you on Wednesday . . ." I advised. "That's a substantial return for 180 days. It's a very substantial return."

Hearing Hill's latest scam was almost refreshing. It was as if Tony would go on forever, and Al Hill would always be there in the shadows, keeping Tony on his toes by coming at him with another preposterous venture.

Ball phoned and said the department was now investigating the people who had allowed their names to be used for bundled checks. If that was the case, the scope of the upcoming arrests would be nearly limitless, and some solid citizens would be in for the shock of their lives.

George Stragalas paged at 11:10 a.m. "Have you seen Goddard's little brochure? He's goin' door to door. It says, 'Don't gamble with Arizona's future' . . . It's hysterical."

"Well, I may use that for mine. 'Gamble with Arizona's future.'"

"So the president's gonna come in, or Reagan," Stragalas relayed, a political junkie to the end. "Former president's gonna come in the last four days for Symington."

"That's a heavy hit."

Stragalas said he was still pushing my gambling issue and had discussed it with Senator Nancy Hill. The senator wasn't receptive, but he thought she could be turned.

". . . She's got a lot of experience. She's married to the former sheriff here, who's always been a friend . . . Nancy's his ninth wife."

"Damn."

"Yeah, but nice guy."

I'll bet.

That afternoon, the mailman brought returned checks of $220 each from Representatives Cindy Resnick and Karen English. I'd never laid eyes on either woman. Since they were Democrats, they must have received their money from the payments Rich Scheffel said he made to Art Hamilton.

At 1:25 p.m., I tracked down Rick DeGraw at Terry Goddard's headquarters. Doc DeGraw had already been tipped that the Phoenix Police was questioning people who allowed their names to be used for falsified contributions. This came ninety minutes after the police had notified me. I made a note to call DeGraw if the fourth room boys ever kept anything from me.

DeGraw's revelation was dizzying. The Phoenix Police's Desert Sting investigation was intertwining with the DPS's wild-goose chase after Tony Vincent. Fact and fiction was starting to blur.

DeGraw added that there were rumors that the *Republic* was going to break the story in two days. "I talked to the reporter. He said no, he doesn't have anything. There's no article," he assured.

Rich Scheffel spoke with Bobby Raymond at 5:35 p.m. The Texan was in good spirits and said he had fought bigger battles in the past.

"I'll tell ya what," Raymond drawled. "This little deal that we were wound up in two years ago was a hell of a lot rougher . . . The one where [Representative Debbie] McCune, [Senator Lela] Alston, and I were wrapped up in . . . That was another one Stephens was involved in . . ."

"I don't even know what that one was about," Scheffel lured. "Tell me about it."

"Well, we had [Mayor Terry] Goddard and [Phoenix Council-woman] Mary Rose Wilcox do this. I don't know, it was about $6,000, do a mailing for us. And this was in '86. And Stephens paid for it."

". . . How? That was after Prop 200. How could he do that?"

"Well, he just did," Raymond laughed. ". . . The city council and the mayor and everybody wound up in this little turkey."

"How'd DeGraw manage this one?"

"Between him and [attorney] Marty Harper, we walked out with a clean bill of health."

". . . I'll be damned. Who investigated that one?"

"The AG [attorney general]."

"And Stephens gave $6,000 to it?" Scheffel repeated. "And this little worm is telling me he knows nothing about any of these bad things that I'm doing. I love it!"

"You know, the only problem I'm still having with this Rich, is I still honestly believe that Hull is the one that's stealing the money."

"Jane?"

"Yeah. I really do . . . Everything seems to be coming out of Jane

Hull . . . Milstead told me the other day that that's where he got onto this. And I honestly believe she thinks this is a Democratic problem and she is just feedin' the fire on this."

". . . I'm still tryin' to figure out how DeGraw and Harper beat the AG on an illegal campaign contribution if they knew that Stephens did it?" Scheffel hammered.

"Oh, they didn't know that Stephens did it . . . They never knew that. Covered that shit up like a rug, man . . . Between DeGraw and them, they did it."

Raymond tossed in that he had also heard the *Arizona Republic* was ready to lay ink on their Tony Vincent story—whatever it was they had.

"Who told you there was gonna be a story?" Rich asked.

"Will you keep it confidential? Joe Lane told me . . . Guess where he got it? Jane Hull."

"Where'd Jane Hull get it?"

"Well, don't ask me."

". . . What do you think we can see in the story?"

"There isn't gonna be one . . . I called Randy Collier and asked him. He said, 'No,' there isn't any story that he can find. He said, 'I'd like to talk with this Vincent guy, but you know, no story as far as I'm concerned.'"

"I'll tell you what, Joe Lane doesn't miss the mark very often," Scheffel warned.

Detective Ball called at 6:30 p.m. to warn me that Collier had uncovered my true name, Joe Stedino. That meant one of my own team was now freely talking. No way could my cover have been blown that deep without the reporter reaching into the tight circle of the fourth room–second apartment boys—or their bosses. Ball stood firm in his stance that it was an unauthorized leak. The rumor was floated that a county attorney had told a defense attorney friend about the sting, and the defense attorney had run to the *Republic*. Hell, Al Hill weaved better bullshit stories than that. The decision had probably been made that the operation was exposed beyond repair, and there was no longer a need to dodge the press.

Scheffel phoned DeGraw at 8:25 p.m. for an update. "It's gotta stay between you and I. Bobby told me that Joe Lane called him yesterday and told him, dead certain, the Speaker had told him there was gonna be an article in the paper on Sunday. Dead certain."

"Yeah, well I talked to Randy Collier," DeGraw countered. "There's no article on Sunday. Randy Collier, he has nothing. He says he has absolutely nothing at all."

The talk turned to the Phoenix Police Department's investigation of the bundled names. That prompted DeGraw to reveal how he acquires advance warning about ongoing Phoenix Police activities.

"I could call the mayor. I could call any member of the Public Safety subcommittee. Or, I could call the head of the union, the police union," DeGraw said.

Scheffel, as directed, asked DeGraw about the $6,000 mailing arrangement Raymond had just revealed. "He told me Alan Stephens was the guy who gave the money in the last deal and Alan went nuts over it."

"That's exactly right," DeGraw confirmed.

Scheffel and DeGraw hooked up again two hours later, at 10:20 p.m. By then, there had been a dramatic change in events. The *Arizona Republic* story had suddenly become definite.

"I called Randy Collier five minutes ago," DeGraw said. "And I said, 'What happened from 4:30 p.m. today to now?' And he said, 'Look, I work for the *Arizona Republic*. I do what I'm told.'"

It wasn't immediately clear whether Collier had been told to stonewall or to rush in on a Friday night, gather together his notes from weeks of intensive, investigative reporting, and knock out an intricate, detailed story from scratch a few hours before deadline.

"What's gonna be in the story?" Scheffel asked.

". . . He wouldn't tell me. Now supposedly it involves Chuy Higuera . . . All I know is that this is not the standard way that even the *Republic* reporters do business. There's a political agenda at work here."

DeGraw, Arizona's top political fixer, was asserting that the local newspaper was in bed with the politicians, dirty dealing with the best of them. That meant the Good Guys—and their point man Joe Stedino—could expect a vicious political backlash fueled by the *Arizona Republic*. Serious ugliness loomed on the desert horizon.

Scheffel phoned Raymond to relay the sour news at 10:30 p.m. Raymond already knew.

"I just got a call from [Debbie] McCune," Raymond said. "Who got a call from Randy Collier. And Randy Collier says, 'Do you know this guy [Vincent]?' And she says, 'No.' And he said, 'You'll be interested to know that tomorrow morning there is going to be a story I'm breaking that this guy, Tony Vincent, has been conducting a double-sting operation. That he is employed by the Phoenix Police Department.'"

That was the kicker. The *Arizona Republic* was now tipping off politicians about the sting before the story was published! And they were doing it without warning the cops and giving us a chance to pull out.

"Bullshit," Scheffel said, clinging to his cover.

"That's what he told her."

"That's what Randy Collier told her?"

"Yeah . . . She just now hung up talking with me."

"What does she mean by 'double sting'?"

"I don't know."

I didn't either.

"What's Rick think?" Scheffel asked.

"He doesn't know . . . Alan . . . has also been told that there's gonna be a story in the morning."

"Who told him?"

"He didn't say."

". . . Why would an investigative reporter call Debbie McCune and tell her that?" Scheffel wondered.

"He said that he wanted to make sure she was gonna be around for comment."

What neither of them noted at the time was that McCune was very close to House Majority Leader Art Hamilton. From my vantage point, that was a saleable explanation. The newspaper wanted to warn Art.

While Scheffel was talking with Raymond, I was hearing the same report from DeGraw.

"I talked to Randy Collier at 4:30 p.m. today," he began. "And he told me there was no story. Then, I'd heard from two or three different places that there was supposed to be a story tomorrow or Sunday. Jane Hull was telling people early this morning there was gonna be a story . . . So tonight, a half an hour ago, I got a call from a legislator who says he had, somebody else had been called by Randy Collier and Randy told them there was gonna be a story tomorrow . . . So I called Randy at home. 'Is there gonna be a story?' 'Yes, tomorrow morning' . . . I said, 'Can you tell me what happened between 4:30 p.m. and now?' He said, 'No. I work for the *Arizona Republic* and they tell me what to do.'"

DeGraw repeated the allegation that Collier had leaked to McCune that it was a "reverse sting." The "sting" rumor was now roaring through the state like a summer monsoon.

". . . Why wouldn't [Collier] tell you what he told Debbie McCune?" I asked.

"I have no idea unless he's still in the fishing stages . . . What's most bizarre to me is that he would get orders from higher up to write a story. I mean, he goes home at 4:30 or quarter to five. And he had no story 'cause I mean, I heard him go through his computer."

If he had no story at 4:30 p.m., at the end of his shift, how come Jane Hull knew about it that morning? How come Joe Lane knew about it the day before? How come you reached him at home, instead of at the office where he seemingly would have been shepherding a last-minute story breaking the biggest sting operation in Arizona history?*

This was going to be a long night.

I called Detective Ball and let him know what I'd heard about the *Republic*. He called me back at 10:45 p.m. and said Romley, Ortega, Keppel, and Click were in a meeting.

"Doing what?"

"Police business," Ball said.

Raymond phoned Scheffel at 10:48 p.m. Half the legislature now appeared to be calling in favors trying to find out what bomb the *Arizona Republic* was going to drop on the city in a few hours. As of 11 p.m., the rumor remained that the article focused on Chuy Higuera.

Bobby Raymond was having a difficult time accepting the Collier-to-McCune report that the operation was a sting.

". . . The thing that I can't, I can't believe is there's just been too much money. Way too much. There's just been too much money gone through."

As I knew all along, the loose purse strings had been a key to the success of Desert Sting. We were fortunate to have a county attorney who believed in letting the cash flow—especially in areas that didn't result in criminal acts. This enabled us to avoid a mistake the FBI sometimes makes. The Feds' stinginess telegraphs to smart criminals that they've been sucked into a sting.

At 1:05 a.m. on February 2, I returned a page from Rick DeGraw. He said he was holding a copy of that morning's *Arizona Republic*. It was all there. The names. The players. Everything. I had received no warning from the newspaper, the county attorney, or the police. The *Arizona Republic* had done the unthinkable. They blew open an ongo-

---

Arizona Republic reporter Randy Collier responds that he spoke to Rick DeGraw between 2 and 3 p.m. on Friday before the story was officially designated to be printed. He said he doesn't recall ever telling DeGraw that "I work for the *Arizona Republic*. I do as I'm told." Collier also denied speaking to Representative Bobby Raymond that day, and denied having ever spoken to Representative Debbie McCune. McCune confirmed the call and said the transcripts are accurate. She had no clue, however, as to why she was singled out to be warned by the reporter. Collier says he spoke to Deputy Police Chief Benny Click at 4 p.m. that Friday, advised him that a story exposing the operation was being printed, and suggested that Click pull the undercover operatives from the field. Chief Click said he regarded the call as a typical *Arizona Republic* bluff. When asked to comment on whether a journalist has the ethical right to shut down an ongoing, undercover police operation, Collier said that was a management decision.

ing, police undercover operation without so much as warning the police operatives in the field that their cover would be destroyed in the morning paper. Without DeGraw's call, I could have shown up in the office that morning thinking it was business as usual. In fact, Jim Davis had pushed me for a meet early Saturday so I could give him a picture of the intended hit victim. The cops had yet to phony a photo, so I had to put him off until Wednesday. Otherwise, he'd have come to the office armed and ready to kill—the same morning as the newspaper ambushed me.

DeGraw reacted strangely to the article. I don't know if he was stunned, or shocked, or what, but rather than acknowledge that it was a sting and dive for cover, he discussed how I would deal with this latest assault upon Tony Vincent's reputation.

"First of all, there are going to be a lot of legislators who are, uh, most upset, if this is true and your office has been wired."

"Who wired my office?" I said, clawing on to my cover to the bitter end.

"I'm just saying if this article is true all those people are going to be saying, you know, we've got to figure out what went on, whether anything that went on was illegal or not."

"You think the attorney general or somebody maybe got a wire in my office?" I said, going as far with it as DeGraw was allowing. Instead of answering, he continued reading parts of the article. He stopped midway to offer more strategy.

". . . I also suggest that . . . if these charges in here are not true, that you consider what action you can take against the *Arizona Republic*," Doc advised. "Because if you are still interested in continuing in the gaming area, then you have to do something or, you know, you have no credibility of any kind left with anybody."

Continuing the gaming issue? Was this guy crazy? Even if the story was wrong and Tony was real, he had effectively been shut down. Cut the losses and get the hell out of town before sundown.

". . . What bothers me is that it just is so crazy," I said truthfully. "It's like watching a science fiction movie in black-and-white from the 1950s."

"In which you are the star."

"Yes, and my supporting cast is the State of Arizona."

I drove to a nearby 7-Eleven and bought the paper. It was as DeGraw had described. The big, black, doubled-decked headline stretched across the front page: "Legislators Under Investigation In Political-Corruption 'Sting.'" The article that appeared under the headline couldn't have been more accurate if I'd written it myself. The only fiction were the denials from the lips of the legislators and hangers on. Among those quoted was the long-forgotten Gary Bartlett.

"I wouldn't have taken [the job] if I thought there was anything illegitimate about it," Bartlett lied.

Representative Raymond described me as "an old-style Italian" who was "a hoot to sit and talk to." Don Kenney said I wore a pinky ring and "looked kind of sleazy."

Upon a second read, the article seemed jumbled. The first third read like the operation was a sting. The remaining two thirds read like an investigation into Tony Vincent's attempt to push casino gambling. It was as if the newspaper had stacked a new top on a story that already existed.

Whatever the journalistic intrigue, one thing was certain. Tony Vincent was dead — murdered by the morning newspaper.*

The article left absolutely no doubt that its information had come from my inner circle. Ball and Mount stood by their stories that it was an unintentional leak. No way, I thought. If it was leaked, it was leaked by design.

It was too late and I was too exhausted to deal with the death of Tony Vincent that morning. I just collapsed into bed and fell into a hard, fevered sleep.

While I slept, Rich Scheffel was trying to put out the fires. He spoke to Bobby Raymond at 6:50 a.m.

"Do you think it's real?" Raymond wondered.

"No. It can't be," Scheffel answered.

"No, I mean do you think he's real? Tony?"

"I don't know. I'm hopin' he is."

"Aren't we all," Raymond sighed. The charismatic representative said he didn't know if he should show up for the legislative session that morning. Scheffel advised him it would look worse if he didn't.

---

*Arizona Republic Managing Editor John Oppendahl said the story exposing the sting had been in the works for months and was virtually complete a week prior to publication. Oppendahl said they intended to hold the story until after the indictments were announced, a date they had been led to believe would be February 4. However, because the newspaper viewed the leaks as so pervasive, they decided to go with their story on Saturday before another news organization scooped them. He said the Republic informed County Attorney Rick Romley and Police Chief Ruben Ortega on "Thursday or Friday." Oppendahl said that because the leaks were so extensive, the issue of exposing an ongoing police undercover operation was no longer a consideration. County Attorney Rick Romley counters that the issue remained very much a consideration and says he asked the Republic not to run the story until the undercover operation was completed. "We wanted to go on," Romley says. "We had another guy coming in to meet with Tony Vincent that week." Romley added that the Arizona Republic in general, and reporter Randy Collier in specific, are always threatening to go with some story or another and he had no reason to believe that this wasn't just another routine bluff.

"The thing is, it's not time to lose nerve now, huh?" Raymond asked. The words were similar, but the wonderful ballsiness had deserted the Texan's voice.

Ernie Hoffman phoned Scheffel at 7:30 a.m. He was in Tucson and had yet to see the story. Rich read it to him. It was then he realized that the one name that wasn't in the story, curiously enough, was that of former Representative Bill English. That supported the theory that Ernie had been Collier's "Deep Throat." Why else would Ernie's boy have been protected?

"Wha . . . do . . . do you think, indeed that Vincent is a sting?" Ernie asked after Scheffel finished reading. Ernie was finally realizing that all his betrayals and double dealings had done nothing but bring the posse down upon him.

"Well, that's what this article says it is," Scheffel responded, turning the knife.

" . . . You know, videotapes, sorting out all this other stuff, and then contribution levels, that could be kind of a nasty situation."

"I would think so," Scheffel understated.

" . . . I certainly have nothing to hide," Hoffman insisted. " . . . So [Tony's] not anywhere to be found probably at this point."

"Well, I talked to him this morning," Scheffel laughed.

"You're kidding me?"

" . . . He denies it vehemently. He's gonna file a lawsuit against the *Republic*."

"You're kidding me!" Ernie said, brightening. " . . . That's a remarkable thing for the guy to deny it once it's in the paper."

The reality of the situation, that Rich Scheffel was also part of the sting, was a surreal twist that was obviously too much for Ernie, or anyone else, to contemplate.

" . . . He took a call?"

"Yeah, no problem."

" . . . Well, that's wilder than hell," Ernie said, wavering between hope and despair. " . . . He just did too many things that were inconsistent . . . Not a very bright person either. But, bright enough that he pulled this off."

As Ernie elaborated, he gave a textbook illustration of why Operation Desert Sting had gone so well.

" . . . Typically, those things work in a manner that, uh, it's pretty sophisticated. This guy . . . as rough and tough as he was, is really out of the norm. 'Cause he's not a, you know, he's not an educated man . . . If he indeed did all of that and it's an internal sting, and spent, evidently, a lot of money on surveys and all this other stuff, it's kind of interesting to me that he would go that far . . . It doesn't make sense . . ."

"No, it boggles my mind," Scheffel said. That comment, I suspect, was truthful.

Hoffman speculated that Tony Vincent had started out real, got caught, and was turned by the cops to save himself.

At 8:50 a.m. on Saturday, February 2, 1991, Tony Vincent received the last phone call of Operation Desert Sting. It was Ron Tapp.

"I'm reading an article in the newspaper," Tapp curtly opened. "It says that you are an undercover police officer."

"I read that, had that read to me at 1 a.m.," I said, shrugging it off as old news.

". . . Well, are you an undercover cop?"

"No," I answered. It was the truth. I wasn't a cop. "Don't pay any attention to what you read in the paper. Don't you know what dogs do on newspapers? I think Bartlett is behind this a thousand percent."

". . . Well, about the only way to solve this newspaper problem is hit 'em with a libel suit," Tapp said.

"I fully intend to go with any legal recourse that I have . . . Nothin's changed. Just some bullshit that a reporter pulled out, plucked out of the air and I'll deal with it."

"Right," Tapp said.

". . . You just relax."

"I'm gonna go to the racetrack, screw it."

". . . Just have an enjoyable day," I said.

Shiree Foster paged shortly before 10 a.m. That would have been one interesting call to return. Unfortunately, she was a few minutes too late. At 9:45 a.m., Sergeant D. P. Davis made it official. I was to stop receiving or returning calls. Tony Vincent was dead.

26

The Phoenix Police fanned out across the desert on the morning of the newspaper story and arrested Jim Davis, Al Hill, and Ron Tapp. They were the three that were thought to be the most dangerous. Tapp was shocked to learn that among the thirty felonies he'd been slapped with, one was a murder conspiracy count.

"What murder?" he protested.

"Bartlett," Detective Ball said.

"Oh shit," Tapp responded, suddenly remembering the long-forgotten request to bump Bartlett. "I should have known. I should have known!"

"You're not alone," Ball said. "Before this is over, a lot of people are going to be saying 'I should have known.'"

According to Ball, Tapp started trying to cut a deal before they even got the cuffs on. He promoted himself as being "a good snitch."

Hill, arrested at his home, told the cops he knew nothing about "exploiting no minors," which was the language of the charges against him.

Jim Davis claimed to be conducting his own investigation. That was fine—as long as he could hand over his undercover tape recordings. And how about the Corvette? If Davis could pull that silver and black rabbit out of his cowboy hat, he might have a better argument. The Corvette, of course, has yet to reappear. Neither have any tapes.

Although he wasn't yet arrested, the cops visited Ernie Hoffman's place with a search warrant. Ernie greeted the officers like lost brothers and professed to have also been conducting his own investigation. He explained the $18,000 he scooped off the table for Bill English as "an advance for public relations work."

The police were in no hurry to arrest the others. They were solid citizens who weren't going anywhere. The cops did send a team of officers to search Don Kenney's home and law office. The search turned up his extortion lists, still in his computer files.

On Sunday, February 3, I returned to the local flea market to purchase identification in the name of Frank Pietro. It was eerie. So much had changed since I'd last transacted business with the ID man. So many lives would forever be altered. Yet the hustle and bustle of the packed morning market was the same. Life goes on.

On Monday, I checked my mail at the office. There was a letter from the Republican party inviting Tony Vincent to a $1,000-a-plate dinner with J. Fife Symington and Ronald Reagan. Wish Tony could've attended. There was also a $220 check from Senator Jim Henderson. The Navajo had returned my legal contribution.

The events that led to the release of the remaining grand jury indictments the following evening remain controversial. I was told that the grand jury had originally approved the indictment of twenty-one people. Among the twenty-one were Senator Alan Stephens, Representative Art Hamilton, and Representative Candice Nagel. County Attorney Rick Romley and his top assistant, Jim Keppel, discussed their strategy. The conversation was spirited. Romley wanted to go full-force and prosecute all those charged by the grand jurors. He was satisfied that the case against Stephens, Hamilton, and Nagel would stand. Keppel was far more cautious. He saw the case against the trio as being the investigation's Achilles' heel. Those cases, in Keppel's eyes, weren't airtight like the others. Romley countered that at the worst, the Good Guys would win 18–3, still an impressive victory. Keppel argued that 18–0 would be much better, and taking a chance with the remaining three could domino into a catastrophe. If Hamilton, Stephens, and Nagel went to trial first and all won, they could create a momentum that might snowball. The prosecutors argued back and forth, eventually settling on a conservative strategy that favored Keppel's position. No criminal indictments would be brought against Stephens, Hamilton, and Nagel.

The Maricopa County Attorney's Office also filed a companion civil lawsuit that sought to recover the money spent during the investigation. It's a complicated process that has become a popular prosecutorial strategy in RICO cases. The civil suit generally sweeps in husbands, wives, and other family members of the accused who may have profited from the money. Both Alan Stephens and his wife were named in this suit. Hamilton and Nagel remained in the clear.

One of the fourth room gang later related that the problem with Nagel, aside from her decision not to take the money, was that the prosecutors feared she'd button her vulgar lip, shift into her Doris Day mode, and sway a jury.

With that straightened out, it was time to drop the bomb. Romley called a press conference for the unlikely hour of 8 p.m. on Tuesday night—barely enough time to make the late news programs that air at 10 p.m. in Phoenix's Mountain Time zone. Romley faced the cameras and announced the first wave of indictments: Representative James A. Hartdegen, Senator Jesus R. "Chuy" Higuera, Representative Donald Kenney, Representative Suzanne Cramton Laybe, Representative James Harris Meredith, Representative Bobby D. Raymond, Senator Carolyn Ann Walker; lobbyists Ernest L. Hoffman, David M. Horwitz, Ronald Tapp, and Richard T. Scheffel; County Democratic Chairman David Manley, former State Democratic Party Executive Director George Stragalas III—and poor Shiree L. Foster.

For myriad legal reasons, Jim Davis' arrest was announced a day earlier, and the indictments of Al Hill, former Representative Bill English, ex-Magistrate Gary Bartlett, and Justice of the Peace Donald Stump were announced later.

What was interesting were the diversity of the counts. The charges varied on each person, and ranged from Tapp's thirty felonies and Kenney's twenty-eight, to Shiree Foster's single count of "conspiring to participate in a crime," that is, lending her name to bundled checks.

Bobby Raymond was slapped with fourteen felonies: conspiring to participate in a crime, participating in a criminal syndicate, seven counts of bribery, two counts of laundering money, making false campaign-finance statements, hindering prosecution, and conspiring to obstruct a criminal investigation.

The others were charged with variations on the same theme. Some more. Some less. All were in deep shit.

The civil suit included all of the above, except Scheffel, plus several spouses: Jane Doe Davis, Dorothy Hartdegen, Lourdes Higuera, Linda Kenney, Michael Laybe, Rexanne Meredith, Sheri Raymond, Karen Stragalas, Jane Doe Stump, and Helen Tapp. Alan Stephens and Stephen's wife, attorney Leslie Hatfield, rounded out the accused.

For some reason, the prosecutors weren't able to nail down the first names of Mrs. Davis and Mrs. Stump, thus the "Jane Doe" designations.

Lobbyist Rick DeGraw wasn't indicted until August 1991—seven months after the operation ended. He was charged with nine felonies: seven counts of obstructing a criminal investigation, one count of conspiracy to obstruct a criminal investigation, and one count of illegally conducting an enterprise. Much of the delay resulted from the fact that

his involvement came late in the investigation and the police and prosecutors focused their early attention on the first wave of defendants.

Another book could be written about what happened after the initial indictments. In short, the politicians, lobbyists, and others jockeyed
for position, some of their defense attorneys let fly wild trial-balloon
defense strategies, and the American Civil Liberties Union screamed
that the police were Nazi storm troopers who entrapped honest citizens. The politicians, indicted or not, yelled that Desert Sting was a
politically motivated scheme to destroy legislators who were soft on
law enforcement issues and was specifically designed to boost the
political careers of Rick Romley and/or Phoenix Police Chief Ruben
Ortega. Since the Desert Sting operation was my idea to begin with,
those accusations were nonsense.

After the screaming died down, most of the accused quietly
gulped their medicine and negotiated pleas. Virtually all the pleas
included provisions to have the indicted politician's wife or husband
dropped from the civil suit. That was the prosecutor's hammer.

Bobby Raymond, as I predicted, was the first legislator to cop a
plea. He waited a little more than two weeks to orchestrate the last
deal of his political career. Raymond owned up to five felonies.

The only holdouts, as of March 1992, were Carolyn Walker, Ron
Tapp, Gary Bartlett, Jim Davis, Rick DeGraw, and, interestingly
enough, Shiree Foster. (On March 20, two weeks before the trial, all
charges were dropped against Bill English in return for his testimony
against Ron Tapp.)

The sentences were as illogical as the charges: Laybe accepted
$24,960 from Vincent and was charged with seventeen felony counts.
She pleaded guilty to a pair and received six months in jail, four years
of probation, and was ordered to pay $14,960 in restitution and com-
plete 600 hours of community service. Higuera took $4,040 and was
charged with eight felonies. He pleaded to a single count of bribery
and was given two months in jail, four years probation, and 640 hours
of community service. Jim Meredith took $9,300 from Vincent and was
indicted on four felony counts. He pleaded to one "undesignated
offense" and was given no jail, three years probation, and ordered to
pay $15,000 in restitution. Meredith also received assurances that his
"undesignated" count, conspiring to make false campaign-contribu-
tion statements, might later be reduced to a misdemeanor. Jim Hartdegen took $660 and was indicted on three felonies. He pleaded to three
misdemeanor counts of campaign-finance law violations and received
eighteen months probation, $2,760 in fines and restitution, and 50
hours of community service. Don Kenney took $60,250 and was

charged with twenty-eight felonies. He pleaded to seven and was given five years in prison, ordered to pay $200,000 in restitution, and perform 500 hours of community service. George Stragalas was slapped with twenty-four felony counts, pleaded to five, and is awaiting sentencing.

Bobby Raymond took $12,105 from Vincent, resulting in fourteen felony counts. He pleaded to five and was sentenced to two years in prison—not jail but state prison—seven years of probation, $34,500 in fines and restitution, and 300 hours of community service. He served part of his time on an agriculture chain gang trimming trees and picking peaches in 100-plus degree heat.

Bobby got screwed.

Among the others, Al Hill's attorney was able to knock the twin, class two felony counts of sexual exploitation of a minor down to the much-less serious "possession of obscene material." Hill then failed to show for his sentencing, claiming a "miscommunication" with his lawyer. That's the last anyone has seen or heard of Fondia Al. He is currently a fugitive, and the original felony charges have been reinstated. Dumb move. Look for Al to show up on "America's Most Wanted." Ernie Hoffman was indicted on nineteen felony counts. He pleaded to three and was given probation and 200 hours of community service. After completing his 200 hours, a judge generously set aside the convictions. Justice Stump was indicted on nine felonies, pleaded to a pair, and was sentenced to six months in jail.

All the elected politicians either resigned or were booted out of office. Those who pleaded guilty to, or were convicted of, felonies can never hold public office again. Those who escaped with misdemeanors, like Hartdegen and possibly Meredith, are free to resume their political careers—if the voters will have them.

Putting aside all the legalese and felony counts, it is hard for me to understand the difference in the $12,105 Raymond took that earned him such a comparatively harsh sentence, and the $9,300 Meredith took for which he skipped away so lightly. Bobby, it seems, might be the first person ever to receive a prison sentence for uttering so many colorful quotes.

Some of the more interesting post–Desert Sting events bear mention. Sue Laybe refused to resign her seat and forced a public hearing. Her mystery advisor surfaced and coughed her up like a cat spitting up a fur ball. The mystery man turned out to be Michael Crusa, one of U.S. Senator Dennis DeConcini's top aides. Crusa testifed that he accepted $10,000 from Laybe, which she wanted laundered through the national Democratic fund-raising committee then funneled back to her. Crusa's testimony in the televised hearing was devastating. A shaken Laybe resigned the next day.

The *Arizona Republic* reported on February 27 that instead of bringing the $10,000 to the party, Crusa spent it. The newspaper stated that he had to borrow the $10,000 he returned to the county attorney's office after Desert Sting blew. Crusa was not charged, but resigned his position as DeConcini's state director. Laybe's attorney, Gary Peter Klahr, charged that Crusa should have been indicted instead of Laybe.

That was a stretch, but consider what poor Sue had been through. Her secret advisor first spent the money, then cut a deal to appear in a televised hearing to rat her out. Politics is a gruesome business.

Speaking of ugly politics, Evan Mecham called a press conference after the indictments to point out that five of the seven sitting legislators indicted had voted to impeach him. If there was a point there, I sure as hell missed it.

Carolyn Walker fought her ouster from the Senate. She marched dramatically out of a Senate Ethics Committee hearing when the committee refused to allot her attorney the unlimited time he felt he needed to present her case. The committee also refused to recognize "entrapment" as a defense in the in-house disciplinary hearing. Shortly thereafter, Walker became the first senator in Arizona history to be expelled from the Senate.

Alan Stephens, on the other hand, continued his run of incredibly good luck. His feisty attorney, Janet Napolitano, not only got him and his wife bounced from the civil suit, she won a subsequent claim that the county was responsible for the $31,525 Stephens allegedly spent in legal fees (on her) to defend himself, and the $8,050 his wife spent. Stephens took more than $4,000 from Tony Vincent, and now the county has to fork over another $40,000. He not only survived Desert Sting, he profited! His case was bolstered by a nationally renowned "tape expert" from the Nixon Watergate days who "determined" that not only had the admittedly muffled recording failed to pick up my statement in the Black Angus that the money was mine, but he concluded that there was no way I could even have made such a statement. The expert also said he knew I was wearing a body mike because he could hear my clothes rustling against the instrument. The bug was in the cellular phone.

It gets better. Stephens has since gained widespread public sympathy as the "wronged man of AzScam." Even the usually hard-biting alternative weekly *New Times* did a fawningly sympathetic feature. Expect to see Alan Stephens ride this wave of support into the United States Congress.

Candice Nagel, although never officially indicted, nevertheless quickly resigned her seat after the sting broke. She cited health reasons, but it is widely believed that she was either forced out because of the blistering comments she made about her fellow lawmakers, or resigned out of embarrassment. I think she overreacted. Everybody ripped on everybody else. She was no worse than the others. You think Bobby Raymond would have resigned over anything he said?

Chuy Higuera, along with Laybe, was allowed to do his jail time on a job release program that enabled him to work on the outside during the day while spending his nights behind bars. However, that deal was quashed when he got caught pinching a $4.55 bottle of nasal spray from a Tucson market. The theft charges were dropped, but he was forced to do the rest of his sentence as a full-time prisoner.

Shiree Foster's ex-boyfriend, Romano Sbrocca, was nailed in the FBI operation two months after Desert Sting broke. Sbrocca was charged with seven counts of laundering drug money. It's a solid case. The money was handed to him by an undercover FBI agent. Romano's son, Angelo, got hit with fifteen felony counts. Twelve others were snared in that sting. The Feds confiscated and closed Ernesto's Backstreet.

According to the prosecutors, Shiree renewed her relationship with Sbrocca following both of their indictments. That lends credence to my initial belief that it had never ended.

On April 3, 1991, a caller phoned Silent Witness, the local citizen crime watch line, to warn that I'd never make it to the trials. The caller claimed that New York Mob boss John Gotti, of the "Gotti family," had given the murder contract to a guy named "Rizzo" from Los Angeles. I wasn't too upset because there were a lot of holes in the caller's short statement. Gotti is the boss of the Gambino family, not the Gotti family, and despite popular belief, the Mafia doesn't contract hits. All sworn Mafia members are killers because one must kill at least once before you can be "made." They are thus able to take care of that kind of business in-house. If Gotti wanted me clipped, he'd quietly dispatch one of his trusted soldiers. In addition, the Mafia is extremely territorial. Although the Gambinos are the largest crime family in America, insiders say they have no interests in Arizona. Despite the flaws in the story, the police were concerned enough to move me to another house.

The most bizarre aspect of the post–Desert Sting fallout involves Phoenix Police Chief Ruben Ortega. In June, after the dust settled,

Ortega found himself in a messy public squabble with the Phoenix City Council over the police force's iron-fisted control of the millions in confiscated RICO cash. The council wanted to get their hands on the money, and also wanted the city manager to be advised how the money was being spent. In other words, they wanted to know in advance if any more political sting operations were in the works. (The Arizona State Legislature is currently trying to pass a similar self-protecting bill.) Ortega correctly protested that such a requirement was crazy. The information would be leaked all over Arizona before the operation could even begin. Chief Ortega was so enraged that he resigned. The council backed down and Ortega un-resigned the next day. But, even while backing down, a few of the council members and legislators in Ortega's district took the opportunity to toss some nasty barbs at the chief. Representative Susan Gerard—Don Kenney's beaver-shot target—accused Ortega of "grandstanding." Councilwoman Linda Nadolski went as far as saying that although Ortega had done a decent job keeping the people of Phoenix safe, "We need to know that we're safe from Chief Ortega."

Incensed anew, Ortega resigned again. This time it held. Although Ortega goes down in the scorebook as a backlash victory for the embittered politicians, others caution that there is far more involved. Many suspect Ortega of maneuvering himself into martyr status as a platform to launch a political career. The whispers are that he has his eye on a congressional seat—possibly the same seat lusted after by Senator Alan Stephens. Stephens is a Democrat. Ortega is a Republican. Wouldn't that be a nifty election?

J. Fife Symington hardly had a chance to settle in as governor before the grinning skeletons in his savings and loan past started leaping out of the closet. On September 13, 1991, the *Washington Post* published an internal memo from lawyers at the government's Resolution Trust Corporation (RTC) that skewered the guv for his handling of a controversial hotel-office-retail project in Phoenix. Symington's "Esplanade" development was said to have cost Southwest Savings and Loan $52 million. Southwest went belly-up in 1989, socking taxpayers for $941 million.

In contrast to the taxpayers' woes, Symington was reported to have invested only $432 of his own money in the enterprise, and came away with more than $8 million in development fees plus a "large" profit from his share in the struggling complex. The language of the memo was harsh: "Symington spent Southwest's funds with reckless abandon. [He] reaped a huge personal financial benefit and then walked away from the project virtually untouched."

The Esplanade development was described as being "replete with breaches of the duty of loyalty, self-dealing, conversion of assets, and breaches of the duty of care by Southwest's officers and directors." It accused Symington of charging "exorbitant" development fees and added: "Symington used Southwest's money as if it were his own, effectively channeling it into his own pocket by overspending on soft development costs on which he earned a 5 percent commission."

Symington sat on Southwest's board from January 1972 until January 1984. The Esplanade deal was cut in 1983. Cute deal. One component was that Southwest agreed to loan Symington and partners $39.6 million to buy eighteen acres of land valued at only $31 million. Small wonder Southwest bit the bullet.

In the memo, four top RTC lawyers recommended taking legal action against Symington and twelve other Southwest officials. On December 16, 1991, the RTC did just that, suing Symington and eleven other ex-Southwest figures for $140 million, charging them with acting with "gross negligence" and "wanton disregard" of their banking duties.

Symington termed the RTC leak and subsequent lawsuit dirty politics, denied he was a bad guy, blamed Southwest's problems on Congress and a "real-estate depression," claimed to still be liable for the financial health of Esplanade, and pointed out that the ravaged savings and loan failed five years after he left the board.

"This incident is unfair, unjustifiable, and despicable," Symington countered following the initial leak. "This is a flagrant attempt to try me in a court of pubic opinion without due process of any official RTC sanctions or communications . . . I want the people of Arizona to know that their governor is proud of his record as a former member of the board of Southwest Savings. I did nothing wrong nor improper. I served the board with honor."

As if Symington's RTC troubles weren't bad enough, a local newspaper published a story in October 1991 accusing the governor of awarding the $60,000-a-year position of Executive Assistant for International Relations to his Mexican mistress—a job the newspaper charged she was woefully unqualified for.

Symington denied that his questionably competent but unquestionably beautiful assistant for international relations was his mistress.

"The man who promised to run the state on business principles is in public disgrace less than a year into his term," decreed *New Times* columnist Tom Fitzpatrick.

The tough times continue for Arizona.

* * *

As for me, the newspapers ripped and tore on me, digging up every bad thing in my past and painting me as the reincarnation of John Dillinger. The ever-ethical *Arizona Republic* published a long feature woven around the comments of a San Francisco private detective hired by defense attorneys in the Reno drug money case to dig up dirt on my background. Even Mother Teresa couldn't withstand that kind of scrutiny and one-sided reporting. Quoting this dick, the *Republic* wrote that I changed my name to "Stedino" so "people would think I was Italian." That was garbage. Stedino is my family's original name. Like millions of other immigrants, it was shortened (to "Stead") when my great-grandparents arrived in America. The man also ripped my movie performances, criticized my talk show interviewing ability, and questioned my motives in the Reno operation. Without citing any attribution, the article went on to say "Police thought they were dealing with a 'loose cannon' that had to be controlled at all times." The article did not bother to contact a single friend or associate who would have said something remotely positive about me.

The Associated Press joined the lynch party and went so far as to write that I had acknowledged "prior convictions for theft, pimping, and white slavery . . ." I couldn't recall any such damning admissions.

Not to be outdone, the television stations leaped into the fray. One tracked down a defense attorney in Las Vegas who described me as a "mouse trying to be a rat" and warned that putting me on the streets of Phoenix was like unleashing a rabid dog on the good citizens of Arizona. If he could make up his mind what kind of animal I was, I'd know which Purina Pet Chow to buy.

While the news vultures were slandering me in public, they were privately clamoring for exclusive interviews.

The one exception was the newspaper in Mesa, the large city just east of Phoenix. Mesa *Tribune* reporter Bill Roberts wrote a fair and balanced account of my life. I called to thank him and we developed a friendship. Roberts subsequently came under attack from his colleagues because of our relationship.

After the journalist took their shots at me, the defense attorneys took theirs. Arizona is a deposition state, meaning lawyers are allowed to question witnesses before the trial in a process known as "discovery." That resulted in hour upon hour upon hour of attorneys browbeating me. One attorney deposed me for more than twenty-five hours before getting around to his client's case. These depositions were then typed and made available to the media, which resulted in more damning stories. Fortunately, by then, Roberts had hooked me up with Dary Matera, a bestselling author who was in Phoenix quietly writing the book *Quitting the Mob,* with Colombo-family Mafia captain Michael Franzese. Matera sent out an S.O.S. to another of his former book subjects, famed Miami defense attorney Ellis Rubin, who donated his legal services as a favor to Matera.

For two days, Rubin roared through Phoenix like a tornado. He conferred with the county attorney; presided over a raucous press conference that ended with me having to hide from the media inside a hotel food cart; helped me tape an interview with Tom Jarriel and producer Martin Clancy of ABC's "20/20"; set ground rules for the remaining depositions; threatened the newspapers and television stations with massive lawsuits if they didn't stop their character assassinations; and warned the county attorney's office that he would refuse to allow me to testify as a witness in the upcoming trials unless the "death by deposition" assaults were curtailed. And that was just the first day! It was great. The next day, Rubin did a live radio show and held another press conference at the airport before leaving town.

Things quieted down considerably after Rubin's tumultuous visit. With the bearded Florida attorney off waving his sword at other legal windmills, I hired Phoenix defense attorney Bill Friedl to carry the ball from there. Friedl filed a protective order that limited the length and scope of the depositions. He also attended them with me to make sure the marauding attorneys cut the shit.

Of course, I wasn't the only one being savaged in the media. The newspaper and television reporters were having a field day with the politicians. That too struck me as being cruel. The accused weren't the slimy low-lifes the public was being led to believe. Bobby Raymond is a prime example. Because he is a larger-than-life character prone toward forcefulness and dramatic language, he's had to bear the brunt of the public's outrage. Yet Bobby Raymond is a talented, charismatic leader with guts. To twist Shakespeare, Raymond played the political game not wisely but too well.

It's a tired cliché to blame someone's offenses on their environment, but in Raymond's case, I think it applies. He merely excelled in an environment of rampant corruption.

Similarly, the others are not without merit. As a black woman, Carolyn Walker overcame a double negative to achieve success in both her professional and political life. Her weakness was the same as her strength—blind ambition. Jim Meredith's insecurities led him to try overly hard to please others to gain their support. Don Kenney had no doubt become unconsciously hardened by the twin professions of law and politics. What others would consider crime had probably become nothing more than routine business to him. Jim Hartdegen was a good ol' boy who temporarily lost sight of the simple pleasures in life. Chuy Higuera, despite his respected political status, seemed to be running just one step ahead of poverty. The money he took gave him some breathing room. Sue Laybe lifted herself from the dead-end world of bartenders and waitresses to become a lawmaker. Her sin was in wanting to climb too high too fast. George Stragalas, after being abandoned by the party he gave his life to, was desperately trying to survive in the political world he loved.

Which is not to say I sit around home wracked with guilt over what I did to these fine, upstanding individuals. Truthfully, I've felt no sense of remorse. For a long time, I couldn't figure out why. Then one evening, it came to me. Joe Stedino never knew them. They were Tony Vincent's friends. And Tony Vincent was gone.

For Joe, being a good guy continues to be tough. I'm not really a cop, so the cops keep their distance. I'm not an attorney, so the county attorneys shy away. I fronted a sting, so the bad guys run at the sight of me. I don't seem to fit anywhere in society at the moment. And I have no idea what will happen to me after the trials.

INDEX